G000144616

A POLITICAL AND ECONOMIC DICTIONARY OF EASTERN EUROPE

A POLITICAL AND ECONOMIC DICTIONARY OF EASTERN EUROPE

Roger East, Catherine Jagger, Carolyn Postgate
and Richard J. Thomas

SECOND EDITION

Routledge
Taylor & Francis Group

LONDON AND NEW YORK

First edition 2002
Second edition 2007

© Cambridge International Reference on Current Affairs (CIRCA) Ltd, 2007
Compiled and typeset by Cambridge International Reference on Current Affairs
(CIRCA) Ltd, Cambridge, England.

Published by Routledge, Haines House, 21 John Street, London WC1N 2BP,
United Kingdom
(Routledge is an imprint of the Taylor & Francis Group, an **informa** business)

ISBN-13 978-185743-334-0

ISBN-10 1-85743-334-3

Printed and bound in Great Britain by MPG Books, Bodmin, Cornwall

FOREWORD

A POLITICAL AND ECONOMIC DICTIONARY OF EASTERN EUROPE is being published in a new edition to reflect the new structure and organization of government, politics, production, international relations and trade across this region, which has been reshaped dramatically in the past two decades. Even the map has been redrawn in this post-communist period. Where once the obvious dividing line across Europe lay at the westernmost reach of Soviet domination, the most coherent definition of 'Eastern Europe' must now be that part of the continent beyond the recent expansion of European Union (EU) membership.

This book accordingly covers the Russian Federation (although much of this vast country is obviously Asian rather than European at all), and those European countries which once formed part of the Soviet Union, namely Belarus, Ukraine, Moldova, and the trans-Caucasian republics of Georgia, Armenia and Azerbaijan. Unlike the previous edition published under the same title in 2002, it leaves for a separate volume (*A Political and Economic Dictionary of Central and South Eastern Europe*) the three Baltic states, the other former communist countries for which the term Central Europe is both more historically appropriate and geographically accurate, and all the Balkan states – among which only Albania and most of the ex-Yugoslav countries have yet to realize the ambition of joining the EU.

Although there can be no 'ideal time' to try to capture the shape of the contemporary political and economic situation in any region of the world, there is a powerful case for trying to establish an overview based on up-to-date information, and this is an objective that this book seeks to serve.

Entries in the dictionary are designed to stand on their own in providing definitions and essential facts, with coverage of recent developments and, where appropriate, full contact details. The broad scope of the dictionary includes political groups, institutions, main government leaders and prominent individuals, financial and trade bodies, religious organizations, ethnic groups, regions, geographical areas and principal cities, as well as essential terms and concepts, flashpoints, and other entries as appropriate.

There is extensive cross-referencing between entries, indicated by the simple and widely familiar device of using a bold typeface for those words or entities which have their own coverage. There is also a listing, by country, of the entries relevant to that country (Appendix, p. 305), and a comprehensive index of personal names (p. 309).

The longest individual entries in this book are those for the region's seven individual countries, giving a succinct structural description and historical survey to place recent events in context. The country entries are followed in each case by entries on that country's economy, again combining up-to-date basic data with a short overview and a focus on recent issues and developments.

Cambridge, March 2007

ACKNOWLEDGEMENTS

The editors gratefully acknowledge the assistance received with the compilation of this book from many of the organizations listed in it. We are also greatly indebted to the staff of Cambridge International Reference on Current Affairs (CIRCA) Ltd for their painstaking work in collecting and revising data, and to two publications in particular, *The Europa World Year Book* and *The International Who's Who*, which have both been used extensively for the cross-checking of detailed factual information.

We also wish to acknowledge the assistance of national statistical offices, government departments and diplomatic missions, as well as the following publications as invaluable sources of statistical information for the present volume: the United Nations Population Fund's *The State of the World Population 2006*, the World Bank's *World Bank Atlas 2006* and *World Development Indicators 2006*, the International Monetary Fund's *Direction of Trade Statistics Yearbook 2006*, the Inter-Parliamentary Union's Parline Database, *The Military Balance* and CIRCA's *People in Power*.

CONTENTS

INTERNATIONAL TELEPHONE CODES

Eastern Europe

Armenia +374
Azerbaijan +994
Belarus +375
Georgia +995
Moldova +373
Russian Federation +7
Ukraine +380

Other countries hosting relevant international organizations

Austria +43
Belgium +32
China +86
Finland +358
France +33
Hungary +36
Iran +98
Italy +39
Netherlands +31
Norway +47
Saudi Arabia +966
Sweden +46
Switzerland +41
Turkey +90
United Kingdom +44
United States of America +1

ABBREVIATIONS

Used in addresses

Al.	Aleja (Alley, Avenue)
Ave	Avenue
bd, blvd, Bul., bulv.	Boulevard (Avenue)
BP	Boîte Postale (Post Box)
c/o	care of
CP	Case Postale (Post Box)
Gen.	General
per.	pereulok (lane/alley)
pl.	place (square)
POB	Post Office Box
pr.	prospect (avenue)
St	strada (street)
Str.	strada (street)
u.,	ut. utca (street)
ul.	ulica/ulitsa (street)
vul.	vulitsa (street)

Miscellaneous

ASSR	Autonomous Soviet Socialist Republic
b/d	barrels per day
c.	circa
GDP	Gross Domestic Product
GNP	Gross National Product
m.	million
PPP	Purchasing Power Parity
SSR	Soviet Socialist Republic
UN	United Nations

A

Abaza

A north Caucasian people situated in **Karachai-Cherkessia**, in the extreme south of **European Russia**. Closely related to the **Abkhaz**, the Abaza migrated north of the **Caucasus** in the 13th century, having converted to Islam. In their new home they became vassals of the local Karachai princes. During the imperial battle for the region between the **Russian** and Ottoman Empires, Abaza communities were often deported *en masse* to Russia or Turkey to quell rebellion. By the end of the 19th century many tens of thousands of Abaza had migrated to Turkey, where their religious affiliations were better suited to the prevailing society. The Abaza left in Russia sided with both the Bolsheviks and **White Russian** forces during the Civil War (1918–20), with famed Abaza horses serving as prestigious cavalry. After the war the Abaza lands were divided between the Karachai and **Cherkess** lands, but were rejoined when the two larger regions were amalgamated in 1957.

Traditional animal husbandry and small-scale farming were forcibly swapped for collectivized agriculture in the 1930s and Abaza culture was heavily slavicized. The Abaz language, originally transcribed using a Latin-based script from 1923, has used the **Cyrillic alphabet** since a decree from the **Soviet** authorities in 1938.

Abkhazia

A nominally autonomous republic within **Georgia** on the eastern coast of the Black Sea. The Abkhaz defeated Georgian forces in a war of secession between 1992 and 1994 and declared independence, which remains unrecognized. *Population*: 250,000 (2000 estimate). The general region was first colonized by the ancient Greeks in the 8th century BC and known as Colchis. The descendants of these first colonists are represented today by the **Pontic Greeks**. The indigenous Caucasian Abkhaz (known to themselves as Apswa) were converted to Christianity in the 6th century AD and became vassals of the Byzantine Empire. A later independent kingdom was absorbed into Georgia until the entire area came under Turkic Ottoman control in the 16th century. Under the Ottomans,

1

some Abkhaz converted to Islam, and today the two religions coexist in relative peace.

The ethnic balance in Abkhazia was permanently undermined in the late 19th century when the new **Russian** masters (since 1810) rejected ideas of autonomy, and fiercely repressed a local uprising. Thousands of Abkhaz fled to Turkey and their land was appropriated by Russian colonists. The strong identity of Abkhaz culture (most closely related to that of the **Abaza** to the north) and the great difference of the language from Georgian or Russian ensured the region's separate status under the Bolshevik/**Soviet** regime after 1917. An Abkhazian republic was declared in 1921 but was lost in 1931 when it was reabsorbed into Georgia. In the 1930s a wave of **Georgian** colonists further diluted the Abkhaz population. However, Abkhaz culture and language were protected and promoted under the Soviet regime.

The growth of Georgian nationalism approaching independence in the late 1980s prompted calls for greater autonomy for Abkhazia. Tensions were exacerbated by Georgian attempts to establish a branch of Tbilisi University in the Abkhaz capital, Sukhumi. This was viewed by the Abkhaz authorities as an attempt to repress Abkhaz culture. Conflict was provoked in 1992 when Georgian troops were despatched to Sukhumi after the restoration of the autonomous Abkhaz 1925 Constitution. In the ensuing war Abkhazian forces, tactically supported by the Russian military and north Caucasian mercenaries, pushed back Georgian troops by October 1993. Abkhaz independence, declared in 1994, remains unrecognized. In 2002 the **Parliament of Georgia** amended the Constitution to recognize Abkhazia as an autonomous region, but several plans for *de jure* autonomy have been rejected by the Abkhaz authorities, who demand full independence.

Political crisis within Abkhazia followed the 2003 presidential poll, when official results announced that opposition candidate Sergei Bagapsh had beaten Russian-backed Raul Khadzhimba. The incumbent President's declaration that the poll should be rerun was met with mass protests. Georgian President Mikhail **Saakashvili** voiced unprecedented recognition of an Abkhaz election, strongly supporting the initial result, while Russia went as far as closing the cross-border rail link that had resumed in 2002. The impasse was resolved when the two rivals agreed to stand on a joint ticket in the re-run in January 2004, with Bagapsh taking the presidency and Khadzhimba the vice-presidency.

In 2006 the Georgian and Abkhaz authorities appeared willing to negotiate—if still from incompatible standpoints. However, a successful offensive by Georgian police against guerrillas in the **Kodori Gorge** in July of that year led Saakashvili to announce the relocation of the Government-in-exile to the area, infuriating the *de facto* Abkhaz Government. In October Abkhazia appealed to Russia to recognize its independence.

Most Abkhaz residents were granted Russian passports in the latter part of the 1990s and the region's economy is heavily dependent on Russia and uses the

Russian rouble as currency. Russia agreed to withdraw from its military bases in Abkhazia by 2001, and now says they are just used for peacekeeping activities, but Georgia alleges that the base at Gudauta is still being used to provide military support to Abkhaz troops.

Abkhaz people remain the minority in Abkhazia, with **Russians** and **Armenians** now constituting the rest of the population. Georgians, the previous majority population in Abkhazia, fled the republic in the fighting of the early 1990s, and their homes and land were occupied by Abkhaz forces. The displaced Georgians have formed a powerful pressure group in Georgia, calling for an immediate restoration of their property.

Economic activity is centred on the major urban centres of Sukhumi and Ochamchire, both on the coast, although restrictions on international commerce have increased the importance of agricultural production. Tobacco, tea, nut oil, silk and citrus fruits are major exports. The Soviet-era tourist industry has greatly diminished.

ABM Treaty *see* **SALT**.

Abrene question

A territorial dispute between the **Russian Federation** and Latvia over the Abrene region along their common border. The 1920 Treaty of **Riga** assigned the Abrene region to Latvia, but in the border reconstruction undertaken by the **Soviet** authorities towards the end of the Second World War, Abrene and its environs were absorbed wholesale into Russia, then becoming known as Pitalovo. Although dissent was muted by the totalitarian Soviet state, the independent Latvian authorities did not officially drop their claim to the district and set out their case in a 1992 resolution. However, the matter was not taken further in order to maintain the nominally cordial relations between the two republics.

Wording for a border treaty recognizing the *de facto* border between Russia and Latvia was formulated in 1997, but it was not until 2005 that both countries declared their agreement to sign this treaty, following Latvia's membership of the **North Atlantic Treaty Organization** and the **European Union**. Even then there was a hold-up just before the signing ceremony, when Latvia attempted to add a reference to the 1920 treaty, and Russia thereupon refused to sign the document at all. A further year of wrangling finally ended with the Latvian Parliament's approval of the signing of the treaty without the contentious reference.

ADA *see* **Armenian Development Agency**.

Adygeya

A constituent republic of the **Russian Federation** situated to the north-east of the Black Sea in southern **European Russia**, north of the **Caucasus region**. *Population*: 447,109 (2002 estimate). The republic is dominated by the Circassian Adygei people, closely related to the **Cherkess** and Kabards (*see* **Kabardino-Balkaria**) and distinguished from them as a separate ethnic group only in the 1920s. The region was included as an autonomous *oblast* (region) in the Krasnodar district by the Bolsheviks in 1922 but separated as a full autonomous republic in 1934. After the collapse of the **Soviet Union**, Adygeya was declared a Sovereign Republic within the Federation in 1991. Aslan Tkhakushinov was elected President of the republic in 2007.

Economic activity is based on food production and exporting. The ancient Adygei were famed for their excellence in horse breeding, and efforts have been made to resurrect this traditional activity in the capital, Maikop.

Adzharia
(or Ajaria)

An autonomous republic within **Georgia** dominated by the **Muslim** Adzharians. *Population*: 376,000 (2002 estimate). The Adzharians were ethnic **Georgians** who converted to Sunni Islam while their homeland was under Turkish dominion between the 17th and 19th centuries. They came under **Russian** control in 1878 and were attached to the Georgian **Soviet** republic in 1922. Recognition as a separate ethnic group was ended after widespread unrest in Adzharia over religious intolerance and enforced collectivization. Large numbers of Adzharians were subsequently deported to central Asia. Since that time they have officially been considered to be Georgians, although their autonomous status was retained.

The rise of Georgian nationalism in the early 1990s prompted authorities in the Adzharian capital Batumi to prepare for the armed protection of their autonomy, should it be revoked. Open conflict in Adzharia was avoided, while a serious debate about its future within Georgia was put off due to hostilities in **Abkhazia** and South **Ossetia**.

Adzharia's long-term President, Aslan Abashidze, an authoritarian and a staunch ally of Moscow, refused to acknowledge the ouster of Georgian President Eduard **Shevardnadze** in November 2003. Tensions mounted with the new regime of President Mikhail **Saakashvili**, who was prevented from entering Adzharia in March 2004 and responded by imposing a land, sea and air blockade on the republic. Crisis talks forced Abashidze to back down, though he subsequently reneged on his pledge to disarm his militias. In early May his militias blew up bridges and a railway line, severing the region's links with Georgia proper. Thousands of people took to the streets of Batumi in protest, in spite of the state of emergency that had been imposed, echoing Georgia's earlier **Rose Revolution**: Abashidze resigned and fled to Russia. In Adzharia's June 2004 election the Saakashvili-Victorious Adzharia bloc went on to win 75% of the vote, giving them 28 of 30 Supreme Council seats; the remaining two were won by the **Republican Party of Georgia**. Mikheil Makharadze was elected President in July.

The economy is based around the key port of Batumi, a major gateway for oil distribution from Kazakhstan, Turkmenistan and **Azerbaijan**. It is noted for shipbuilding and its oil refinery. Agriculture centres on tobacco, tea and citrus fruits. The tourism industry elsewhere on the Black Sea coast has benefited from instability in Abkhazia.

Agrarian Party of Belarus
Agrarnaya Partiya Belarusi (APB)

A party in **Belarus** representing those agrarian interests which derived from the Soviet-era agricultural system, and opposing the restoration of individual peasant ownership of the land. Established in 1994, the APB emerged as the most powerful agrarian party in the 1995 legislative elections, winning 33 seats. In January 1996 APB leader Syamyon Sharetski was elected Chairman of the then unicameral legislature, but he later fled the country after rifts within the party emerged over Sharetski's opposition to constitutional changes in 2000. In March that year, the APB officially aligned itself with President Alyaksandr **Lukashenka**. In legislative elections held since then, the APB has secured a handful of seats, gaining five in October 2000 and three in October 2004.

Leadership: Mikhail Shymanski (Chair).
Address: vul. Kazintsa 86/2, 220050 Minsk.
Telephone: (17) 2203829.
Fax: (17) 2495018.

Agrarian Party of Russia
Agrarnaya Partiya Rossii (APR)

A small party in the **Russian Federation** which has swung from left to right and now supports the Government of President Vladimir **Putin**. Formed in February 1992, the APR's main policy platform at that time was opposition to the privatization of land. It naturally inclined to the left-wing **Communist Party of the Russian Federation** (KPRF), and pledged the party its support after winning 7.7% of the vote in the 1993 elections. Perhaps overshadowed by its partner, and jostled by newer parties seeking to claim the attention of the disaffected, the APR slumped to just 3.8% of the vote in the 1995 poll, though it claimed 20 constituency seats. It remained loyal to the KPRF, backing that party's leader Gennadii **Zyuganov** in his unsuccessful presidential bid in 1996.

At this juncture the APR jumped across the political spectrum. It dropped its opposition to privatization and joined forces in August 1999 with the rightist Fatherland electoral alliance, at that time still in opposition.

Fighting the 2003 elections alone (Fatherland having become part of the pro-Putin **United Russia** in 2001), the APR dwindled to just two seats with only 3.8% of the vote. Party Chairman Mikhail Lapshin was ousted and the APR cemented an alliance with the Government by electing pro-Putin deputy Vladimir Plotnikov in his place in April 2004.

Leadership: Vladimir Plotnikov (Chair).
Address: B. Golovin per. 20/21, 107045 Moscow.
Telephone: (495) 2079951.
Fax: (495) 2079901.
E-mail: press@agroparty.ru
Internet: www.agroparty.ru

AIDS
(acquired immunodeficiency syndrome)

Discussion of the impact of AIDS in **eastern Europe** has generally focused on the poorer sections of society, and particularly on drug users. The prevalence of HIV (human immunodeficiency virus, the virus responsible for AIDS) varies across the region but the explosion of numbers in some countries is considered an epidemic. The situation is worst in **Ukraine**, where UN figures for 2005 recorded that 1.4% of adults aged 15–49 were infected with HIV, a total of over 600,000 people. Also badly affected are the **Russian Federation** and **Moldova** (1.1% each). The situation in other countries is an increasing problem, but one which is often not fully appreciated. The fact that the epidemic has its roots among the socially excluded—drug users, sex workers and homosexuals—has made raising awareness, and prompting government action, disproportionately difficult.

Ajaria *see* **Adzharia**.

Alania *see* **Ossetia question**.

Aleksishvili, Aleksi

Minister of Finance, **Georgia**. Aleksi Aleksishvili is a trained economist who became a member of the Council of Ministers at just 30 years of age as Minister of Economic Development in December 2004. He was appointed Finance

Minister on 30 June 2005.

Born in **Tbilisi** in 1974, Aleksishvili graduated in economic relations from Tbilisi State University in 1996. During his student years he became president of the NGO Young Economists' Society, a post he held until 2001. On graduation, he got a post at the Tbilisi Economical Relations Institute, while also becoming a senior specialist at the **Parliament of Georgia**. In January 1999 he became assistant to Zurab Zhvania, the Chair of Parliament. Two years later he was appointed Deputy Finance Minister, a post he held for just over a year. In the summer of 2002 he moved to the USA where he studied at Duke University for two years. On his return in 2004 he was made First Deputy Finance Minister, and also became involved again with the Young Economists' Society, this time as a consultant. In December 2004 he was promoted to full Minister, holding the Economic Development portfolio, before being transferred to the Finance Ministry six months later.

Aleksi Aleksishvili is married and has two children. He speaks Russian and English.

Address: Ministry of Finance, Abashidze 70, 380062 Tbilisi.

Telephone: (32) 292077.

Fax: (32) 292368.

E-mail: minister@mof.ge

Internet: www.parliament.ge/gov/ministries/finance.html

Aleph *see* **Aum Shinrikyo**.

Alfa-Bank

Rapidly growing independent bank network in the **Russian Federation**, founded in 1991. As of December 2003 the Bank held reserves of US $386.2m. and had 39 branches.

President: Petr Aven.

Chief Executive: Petr Smidr.

Address: ul. M. Poryvayevoi 9, 107078 Moscow.

Telephone: (495) 9742515.

Fax: (495) 7455784.

E-mail: mail@alfabank.ru

Internet: www.alfabank.ru

Aliyev, Heydar

President of **Azerbaijan** from 1993 to 2003. Born in May 1923 in the Azeri enclave of **Nakhichevan**, Heydar Alirza oglu Aliyev went to university in **Baku** to study architecture, but his studies were interrupted when the **Soviet Union** entered the Second World War in 1941. He later successfully completed a history degree. A member of the **Communist Party of the Soviet Union** (KPSS) from 1945 to 1991, he was Vice-Chairman and then Chairman of the Azerbaijan KGB (*see* **Federal Security Service**) between 1967 and 1969, when he was elected First Secretary of the Party Central Committee at republican level. In 1982 he became a member of the Politburo of the KPSS, the highest rank in the Soviet power structure ever achieved by an Azeri, and also First Deputy Chairman in charge of transport in the Soviet Council of Ministers. However, in 1987 he left the KPSS Politburo following disagreements with (and accusations of corruption from) Mikhail **Gorbachev**, who was implementing a controversial reform programme as KPSS General Secretary. In 1991, the year of Azerbaijan's declaration of independence, Aliyev resigned outright from the KPSS. A year later he founded the **New Azerbaijan Party** (YAP) and became its Chairman.

On 15 June 1993, after a rebellion had forced the incumbent President Abulfaz Elchibey to flee the capital, the **National Assembly** elected Aliyev as its Chairman and he assumed the duties of State President. Following an August referendum supporting the removal of Elchibey, presidential elections were held on 3 October 1993. Aliyev was recorded as having won 98.8% of votes in a turnout of 97%. However, no major opposition candidates had stood for election, while human rights' monitors described the poll as undemocratic and said that the media had been closely controlled by Aliyev.

The YAP, closely aligned with Aliyev, continued to dominate the legislature, while Aliyev himself secured a second term at the October 1998 presidential elections. On this occasion, although many opposition parties boycotted the poll, there were at least real rival candidates. Aliyev's recorded share of the vote— 76%—was widely regarded as having been inflated by 'irregularities' in the conduct of the election, although it was at least generally recognized as more credible than the 1993 poll. Crucially, 76% was above the necessary two-thirds majority required to have Aliyev declared the outright victor rather than have to face a second round run-off.

The cult of personality built up around Aliyev presented him as a father of the Azeri nation, with his portrait omnipresent and his sayings prominently displayed on posters in public places. The state propaganda machine also emphasized the image of Aliyev as a major international statesman, exploiting to the full his foreign visits—to the USA in particular.

He groomed his son, Ilham, for the succession and in November 2001 the YAP voted to give its backing to Ilham as his father's eventual successor. Heydar Aliyev collapsed in April 2003 during a military ceremony, and during the subsequent months Ilham was manoeuvred into position. Heydar withdrew his candidacy just before the presidential elections in October, and support swung behind his son, who easily secured victory. Heydar Aliyev died on 12 December 2003, while seeking medical treatment in the USA.

Aliyev, Ilham

President of **Azerbaijan**. Ilham Aliyev is the son of Heydar **Aliyev**, the long-time President of Azerbaijan. He took over the post from his father following disputed elections just two months before the latter's death in December 2003; Heydar had been ill and had been considering his succession for some time. Ilham had once wanted to become a Soviet diplomat, but the collapse of the **Soviet Union** led him to become a roving businessman and minor oil magnate. He is a sports fan with a reputation as a 'playboy' and remains President of the National Olympic Committee.

Ilham Heydar oglu Aliyev was born on 24 December 1961 in the Azeri capital, **Baku**. His father had at that time just become head of the Azeri KGB (*see* **Federal Security Service**). Ilham Aliyev was educated in Baku until 1977 when he entered the Moscow State University of International Relations (MSUIR), graduating in 1982, the year his father joined the Soviet Politburo. Ilham received his doctorate in history in 1985. He remained at MSUIR as a lecturer until 1990.

From 1991 until 1994 Aliyev ran a number of private industrial and commercial enterprises, spreading his time between **Moscow** and Istanbul. It was during this period that he gained a reputation as a roulette-loving 'playboy'. His father was elected President of Azerbaijan in 1993, and by 1994 Ilham had become Vice-President of the State Oil Company of the Azerbaijani Republic (SOCAR) and was actively promoting his father's oil strategy. The following year he was elected to the **National Assembly** for the first time.

In 1997 he became the President of the National Olympic Committee of Azerbaijan. In 1999 he was elected Deputy Chairman and in 2001 First Deputy Chairman of the ruling **New Azerbaijan Party** (YAP). From 2001 until 2003 he served as the head of the Azeri parliamentary delegation to the Parliamentary Assembly of the Council of Europe (PACE). He was appointed Prime Minister on 4 August 2003; his father had collapsed in the spring of the same year and was openly considering his succession. In early October Heydar withdrew his own candidacy from the forthcoming presidential elections to allow Ilham to take his place. The polls on 15 October were allegedly marred by voter intimidation, media bias and violence; Ilham Aliyev won 80% of the vote and was sworn in on 31 October.

Though some Western observers, particularly those with an interest in Azerbaijan's oil industry, have made much of Aliyev as an urbane pro-Western modernizer, others consider this account false and claim he has inherited his father's corrupt police state intact.

Ilham Aliyev is married with one son and two daughters.

> *Address*: Office of the President, Istiklal küç 19, 370066 Baku.
> *Telephone*: (12) 4927906.
> *Fax*: (12) 4980822.
> *E-mail*: office@apparat.gov.az
> *Internet*: www.president.az

All Armenian Labour Party

A small party in **Armenia**. A social-democratic formation, the All Armenian Labour Party won one seat in parliamentary elections in May 2003.

AMN *see* **Our Moldova Alliance**.

APB *see* **Agrarian Party of Belarus**.

APR *see* **Agrarian Party of Russia**.

Archangel

A major city and region in the north of **European Russia**, 50 km south of the often frozen White Sea. *Population*: 355,500 (2002 estimate). The city was founded as a fortified monastery dedicated to the Archangel Michael in 1584 at the start of **Russia**'s great expansion into the Eurasian wilderness. As the Russian Empire established itself as an important European power in the 17th century, Archangel (Arkhangelsk in Russian) became a vitally important trading port. It was the base for the first trade with Britain, supplying vital timber for the shipbuilding industry. Archangel's fortunes declined with the opening of **St Petersburg** in 1703 and the introduction of heavy tariffs to favour Peter the Great's new city. It regained its place as Russia's major centre for timber exporting after the completion of a railway in 1898. This role was preserved throughout the **Soviet** period until the present day. The local Bolsheviks took control of the city in February 1918, only to be temporarily ousted by Allied forces in the opening years of the Russian Civil War. Industrialization in the 1930s brought a wave of migration from further south, swelling the population by more than 150,000 by 1939. Archangel's working population has long been at the forefront of industrial action and held the greatest number of strikes in European Russia in 1998 with 374 separate recorded actions.

Arctic Council

A body in which the **Russian Federation** co-operates with Scandinavian and North American countries on Arctic issues. It was founded in 1996, and promotes sustainable development—addressing social, economic and environmental issues. The chairmanship of the organization rotates on a biennial basis: Norway took over the Chair from Russia in October 2006.

Members: Canada, Denmark, Finland, Iceland, Norway, Russian Federation, Sweden, USA.

Address: Arctic Council Secretariat, c/o Ministry of Foreign Affairs, POB 8114 Dep., N-0032 Oslo, Norway.

Telephone: (22) 243243.

Fax: (22) 249580.

E-mail: ac-chair11@npolar.no

Internet: www.arctic-council.org

Ardartyun *see* **Justice**.

Armenia

Hayastany Hanrapetoutioun

A landlocked republic in the south-western **Caucasus region**, bounded by Turkey to the west, Iran to the south, **Azerbaijan** to the east and **Georgia** to the north. The country is divided administratively into 11 regions (*marzer*).

Area: 29,800 sq km; *capital*: **Yerevan**; *population*: 3m. (2005 estimate), comprising ethnic **Armenians** 93%, **Azeris** 3%, **Russians** 2%, others 2%; *official language*: Armenian; *religion*: **Armenian Apostolic Church** 88%, Catholic Church of Armenia 6%, others (including **Russian Orthodox**, **Protestant**, **Muslim** and Yezidi (*see* **Kurds**) communities) 6%.

A new Constitution approved in July 1995 established a democratic presidential system, with an executive President as Head of State elected by popular vote for a term of five years, renewable once. The President appoints the Prime Minister and Cabinet subject to approval by the **National Assembly** (Azgayin Joghov). Legislative authority is vested in the unicameral Assembly of 131 members elected for a four-year term by universal adult suffrage, 75 by majority voting in single-member constituencies and 56 by proportional representation from party lists obtaining at least 5% of the vote. Constitutional amendments passed in November 2005 restricted the President's powers, limiting his freedom to choose the Prime Minister and to dissolve the Assembly, and lengthened the term of the Assembly to five years after the 2007 election.

History: Settled in ancient times by Indo-European tribes, and claiming to have been the first state to adopt Christianity as its official religion (in 301), Armenia was dominated for centuries by conflicts between larger neighbouring powers. Once a Roman province, it was caught in the struggle between the Byzantine and Persian Empires, before being conquered by the Seljuk Turks in the 11th century, overrun by the Mongols in the 13th and incorporated into the Ottoman Empire in the 16th. In 1639 Armenia was partitioned, the Ottoman Turks retaining the larger, western region while the eastern region (the present-day republic) became part of the Persian Empire. In 1828 Persia ceded eastern Armenia to **Russia** and in 1878 the Congress of Berlin transferred the Kars province, a large territory in western Armenia, to Russian control. From the late 19th century the Ottoman Turks persecuted their Armenian subjects, and in 1915 over a million people were murdered or deported (*see* **Armenian question**). In 1918, following the 1917 Bolshevik Revolution in Russia, Armenia declared its independence, but this was short-lived in the wake of subsequent Turkish and Soviet occupation. In 1920 the area under Bolshevik control was proclaimed a Soviet Republic and in 1922 became a member (with Azerbaijan and Georgia) of the Transcaucasian Soviet Federative Socialist Republic (TSFSR). The TSFSR was dissolved in 1936 and Armenia became a full union republic of the **Soviet Union**.

In the late 1980s the influence of the *glasnost* (openness) initiative in the Soviet Union and the nationalist tensions caused by the military conflict in **Nagorno-Karabakh** (an ethnic Armenian enclave ceded to Azerbaijan in the early 1920s) gave expression to Armenian historical and political grievances. In mid-1990 the pro-independence **Pan-Armenian National Movement** (HHSh) achieved the largest number of seats in the elections to the then Armenian Supreme Soviet. This legislature made a declaration of sovereignty, renamed the country the Republic of Armenia and in 1991 refused to participate in negotiations to renew the union treaty of the Soviet Union. Alleged Soviet support for Azerbaijan in the worsening Nagorno-Karabakh conflict, and the effects of political disintegration in Moscow, led to a huge majority in favour of full secession from the Soviet Union in a referendum on independence in September 1991. Levon Ter-Petrossian, the incumbent candidate of the HHSh, was elected President the following month with overwhelming support. In December 1991 Armenia became a fully sovereign member of the **Commonwealth of Independent States** (CIS).

In the first post-Soviet legislative elections in July 1995 the Republican Bloc, an alliance of six groups led by the HHSh, won 119 of the 190 seats and accordingly dominated subsequent Governments. In presidential elections in September 1996 Ter-Petrossian was re-elected outright in the first round. Robert **Kocharian**, who had been President of the 'independent' republic of Nagorno-Karabakh proclaimed unilaterally a year earlier, was appointed Prime Minister in March 1997. Ter-Petrossian's willingness to consider an agreement for the enclave which recognized Azerbaijan's sovereignty brought him into increasing conflict with Kocharian and the Armenian military, the outcome being the

President's resignation in February 1998.

New presidential elections in March 1998 resulted in a narrow second-round victory for Kocharian, standing as a non-party candidate. His main opponent, the veteran former communist Karen Demirchian, went on to found the **People's Party of Armenia** (HZhK). Kocharian's lack of support in the Assembly prompted him to call legislative elections in May 1999, contested by a proliferation of new and realigned parties. The Unity (Miasnutiun) bloc emerged as the biggest grouping; an alliance of Demirchian's HZhK and the **Republican Party of Armenia** (HHK), it gained 55 of the 131 available Assembly seats.

Efforts to build a unity government around this bloc, with HHK leader Vazgen Sarkissian as Prime Minister, were dramatically derailed in October 1999 when gunmen invaded the legislative chamber and shot and killed eight people including Sarkissian and Demirchian. Subsequent investigation of the shootings made slow progress. Six people were eventually jailed for life in December 2003, amidst continuing rumours that the attack had been an attempt by hardliners to sabotage a prospective peace agreement on Nagorno-Karabakh (see below).

Sarkissian was succeeded as Prime Minister by his younger brother, Aram Sarkissian, and Demirchian's role as HZhK party leader went to his son Stepan Demirchian. Friction between Kocharian and the new Prime Minister, however, led to the latter's replacement in May 2000 by new HHK Chairman, Andranik **Markarian**. The anti-Kocharian elements of the HHK became increasingly vocal, and this, combined with serious strains with the HZhK, rendered the Miasnutiun alliance unworkable. The HZhK left the coalition in September 2001. Kocharian and the HHK faced mounting accusations of authoritarianism. When the Government closed the A1+ telecommunications agency over a technicality in April 2002, thousands of opposition supporters came onto the streets to protest, but with little effect.

Latest elections: Presidential elections in February–March 2003 resulted in re-election for Kocharian, standing again as a non-party candidate. He won 48.3% in the first round on 19 February, while his nearest rival Stepan Demirchian won 27.4%. Kocharian was elected in the second round on 5 March with 67.5% of the vote, against 32.5% for Demirchian. National Assembly elections on 25 May 2003 (with three seats contested on 14–15 June) produced a relative victory for the HHK, which won 33 of the 131 seats with 23.7% of the vote. Other seats and vote shares were won as follows: **Country of Law Party** (OY) 19 (13%), **Justice** (Ardartyun) bloc 14 (13.7%), **Armenian Revolutionary Federation** (Dashnak) 11 (11.5%), **National Unity Party** (AzM) 9 (8.9%), **United Labour Party** (MAK) 6 (5.7%), **All Armenian Labour Party** 1, **Republic** (Hanrapetutiun) 1, independents 37.

Recent developments: Prime Minister Markarian was reappointed following the May 2003 legislative elections amidst countrywide protest over apparent irregularities in both the presidential and parliamentary votes. The claims were partially substantiated by international observers. None the less, the legitimacy of the new coalition, headed by the HHK and including the populist OY, was confirmed by the Constitutional Court. Meanwhile, former Prime Minister Aram Sarkissian, now head of the defeated **Democratic Party of Armenia** (part of the Justice bloc), was jailed for 15 years in November 2003 for ordering the murder of public television chief Tigran Naghdalian. Protests organized by the opposition (which was boycotting the Assembly) in April 2004 were brutally suppressed, and further demonstrations were curtailed by severe legal restrictions put in place in May. Thousands returned to the streets in November 2005 calling for Kocharian's resignation amidst scepticism of the apparent 94% vote in favour of a new constitution. (The new constitution promised to better define the roles of the executive and to allow diaspora Armenians to vote.) Among those voicing accusations of improper conduct during the plebiscite was the outspoken OY leader, and Assembly Speaker, Artur Bagdasarian, and even Prime Minister Markarian himself.

International relations and defence: Having joined the CIS at independence in December 1991, Armenia was admitted to the **Organization for Security and Co-operation in Europe** (OSCE) and the UN early in 1992. It also became a member of the **Organization of the Black Sea Economic Co-operation** and obtained observer status in the **Non-Aligned Movement**. In 1994 it became a member of NATO's **Partnership for Peace** programme, while an agreement on partnership and co-operation with the **European Union** was signed in 1996 (also covering Azerbaijan and Georgia). A Treaty of Friendship, Co-operation and Mutual Understanding signed with the Russian Federation in August 1997 highlighted a continuing close security relationship, reflecting in part Armenia's historic antagonisms with Turkey, aggravated by the recent success of the Armenian diaspora in persuading the USA and other Western legislatures to issue condemnations of the 1915 Armenian massacres. Turkish efforts to head off international criticism led to a commitment to rebuild political relations in April 2005 while the genocide claims were 'investigated' by Turkish specialists. A policy of accommodating the USA, such as allowing access to Armenian airspace during the Afghan conflict in October 2001, and sending a small contingent of troops to aid the occupation of Iraq in 2003, had the side effect of cooling Armenia's formerly close relations with Iran.

In January 2001 the **Council of Europe**'s Ministerial Committee voted unanimously to admit Armenia (and Azerbaijan) to membership. Armenia's membership was briefly threatened by an early insistence that a ban on the death penalty would not apply to pre-2001 sentences for paedophile and terrorist acts. This final loophole was closed in September 2003 when the death penalty was completely abolished.

Armenia's military successes against Azerbaijan in the Nagorno-Karabakh conflict in the mid-1990s failed to produce a peace agreement on the disputed enclave, despite the efforts of the OSCE's **Minsk Group** and other bodies. A series of meetings between Kocharian and President Heydar **Aliyev** of Azerbaijan in 1999–2000 gave some impetus to the deadlocked negotiations, raising the possibility of a settlement based on an exchange of territory under which Azerbaijan would obtain a corridor to its **Nakhichevan** enclave in return for making concessions on the status of Nagorno-Karabakh. A high-water mark in hopes came in December 2003 when talks in Scotland (UK) confirmed that peace would be the only acceptable solution to the issue. Tensions returned, however, as the 10th anniversary of the conflict's start was marked in 2004. Subsequent negotiations between Kocharian and the new Azerbaijani President Ilham **Aliyev** have made no progress.

Armenia's defence budget totalled the equivalent of some US $194m. in 2006, equivalent to about 3.2% of GDP. Total armed forces at August 2006 were 43,641, including those drafted under compulsory conscription of 24 months. Since mid-2004, conscripts have had the alternative of doing 42 months of civilian service. Reservists number an estimated 210,000.

Armenia, economy

A small and still largely agricultural economy, afflicted in the 1990s with familiar post-Soviet difficulties but posting double-digit growth in 2001–05, helped by financial inflows from **Armenians** abroad. The main transport and communications links between landlocked Armenia and the outside world are currently confined to those through **Georgia** and Iran, since Turkey maintains a closed border with its eastern neighbour and Armenia remains effectively at war with **Azerbaijan** over **Nagorno-Karabakh**.

GNP: US $4,441m. (2005); *GNP per capita*: $1,470 (2005); *GDP at PPP*: $15,121m. (2005); *GDP per capita at PPP*: $5,013 (2005); *exports*: $1,320m. (2005); *imports*: $1,958m. (2005); *currency*: dram (plural: drams; US $1=D364 at the end of December 2006).

In 2005 agriculture accounted for 20.5% of GDP, services 35.2% and industry 44.3%. Some 47% of the 1.3 million workforce are engaged in agriculture, 38% in services and 15% in industry (manufacturing, mining and construction). About 18% of the land is arable, 2% under permanent crops, 28% permanent pasture and 10% forests and woodlands. The main crops are potatoes, grapes and other fruit and vegetables, with animal husbandry in the upland areas. Mineral resources include small deposits of gold, copper, molybdenum, silver, lead, zinc and iron. The main industries are relatively small-scale manufacturing, cigarettes and textiles, with computer software rising from 2000. Energy sources include hydroelectric power and energy from a reopened nuclear power plant at Medzamor, while petroleum and gas are imported from the **Russian Federation**, Iran and Turkmenistan.

Armenia's main exports by value in 2004 were jewellery (about 40% of the total), iron, steel and other base metals (19%), mineral products (14%) and food, beverages and tobacco (10%). The principal imports that year were precious stones (about 22% of total), food and agricultural products (19%) and mineral products (16%). In 2004 about 15% of Armenia's exports went to Belgium, 14% to Israel, 12% to Germany and 11% to the Russian Federation. The main sources of imports that year were the Russian Federation (13%) and Belgium, the UK and the USA (8% each).

Prior to the dissolution of the **Soviet Union** in 1991, Armenia supplied a range of manufactured goods and textiles to the rest of the Soviet Union in exchange for raw materials, but this arrangement fell away after the end of 1991 and the external balance deteriorated sharply. The economic situation at that time had already been made more serious by the repercussions of the severe earthquake of December 1988, while further difficulties were experienced as a result of the ongoing conflict with Azerbaijan over Nagorno-Karabakh. As a result, output dropped drastically and there was a huge wave of emigration from Armenia in the 1990s, although this latter factor resulted in an increased flow of remittances from Armenians working abroad. In the early 1990s GDP fell by an average of around 10% annually and there was massive inflation.

From 1995 there was improvement on many fronts as Armenia began implementing a comprehensive programme of macroeconomic reform with the support of international financial institutions and donors. In 1996 GDP showed an annual growth of 5.8%, and by 1997 inflation had fallen to 13.2%. Nevertheless, in 1998–99 Armenia felt the effects of the Russian economic crisis (*see* **Russian Federation, economy**), with delays in flows of financing from Russia, reductions in net transfers from Armenian workers in Russia and cancellation of some private investment. The problems were compounded by a severe trade and balance-of-payments deficit, huge external debt service requirements, high rates of interest and persistent depreciation of the dram. Real GDP growth slowed to 3.3% in 1999, during which the average officially-registered rate of unemployment was 10.9%, although large numbers were effectively underemployed. The Government responded with new plans for avoiding over-dependence on the Russian Federation and the other former Soviet republics, and by seeking inward investment to help modernize its industry and other sectors of the economy. Foreign loans were used to finance a budget deficit that reached 5.3% of GDP.

From 2001, the Government focused on strengthening the business environment, and five years of spectacular double-digit growth of real GDP followed, reaching 13.9% in 2005 on the back of a good harvest. The rapid growth was spurred by the expanding construction sector, promotion of investment and the export sector, particularly manufacturing. By 2004 Armenia's GDP had finally recovered to its pre-independence level, but this masked a decade of widening wealth inequalities, and a persistently high rate of unemployment and underemployment—resulting in increasing poverty in rural areas especially. Real GDP growth slowed in 2006 to 7.5%, as the construction boom slackened and energy prices increased, though inflation was under control at around 3% and the budget deficit had narrowed to around 2%.

The privatization of arable land, instituted immediately after independence in 1991, was almost complete by the end of 1996, so that private farms accounted for some 95% of agricultural production in 1997. By 1998 most small enterprises had also been privatized, as were some 90% of medium and larger enterprises (after a slower start), following the launch of a major new programme in 1995. The electricity distribution system was privatized in 2002.

Armenian Apostolic Church

A denomination of 'Lesser' or 'Oriental' **Orthodox Christianity** intrinsically linked to the state of **Armenia**. Christianity was brought to Armenia by SS Thaddeus and Bartholomew in the 1st century AD, and the apparent adherence to their tradition lends the Church its 'Apostolic' title. Armenia became the first Christian state in the world in 301. Armenian Christianity soon diverged from the dominant traditions of western **Roman Catholicism** and eastern Orthodox Christianity, and the history of its Apostolic Church and the country have since been interwoven.

The unique Armenian script was devised in the early years of the 5th century by St Mesrob as a means of religious instruction. Ties between the Church and Armenian culture remain strong and in 2001 the country celebrated 1,700 years of Christianity. Karekin II has been Supreme Patriarch and Catholicos since 1999.

Armenian Development Agency (ADA)

Set up by the Government of **Armenia** in 1998 to facilitate foreign direct investments and promote exports.

General Director: Dr Vahagn Movsisyan.
Address: Charents St 17, 375025 Yerevan.
Telephone: (10) 570170.
Fax: (10) 542272.
E-mail: info@ada.am
Internet: www.ada.am

Armenian question

The issue of whether the massacres of **Armenians** in the last years of the Ottoman Empire should be recognized as genocide. Turkey strongly resists this. It regards the deaths as part of a general loss of life arising from the collapse of the Ottoman Empire, and emphasizes that many Turks were also killed by Armenian groups at this time. **Armenia**, as an independent state since 1991, has lobbied persistently for 'the Armenian genocide' (Armenians use the term *metz yeghern*, meaning 'great crime' or 'great evil') to become an internationally-accepted part of the historical record. The Armenian case is that the treatment of the Armenian minority in areas under Ottoman control, in a period beginning with the Russo-Turkish war in the 1870s and including the large-scale massacres of 1894–96 and 1915, represented an attempt at their extermination. Armenia wants an apology from Turkey, in particular for the events of 1915, when the Armenians were accused of aiding the **Russian** invaders during the First World War, and many hundreds of thousands of Armenians (1.5 million is a commonly-cited estimate) were killed by Turkish soldiers or died of starvation during their forced deportation from eastern Turkey to Syria and Mesopotamia. Resolutions proposing the explicit recognition of 'the Armenian genocide' are debated frequently in legislatures in Europe and North America. Turkey is particularly sensitive to the possibility of such a resolution being passed by the European Parliament, because of the implications for its efforts to gain membership of the **European Union**.

Armenian Revolutionary Federation
Hai Heghapokhakan Dashnaktsutyun (HHD/Dashnak)

The historic Armenian nationalist political movement/party originally founded in 1890, which was the governing party in pre-Soviet independent **Armenia** (1918–20) and retained a large following in the **Armenian** diaspora after being proscribed by the Bolsheviks in 1920. Dashnak is affiliated to the **Socialist International**, having been a member of the pre-First World War Second International.

Re-established in 1990 as a nationalist opposition party of socialist orientation, Dashnak strongly criticized the conduct of the **Nagorno-Karabakh** war by the Government of the **Pan-Armenian National Movement** (HHSh), which claimed in response that Dashnak leaders in exile had co-operated with the **Soviet** security authorities. At the end of 1994 the party was suspended by presidential decree, on the grounds that it had engaged in terrorism and drug-trafficking. Some 30 Dashnak activists were put on trial in March 1996 charged with involvement in an alleged coup attempt during the elections. Chairman Vahan Hovhanissian was among those convicted and sentenced to prison, but all were released in February 1998 when the ban on the party was lifted, a week after the resignation of President Ter-Petrossian (HHSh).

Dashnak backed the successful candidacy of Robert **Kocharian** (non-party) in the March 1998 presidential elections, following which Hovhanissian became a presidential adviser and the party obtained two ministerial portfolios in the new Government. In the May 1999 **National Assembly** elections Dashnak achieved third place with nine of the 131 seats and 7.8% of the proportional vote, subsequently obtaining one portfolio in the new government coalition.

In February 2000 Dashnak held its 28th world congress in Tsaghkadzor (its first in Armenia since 1919), deciding to establish the party's head office in Yerevan. (The party has significant branches active in Lebanon and Nagorno-Karabakh.)

Continuing to back Kocharian, Dashnak secured fourth place in legislative elections held in May 2003 with an increased share of 11 seats and 11.5% of the vote. It remains a key member of the governing coalition.

Leadership: Ruben Hagobian, Vahan Hovhanissian (Chairs);

Hrand Margaryan (Chair of World Bureau).

Address: Mher Mkrtchyan St 30, 375010 Yerevan.

Telephone: (10) 521502.

Fax: (10) 520426.

E-mail: info@arfd.am

Internet: www.arfd.am

Armenian Stock Exchange (Armex)

First established as the Securities Market Members' Association, and registered in 2001 as a self-regulated organization.

Executive Director: Armen Melikyan.

Address: 3rd and 4th Floors, Mher Mkrtchyan St 5B, 375010 Yerevan.

Telephone and Fax: (10) 543324.

E-mail: info@armex.am

Internet: www.armex.am

Armenians

An Indo-European people concentrated in the modern republic of **Armenia** but spread throughout neighbouring states. The name Armenian is derived from the Greek and Persian names—Armenioi and Armina respectively—given to a people known to themselves as the Hayq (singular: Hay). The Armenian language is Indo-European but has many phonetic and grammatical similarities to the neighbouring Caucasian tongues. Armenians pride themselves that their country was the first to adopt Christianity officially as a state religion (in 301) and modern Armenians are mostly either of the **Armenian Apostolic Church** or part of the Catholic Church of Armenia.

Armenians dominated their historic region—now mostly occupied by modern Turkey—until Muslim conquerors gained ascendancy from the 7th century. In the 19th century historic Armenia was divided between the Ottoman Turks and the

Russian Empire. The division prompted a mass migration of Armenians from Turkey, including many to Europe and the USA as well as to Russian Armenia. Those remaining in Turkey faced mass persecution in 1915 as the Ottoman Empire viewed them as a potential 'fifth column'. Many were deported to areas further south. The Armenians claim many hundreds of thousands were killed and consider this episode a purposeful genocide (*see* **Armenian question**).

The Armenians in Russia were concentrated (a) in what is now the Armenian Republic, (b) in what is now the disputed enclave of **Nagorno-Karabakh** in neighbouring **Azerbaijan**, and (c) to a lesser extent in parts of what is now **Georgia**. In the **Soviet** era they largely abandoned their traditional agricultural lifestyle and became urbanized through industrialization drives. Those who live in what is now Georgia, estimated to number some 250–300,000, have no separate representation and the Georgian authorities are not keen to develop this, although there are Armenian-language facilities throughout the country. The Armenians live mainly in urban centres, where they have been greatly russified, but there are also significant rural communities in southern Georgia, particularly **Javakheti**, and the coastal regions of **Abkhazia** and **Adzharia**.

Armenpress

Armenia's main and oldest-established news agency, which was restructured as a joint-stock company in 1997 but remains in state ownership. It was originally founded in 1922, and holds a large photographic archive on Armenian history. Armenpress provides a daily news service in Armenian, English and Russian.

Director: Hrayr Zoryan.
Address: 4th Floor, Isaahakian St 28, 375009 Yerevan.
Telephone: (10) 526702.
Fax: (10) 525798.
E-mail: contact@armenpress.am
Internet: www.armenpress.am

Armex *see* **Armenian Stock Exchange**.

Aromani *see* **Vlachs**.

Astrakhan

A historic city—and a similarly-named *oblast* (region)—at the mouth of the **Volga** river in south-eastern **European Russia**. *Population*: 501,000 (2005 estimate). The original settlement became a key trading city in the Mongol

Golden Horde in the 14th century and was the capital of the **Tatar** Astrakhan khanate until it was conquered by the Russian Tsar, Ivan the Terrible, in 1556. It has been an integral part of **Russia** ever since.

Economic activity centres on the use of the Volga as access for goods flowing in and out of the Russia's industrial heartland and the bountiful products of the Caspian Sea. However, the shallow depths of the sea's northern waters mean that seagoing vessels cannot reach the city's main port. Astrakhan is home to a large fishing fleet and fish processing and **caviar** preserving are major activities.

August coup

In the **Soviet Union**, the attempted *coup d'état* of 19–21 August 1991 to oust President Mikhail **Gorbachev** and install a hardline communist regime. The hardliners were seeking to prevent the continuation of the reform and devolution policies which they saw as destroying the Soviet communist system. A new Union treaty for the Soviet Union was about to be signed the following day, when members of the Politburo of the **Communist Party of the Soviet Union** (KPSS) and the heads of the Soviet military and security services detained Gorbachev at his villa in the **Crimea**. Announcing Gorbachev's removal on health grounds, they set up a Committee of the State of Emergency, but were met by strong popular resistance in **Moscow**, spearheaded by the then Russian President Boris **Yeltsin** who took a public stand with demonstrators outside the Russian parliament building (the **White House**). Soldiers sent in with tanks either switched sides or turned back, and without full military backing the August coup quickly collapsed. It marked a critical moment, however, in the passing of effective power from Gorbachev to Yeltsin and, ironically, precipitated the rapid disintegration of the Soviet Union and the banning of the KPSS.

Aum Shinrikyo
(or Aleph)

A Japan-based religious cult, notoriously responsible for the 1995 sarin nerve-gas attack in Tokyo. At its peak it claimed around 30,000 followers in the **Russian Federation**. The cult is based loosely on **Buddhism** and Hinduism and teaches enlightenment through meditation and austerity. It changed its name to Aleph in January 2000 as part of its efforts to distance itself from its founder Shoko Asahara, who, it admits, was responsible for the 1995 attack. The political/violent nature of the sect has led to close monitoring of its adherents. Since 1995 it has lost support worldwide and has dwindled in numbers, and supporters in Russia number only around 300.

Avars

A Caucasian people who make up the largest group in the ethnically diverse **Russian** republic of **Dagestan**. Numbering around 750,000 the Avars account for about 29% of the republic's population. Unconnected to the historic Avars of central Asia who invaded **central Europe** from the 7th century, the Dagestani Avars were effectively created from an assortment of local groups in the 1930s. They were employed by the Russian and **Soviet** authorities as the ruling elite in Dagestan, but the introduction of a democratic system in 1992 has diluted this dominance. In 1993 ethnic Avars clashed with **Chechens** and Laks over land rights. Like most Dagestanis they are Sunni **Muslims**, and mainly absorbed in agricultural activity. The cultural predominance of the Turkic **Kumyk** group in the region has seen some Avars assimilated.

AXCP *see* **Azerbaijan Popular Front Party**.

Axlebi *see* **New Rights**.

Azadliq *see* **Freedom**.

Azarov, Mykola

First Deputy Prime Minister and Minister of Finance, **Ukraine**. **Russian**-born Azarov is a leading figure in Prime Minister Viktor **Yanukovych**'s **Party of Regions** (PR). A geologist by training, he spent six years as head of the State Tax Administration, before his first appointment as Finance Minister in November 2002 during the presidency of Leonid **Kuchma**, a long-time ally. He returned to office in August 2006, following the reappointment of Yanukovych as Prime Minister.

Mykola Azarov was born Nikolay Yanovych Pakhlo on 17 December 1947 in Kaluga, Russia. He took his wife Lyudmila Azarova's family name after their marriage; they have one son. He graduated in geology from the Lomonosov Moscow State University in 1971, and further study later in life earned him a doctorate and a professorship, plus full membership of Ukraine's National Academy of Sciences. From 1971 he worked for five years at the Tula coal mine, before joining the Moscow Research Design Coal Institute.

In 1984 he moved to Ukraine, becoming Deputy Director and then Director of the Ukrainian State Research and Design Institute of Mining Geology, Geomechanics and Mine Survey, based in Donetsk, where he has built up much support among the business community. A decade later he won election for the first time to the **Supreme Council**, and became head of the Budget Committee and a member of other economic and financial councils. In 1996 he was appointed head of the State Tax Administration, a post he was to hold for six years.

A member of the forerunner party to the PR since 1994, he was appointed as the reformed party's first leader in March 2001, but resigned at the end of the year, fearing that his job as tax chief might be seen to conflict with his party role in the run-up to the 2002 elections.

When the Donetsk Governor Yanukovych was appointed Prime Minister in November 2002, he chose Azarov as his First Deputy Prime Minister and Finance Minister. At the time of the disputed presidential elections of 2004, he briefly acted as Prime Minister, in 7–28 December and 5–24 January 2005. He was then out of government until the electoral success in March 2006 of the PR (in which he now heads the Political Council); Yanukovych returned as Prime Minister in August and he brought Azarov back into his team to fill the same roles as in 2002–04, namely First Deputy Prime Minister and Finance Minister. He has on occasion been criticized for his authoritarian approach and for retaining too much of his Russian background: he gives many speeches in Russian, despite being fluent in Ukrainian. He has campaigned strongly for the creation of the **Single Economic Space**, joining Russia, Ukraine, **Belarus** and Kazakhstan.

Address: Ministry of Finance, M. Grushevskogo St 12/2, 01008 Kiev.
Telephone: (44) 2935293.
Fax: (44) 2938243.
E-mail: infomf@minfin.gov.ua
Internet: www.minfin.gov.ua

AzarTAc (or AzerTAj)
Azarbaycan Dövlat Teleqraf Agentıy

The state news agency in **Azerbaijan**, originally founded in 1920 as AzerTAg.
Director-General: Aslan Aslanov.
Address: Bül-Bül pr. 18, 1000 Baku.
Telephone: (12) 4935929.
Fax: (12) 4936265.
E-mail: azertac@azdata.net
Internet: www.azertag.net

Azerbaijan
Azarbaycan Respublikasi

An independent republic in the eastern **Caucasus**, bordering Iran to the south, **Georgia** and the **Russian** republic of **Dagestan** to the north, **Armenia** to the west and the Caspian Sea to the east. Administratively, the country is divided into 74 districts (*rajons*), an autonomous republic and an autonomous region (*oblast*). The autonomous republic, **Azeri**-populated **Nakhichevan**, is separated geographically from the rest of Azerbaijan by Armenian territory. The autonomous region, the mainly **Armenian**-populated enclave of **Nagorno-Karabakh**, has been the focus of lengthy conflict with **Armenia** (see below).

Area: 86,600 sq km; *capital*: **Baku**; *population*: 8.4m. (2005 estimate), comprising ethnic **Azeris** 90.6%, **Lezghins** 2.2%, **Russians** 1.8%, Armenians 1.5%, others 3.9%; *official language*: Azeri; *religion*: **Muslim** 93.4%, **Russian Orthodox** 2.5%, **Armenian Apostolic Church** 2.3%, others 1.8% (1995 estimate).

Under the new Constitution adopted in November 1995, legislative authority is vested in the **National Assembly** (Milli Majlis), which has 125 members elected for a five-year term. (Constitutional amendments in 2002 made all 125 seats into single-member constituencies, whereas previously 25 had been elected by proportional representation according to party lists.) Executive power rests with the President, who is directly elected by universal adult suffrage for a non-renewable five-year term, and who appoints the Cabinet of Ministers, subject to approval by the Assembly.

History: Having from ancient times experienced rule by the Medes, Greeks and Persians, Azerbaijan came under Arab control in the 7th century, heralding the rise of Islam as the principal religion. Penetration by **Turkic** tribes from the 11th century onwards had a significant impact on the ethnic evolution of the population before the region fell again under Persian control in the 1500s. In the second half of the 18th century political fragmentation and internecine conflicts encouraged Russian encroachment. Two Russo-Persian wars followed, in 1804–13 and 1826–28, resulting in the division of the territory; the northern part (now independent Azerbaijan) was integrated into the Russian Empire while the southern area remained in Persian (Iranian) hands.

After the Russian Revolution of October 1917, there was a brief period of pro-Bolshevik rule in Azerbaijan before an anti-Soviet nationalist Government took power and declared the country an independent state in May 1918. However, Azerbaijan was reconquered by the Red Army in 1920 and joined the **Soviet Union** in 1922 as part of the Transcaucasian Soviet Federative Socialist Republic (together with Armenia and Georgia). In 1936 it became the Azerbaijan Soviet Socialist Republic with full union republic status. During this period religious intolerance was severe (reflecting Soviet efforts to reduce the influence of Islam in the republic), collectivization of agriculture led to peasant uprisings and their suppression, and political purges of perceived opponents of Stalin's regime took a heavy toll.

During the Second World War Soviet troops occupied Iranian Azerbaijan, rekindling pan-Azerbaijani sentiments. However, they were forced to withdraw under pressure from the USA and UK in 1946, in one of the first confrontations of what became the **Cold War** between the Soviet Union and the West.

Since the 1960s Azerbaijan's political course has revolved around the fortunes of its most influential figure, Heydar **Aliyev** (until his death in 2003), and the long-standing ethnic tension with neighbouring Armenia, particularly over the disputed territory of Nagorno-Karabakh.

Aliyev, installed as First Secretary of the Azerbaijan Communist Party (AKP) in 1969, was appointed to the Politburo in **Moscow** from 1982, the highest position ever reached by an Azeri in the Soviet Union. In 1987, however, he was removed by the then leader Mikhail **Gorbachev** for alleged corruption. The following year fighting escalated in Nagorno-Karabakh between Azerbaijani forces and ethnic Armenian separatists.

The ensuing protracted military conflict took place against the backdrop of the collapse of the Soviet Union and the re-establishment, in 1991, of Azerbaijani independence under President Ayaz Mutalibov (the last AKP First Secretary).

Mutalibov was re-elected President unopposed in September 1991. However, unrest in Azerbaijan over defeats by Armenia in Nagorno-Karabakh led to his resignation in March 1992. His successor Abulfaz Elchibey of the nationalist **Azerbaijan Popular Front Party** (AXCP), elected in June 1992, was in turn forced to resign a year later. At this point Aliyev, now leading the **New Azerbaijan Party** (YAP), again took up the political reins, claiming a conclusive victory in the presidential election of October 1993. A ceasefire agreement with Armenia, brokered by the Russian Federation, was reached in May 1994, although Azerbaijan by this time had lost control of almost 20% of its territory and was facing a serious refugee problem.

Restrictive registration requirements for the first post-Soviet elections to the National Assembly in November 1995 meant that only eight parties were allowed to take part. Official results (after further polling in February 1996) gave the YAP and independent candidates supporting President Aliyev an overwhelming majority, but international observers declared that the elections had not been conducted fairly, while opposition groups demanded fresh balloting.

In further presidential elections held in October 1998, Aliyev easily secured re-election, while his son Ilham **Aliyev** headed the YAP list in a resounding electoral victory in November 2000. The conduct and outcome of the polling again attracted censure from the opposition parties and international observers. Despite his dubious success, questions arose early in this new term over Aliyev's health and the succession of power. A new Constitution was confirmed by plebiscite in August 2002. Among reforms was the abolition of the partial proportional representation system for elections and contingencies to transfer executive power to the presidentially-appointed Prime Minister in times of the President's incapacity, rather than the parliamentarily-elected Speaker. The 96% approval in the referendum was widely questioned and met with large-scale protests in September 2002 which saw calls for Aliyev's resignation.

President Aliyev collapsed during a televised debate in April 2003 and failed to return to active duty. His son was approved as Prime Minister, and thereby

25

acting Head of State, in August 2003 and began actively campaigning as a presidential candidate within days; Artur **Rasizade**, who had previously held the post of Prime Minister since 1996, continued to fulfil the day-to-day role. Ongoing demonstrations led to fierce clashes with security forces in September. In presidential elections held on 15 October, Ilham Aliyev secured 76.8% of the votes cast to win on the first ballot against seven other candidates, following which Artur Rasizade was reappointed Prime Minister of a YAP-dominated Government. Heydar Aliyev died in December.

The new President Aliyev, concerned by how fragile the regimes of several other post-Soviet countries were proving in the face of popular opposition movements (the '**colour revolutions**'), moved to silence protest in Azerbaijan with a series of crackdowns on demonstrators and the press. Domestic and international anger, however, soon prompted him to seek a rapprochement with his detractors. The newly formed opposition alliance **New Policy** (YeS) was invited to talks with the Government in May 2005, though continued harsh treatment of demonstrators undermined Aliyev's apparent goodwill. Ruslan Bashirli, leader of the opposition youth movement New Thinking (Yeni Fikir), was arrested in August 2005 on suspicion of plotting an Armenian-financed coup. Several former ministers were arrested over further coup rumours in the run-up to legislative elections in November of that year.

Latest elections: In official results from the 6 November 2005 legislative elections, the YAP claimed 56 of the 115 seats up for contest (out of 125), the **Freedom** (Azadliq) bloc 9, eight other parties 10 between them and independents 40. The election again attracted censure from the opposition parties and international observers.

Recent Developments: Serious doubts over the legitimacy of the 2005 elections sparked yet more protests, and prompted a predictable clampdown by the Government including the arrest of senior opposition leaders. Nevertheless, opposition to Aliyev began to weaken through the course of 2006 as internal differences emerged within the Freedom bloc over its level of participation in electoral re-runs in May.

International relations and defence: Since independence, Azerbaijan has been admitted to the UN, the **Organization for Security and Co-operation in Europe** (OSCE), the **Commonwealth of Independent States** (CIS), the **Organization of the Islamic Conference** (OIC), the **Economic Co-operation Organization** (ECO), the **Non-Aligned Movement** (as an observer) and the **Organization of the Black Sea Economic Co-operation**. It is also a member of NATO's **Partnership for Peace** and in 1996 signed a partnership and co-operation agreement with the **European Union** (together with Armenia and Georgia). In February 1999 Foreign Minister Tofik Zulfagarov stated that integration into European and trans-Atlantic institutions was a priority for Azerbaijan. In January 2001 the **Council of Europe**'s Ministerial Committee voted unanimously to admit Azerbaijan (and Armenia) to membership. Since then, Azerbaijan has moved towards closer ties with the USA, which saw restrictions on trade lifted in January 2002, and an official visit for President Ilham Aliyev to Washington, DC, in April 2005.

At regional level, Azerbaijan has pursued the delimitation of Caspian Sea boundaries with the other littoral states (Iran, Kazakhstan, Russian Federation and Turkmenistan) with a view to determining the ownership of the rich oil and gas resources in the area (*see* **Azerbaijan, economy**). A convention on the environmental protection of the sea was signed by the affected states in November 2003. Ties to Iran have been reinforced, with an agreement on a new oil pipeline signed in October 2002, and strengthened in the face of US aggression towards Iran from 2005.

Despite continuing negotiations between Azerbaijan and Armenia over Nagorno-Karabakh, under the aegis of the OSCE's **Minsk Group**, no real progress has been made on a settlement. The 1994 ceasefire broadly held, and a series of meetings in 1999–2000 between President Heydar Aliyev and his Armenian counterpart, Robert **Kocharian**, gave some impetus to the quest for an agreement. A suggested possibility of an exchange of territory under which Azerbaijan would obtain a corridor to its Nakhichevan enclave in return for concessions on the status of Nagorno-Karabakh has been rejected. Though talks appeared promising in December 2003, tensions returned in 2004 as the 10th anniversary of the conflict approached. Negotiations between new President Ilham Aliyev and Kocharian have made no progress.

Azerbaijan's defence budget totalled some US $306m. in 2006, equivalent to about 3.1% of GDP. Total armed forces at August 2006 were 66,740, including those drafted under compulsory conscription of 17 months, while reservists numbered an estimated 300,000.

Azerbaijan, economy

An economy until recently relatively undeveloped, which shrank dramatically in the first half of the 1990s but has posted double-digit growth since 2001. Its future is heavily based on exploitation of the rich hydrocarbon reserves beneath the Caspian Sea, the prospects for which have begun to alleviate the familiar post-**Soviet** transition problems.

GNP: US $10,399m. (2005); *GNP per capita*: $1,240 (2005); *GDP at PPP*: $47,036m. (2005); *GDP per capita at PPP*: $5,607 (2005); *exports*: $4,235m. (2004); *imports*: $6,310m. (2004); *currency*: new manat (plural: new manats; US $1=M0.875 at the end of December 2006).

In 2004 industry accounted for 55.4% of GDP, agriculture 12.3% and services 32.3%. Some 39.9% of the 4.1 million workforce are engaged in agriculture and fisheries, 11.6% in industry and 48.5% in services. About 21% of the land is arable, 3% under permanent crops, 31% permanent pasture and 11% forests and woodland. The main crops are grain, apples, watermelons and other fruit, vegetables and cotton. Mineral resources include petroleum, natural gas, iron ore, non-ferrous metals and alunite (alum-stone). The main industries include petrochemicals, iron and steel, aluminium and glass and ceramics, while parts of the traditional textiles and clothing sector have declined in the face of external competition. In 2003 about 12% of domestic electricity generation was produced from hydroelectricity and the other 88% from thermal power stations.

Azerbaijan's main exports by value in 2004 were mineral products (accounting for 82% of the total). The principal imports were machinery and electrical equipment (31%), as well as metals and metal products (17%) and mineral products (14%). In 2004 45% of Azerbaijan's exports went to Italy, 9% to Israel and 6% to the **Russian Federation**. The main sources of imports were the Russian Federation (16%), the UK (12%) and Kazakhstan (7%).

Azerbaijan has long exploited its oil and gas resources in the Caspian Sea, with the result that the Apsheron peninsula (including **Baku**) is one of the most polluted land areas in the world. Production fell sharply in the 1980s, but following independence in 1991 major agreements were concluded for development of Caspian Sea reserves, notably the US $8,000m. 'deal of the century' signed by the Azerbaijan International Operating Company (AIOC) in September 1994. Although some exploring consortia achieved disappointing results, oil production rose to 452,000 barrels per day (b/d) by 2005, of which over three-quarters was exported. By 2005 Azerbaijan's oil reserves were put at 7,000m. barrels, depending in part on the still-unresolved issue of delimitation of littoral states' rights in the Caspian: Russia, Azerbaijan and Kazakhstan signed an agreement in 2003 to divide the northern section of the Caspian, but Iran and Turkey did not back the deal. Azerbaijan's production capacity has risen significantly since the completion in 2005 of the main export pipeline (MEP), a 1,768-km link between Baku and the Turkish Mediterranean port of Ceyhan via **Georgia** (*see* **Baku–Tbilisi–Ceyhan (BTC) pipeline**) and of other major investment projects at the Azeri-Chiraq-Guneshi oil field and the Shah Deniz gas fields in 2006.

Azerbaijan emerged from Soviet rule with an economy relatively less developed than those of neighbouring **Armenia** or Georgia and with its trade closely tied to the other Soviet republics. Economic difficulties were aggravated by the ongoing conflict with Armenia over **Nagorno-Karabakh**, which adversely affected agricultural production and caused huge refugee flows. At the same time, transport communications through Georgia and the southern Russian republics of **Dagestan** and **Chechnya** were disrupted by conflict in those areas. Accordingly, officially recorded GDP contracted by nearly 60% in 1990–95 and in 1996 was only half that of 1990.

Assisted by a ceasefire in Nagorno-Karabakh and large foreign investment in the oil sector, the economy showed substantial improvement from 1997 on the basis of a comprehensive stabilization programme drawn up by the Government and backed by the **International Monetary Fund**. Inflation was reduced to around zero by the end of 1997, during which real GDP expanded by 5.8%, followed by growth of 10% in 1998 (including 23% growth in the oil sector). Azerbaijan was little affected by the 1998 Russian financial crisis (*see* **Russian Federation, economy**), although the decline in world oil prices in 1998–99 and sharply reduced oil investment resulted in GDP growth slowing to 7.4% in 1999. Growth in the agriculture sector was around 7% in 1999, but non-oil industrial output continued to decline, with previously dominant sectors such as metallurgy and machine-building having come to a virtual standstill. The unemployment rate was given as 14% in 1999 but it was unofficially estimated to be considerably higher, reaching at least 20%.

The rapid expansion of the oil sector from 2000 spurred strong GDP growth, consistently over 10% and reaching a staggering 26% in 2005. The Government struggled to keep inflation under control: it rose to 6% in 2004 and 10% in 2005. The exchange rate also fluctuated significantly, with a 10%-plus appreciation of the manat against the dollar within just two hours on 17 September 2005; a new manat was issued on 1 January 2006 worth 5,000 old manats. Strong growth is expected to continue, though foreign direct investment is likely to decline following the completion of several major infrastructure projects. Domestic investment is growing, but it is vital for the Government to channel funds into the non-oil sector of the economy. If no new oil reserves are found, production is expected to peak in 2011 and last for only 20 more years after that.

Membership of the **World Trade Organization**, which has been under discussion since 1997, would accelerate economic reform and open up foreign markets.

Privatization effectively began only in 1995, with many shops and small enterprises passing into the private sector in 1996–97 and more medium-sized businesses in 1997–99 mainly through an auction process; however, the Government has kept certain major strategic businesses within the public sector, including the state oil company SOCAR.

Azerbaijan Popular Front Party
Azarbaycan Xalq Cabhasi Partiyasi (AXCP)

A broad-based political party in **Azerbaijan** founded in 1989 under the leadership of Abulfaz Elchibey, which opposes the Governments of Heydar and Ilham **Aliyev** of the **New Azerbaijan Party** (YAP).

The Azerbaijan Popular Front (AXC) originally came into being to demand reform of the then communist-run system. It took a **pan-Turkic** line, supporting nationalist calls for the acquisition of **Azeri**-populated areas of northern Iran, and in January 1990 some of its members were among 150 people killed by the security forces in **Baku** and elsewhere in disturbances arising from AXC-led anti-

Armenia demonstrations.

Allowed to contest the Supreme Soviet elections of autumn 1990, the AXC-led opposition won only 45 of the 360 seats (with a vote share of 12.5%). Together with other opposition parties, the AXC boycotted the direct presidential election held in September 1991 but subsequently brought about the resignation of President Ayaz Mutalibov of the Azerbaijan Communist Party (AKP) in March 1992. In a further presidential election in June 1992, Elchibey was victorious with 59.4% of the vote against four other candidates.

The AXC-led Government blocked ratification of Azerbaijan's membership of the **Commonwealth of Independent States** but came under increasing pressure from opposition groups, notably Heydar Aliyev's recently-formed YAP. Replaced as Head of State by Aliyev in June 1993, Elchibey fled to **Nakhichevan** and disputed the official results of an August referendum (boycotted by the AXC) in which only 2% of voters were said to have expressed confidence in Elchibey. Aliyev secured popular endorsement as President in October 1993, in direct elections which were also boycotted by the AXC. The authorities subsequently launched a crackdown on the AXC, raiding its headquarters in Baku in February 1994 and arresting 100 AXC activists. Nevertheless, the AXC was able in 1994-95 to command substantial popular support for its opposition to the Aliyev Government's policy of seeking a **Nagorno-Karabakh** settlement through the mediation of the **Russian Federation**. (It was in 1995 that the AXC officially changed its name to the AXCP.)

In May 1995 Elchibey repeated the AXCP's call for the creation of a 'greater Azerbaijan', to include the estimated 15 million ethnic Azeris inhabiting northern Iran. In the same month Shahmerdan Jafarov, an AXCP deputy, was stripped of his parliamentary immunity and accused of setting up illegal armed groups in Nakhichevan, where Elchibey's residence was reportedly surrounded by government troops. In June 1995 Jafarov was shot in a clash in the enclave, later dying of his injuries.

In the November 1995 **National Assembly** elections the AXCP was officially credited with winning three proportional seats on the basis of a national vote share of 10%, and it took a fourth seat in balloting for unfilled seats in February 1996. Proceedings against AXCP members early in 1996 included the sentencing to death *in absentia* of former Defence Minister Rakhim Gaziyev for treason, although his sentence was commuted to life imprisonment on his extradition from **Moscow** to Baku in April. Some AXCP leaders were released under a presidential amnesty in July 1996, while in October 1997 Elchibey returned to Baku after four years in internal exile.

The AXCP also boycotted the October 1998 presidential elections, following which Elchibey was put on trial for insulting the Head of State. The cancellation of these proceedings in February 1999 on the initiative of President Aliyev was widely attributed to international pressure. Thereafter the AXCP continued to be the leading component in various opposition fronts. However, increasing internal divisions led to an open split in August 2000, coinciding with the death of Elchibey in Turkey from cancer. A 'reformist' faction led by former AXCP Deputy Chairman Ali Kerimli advocated accommodation with the regime, while the 'conservative' wing led by Murmahmud Fattayev maintained an uncompromising opposition line.

The Fattayev faction of the AXCP was barred from presenting candidates in the November 2000 Assembly elections, instead forming an alliance with the **Equality** (Musavat) party. The Kerimli faction of the AXCP was allowed to stand, however. It was credited with 10.9% of the vote in the proportional section and six seats, including one won in re-runs in early January 2001. In the wake of the balloting both factions joined in opposition condemnations of its validity. In mid-January 2001 the Kerimli AXCP announced jointly with the Civil Unity Party that its deputies would participate in the work of the new Assembly, though only in order to campaign for new elections. AXCP candidate Gudrat Hasan-Guliyev came a distant seventh in presidential elections in October 2003.

Both sides of the AXCP were reconciled in their opposition to the Government in the lead up to the November 2005 legislative elections, with the party joining the **Freedom** (Azadliq) bloc with Equality and the Azerbaijan Democratic Party. After winning only a single seat (of the nine won by the Freedom bloc), the AXCP was at the forefront of a strong protest campaign against apparent irregularities in the vote. Karimli in particular was vociferous in urging sit-ins and prolonged campaigning, including withdrawing from the May re-runs of officially disputed seats. His stance pitted the AXCP against Equality and the latter withdrew from the Freedom alliance in February 2006.

Leadership: Ali Kerimli (Chair of 'reformist' faction); Murmahmud Fattayev (Chair of 'conservative' faction).

Address: Metti Hussein küç. 2, Milli Majlis, 1152 Baku.

Telephone: (12) 4980794.

E-mail: axcp@axcp.org

Internet: www.axcp.org

Azerbaijani Export and Investment Promotion Foundation
(Azpromo)

Set up as a joint public-private initiative by the Ministry of Economic Development of **Azerbaijan** in 2003 as an independent organization for the promotion of foreign investment and export of non-oil products.

Chair: Heidar Babaev.
Address: U. Hajibayov St 40, 1000 Baku.
Telephone: (12) 5980147.
Fax: (12) 5980152.
E-mail: office@azerinvest.com
Internet: www.azpromo.org

Azeris

A **Turkic people** concentrated in **Azerbaijan,** descended from Seljuk Turks who invaded the region in the 11th century and incorporated the ethnic Iranian and Caucasian groups around the southern shores of the Caspian Sea. Their language belongs to the Turkmen or Oguz group of Turkic languages, similar to that spoken by Turkic people throughout the region. Until the 20th century Azeri was transcribed using Arabic script. Under **Soviet** domination, between 1939 and 1992, the **Cyrillic alphabet** was used but since independence Azeri has been written with the Latin alphabet. Most Azeris are **Muslim,** with roughly two-thirds following the Shi'a sect and one-third the Sunni sect. The 15–20 million Azari Turks living in northern Iran, ethnically identical to Azeris, have embraced Shi'a Islam and are well integrated into Iranian society.

AzerTaj *see* **AzarTAc.**

Azgayin Joghov *see* **National Assembly (Armenia).**

AZhD *see* **National Democratic Alliance Party.**

AZhK *see* **National Democratic Party.**

AZhM *see* **National Democratic Union.**

AZM *see* **National Unity Party.**

Azpromo *see* **Azerbaijani Export and Investment Promotion Foundation.**

B

Baku

The capital city and major urban centre of **Azerbaijan**. *Population*: 1.8m. (2003 estimate). The natural Baku harbour provides the best port on the Caspian Sea. Settlement at the site dates back to several centuries BC but the first historical reference dates from 885 AD. Long dominated by the Persian Empire, Baku became an important economic and administrative centre. **Russian** rule first came in a 12-year spell from 1723 and was finally established permanently in 1806. After the Russian Revolution Baku was made the capital of the Azeri republic, a role it maintained after the country's independence in 1991.

The oil industry has long dominated Baku's economy. Surface wells have been exploited for fuel since the 15th century. Modern commercial collection began in 1872, the second such venture in the world (after that in Ploieşti in Romania). Although the city's surrounding sources have largely dried up, Azerbaijan's claims in the Caspian remain bountiful and there are other sites inland. Along with extraction Baku has specialized in associated manufacture, producing equipment and machinery for the oil and chemical industries.

Baku Stock Exchange
Baki Fond Birjasi

The stock exchange for **Azerbaijan**, based in **Baku**. Founded in 2000, it is a closed joint-stock company trading in securities.

President: Anar Akhundov.
Address: Bül Bül pr. 19, 1000 Baku.
Telephone: (12) 4988522.
Fax: (12) 4937793.
E-mail: info@bse.az
Internet: www.bse.az

Baku–Tbilisi–Ceyhan (BTC) pipeline

Azerbaijan's main oil export pipeline. It runs for 1,768 km from the Azeri-Chirag-Guneshli oil field in the Caspian Sea to the Mediterranean, the second longest pipeline in the world, with the capacity to deliver a million barrels per day. The first quarter of its total length is through Azerbaijan, then it runs for 259 km through **Georgia**, and 1,076 km through Turkey to the transhipment terminal at Ceyhan on the Mediterranean coast. Discussion on the route of the pipeline began in the late 1990s, and the Baku–Tbilisi–Ceyhan route was approved in November 1999. Construction began in September 2002. The Baku end of the pipeline was inaugurated on 10 May 2005, but as 10 million barrels of oil were required to fill the pipeline the first oil only reached Ceyhan on 28 May 2006. The whole pipeline was inaugurated on 13 July 2006, though it will take around two years to reach normal working capacity. BP (UK) holds a 30% share in the pipeline; other shareholders are the State Oil Company of Azerbaijan (SOCAR); Unocal, ConocoPhillips and Amerada Hess (USA); Statoil (Norway); TPAO (Turkey); Eni/AGIP (Italy); Total (France); and Itochu and Inpex (Japan). Transit fees will be payable to Georgia and Turkey. Both Kazakhstan and Turkmenistan are considering building pipelines across the Caspian to link with the BTC pipeline.

Balkans

The south-east peninsula of Europe. The name derives from the Turkish for mountain and the area is traversed by various mountain chains, particularly in the west. The Balkans stretch south from the Pannonian plain (mainly in Hungary) to the northern highlands of Greece, and from the Italian Alps in the west to the Ukrainian plain in the east. Politically, the name Balkans is commonly used as a collective term for the countries of the region: Albania, Bosnia and Herzegovina, Bulgaria, Croatia, Greece, Macedonia, **Moldova**, Montenegro, Romania, Serbia and Slovenia. The region's collective history has often set these countries apart from the rest of Europe, from the Ottoman domination of the 14th to 19th centuries, at least until the communist-dominated post-1945 period. More recently the Balkans have suffered some of the continent's most bitter wars, pitting diverse yet often closely-related ethnic groups and various religions against one another. The fragmentation of previously homogenous groups, particularly the south **Slavs**, has spawned the concept of Balkanization.

Balkars *see* **Kabardino-Balkaria**.

Baltic Marine Environment Protection Commission
(or Helsinki Commission, HELCOM)

The main regional organization co-ordinating environmental protection efforts in the Baltic and seeking to combat pollution of the Baltic. Its original Helsinki Convention, signed in 1974 by the then seven Baltic coastal states and entering into force on 3 May 1980, marked the first time ever that all the sources of pollution around an entire sea were made subject to a single convention. In the light of political changes, and developments in international environmental and maritime law, a new convention was signed in 1992 by all the states bordering on the Baltic Sea and by the European Community. After ratification this new convention entered into force on 17 January 2000. It covers the whole of the Baltic Sea area, including inland water, and also commits its signatories to take measures in the whole catchment area of the Baltic Sea to reduce land-based pollution. A new Baltic Sea Action Plan to reduce pollution and reverse the degradation of the marine environment is due to be approved in November 2007. The chairmanship of the Commission rotates on a biennial basis; Poland has held the position since 30 June 2006.

  Members: Denmark, Estonia, **European Union**, Finland, Germany, Latvia, Lithuania, Poland, **Russian Federation** and Sweden.

  Chair: Mieczyslaw Ostojski.

  Address: Katajanokanlaituri 6в, FIN-00160 Helsinki, Finland.

  Telephone: (207) 412649.

  Fax: (207) 412639.

  E-mail: helcom@helcom.fi

  Internet: www.helcom.fi

Baltic States

The three countries—Estonia, Latvia and Lithuania—along the eastern shore of the Baltic Sea. Although ethnically, linguistically and culturally very distinct, these three territories have had a common history facing German, Swedish and ultimately Russian encroachment. In particular the Baltic States were grouped together as the first three countries to break free from the **Soviet Union** in 1991 and the only three to emerge with relatively stable and prosperous economies. As such they occupy a unique place on the European political map, squashed between the aspirations of **central Europe**, the political hegemony of the **Russian Federation** and the economic success of Scandinavia. All three have now forged greater ties with the West including membership of the **North Atlantic Treaty Organization** and the **European Union**—thereby causing concern in the neighbouring Russian Federation and straining regional relations.

Bank for Foreign Trade
Vneshtorgbank (VTB)

Founded in 1990. As of December 2003 the Bank held reserves of US $220m. and had 39 branches in the **Russian Federation**.
Chair and Chief Executive: Andrei L. Kostin.
Address: ul. Plyushchka 37, 119992 Moscow.
Telephone: (495) 7397799.
Fax: (495) 2584781.
E-mail: info@vtb.ru
Internet: www.vtb.ru

Bank for International Settlements (BIS)

One of the institutions of the international financial and monetary system, originally founded pursuant to The Hague Agreements of 1930 to promote co-operation among national central banks and to provide additional facilities for international finance operations. As of 2006 the central banks of 53 countries and Hong Kong, together with the European Central Bank, were entitled to attend and vote at general meetings, held annually in late June/early July. Of the countries of **central** and **eastern Europe**, Bosnia and Herzegovina, Bulgaria, Croatia, the Czech Republic, Estonia, Greece, Hungary, Latvia, Lithuania, Macedonia, Poland, Romania, the **Russian Federation**, Slovakia, and Slovenia all participate and hold shares in the BIS. The legal status of the Yugoslav issue of the capital of the BIS is still under review.
Chair of the Board: Jean-Pierre Roth.
General Manager: Malcolm D. Knight.
Address: Centralbahnplatz 2, 4002 Basel, Switzerland.
Telephone: (61) 2808080.
Fax: (61) 2809100.
E-mail: email@bis.org
Internet: www.bis.org

Barents Euro-Arctic Council (BEAC)

A regional grouping officially established in January 1993 in Kirkenes, Norway, as a forum for co-operation between the central governments of the member countries. Its existence testifies to the notion of a common history of the peoples of northern Scandinavia and north-western **Russia** (the Barents region), interrupted by the closed borders regime of the 1917–91 era. The Kirkenes Declaration set out five principal objectives, relating to peace and stability, cultural ties, better bilateral and multilateral inter-state relations, sustainable economic, social and environmental development, and active participation by indigenous peoples of the region. The chairmanship of the Council rotates every two years between Norway, Finland, the Russian Federation and Sweden; it passed to Finland in 2005.

Members: Denmark, Finland, Iceland, Norway, the Russian Federation, Sweden and the European Commission (of the **European Union**).

Address: Barents Regional Council Secretariat, c/o Ministry of Foreign Affairs, Merikasarmi, Laivastokatu 22, POB 176, FIN-00161, Helsinki, Finland.

Telephone: (9) 16005.

Fax: (9) 1629 840.

E-mail: ita-25@formin.fi

Internet: www.beac.st

Bashkirs *see* **Bashkortostan**.

Bashkortostan

A heavily-industrialized constituent republic of the **Russian Federation** situated at the southern end of the Ural mountain chain. Bashkortostan, with a population of 4.1 million (2002 estimate), is the most heavily populated of the non-Russian republics in **European Russia**. The Bashkir people are ethnically **Turkic** and similar to the **Tatars**, but are differentiated by the assimilation of local **Finno-Ugric peoples**. Like the Tatars they are largely **Muslim** in religion.

The lands of the Bashkirs came under the suzerainty of the Russian Empire in 1552 after the collapse of the Kazan khanate. Along with the Tatars the Bashkir population largely supported the 'Whites' during the Russian Civil War. Bashkortostan (known to the Russians as Bashkiria) was granted the status of an Autonomous Republic by the Bolsheviks in 1919 after attempts to merge it with **Tatarstan** were defeated. The Sovereign Republic of Bashkortostan was declared in October 1990, and secured a favourable federal treaty with Russia in August 1994. Heavily industrialized, the republic now accounts for around 3% of the Federation's total industrial output.

While **Russians** form the largest ethnic group, the 1.2 million Bashkirs are now the second largest, outnumbering the **Tatars**, whose population has shrunk to just under one million. The political dominance of the Bashkirs, and the official promotion of the Bashkir language over Tatar, has led to tensions. Murtaza Rakhimov has been President of Bashkortostan since December 1993, and before that was the Chairman of the Bashkir Supreme Council from April 1992.

BEAC *see* **Barents Euro-Arctic Council**.

Belarus
Respublika Byelarus

A landlocked independent republic in north-eastern Europe, bounded by Lithuania and Latvia to the north-west, **Ukraine** to the south, the **Russian Federation** to the east and Poland to the west. The country is divided administratively into six *oblasti* (regions) and one municipality.

Area: 207,600 sq km; *capital*: **Minsk**; *population*: 9.8m. (2005 estimate), comprising ethnic **Belarusians** 81%, **Russians** 11%, **Poles** 4%, **Ukrainians** 2%, others 2%; *official languages*: Belarusian and Russian; *religion*: **Orthodox Christianity** 60%, **Roman Catholic** 8%, others (including **Protestant**, **Jewish** and **Muslim**) 32%.

Under the Constitution adopted in March 1994 and amended in November 1996, legislative power is vested in the bicameral **National Assembly** (Natsionalnoye Sobranie). This consists of a 110-member lower chamber, the House of Representatives (Palata Predstaviteley), elected by universal adult suffrage for a four-year term, and a 64-member upper chamber, the Council of the Republic (Soviet Respubliki). Eight members of the upper house are appointed by the President and 56 are indirectly elected by local administrative bodies. The executive President, directly elected for a five-year term, is Head of State. A two-term limit on the President's tenure was removed in 2004. The President appoints the Prime Minister and the Council of Ministers; they are accountable to the President, and responsible to the National Assembly.

History: Settled by east **Slavic** tribes in the 5th century, Belarus was controlled by the Princes of **Kiev** from the 9th to 12th centuries. Following the Mongol invasion in the 1200s, the territory was absorbed into Lithuania before coming under Polish rule in the mid-16th century. Between 1772 and 1795 Poland suffered three successive partitions between Russia, **Prussia** and Austria, resulting in the integration of Belarus into the Russian Empire under Catherine the Great. A battleground in the Napoleonic invasion of Russia in 1812, Belarus suffered this fate again in both World Wars. At the time of the Russian Revolution of 1917, much of the country was under German control. The withdrawal of German forces was followed by the declaration of the Byelorussian Soviet Socialist Republic in 1919. The western part of the region, ceded to Poland in 1921 after Soviet defeat in the Polish–Soviet war of 1919–20, was retaken by Soviet forces in 1939, but the republic as a whole was subsequently devastated by German invasion and occupation. In 1945, at the end of the Second World War, the Byelorussian SSR was restored. Part of the **Soviet Union**, it was also given membership of the UN in its own right.

Post-war reconstruction needs led to a rise in Russian immigration into the republic. As the process of 'russification' continued in the 1960s and 1970s, there was decreasing use of the Belarusian language. The republic did, however, enjoy relative economic prosperity within the Soviet Union.

With the imminent collapse of the Soviet Union, the republic declared its sovereignty in July 1990, and then its independence in August 1991 after the failed coup by hardliners in **Moscow** (*see* **August coup**). In September 1991 the official name of the new nation was changed to the Republic of Belarus. A reformist, Stanislau Shushkevich, assumed the leadership of the country as Chairman of the Supreme Council (parliament) elected in March 1990. However, conflict with the communist-dominated Council led to Shushkevich's resignation in January 1994 and his replacement by Mechislau Gryb, a hardliner. Following the adoption of a new presidential Constitution in March 1994, elections for the presidency were held in June and July. Alyaksandr **Lukashenka**, an independent campaigning against corruption, won on the second ballot, taking 85% of the vote.

Against a background of ongoing confrontation between the new President and the Supreme Council over constitutional issues, a referendum on four policy questions was held in May 1995. Voters expressed strong support for an extension of presidential powers, closer integration with the Russian Federation, equal status for Russian and Belarusian as official languages and the introduction of a new flag. At the same time as the referendum, Belarus's first post-Soviet legislative elections were held. Under half of the 260 seats in the Supreme Council were filled owing to the stringent electoral regulations and, since this failed to produce the necessary two-thirds quorum, further rounds of voting took place in November and December 1995 (although 62 seats still remained unfilled).

Tensions between Lukashenka on the one hand and the Supreme Council and Constitutional Court on the other escalated in 1996. In a further controversial referendum held on 24 November, 70.5% of voters backed changes to the 1994 Constitution that significantly strengthened Lukashenka's presidential authority. In addition to lengthening his term of office from 1999 to 2001, the amendments also granted him extensive powers of appointment and provided for a new bicameral National Assembly to replace the Supreme Council. At the end of November 1996 a majority of parliamentary deputies supporting Lukashenka (mainly independents) adopted legislation reconstituting themselves as the House of Representatives, or lower chamber of the new Assembly, and abolishing the Supreme Council. A new upper chamber, the Council of the Republic, was convened in January 1997. Doubts about the legitimacy of the November 1996 referendum were expressed by international organizations, including the **Council of Europe** (which suspended Belarus's 'guest status') and the **Organization for Security and Co-operation in Europe** (OSCE).

Elections to the House of Representatives, once again highly controversial in the manner of their conduct, were held in October 2000. They were boycotted by most of the opposition parties on grounds of their perceived fraudulence, which was confirmed by international observers. The official results gave pro-Lukashenka candidates all but three of the 110 seats.

In a presidential election held in September 2001, Lukashenka was credited with winning 75.6% of the vote. The opposition parties continued to protest that he had no legitimate mandate but were met with repression and intimidation. The media were particularly targeted, with opposition papers closed down and journalists persecuted. The Federation of Trade Unions was purged of its opposition-leaning hierarchy and a pro-Lukashenka candidate was positioned at its head in July 2002. Opposition efforts centred now around forming united blocs ahead of the 2004 parliamentary elections. The alliances were unwieldy, however, with three separate groups forming, serving only to dilute effective electoral opposition.

Latest elections: Elections to the House of Representatives were held on 17–18 October 2004, along with a referendum on a constitutional amendment to allow Lukashenka a third term in office. International observers criticized the lack of access to the media for opposition parties, and the OSCE highlighted problems with the vote count and the independence of the election commission, but observers from the **Commonwealth of Independent States** (CIS) declared the election free and fair. Two seats were rerun on 27 October, and one went to a third round on 20 March 2005. The official results gave pro-Lukashenka candidates all of the 110 seats (of which the **Communist Party of Belarus** won eight seats, the **Agrarian Party of Belarus** won three and the **Liberal Democratic Party of Belarus** won one). Meanwhile the referendum produced an 86% vote in favour of allowing Lukashenka to stand for a third term. Indirect elections for the Council of the Republic in October–November 2004 also confirmed the entrenched power of Lukashenka's supporters.

In a presidential election held in March 2006, Lukashenka was credited with winning 83% of the vote, defeating the independent candidate Alyaksandr Milinkevich. The results were not independently verified. Opposition to the election, and to Lukashenka in general, continued to lack clear leadership, rendering futile the demonstrations that formed on the streets of the capital. Lukashenka had warned before the poll against any attempt at a '**colour revolution**' as seen recently in **Georgia** and Ukraine.

International relations and defence: On the break-up of the Soviet Union in 1991, Belarus retained close links with other former constituent republics through its accession to the CIS. In particular, Belarus under Lukashenka has pursued greater economic, political and military integration with the Russian Federation. In April 1996 and April–May 1997 the two countries signed initial union treaties and a charter establishing a structure for the co-ordination of joint affairs. This was followed in December 1998 by agreements envisaging a staged convergence of their economic and political systems, leading to the signature in December 1999 of a full **Belarus-Russia Union** treaty. Although this process has stalled,

Belarus's pursuit of formal links with the Russian Federation, together with the question marks over its commitment to democratic processes, soured relations with the West, notwithstanding its post-Soviet admission to European structures such as the OSCE, the **Central European Initiative** and NATO's **Partnership for Peace** programme. In 2005 the USA listed Belarus among the six remaining 'outposts of tyranny'.

Belarus's official defence budget totalled some US $279m. in 2006, equivalent to 0.8% of GDP. The armed forces at August 2006 were 72,940, including those drafted under compulsory conscription of 9–12 months, while reservists numbered an estimated 289,500. Under the proposed Belarus-Russia Union it was envisaged that a joint military force would be created, although the Russian side ruled out a joint military command.

Belarus, economy

An economy operating in a landlocked country which has close political and economic links with the neighbouring **Russian Federation**.

GNP: US $26,975m. (2005); *GNP per capita*: $2,760 (2005); *GDP at PPP*: $77,059m. (2005); *GDP per capita at PPP*: $7,883 (2005); *exports*: $18,153m. (2005); *imports*: $17,851m. (2005); *currency*: Belarus rouble; US $1=BR2,142 at the end of December 2006).

In 2005 industry contributed 41.2% of GDP, agriculture 9.5% and services 49.3%. Of the workforce of 4.8 million, industry accounts for 34.8%, agriculture and forestry for 10.7% and services for 54.8%. Some 27% of land is arable, 1% under permanent crops, 15% permanent pasture and 38% forests and woodland. The main agricultural products are grain, potatoes and sugar beet. There are small identified reserves of oil and natural gas, while other principal natural resources include forests and peat. (Since the 1986 **Chernobyl** nuclear reactor disaster just over the border in **Ukraine**, peat cannot be used for fuel in Belarus for fear of dispersal of contaminated ash.) The principal industries include machine-building, chemicals, power generation and textiles. In view of the lack of mineral resources, most of Belarus's energy requirements are met through imports of petroleum and natural gas (the latter in particular from the Russian Federation).

Belarus's main exports by value (2003) are mineral products (22%), machinery and transport equipment (22%) and basic manufactures (19%). Principal imports include petroleum and natural gas (23%), machinery and transport equipment (19%), and basic manufactures (19%). In 2004 49% of Belarus's exports, and 66% of its imports, were to/from the Russian Federation.

As part of the **Soviet Union**, Belarus had a relatively prosperous economy, with a substantial engineering basis linked to the military-industrial complex. After the 1991 dissolution of the Soviet Union, however, the economy declined sharply, with political instability aggravating the situation and with little outside investment. In the five years to 1996 GDP fell by an annual average of over 6%, while inflation escalated to around 2,000% in both 1993 and 1994.

The advent to power of President **Lukashenka** in 1994 led to the readoption of centralist policies of regulatory 'market socialism' and a slowing-down of market-related reforms in the interests of preserving jobs and minimizing social problems. A stabilization plan agreed with the **International Monetary Fund** (IMF) in September 1995 was quickly suspended when performance criteria were not met. Inflation was initially curbed but resumed an upward path from 1996, rising to 182% in 1998 and 250% in 1999. In 1998 Belarus's currency came under severe pressure as a result of financial crisis in the Russian Federation (*see* **Russian Federation, economy**), again worsening the general economic position. A further attempt by the IMF to agree a contingency facility with Belarus broke down in May 1999. Although GDP was officially stated to have risen by 8.5% in 1998 (and industrial output by 11%), growth slowed in 1999 to 3.5%.

In January 2000 new bank notes were issued converting 1,000 roubles into one new currency unit, while in September 2000 the official rate of the rouble against the US dollar was set at close to the unofficial market rate. In February 2001 President Lukashenka claimed that in the period 1996–2000 GDP had increased by 36%, industrial production by 60% and real incomes by 70%, although there was no independent confirmation of such figures.

Since 2000 GDP growth has recovered, reaching 11% in 2004 (second highest among the **Commonwealth of Independent States**—CIS) and 9% in 2005. This was spurred by growth in demand for exports by Russia and other CIS members, and by rising internal demand as the Government's social spending programme boosted salaries and reduced levels of poverty. The high inflation rate was gradually brought under control, coming down to 10% by 2005.

Growth is expected to continue in the near future, though the level of state intervention in the economy makes the business environment unconducive to private and foreign investment. The threatened removal of Russian subsidies on fuel imports caused major political disputes with Russia in 2006 and 2007; it was agreed that subsidies will reduce gradually until 2011 when Belarus will have to pay the European market price for oil and gas—this will have serious consequences on the potential for continued growth.

The legacy of the Chernobyl disaster has put a huge burden on Belarus's economy. In 2006 the **World Bank** provided a US $50m. loan for an energy efficiency project targeted at people living in Chernobyl-affected areas. The project marks a shift from humanitarian assistance towards longer-term sustainable development.

Certain industries and enterprises were privatized after 1991, but progress was limited because of rampant corruption combined with a preference after the 1994 change of government for maintaining a dominant state sector. Even the privatization of smaller enterprises was suspended in 1996, so that by the end of the 1990s only about 10% of all enterprises under central control had been privatized. In April 2000 President Lukashenka declared that the collective farm system would 'always' be the basis for the country's agricultural production. The private sector's share of GDP remains low at around 25%. The 'golden share' rule was expanded in 2004, giving the Government a unique power to intervene in any company which used to have state ownership.

Belarus's already close economic links with the Russian Federation were solidified by the 1996 CIS customs union agreement (together with Kazakhstan, Kyrgyzstan and subsequently also Tajikistan). Subsequent bilateral agreements and treaties, culminating in the signature of the **Belarus-Russia Union** treaty in December 1999, envisaged full-scale economic and monetary union by 2005. A draft agreement on monetary union was signed on 8 June 2003, but the rouble introduction was postponed first for one year and then repeatedly, with no firm date now proposed. The Union budget was 3,100m. Russian roubles in 2006, and increased by 30% in 2007; Belarus is expected to contribute 35% and the Russian Federation 65%.

Belarus-Russia Union

The structure under which **Belarus** and the **Russian Federation** are supposedly to merge eventually into a single confederal entity. The Belarus-Russia Union is based in **Minsk**. Belarus has been independent since the collapse of the **Soviet Union** in 1991. However, from the earliest days of its independence the idea of returning to the Russian fold has been popular among the ruling elite. Under the guidance of Belarusian President Alyaksandr **Lukashenka** and the then Russian President Boris **Yeltsin**, the two countries signed a preliminary Union agreement on 2 April 1996, and a second agreement a year later. The basis of the Union lies in the relative weakness of the independent **Belarusian economy**, the country's long historical connection to Russia and the ethnic similarity between the two dominant east **Slavic peoples**. Under the agreement, the two countries would retain their nominal independence—with separate representation at the UN—after entering into a confederal Union with each other, but would share government policy in all fields.

The agreement was refined at the end of the Yeltsin presidency through the signing of a draft Union Treaty on 8 December 1999. This finalized the eventual structure of the Union and set a deadline, 2005, for the harmonization of currencies, legislatures, tax policies, border security, customs and defence policies. A Supreme State Council was established to form Union agencies. Eventually it is envisaged that the Union will have an upper House of Union, with delegates from the National Assemblies of both Belarus and the Russian Federation, a directly-elected lower House of Representatives and an executive Council of Ministers whose role remains undefined.

Since the election of Vladimir **Putin** as Russian President in May 2000, however, the pace of the Union preparations has been considerably reduced. Putin has taken the emphasis away from the Union in matters of regional policy, and in December 2001, Belarusian Prime Minister Gennadz Novitski was reported as suggesting that Putin had even unofficially requested the Treaty's revision. In April 2001 the upper house of the Belarusian **National Assembly** approved plans to introduce the Russian rouble in Belarus on 1 January 2005, and the proposed Union currency in 2008. A draft agreement on monetary union was signed on 8 June 2003, but the introduction of the Russian rouble was postponed first by one year and then repeatedly, with no firm date now proposed. Meanwhile a customs union, introduced in March 2001, soon crumbled, with both countries reintroducing customs controls within a year.

The two parties appeared to be unable even to reach agreement on the form of the Union. Lukashenka favoured a Soviet Union-style structure, while Putin proposed a looser EU-style confederation or even just the subsuming of Belarus within the Russian Federation. Lukashenka railed against the idea of Belarus losing its independence. A meeting between the two Presidents in December 2005 appeared not even to touch on the subject of union—despite the passing of the 2005 deadline for unity of political and economic structures. Instead it focused on the cutting of gas subsidies for Belarus, though this was postponed at least until 2007. Meanwhile, Belarus-Russia Union State Secretary Pavel Borodin revealed that his Secretariat was working on nine different versions of a possible constitution for the Union.

Couched in Article Seven of the 1996 Agreement was also an invitation for other countries to join the proposed Union. The offer has not been taken up by any Governments, but has been seriously mooted by **Ukraine** and, soon after the election of a communist Government there, by **Moldova**. The possibility of extending the Union was boosted in late 2001 when the Russian Government passed laws allowing the theoretical membership of new Republics to the Russian Federation itself—a proposition welcomed in particular by the Georgian Republics of **Abkhazia** and South Ossetia (*see* **Ossetia question**).

However, with European integration beckoning, Ukraine and Moldova turned their interests away from greater unity with Russia, and as Russia's economic support for Belarus dwindled during 2006 even Lukashenka decried his former ally. In the face of the ongoing gas price wars in late 2006, Lukashenka even proposed a Belarus-Ukraine union to stand against Russia.

Belarusian Chamber of Commerce and Industry

The principal organization in **Belarus** for promoting business contacts, both internally and externally, in the post-communist era. Originally founded in 1952.

President: Uladzimir N. Bobrov.
Address: pr. Pobeditelei 14, 220035 Minsk.
Telephone: (17) 2269127.
Fax: (17) 2269860.
E-mail: mbox@cci.by
Internet: www.cci.by

Belarusian Currency and Stock Exchange

The exchange in **Belarus** created by the merger in 1998 of the Belarusian Stock Exchange (BSE) and the Interbank Currency Exchange (ICE). The BSE had been 40% owned by the Ministry of State Property but had a total of 490 stockholders, while the ICE was a department of the **National Bank of the Republic of Belarus**.

General Director: Pavel Tsekhanovich.
Address: vul. Surganova 48A, 220013 Minsk.
Telephone: (17) 2063469.
Fax: (17) 2094110.
E-mail: bcse@bcse.by
Internet: www.bcse.by

Belarusian Popular Front-Renaissance
Narodni Front Belarusi-Adradzhennie (NFB-A)

A major political movement in **Belarus** with a strong Christian democratic current, seeking post-Soviet reform, which has opposed the Government of President Alyaksandr **Lukashenka** since 1995. It no longer has parliamentary representation.

What became the NFB-A was launched in June 1989 at a conference of pro-independence groups in Vilnius (Lithuania), after the communist authorities had refused to allow it to be held in the republic and had denounced its organizers as 'extremists'. Founding or subsequent NFB-A participating parties included the Belarusian Peasants' Party, the Belarusian Social Democratic Party, the National Democratic Party of Belarus, the Belarusian Christian Democratic Union, the Movement for Democratic Reforms and the United Democratic Party of Belarus.

Elected leader at the Vilnius session was Zyanon Paznyak, an archaeologist who in 1988 had published evidence of mass graves found near **Minsk** on the site of a detention camp established on Stalin's orders in 1937. With monolithic communism crumbling across **eastern Europe**, the changing atmosphere had some impact in Belarus, where opposition candidates were allowed to run in the April 1990 Supreme Council elections. However, the entrenched position of the

Communist Party of Belarus (KPB) enabled it to win a large majority, the NFB-A winning only 34 seats out of 360. In August 1991 the NFB-A was strongly critical of the Government's initial support for the attempted coup by hardliners in **Moscow** (*see* **August coup**). It therefore welcomed the resultant downfall of the Minsk conservatives and the accession of the Shushkevich Government, supporting the latter's declaration of Belarus's independence in late August 1991.

Remaining in opposition, the NFB-A in 1992 and 1993 twice collected the requisite 350,000 signatures for a referendum on early multi-party elections, but neither petition was accepted by a legislature dominated by conservative elements. The NFB-A opposed the new presidential Constitution introduced in March 1994, on the grounds that a democratic parliament had not yet been elected. It also opposed the treaty on monetary union with the **Russian Federation**, signed by the Government in April, and Belarus's participation in the security arm of the **Commonwealth of Independent States** (CIS). In the direct presidential elections of June–July 1994, Paznyak stood as the NFB-A candidate but received only 13.5% of the first-round vote and was eliminated. In the second round, NFB-A support swung overwhelmingly behind Lukashenka as being the more reformist candidate.

By the time of the 1995 parliamentary elections, the NFB-A was as clearly opposed to President Lukashenka's Government as it had been to the predecessor, the main issue being once again the President's policy of close integration with the Russian Federation. The NFB-A won no seats in the 1995 elections, following which Paznyak went into exile in the USA. Following the signature of an initial **Belarus-Russia Union** treaty in April 1996, NFB-A leaders came under pressure from the authorities for organizing protests against constitutional amendments tabled by the Government to replace the unicameral Supreme Council with a bicameral legislature. The approval of the amendments in a referendum in November 1996 was rejected as invalid by the NFB-A.

The political impasse continued in the late 1990s, during which the NFB-A mounted regular opposition demonstrations. In May 1999 the NFB-A was a principal organizer of 'alternative' presidential elections, which according to the opposition attracted over 60% voter participation and which, they further claimed, yielded a two-thirds majority for Paznyak. Thereafter the Government combined repression of NFB-A leaders and other opponents with periodic attempts, under pressure from Western governments, to initiate a dialogue with the opposition, although little progress was made.

The sixth NFB-A congress held in Minsk in August 1999 precipitated a split between critics of Paznyak's leadership in exile and his supporters. The following month the pro-Paznyak (minority) faction broke away to form the Conservative Christian Party, of which Paznyak was declared leader, while Vintsuk Vyachorka was elected NFB-A Chairman. The NFB-A boycotted the October 2000 legislative elections on the grounds that there was no prospect of their being free and fair.

Re-engaging with the electoral system ahead of polls in October 2004, the party was at the forefront of the **People's Coalition Five Plus**. Despite strenuous campaigning, this coalition failed to win a single seat in the highly controversial poll. Struggling on, the NFB-A nominated the independent, Alyaksandr Milinkevich, as the coalition's unsuccessful presidential candidate for the March 2006 leadership contest.

Leadership: Vintsuk Vyachorka (Chair).
Address: vul. Varvasheni 8, 220005 Minsk.
Telephone and Fax: (17) 2845012.
E-mail: pbnf@pbnf.org
Internet: www.pbnf.org

Belarusians
(literally, White Russians)

A **Slavic people** dominant in **Belarus** (White Russia) and known as **White Russians** (not to be confused with the anti-Red, i.e. anti-Bolshevik, 'White' Russian forces of the Russian Civil War, 1918–20). Ethnically Belarusians are very closely related to the other east Slavs, namely **Russians** and **Ukrainians**. During the 20th century the political domination of the former led to intense russification of the Belarusians. The Belarusian language is central to the notion of Belarusian nationalism. It was revived after the country's independence in 1991 and became the official state language (although most Belarusians are fluent in Russian). It is written using the **Cyrillic alphabet** and contains many loan words from Polish (reflecting the region's history). Like other east Slavs most Belarusians embrace **Orthodox Christianity** although some follow the **Roman Catholic Church** (*see* **Uniate Church**). Around 808,000 Belarusians live in the **Russian Federation**.

BelTA

The state news agency in **Belarus**. Originally founded in 1918, it was overshadowed throughout the Soviet era by the Telegraph Agency of the Soviet Union (TASS—*see* **ITAR-TASS**). It is owned, controlled and run by the Government.

Director: Dimitriy A. Zhuk.
Address: vul. Kirava 26, 220030 Minsk.
Telephone: (17) 2271692.
Fax: (17) 2271346.
E-mail: oper@belta.by
Internet: www.belta.by

Beslan school siege

A hostage crisis in North **Ossetia** in the **Russian Federation**. At 09:30 on 1 September 2004, the first day of the school year, militants from the neighbouring republics of **Ingushetia** and **Chechnya** entered School Number One in the town of Beslan in North Ossetia. Armed with guns and explosives, the 32 attackers took hostage over 1,200 teachers, parents and children, holding them in the school gymnasium. Several male hostages were killed at once and their bodies thrown outside the buildings. The remaining hostages were denied food or water, and the heat and fear caused many children to lose consciousness.

At 13:04 on 3 September the hostage-takers allowed Russian emergency servicemen to enter the school grounds to collect bodies. As they approached, an explosion occurred inside the gymnasium and firing began: it remains unclear whether the explosion was an accidental activation of one of the many mines laid by the militants, a suicide blast by one of the female militants, or a rocket attack by Russian special forces. In the chaos that ensued many children were too weak even to flee. Fighting continued for several hours, but eventually 31 of the militants were killed and one was captured—at a cost of 311 lives of innocent adults and children and 20 Russian servicemen. The situation was so chaotic that many families were unable to discover for some time whether their children had lived or died.

On 16 September an international terrorist group led by Chechen militant Shamil Basayev claimed responsibility for the attack. Basayev's group was also responsible for the **Moscow theatre siege** in 2002.

In the days and months of grief and mourning that followed, the Russian authorities were heavily criticized for their handling of the crisis and its chaotic aftermath. A parliamentary inquiry investigating the siege accused local officials of several blunders and shortcomings. Three policemen were charged with incompetence. North Ossetian President Aleksandr Dzasokhov resigned in June 2005 after intense pressure from the Mothers of Beslan. The one surviving terrorist was sentenced to life imprisonment in May 2006.

President Vladimir **Putin** announced sweeping changes to Russia's political system as part of the fight against terrorism in the wake of the Beslan school tragedy. The changes strengthened the power of the major parties in the State Duma (lower house of the **Federal Assembly**) and made the posts of regional Governors directly appointable by the President.

Bessarabia question

A historical territorial dispute between Romania and **Russia**, arising from the artificial division of the Romanian principality of Moldavia between Romania and Russia in the 1812 Treaty of Bucharest. Resurrecting the medieval title

Bessarabia for the eastern half of Moldavia, between the Rivers Prut and Dnester, the tsarist authorities attempted to distance the ethnic **Romanian** population from their connections with the state of Romania, and thus foster a separate sense of Bessarabian identity. The division, however, laid the foundation for Romanian claims to the area, and for conflict with future Russian Governments.

With the rise of the **Soviet Union** the Bessarabia question was aggressively revisited. The temporary reunification of Bessarabia and Romania during the inter-war years (1918–39) flew in the face of Soviet insistence that Bessarabia remained an integral part of the Soviet Union. With the onset of hostilities at the start of the Second World War the Romanian Government conceded the Soviet annexation of Bessarabia. The Moldavian Soviet Socialist Republic (already created east of the Dnester to substantiate Russia's claims) was redrawn to include part of Bessarabia and thus to cover the area of what is now **Moldova**. On the other hand southern and northern Bessarabia, known as Bukovina (*see* **Bukovina question**), were ceded to the Ukrainian Soviet Socialist Republic. A program of russification of the Bessarabian Romanians resulted in the creation of a **Moldovan** identity, based on communist social policies and the use of the **Cyrillic alphabet**. The authorities also encouraged the influx of non-Romanians.

The collapse of the Soviet Union in 1991 unleashed a wave of pro-Romanian sentiment in Moldova and reignited the Bessarabia question, which the pre-1989 Romanian communist regime had preferred to leave dormant. Political parties on both sides of the Prut called for the reunification of the Moldavian lands, despite initial hesitation in Romania. Claims to the southern and northern districts were not included. However, attempts to move towards unification led to uprisings in the non-Romanian/Moldovan areas of Moldova, known as **Transdnestria** and **Gagauzia**, in the same year. By the mid-1990s the concept of unification was irrevocably entwined with the idea of the division of Moldova and was thus popularly rejected by the Moldovan people. Aspirations for unification remain dormant for the time being and the notion of Bessarabia seems dead and buried.

Bessarabian Church

A Church of the **Orthodox Christian** denomination in **Moldova** which is subordinate to the **Romanian Orthodox Church**. It claims to have around 400,000 adherents. Bishop Petru Paduraru is the current Metropolitan.

The Bessarabian Church was formed in 1992 when priests broke away from the Autonomous Moldovan Church (which is subordinate to the **Russian Orthodox Church**), claiming lineage instead from the pre-Second World War Romanian Church in **Bessarabia**. Until 2002, however, the Moldovan Government branded the new Church as 'schismatic' and repeatedly refused to register it, partly because of issues of Moldovan national identity (and more specifically the close relationship between the Government and the Moldovan

Church), and partly because of unresolved property issues. The Bessarabian priests appealed, first to the **Chişinau** court in 1997 and then to the **European Court of Human Rights** in 1998. Both courts ruled in their favour, with the latter reaching its verdict in late 2001. In July 2002 in the face of condemnation from the **Council of Europe**, the Moldovan Government agreed to back down and register the Bessarabian Church.

Bezhuashvili, Gela

Minister of Foreign Affairs, **Georgia**. Gela Bezhuashvili worked in international relations before joining the Council of Ministers in 2004 as Georgia's first civilian Defence Minister. He was appointed Foreign Minister on 19 October 2005.

Born on 1 March 1967, he graduated from the Ukrainian Institute of International Relations and International Law at Kiev State University in 1991. He has since taken several courses in law and public administration at major European universities, and a Master's degree at Harvard. He joined the Ministry of Foreign Affairs in 1991 and was appointed as an envoy to Kazakhstan from 1993 to 1996. During the ensuing three years he headed the Ministry's International Law Department while chairing expert forums on Georgia's accession to the **Council of Europe** and the drafting of laws on International Treaties and the Diplomatic Service. He also authored the Organic Law on the National Security Council and became involved with several Council of Europe committees.

In 1999 he led the Georgian delegation to several **Organization of the Black Sea Economic Co-operation** (BSEC) high-level negotiations and headed the conference of Justice Ministers in **Moldova**. The following year, despite his civilian background, he was appointed Deputy Defence Minister, and four years later was promoted to full Minister. He was soon moved to become an assistant to the President on national security issues and Secretary of the National Security Council. On 19 October he returned to the Council of Ministers as Minister of Foreign Affairs.

Gela Bezhuashvili is married with two sons. He speaks English, Russian and Spanish. He continues to research into international law and has published several papers and books.

Address: Ministry of Foreign Affairs, Sh. Chitadze 4, Tbilisi.
Telephone: (32) 284747.
Fax: (32) 284761.
E-mail: inform@mfa.gov.ge
Internet: www.mfa.gov.ge

BIS *see* **Bank for International Settlements**.

Black Sea Fleet (BSF)

The Russian naval fleet based in the Black Sea and harboured in the Ukrainian port of **Sevastopol**. The housing of the original Soviet BSF in the Crimean port made it the focus of strained relations between **Ukraine** and the **Russian Federation** in the early 1990s despite its dilapidated state and crippling maintenance costs. The newly independent Ukraine was eager to assert its separation from the Russian Federation and its sovereignty over **Crimea**, which had been transferred to Ukraine as a goodwill gesture in 1954. However, it could not afford the upkeep of even half of the cumbersome Fleet or the potential economic costs of losing its associated Russian sailors and their families from Sevastopol. For the Russians, the BSF has historical significance in maintaining strategic dominance across the country's southern flank and also in upholding its image as an international power.

From 1991 to 1994 a series of potentially serious incidents involving the BSF and its bases in Sevastopol threatened to bring the two countries into direct conflict. Tensions were invariably cooled, however, by the intervention of the two Governments. Draft agreements regarding the BSF in 1992 placed it first under the auspices of the newly-created **Commonwealth of Independent States** and later under joint Ukrainian-Russian control.

A definitive solution was agreed between the then Ukrainian Prime Minister Pavlo Lazarenko and his Russian counterpart Viktor Chernomyrdin on 28 May 1997. This consolidated proposals to split the BSF nominally 50–50 between the two countries, but granted the Russian Federation the facility to 'buy' an extra third from Ukraine in return for debt relaxation. It also agreed to grant the Russian Federation a 20-year lease on the port and surrounding areas of Sevastopol at a cost of US $97.75m. a year, and secured the recognition by both countries of Ukraine's inalienable sovereignty over Crimea. The remaining one-sixth of the Fleet, left in Ukrainian hands and to be housed in alternative Crimean harbours, was redesignated as the new Ukrainian navy.

BMD *see* **Democratic Moldova Bloc**.

BSEC *see* **Organization of the Black Sea Economic Co-operation**.

BTC pipeline *see* **Baku–Tbilisi–Ceyhan pipeline**.

Buddhism

The fourth biggest religion in the world based almost entirely in Asia. The **Russian** republic of **Kalmykia** is the only Buddhist territory in Europe. The followers of Buddhism venerate the founder, Buddha, his teachings and his relics. It is more a philosophy than a religion in the Western sense, with no God and no concept of Heaven or Hell, but instead Buddhists believe in successive reincarnation, until enlightenment brings the faithful to *Nirvana*. Buddhism is divided into three main branches and the Kalmyks follow the Tibetan strain which is headed by the Dalai Lama. The religion was persecuted along with other creeds by the **Soviet Union** and the Kalmyks, in particular, were targeted by Stalin. They were deported *en masse* to **Siberia** in 1943 (*see* **deported nationalities**). They were rehabilitated in the 1950s and the first Buddhist temple was rebuilt in the republic in 1988. Like other religions Buddhism has undergone a revival in the post-Soviet period.

Bukovina question

A dispute between Romania and **Ukraine** over the division of the Bukovina region, which was rather arbitrarily divided between the two at the end of the Second World War. The northern part of Bukovina had, under Austrian suzerainty, become home to a large **Ukrainian** (**Ruthenian**) population and is contiguous with the similarly-populated regions of **Transcarpathia** and eastern **Galicia**. At the end of the Second World War the **Soviet** authorities incorporated it into the Ukrainian Soviet Socialist Republic. Owing to unclear instructions at the time, the cession included the principally Romanian town of Herta. The region is now known as the Chernovtsy *oblast* (region). The southern region of Bukovina is traditionally the cradle of Moldavian civilization (*see* **Bessarabia question**) and was consequently incorporated into Romania's Moldavian region. Romanian nationalists have long cherished the aspiration of obtaining the return of northern Bukovina, especially Herta. However, since the normalization of relations between Romania and Ukraine after 1991 the claim has not been pursued.

Bulgarians

A modern people of south-eastern Europe, usually considered south **Slavic**. The Bulgars, from whom their name is derived, actually originated as a **Turkic** tribe from central Asia, who settled in the 7th century in what is now **Ukraine**, where they established a Great Bulgarian Empire. On the disintegration of this empire a group of Bulgars migrated south and west into the southern **Balkans** where they merged with the earlier immigrant Slavs, and to a lesser extent with local **Vlachs**, to form the modern Bulgarian people. As such they are considered most closely related to the neighbouring Macedonians; indeed it is sometimes said there is no discernible ethnic difference between Bulgarians and Macedonians. The further advance of the Bulgarians into what is now Macedonia in the 9th century led to their adoption of Christianity, the spread of the Slavic Macedonian language and ultimately the spread of the **Cyrillic alphabet**.

Outside Bulgaria itself, there are some 200,000 Bulgarians concentrated in the Odessa region of Ukraine, with whom the Bulgarian Government has striven to forge links. The second largest group outside Bulgaria consists of 93,000 who live in Spain; 84,000 live in **Moldova**, and form a majority in the rural southern **Taraclia** district, where they have sought some regional autonomy.

BYT *see* **Yuliya Tymoshenko bloc**.

C

Carpatho-Ukraine *see* **Transcarpathia**.

Catholicism *see* **Roman Catholic Church**.

Caucasus region

The mountainous and ethnically diverse region at the extreme south of **European Russia** which forms a natural and political boundary between Europe and Asia. The Greater and Lesser Caucasus ranges rise sharply from the southern Russian steppe and plunge precipitously into the Black and Caspian Seas to the west and east, slicing the land and people into different cultural, linguistic and religious pockets. The region has had a rich and varied history. It has often been overrun by regional powers, only to shake off centuries of domination time and again. It serves effectively as a volatile buffer between the Middle East and Europe, and particularly between Christianity and Islam.

The region can be usefully divided into two. The northern Caucasus lies within the **Russian Federation**, while the southern areas (known collectively as **Transcaucasia**) are split between the **Soviet** successor states of **Armenia**, **Azerbaijan** and **Georgia**. Within the Russian north Caucasus lie the republics of (from west to east) **Adygeya**, **Karachai-Cherkessia**, **Kabardino-Balkaria**, North **Ossetia** (Alania), **Ingushetia**, **Chechnya** and **Dagestan**. Two crossover regions—**Abkhazia** and South Ossetia—are within Georgia.

The most recent overlords, the **Russians**, first attempted to stake their imperial claim to the 'land of mountains' in the late 18th century, having beaten back rival claims from the Ottoman Turks and the Persians (Iranians). Many of the **Muslim peoples** of the north Caucasus took a prominent part in a rebellion against Russian rule in the mid-19th century. At first they succeeded while Russian forces were preoccupied in the **Crimea**, but the revolt was crushed in 1864 and Russian rule was secured. Attempts by the region's larger ethnic groups to assert autonomy after the fall of the Russian Empire in 1917 were crushed by the new Soviet authorities, particularly under the Commissar for Nationalities, and future Soviet leader, Josef Stalin (a Georgian himself). The various republics of today were established after the failure of Stalin's pet Transcaucasian Republic and Mountain Peoples' Republic projects.

The collapse of the Soviet Union in 1991 opened a Pandora's box of nationalist aspirations and religious fervour. The war in Chechnya has threatened to destabilize the entire north Caucasus while Georgia has lost effective control of Abkhazia and South Ossetia. Armenia and Azerbaijan, traditional enemies held together under communism, soon fell dramatically apart with open conflict in **Nagorno-Karabakh** remaining unresolved.

The autochthonous Caucasian peoples (Abaza, Abkhaz, Adygei, Adzharians, Avars, Chechens, Cherkess, Dargins, Georgians, Ingush, Kabardins, Lezghins, Meskhetians, Ossetes and Tabasarans, to name the ones covered in this dictionary) form the dominant ethnic group although their many languages are, in varying degrees, mutually unintelligible and transcribed using various scripts. There are also large communities of **Turkic** origin (Azeris, Balkars and Kumyks) and other non-indigenous Armenian and Iranian peoples.

Caviar

The eggs of the sturgeon fish, highly prized as a gourmet delicacy. High prices have made the trade in top-quality caviar from the Caspian Sea especially lucrative, but led to severe over-exploitation, with quotas seriously undermined by illegal fishing. Both **Azerbaijan** and the **Russian Federation** have borders on the Caspian Sea, along with three other Asian states, and almost all of the world's caviar supply originates from that body of water, with Russian fishermen harvesting 27%. Over-fishing damaged sturgeon stocks there so badly that little over 1,000 metric tons of caviar a year could be obtained in the late 1990s, compared with 22,000 tons in the 1970s. Regulations imposed on the industry from 1998, within the terms of the Convention on International Trade in Endangered Species (CITES), and nominally enforceable in all Caspian Sea countries, did have some impact on the trade but proved insufficient to protect the sturgeon, particularly because of the existence of a flourishing illegal smuggling network via the Middle East. In June 2001 a temporary moratorium on all sturgeon fishing in the Caspian and associated rivers was introduced, and the Caspian states and CITES Secretariat signed the Paris Agreement, an action plan to improve the co-ordination of sturgeon fishing. The moratorium was ended in March 2002, but lack of progress with the co-ordination plan led to several more short-term bans on caviar exports. In 2005 the USA, hitherto the largest importer of caviar, approved a ban on Caspian beluga caviar imports.

CITES set quotas in 2007 for all types of caviar from the Caspian totalling just 90 tons, but illegal catches are estimated to amount to as much as 12 times more than this amount.

CBSS *see* **Council of the Baltic Sea States**.

CDI *see* **Centrist Democrat International**.

CEI *see* **Central European Initiative**.

Central Bank of the Republic of Armenia

The **Yerevan** branch of the Russian State Bank was redesignated the People's Bank of the Soviet Socialist Republic of **Armenia** in December 1920. With the collapse of the **Soviet Union** in 1991 the Bank was transformed into the National Bank of Armenia. For two years Armenia continued to use Soviet roubles despite their withdrawal across the **Commonwealth of Independent States** (CIS). The situation was rectified when the Bank was renamed the Central Bank in March 1993 and the country's new currency, the dram, was introduced in note form: coins followed in January 1994. As at December 2002 the Bank had reserves of 21,938m. drams.

Governor: Tigran Sarkissian.
Address: V. Sarkissian St 6, 375010 Yerevan.
Telephone: (10) 583841.
Fax: (10) 523852.
E-mail: mcba@cba.am
Internet: www.cba.am

Central Bank of the Russian Federation
Centralnyj Bank Rossijskoj Federacii or *Bank Rossii* (CBR)

The Russian central bank, not to be confused with the commercial (joint-stock) Bank Rossiya. An imperial State Bank had first been created in 1860 as part of the emerging capitalist system. Renamed as the People's Bank, it effectively remained in place until 1920 when it was finally dissolved, to be replaced the following year by the Gosbank created under Lenin's New Economic Policy (NEP). From 1921 until 1987 the Gosbank financed the planned economy of the **Soviet Union**. A two-tier system was introduced in 1987–88 in which the Russian republic's state bank had a growing role. It was this republic-level bank which was transformed into the precursor of the CBR in 1990, and found itself increasingly in conflict with its Union-level counterpart. As the Soviet Union broke up in November–December 1991 it took over the (previously Union-level) functions of issuing money and controlling exchange rates. It took on the name CBR in early 1992 and the following year was given regulatory control of the country's banking system. It struggled to fulfil this role amidst the upheavals of the **Russian economy** in its return to capitalism. The rouble was revalued in 1997 and the CBR undertook a major revision of the banking sector in 1998–2001, to restore its viability after the crippling financial collapse of the mid-1990s. The CBR's involvement with tackling criminal money 'laundering' was widely thought to underlie the high-profile assassination of its First Deputy Chairman Andrei Kozlov in September 2006.

As at 1 January 2007 the Central Bank had gold and foreign currency reserves of 303,732m. roubles, an increase of 65% over the previous year.

Chair: Sergei M. Ignatiev.

Address: ul. Neglinnaya 12, 107016 Moscow.

Telephone: (495) 7719100.

Fax: (495) 6216465.

E-mail: webmaster@www.cbr.ru

Internet: www.cbr.ru

Central Europe

An ill-defined term used generally of the countries between the Baltic and Adriatic Seas, and in its adjectival form to describe historic cities such as Prague and Vienna. Changing borders and geopolitical configurations in the area have confused the usage of terms such as central Europe, and indeed eastern and western Europe. **Eastern Europe** would have been generally taken to include East Germany during the communist period, whereas reunified Germany after 1990 would now be considered an integral part of western Europe. In intellectual terms central Europe existed in the 1990s as a transitional zone somewhere between the liberal economies of the 'West', with their apparent security, prosperity and established democratic pluralism, and the largely authoritarian and struggling states of the 'East'—the former **Soviet Union** and the **Balkans**—with their so-called 'economies in transition'. In this sense, to become 'central European' was an aspiration, and suggested a greater suitability for entry into the Western-dominated world economy, particularly the **European Union**. This loose use of the term was most frequently applied to a group consisting of the **Baltic States**, Poland, the Czech Republic, Hungary, and Slovenia. However, this was by no means definitive, and by varying political, cultural and geographic criteria Croatia, Slovakia, Austria, and even parts of Germany and Italy could be considered central European.

Central European Initiative (CEI)

A sub-regional co-operation initiative in **central** and **eastern Europe**, which originated in 1989 as the 'Pentagonale' group (Austria, Czechoslovakia, Italy, Hungary, Yugoslavia). It became 'Hexagonale' with the admission of Poland in

July 1991, and adopted its present name in March 1992. It aimed to encourage regional and bilateral co-operation, working within the **Organization for Security and Co-operation in Europe** (OSCE), and to assist in the preparation process for **European Union** (EU) membership. Since the accession of five CEI member states to the EU in 2004 and two more in 2007, the CEI's focus has shifted to its non-EU member states.

Members: 18 eastern and central European countries: Albania, Austria, **Belarus**, Bosnia and Herzegovina, Bulgaria, Croatia, Czech Republic, Hungary, Italy, Macedonia, **Moldova**, Montenegro, Poland, Romania, Serbia, Slovakia, Slovenia, **Ukraine**.

Director-General: Harald Kreid.

Address: CEI Executive Secretariat, Via Genova 9, 34132 Trieste, Italy.

Telephone: (040) 7786777.

Fax: (040) 360640.

E-mail: cei-es@cei-es.org

Internet: www.ceinet.org

Centre for the Prevention of Conflict (CPC)

One of the two main departments of the **Organization for Security and Co-operation in Europe** (OSCE). The Centre was established in Vienna, Austria, in March 1991, following the decision of a summit meeting the previous November. Its main function is to support the OSCE Chairman-in-Office in the implementation of OSCE policies, in particular the monitoring of field activities and co-operation with other international bodies.

Director: Herbert Salber.

Address: Kärntner Ring 5–7, 1010 Vienna, Austria.

Telephone: (1) 51436122.

Fax: (1) 5143696.

E-mail: info@osce.org

Internet: www.osce.org

Centrist Democrat International (CDI)
(formerly known as Christian Democrat International)

An organization founded in 1961 as a platform for the co-operation of political parties of Christian Social inspiration. It is now also known as the Christian Democrat and People's Parties International.

Members: Over 100 parties worldwide.
President: Pier Ferdinando Casini.
Address: rue d'Arlon 67, B-1040 Brussels, Belgium.
Telephone: (2) 2854160.
Fax: (2) 2854166.
E-mail: idc@idc-cdi.org
Internet: www.idc-cdi.org

CERN *see* **European Organization for Nuclear Research**.

CFE *see* **Conventional Forces in Europe**.

Chamber of Commerce and Industry of Armenia

The principal organization in **Armenia** for promoting business contacts, both internally and externally, in the post-communist era. Originally founded in 1959.
Chair: Martin Sarkissian.
Address: Khanjian St 11, 375010 Yerevan.
Telephone: (10) 560184.
Fax: (10) 587871.
E-mail: armcci@arminco.com
Internet: www.armcci.am

Chamber of Commerce and Industry of Azerbaijan

The principal organization in **Azerbaijan** for promoting business contacts, both internally and externally, in the post-communist era.
President: Suleyman Bayram oglu Tatliyev.
Address: Istiklal küç 31/33, 1601 Baku.
Telephone: (12) 4928912.
Fax: (12) 4989324.
E-mail: expo@chamber.baku.az
Internet: www.exhibition.azeri.com

Chamber of Commerce and Industry of Georgia

The principal organization in **Georgia** for promoting business contacts, both internally and externally, in the post-communist era. Originally founded in 1963.

Chair: Jemal Inaishvili.
Address: Chavchavadze 11, 380079 Tbilisi.
Telephone: (32) 230045.
Fax: (32) 235760.
E-mail: gcci@access.sanet.ge
Internet: www.gcci.ge

Chamber of Commerce and Industry of Moldova

The principal organization in **Moldova** for promoting business contacts, both internally and externally, in the post-communist era. Originally founded in 1969.
Chair: Gheorghe Cucu.
Address: Blvd Ştefan cel Mare 151, 2004 Chişinau.
Telephone: (22) 221552.
Fax: (22) 234425.
E-mail: camera@chamber.md
Internet: www.chamber.md

Chamber of Commerce and Industry of the Russian Federation

The principal organization in the **Russian Federation** for promoting business contacts, both internally and externally, in the post-communist era. Founded in 1991.
President: Yevgenii M. Primakov.
Address: ul. Ilinka 6, 109012 Moscow.
Telephone: (495) 9290009.
Fax: (495) 9290360.
E-mail: dios-inform@tpprf.ru
Internet: www.tpprf.ru

Charter of Paris for a New Europe

An agreement signed in November 1990 by Heads of Government of the member states of the Conference on Security and Co-operation in Europe (CSCE—*see* **Organization for Security and Co-operation in Europe**) which undertook to strengthen pluralist democracy and observance of human rights, and to settle disputes between participating states by peaceful means.

Chavash Republic

A constituent republic of the **Russian Federation** situated on the west bank of the Volga river in central **European Russia**. It was renamed the Chavash Republic in June 2001, having been previously known as Chuvashia. *Population*: 1.3m. (2002 estimate). The region was incorporated into the Russian Empire in the 16th century. Unlike in other ethnic republics, **Russians** form only a small minority, less than 30%, and the republic is dominated by the agriculturalist Chavash people, a mixed ethnic group combining Bolgars, **Turkic peoples** and **Finno-Ugric** groups. The Chavash language is of the Uralo-Altaic branch of Turkic, and is renowned as the only surviving dialect of the ancient language of the Bolgars. Alone among Europe's Turkic peoples the Chavash follow Eastern **Orthodox Christianity**. Outside the Chavash Republic there are significant Chavash minorities in **Tatarstan** (126,500) and **Bashkortostan** (117,000).

Chavashia became an autonomous *oblast* (region) within the **Soviet Union** in 1920 and achieved full republic status in 1925. The republic escaped the excesses of industrialization as visited upon some of the other **Volga region** states but its urban areas did undergo considerable development. However, the economy is still largely based on exploitation of key natural resources, particularly the abundant forest, which covers one-third of the land area, and mineral deposits such as phosphorites and carbonates. The revival of Chavash culture in the 19th century was suppressed by the Soviet regime and only revived during *glasnost* in the late 1980s. A Chavash Sovereign Republic within the Russian Federation was declared on 31 March 1992. The capital is Cheboksary. Nikolay Vasilyevich Fyedorov was re-elected for a fourth four-year term as President of the Chavash Republic in 2005.

Chechnya
Ichkeria

A constituent republic of the **Russian Federation** situated in the north-east **Caucasus region**, and the scene of two protracted wars with **Russian** forces from 1994. Known in Chechen as Ichkeria. *Population*: 1.1m. (2002 estimate).

Dominated by the Caucasian and **Muslim** Chechen people (known to themselves as the Nokhchuo), the region resisted Russian control in the mid-19th century and again in the Russian Civil War (1918–20), but succumbed to the Bolshevik victory and was constituted as an autonomous *oblast* (region) in 1922, before being amalgamated with neighbouring **Ingushetia** in 1934. The two remained joined as a Checheno-Ingush republic from 1936 until 1992. Chechens and Ingush were deported *en masse* by Stalin in 1944 but rehabilitated under Nikita Khrushchev in 1956 (*see* **deported nationalities**).

A Chechen nationalist movement arose in the late 1980s. In 1991, in the face of nationalist opposition led by former Soviet air force general Dzhokhar Dudayev, the communist Government of Checheno-Ingushetia collapsed and a separate Chechen republic, known as Ichkeria, was declared. Plans by Russian President Boris **Yeltsin** to despatch forces to restore 'order' in the republic were undermined by the strongly independent Supreme Soviet, which refused to endorse the strategy. Tensions between Chechens and Ingush in the republic led to the creation of a separate Ingush republic in 1992.

Dudayev's increasingly authoritarian rule provoked strong internal division in Chechnya. His dissolution of the Chechen parliament in 1993 led to a full-scale civil war. The anti-Dudayev forces received covert support from the Russian Federation, but by December 1994 the campaign to oust Dudayev had failed. Yeltsin, his leadership in Russia re-energized by the defeat of an attempted hardline coup, ordered a full-scale invasion of the breakaway republic, refusing to be restrained by the newly-resurrected Duma (lower house of the **Federal Assembly**). Despite very heavy losses on both sides, the Russian army emerged ostensibly victorious, having effectively levelled the Chechen capital Grozny in a prolonged siege. A ceasefire was signed in 1996 and by early 1997 Russian forces had been largely withdrawn. Later that year Aslan Maskhadov was elected as the new President of Chechnya.

By 1999 the situation had deteriorated once again. The declaration of an Islamic state in Chechnya, the lending of Chechen tactical support to Islamic insurgents in nearby **Dagestan**, and terrorist attacks in the Russian Federation blamed on Chechen extremists, prompted Yeltsin's new Prime Minister (and future successor) Vladimir **Putin** to order another full-scale invasion that winter. By early 2000 Russian forces again proclaimed victory but intense Chechen guerrilla activity subsequently told another story. It was estimated in mid-2000 that an average of 160 Russian soldiers were being killed every day by Chechen guerrillas. Direct rule of the republic was imposed from Moscow and the pro-Russian Mufti Akhmed Kadyrov was appointed as administrator, later becoming President (though a parallel regime continued under Maskhadov). Putin capitalized on the Russian nationalism generated by the rapid 'success' of his invasion, securing his own election as President in March 2000, but by the end of the year he was suffering the same negative press as had Yeltsin in 1995–96.

By January 2001 the security situation had worsened to the stage where Putin handed over control of Chechnya's security to the **Federal Security Service** (FSB), under its Director Nikolai Patrushev. Human rights campaigners and the international community joined to condemn the 1999–2000 invasion and continuing human rights abuses by Russian troops. However, the global political climate changed after the 11 September 2001 terrorist attacks on the USA. Putin capitalized on this situation to press for international condemnation of the Chechen militants as terrorists, and thereby to swing global opinion behind the military action. April 2002 saw another grand announcement that the war was 'over', despite ongoing fighting and Russian attacks on Chechen militants who had taken refuge in neighbouring Russian republics and across the border in **Georgia**. In 2003 95% of voters supported a referendum on a new constitution for Chechnya which redefined the region as an autonomous republic within the Russian Federation; the result was rejected by separatists.

Terrorist attacks by pro-Chechen militants included the high-profile **Moscow theatre siege** in 2002, the assassination of Kadyrov during a military parade in Grozny in 2004 and the tragic **Beslan school siege** later in 2004. After Beslan, Putin declared that he would never negotiate with Chechen extremists, and US $10m. rewards were put on the heads of Chechen rebel leaders Shamil Basayev and Aslan Maskhadov. Maskhadov was killed in March 2005, and his successor was shot in June 2006. Basayev was killed in Ingushetia in 2006. Doku Umarov now heads the Chechen rebel administration, while Ramzan Kadyrov is the President of the Russian-backed regime, which has now returned to Grozny after its relocation to Gudermes in 1996.

The first war left Grozny in ruins, and reconstruction of the city will take many years. Economic activity has traditionally focused on oil refining, for which Grozny's facilities had been among the largest in the **Soviet Union**.

Cherkess
(also known as Circassians)

A **Muslim** Caucasian people closely related to other north Caucasian groups, particularly the Adygei (*see* **Adygeya**) and Kabards (*see* **Kabardino-Balkaria**), and concentrated in the **Russian** republic of **Karachai-Cherkessia**. 'Circassian' is a term originally used to describe all related north-west Caucasians, but later limited to these related three, and finally just the Cherkess. They are considered indigenous to the region and have a long chronicled history of interaction with local power brokers. When the Russian Empire exerted its influence over the entire region the Cherkess were among the peoples who resisted. By 1864 the Caucasian rebellion was suppressed and the Cherkess became Russian vassals. Thousands fled to Muslim countries to the south. Under **Soviet** rule the Cherkess were classified as a distinct ethnic group and given the opportunity to develop their language and culture within the repressive bounds of the regime. The Cherkess of Karachai-Cherkessia have led calls for the unification of the 'Circassian' peoples.

Chernobyl
(Chornobyl)

A now defunct nuclear power station in northern **Ukraine** which was the scene of the world's worst nuclear accident in 1986. Human error and poor design

(Chernobyl used RBMK water-cooled graphite-moderated reactors of a **Soviet** design) led to two explosions during a safety test at the plant's No. 4 reactor on 25 April 1986. The resultant release of radioactive material contaminated the atmosphere, sent a cloud of pollution across northern Europe and led to the eventual evacuation of over 200 villages in the surrounding area. Neighbouring **Belarus** was particularly badly affected by radioactive contamination and loss of agricultural land. In dealing with the emergency, containing and extinguishing the fire and conducting a clean-up operation, over 600,000 'liquidators' were exposed to high levels of radiation, leading to at least 31 deaths. Estimates of longer-term casualties from exposure to radiation varied widely. Incidences of treatable thyroid cancer among 1,750 local children appear to have been a direct effect of the disaster, and scientists reported in October 2000 an alarmingly high number of genetic mutations among plant life in the region. However, a report by the UN-backed Chernobyl Forum in 2005 estimated that the accident would cause a total of 'only' 4,000 deaths.

While the remains of the No. 4 reactor were encased in a concrete shell, the other reactors at Chernobyl continued to operate for years after the accident, providing much-needed energy to Ukraine. A timetable for the plant's complete closure was not agreed until April 2000 and the last operational reactor was finally shut down on 15 December 2000. International donors have pledged US $768m. to help safeguard the plant, and the **European Union** has provided funding for the construction of new nuclear power plants to make up the shortfall in the energy supply.

Chişinau

Capital city of **Moldova**, situated on a tributary of the Dnester river. *Population*: 592,600 (2005 estimate). The city was sacked during the retreat of German and Romanian troops at the end of the Second World War. Like many industrialized centres in the country it attracted a large population of ethnic **Russians** during the period of **Soviet** rule.

Christian Democrat International *see* **Centrist Democrat International**.

Christian Democratic People's Party
Partidul Popular Creştin şi Democrat (PPCD)

A centre-right party in **Moldova** which originally favoured unification with Romania but now accepts the post-**Soviet** status quo. The party was founded in 1992 as the Christian Democratic People's Front (*Frontul Popular Creştin şi Democrat*—FPCD) and the successor of the radical pan-Romanian wing of the

Popular Front of Moldova, which had been the dominant political grouping during the collapse of Soviet communist rule in mid-1991. Preferring to call Moldova by the historic name **Bessarabia**, the FPCD saw independence as the first step towards the 'sacred goal' of reunification with Romania. Under the new leadership of Iurie Roşca, the FPCD suffered defeat alongside other pro-Romanian parties in the first multi-party **Parliament** elections in February 1994, winning nine seats on a vote share of 7.5%.

Having backed the unsuccessful re-election bid of Mircea Snegur in the late 1996 presidential elections, the FPCD was in June 1997 a founder component of the Democratic Convention of Moldova (CDM), which included Snegur's Party of Revival and Accord of Moldova (PRCM). In the March 1998 legislative elections the CDM won only 26 seats with 19.2% of the vote and was outpolled by the revived **Communist Party of the Moldovan Republic** (PCRM); but the CDM and other centre-right formations were able to form a coalition Government which included FPCD representation.

The FPCD broke with the CDM and the centre-right coalition in March 1999 when it joined the PCRM in voting against the installation of Ion Sturza as Prime Minister. In opposition, the FPCD in December 1999 changed its name to the PPCD and adopted a new basic programme calling for 'integration within a Europe of nations and the fulfilment of national unity' (instead of its previous advocacy of 'the national unity of all **Romanians** in Romania and Moldova'). In early parliamentary elections in February 2001, in which the PCRM obtained a landslide majority, the PPCD was one of only two other parties to gain representation, winning 11 seats with 8.3% of the vote. This tally remained unchanged at the March 2005 elections, achieving 9.1% of the vote.

Leadership: Iurie Roşca (Chair).
Address: Str. Nicolae Iorga 5, 2009 Chişinau.
Telephone: (22) 233356.
Fax: (22) 238666.
E-mail: magic@ppcd.md
Internet: www.ppcd.md

Chuvash Republic (Chuvashia) *see* **Chavash Republic**.

Circassians *see* **Cherkess**.

CIS *see* **Commonwealth of Independent States**.

Citizens' Union of Georgia
Sakartvelos Mokalaketa Kavshiri (SMK)

Georgia's ruling party for most of the post-independence period prior to 2003, essentially a **nomenklatura**-based formation although it is an observer member of the **Socialist International**.

The SMK was established in November 1993 by Head of State Eduard **Shevardnadze**. Initially an umbrella organization, it quickly attracted support from other pro-democracy and pro-market formations. In November 1995, when Shevardnadze was re-elected President by an overwhelming popular majority, the concurrent legislative elections gave the SMK the dominant position in the new **Parliament** with almost half of the seats. It increased its advantage in the 1999 parliamentary elections, winning 130 of the 227 seats filled (with 41.7% of the vote) on a platform promising an improvement in economic conditions, increased wages and prompt payment of pensions.

In the April 2000 presidential election, which was boycotted by the main opposition leader, Shevardnadze again set the improvement of economic and social conditions as a primary goal and was re-elected with an overwhelming 78.8% of the vote. Following the presidential contest, a number of SMK and allied members of Parliament, including the 12-strong Abkhazeti Bloc representing ethnic **Georgian** refugees from **Abkhazia**, resigned from the SMK parliamentary group in protest against various decisions by the leadership. The SMK factionalized into a pro-Shevardnadze group and a reformers group led by the party's General Secretary Zurab Zhvania and Mikhail **Saakashvili**. In 2001 Saakashvili resigned from the Government and the party over government corruption, and formed the opposition United National Movement (now the **National Movement-Democrats**—NM-D). Many others also quit the party, not assuaged by Shevardnadze's resignation from the party chairmanship. Zhvania initially remained within the SMK, but he too left it in mid-2002 and formed the United Democrats (now also part of the NM-D).

The SMK became the central component of the pro-Shevardnadze 'For a New Georgia' bloc ahead of the November 2003 elections. Official results gave victory to Shevardnadze and the pro-presidential bloc, but protests (the **Rose Revolution**) forced him out of office. The SMK had won 19 of the single seats in the Parliament, but voting for the proportional representation seats was deemed invalid. When they were rerun in March 2004, following the January election of Saakashvili as the new Georgian President, the SMK won none of them.

Leadership: Avtandil Dzhorbenadze (Chair).
Address: Chavchavadze 55, Tbilisi.
Telephone: (32) 999479.
Fax: (32) 931584.
E-mail: cug@access.sanet.ge

CMEA *see* **Council for Mutual Economic Assistance**.

Cold War

A phrase in common usage from 1947, describing the protracted period of post-war antagonism between the communist bloc, particularly the **Soviet Union**, and the West, led by the USA. Sir Winston Churchill's March 1946 speech at Fulton in Missouri, USA, when he warned of the threat of Soviet expansion and of an 'iron curtain' falling across Europe, and the subsequent Soviet imposition of communism in east-central Europe, are usually offered as starting points of the Cold War. The two blocs fought a vigorous propaganda battle in which each sought to discredit its rival and to gain prestige for itself. The balance of terror which followed the Soviet Union's development of the atomic bomb led the blocs to avoid direct military conflict, although there were several dangerous confrontations. Much conflict took place by proxy: one bloc funded and trained indigenous military groups to engage opposing forces when it appeared that the rival bloc was likely to extend its sphere of influence, for instance in Afghanistan. The Cold War forced the two blocs to maintain their readiness for a possible 'hot war'; the expense of the resulting arms race eventually helped to bankrupt the Soviet Union. The appointment in 1985 of Mikhail **Gorbachev** as General Secretary of the **Communist Party of the Soviet Union** marked the beginning of a rapprochement with the West, which was confirmed with the Soviet decision in 1989 not to intervene when the communist regimes in **eastern Europe** were collapsing. Three of the clearest symbols of the ending of the Cold War were the beginning of work on 2 May 1989 to dismantle the 'iron curtain' barrier between Hungary and Austria, the opening in November 1989 of the Berlin Wall, and the final dissolution in 1991 of the **Warsaw Pact**—the military alliance between the former communist-bloc countries.

Collective Security Treaty Organization (CSTO)

A security agreement signed by several members of the **Commonwealth of Independent States** (CIS). An initial six countries—**Armenia**, Kazakhstan, Kyrgyzstan, **Russia**, Tajikistan and Uzbekistan—signed the Collective Security Treaty (CST) on 15 May 1992, and **Azerbaijan**, **Georgia** and **Belarus** joined the following year. The Treaty came into force in April 1994, for an initial five-year period. All signatories agreed to abstain from the use or threat of force against one another and not to join any other military alliances. Only Armenia, Belarus, Kazakhstan, Kyrgyzstan, Russia and Tajikistan renewed the Treaty in 1999, whereas Uzbekistan joined the **GUAM group**, which already included Azerbaijan and Georgia. In October 2002 the CST was reformed as the Collective

Security Treaty Organization, which took effect in September 2003. Uzbekistan returned to the group in 2006 after quitting GUAM the previous year.
Secretary-General: Nikolai Bordyuzha.

Colour revolutions

A series of non-violent pro-democracy popular uprisings against authoritarian regimes in former Soviet states from late 2003 onwards, usually following disputed elections. In each case the protesters adopted a colour or a flower as the symbol for their clothing and banners. The 'colour revolution' terminology recalled the Velvet Revolution in Czechoslovakia in 1989, which brought down the communist Government there. The **Rose Revolution** in **Georgia** in November 2003 resulted in the ouster of Eduard **Shevardnadze**; the **Orange Revolution** in **Ukraine** in November 2004 led to the annulment of the second round presidential election, quashing the victory of President **Kuchma**'s chosen successor; the Tulip Revolution in Kyrgyzstan in March–April 2005 ended with the removal of President Askar Akayev. President **Lukashenka** of **Belarus** warned the opposition against attempting a colour revolution during the March 2006 elections.

Comecon *see* **Council for Mutual Economic Assistance**.

Common Economic Spaces

Four proposed areas of co-operation between the **European Union** and the **Russian Federation**, adopted in May 2003:

The Common Economic Space will open up and integrate the Russian and EU markets by removing barriers to trade and investment and improving regulatory policy and competitiveness.

The Common Space of Freedom, Security and Justice will focus on combating internal terrorism, smuggling of drugs and people, and money 'laundering', and could ultimately lead to the removal of visa restrictions.

The Common Space on External Security will co-ordinate co-operation with UN peacekeeping efforts and responses to the threat of global terrorism and proliferation. It will also address the 'frozen conflicts' in areas adjacent to EU or Russian borders such as **Transdnestria**, **Abkhazia**, and **Nagorno-Karabakh**.

The Common Space on Research, Education, and Culture will enhance co-operation in science and innovation and encourage convergence of university-level educational content.

See alternatively **Single Economic Space**.

Commonwealth of Independent States (CIS)

The Commonwealth of Independent States is a voluntary association of 12 states (though Turkmenistan is now only an associate member). It was established by 11 newly independent states at the time of the collapse of the **Soviet Union** on 21 December 1991, and joined by a 12th country, **Georgia**, in December 1993. Its Charter was adopted formally by the Council of Heads of States on 22 January 1993. Preoccupied initially with arms control and collective security issues, the CIS developed institutionally with the signature of treaties on **Collective Security** (Tashkent, May 1992) and on Economic Union (Moscow, September 1993). CIS peacekeeping forces operated in Tajikistan until the end of the 1990s and also in **Abkhazia**. A programme on combating terrorism was adopted at the CIS's Moscow summit in June 2000, including the establishment of a CIS anti-terrorism centre.

The spate of '**colour revolutions**' from 2003 replaced several pro-Russian governments with pro-Western ones, seeking integration with Europe and the **North Atlantic Treaty Organization** (NATO). This has raised questions over the future significance of the CIS, especially since the creation of the new regional groupings of **GUAM** (**Georgia**, **Ukraine**, **Azerbaijan** and **Moldova**), the **Eurasian Economic Community** and the **Single Economic Space**. Georgia has withdrawn from the CIS Council of Defence Ministers to avoid conflict with its desire to join NATO, and has threatened to end its membership completely, as have **Azerbaijan**, **Moldova** and **Ukraine**, though Ukraine's position has been complicated by the return to power in 2006 of pro-Russian Prime Minister Viktor **Yanukovych**. Turkmenistan, which had never favoured political, military or economic integration, reduced its status to that of associate member in 2005.

Members: **Armenia**, Azerbaijan, **Belarus**, Georgia, Kazakhstan, Kyrgyzstan, Moldova, **Russian Federation**, Tajikistan, Turkmenistan (associate member only), Ukraine and Uzbekistan.
Executive Secretary: Yurii Yarov.
Address: vul. Kirava 17, 220000 Minsk.
Telephone: (17) 2223517.
Fax: (17) 2272339.
E-mail: postmaster@www.cis.minsk.by
Internet: www.cis.minsk.by

Communist Party of Armenia
Hayastani Komunistakan Kusaktsutyun (HKK)

Armenia's sole ruling party in the **Soviet** era, whose influence has declined since it lost power in 1990; many of its former members in the state bureaucracy have joined other parties.

The HKK managed only second place in multi-party legislative elections in 1990 and was suspended in September 1991. Relegalized in 1994, it came a poor third in the 1995 **National Assembly** elections. In the 1996 presidential elections the then party leader Sergei Badalian also came third, with 6.3% of the vote. He stood again in the 1998 presidential contest, winning 11% in the first round but coming only fourth.

The HKK's call for Armenia's accession to the new **Belarus-Russia Union** was an important plank in its platform for the May 1999 Assembly elections, in which it took second place with 12.1% of the proportional vote and 11 of the 131 seats. Badalian died of a heart attack in **Moscow** in November 1999 and was succeeded in January 2000 by Vladimir Darbinian, who had been Armenian SSR Interior Minister in the 1970s. The following month the HKK joined the Government (headed by the **Republican Party of Armenia**) for the first time since losing power in 1990. Arguments over the party's level of support for the Government led to several expulsions.

At the May 2003 election the HKK won only 2% of the vote and therefore did not qualify for any seats in the new legislature. Ruben Tovmassian was appointed as the party's new leader the following August. Allegations of corruption against Tovmassian and other issues have caused further splits in the party's ranks.

Leadership: Ruben Tovmassian (Chair).
Address: Baghramian Avenue 10, 375095 Yerevan.
Telephone: (10) 567933.
Fax: (10) 533855.

Communist Party of Belarus
Kommunisticheskaya Partiya Belarusi (KPB)

The largest party in **Belarus** since 1995, directly descended from the Soviet-era ruling party. The KPB had originated as a regional committee of the Russian Social Democratic Labour Party (formed in 1904) covering both Belarus and Lithuania. Established as the ruling Communist Party of the Soviet Socialist Republic of Byelorussia in 1920, the party suffered greatly during Stalin's purges of the 1930s, when almost all of its leaders were liquidated and party membership fell by more than half. Enlarged by Soviet territorial acquisitions from Poland in the Second World War, the Byelorussian SSR was given UN membership in 1945, but its ruling party and Government remained wholly subservient to Moscow.

From mid-1989 the republican leadership came under official Soviet criticism for not being ready to make compromises with the pro-democracy movement. It therefore allowed candidates of what became the **Belarusian Popular Front-Renaissance** (NFB-A) to contest the April 1990 Supreme Soviet elections, while ensuring that a decisive KPB victory was recorded. The conservative Minsk leadership, however, then unwisely backed the abortive **August coup** by hardliners in Moscow in 1991, following which the hardline republican Head of State, Mikalay Dzemyantsei, was replaced by the reformist Stanislau Shushkevich, who declared independence from the Soviet Union. The KPB itself was suspended and its property was nationalized.

The party remained under suspension for 18 months, although the government structure and the legislature continued to be under the control of persons appointed or elected as communists. At government level, Shushkevich came into increasingly bitter dispute with the hardline Prime Minister, Vyacheslau Kebich, who commanded majority support from the so-called Belarus Group of conservative deputies for his resistance to political and economic reform. The relegalization of the KPB in February 1993 did little to clarify political allegiances, in part because government members preferred to retain the 'independent' label. Moreover, a KPB leadership dispute led to the creation by Viktar Chykin in October 1993 of the Movement for Democracy, Social Progress and Justice as a merger of seven hardline communist groups. At the same time, the various KPB factions came under the umbrella of the Popular Movement of Belarus (NDB), a loose alliance of conservative parties which backed the ousting of Shushkevich as Head of State in January 1994 and his replacement by hardliner Mechislau Gryb.

Having embraced multi-partyism, the mainstream KPB contested the June–July 1994 presidential elections in its own right. Its candidate was its then Chairman Vasil Novikau, who was placed last of six contenders in the first round, winning only 4.5% of the vote. However, forecasts that '**nomenklatura** power' would ensure victory for Kebich (standing as an independent) proved to be badly mistaken: relegated to a poor second place in the first round, he was heavily defeated in the second by another independent, Alyaksandr **Lukashenka**, a moderate but increasingly authoritarian conservative who as anti-corruption supremo had played a key role in the ousting of Shushkevich.

The KPB's organizational strength enabled it to become the largest formal party in the 1995 legislative elections to the new **National Assembly**. It won 42 seats in the lower House of Representatives. Having established his leadership of the rump KPB, Chykin in September 1998 became Executive Secretary of the pro-Lukashenka Belarusian People's Patriotic Union (BNPS), grouping some 30 conservative parties which backed the **Belarus-Russia Union** treaty. In elections to the House of Representatives in 2000 and 2004 the BNPS and its allies obtained near-total ascendancy, amidst opposition and external claims of electoral manipulation and fraud. In the latter poll, the KPB received the largest number of seats for a single party—eight. It remains staunchly pro-Lukashenka.

Leadership: Tatsyana Holubeva (Chair).
Address: Varanyanskaga Street 52, 220007 Minsk.
Telephone: (17) 2266422.
Fax: (17) 2323123.

Communist Party of the Moldovan Republic
Partidul Comunistilor din Republica Moldova (PCRM)

One of the few parties of **central/eastern Europe** which has retained the communist designation and been electorally successful. The PCRM obtained registration in 1994 as effectively the successor to the **Soviet**-era Communist Party, which had been banned in August 1991. Although not legalized in time for the 1994 **Parliament** elections, the PCRM subsequently attracted defectors from other parties and formed the Popular Patriotic Forces front to support the candidacy of party leader Vladimir **Voronin** in the 1996 presidential elections. He came third in the first round with 10.3% of the vote, whereupon the party backed the victorious Petru Lucinschi in the second and was rewarded with two ministerial posts in the resultant coalition Government.

In its first parliamentary elections in March 1998 the PCRM advocated 'the rebirth of a socialist society' and became the strongest single party, with 40 seats and 30.1% of the vote, but went into opposition to a centre-right coalition. In one of a series of subsequent government crises, Voronin was in late 1999 nominated by President Lucinschi to take over the premiership, but he failed to obtain sufficient parliamentary support.

In early legislative elections in February 2001 the PCRM swept to a landslide victory by winning 71 of the 101 seats with 49.9% of the vote. In early April Moldova became the first former communist country democratically to elect a communist as Head of State, when Voronin was elected President by the new Parliament. Vasile Tarlev became Prime Minister of a PCRM Government committed to a strong state role in the economy and the re-establishment of close ties with the Russian Federation. Later in April the new President was re-elected PCRM Chairman, after the Constitutional Court had ruled that the two posts were not incompatible.

In legislative elections held in March 2005, the PCRM was returned to power with a significantly reduced majority, retaining just 56 seats. It was forced to rely on the support of the pro-Western **Christian Democratic People's Party** to ensure Voronin the 61 votes necessary for re-election.

Leadership: Vladimir Voronin (Chair).
Address: Str. Nicolae Iorga 11, 2012 Chişinau.
Telephone: (22) 234614.
Fax: (22) 233673.
E-mail: sava_valeriuion@yahoo.com
Internet: www.pcrm.md

Communist Party of the Russian Federation
Kommunisticheskaya Partiya Rossiiskoi Federatisii (KPRF)

The successor to the **Soviet**-era ruling communist party, in opposition in the post-Soviet period but remaining the **Russian Federation**'s largest single party until a spate of mergers in the period after the 1999 elections. The KPRF was registered in March 1993 following a Constitutional Court ruling in December 1992 that the banning in November 1991 of the **Communist Party of the Soviet Union** (KPSS) had been illegal.

A revived party, using the KPRF name, held a congress in Klyazm near **Moscow** in February 1993 and elected as its leader a former Soviet apparatchik, Gennadii **Zyuganov**, who had been Co-Chairman of the National Salvation Front formed the previous year by communists and Russian nationalists who deplored the passing of the Soviet empire. The KPRF was thus placed in uneasy alliance with the nationalist right, in opposition to the reformist pro-market forces in power in Moscow under the presidency of Boris **Yeltsin**. The manifest negative effects of rapid economic transition, including unemployment, inflation, rampant corruption and organized crime, provided the KPRF with powerful ammunition in the unfamiliar task of seeking electoral support in a democratic system.

In the elections of December 1993 to the State Duma (lower house of the **Federal Assembly**) the KPRF took third place with 65 seats and 12.4% of the proportional vote, thereafter becoming the principal focus of opposition to the Yeltsin administration. Despite the appointment in January 1995 of an acknowledged communist as Justice Minister, the KPRF continued to be essentially an opposition party, its platform for the December 1995 State Duma elections promising the restoration of 'social justice'. Its reward was 157 seats (with 22.3% of the proportional vote), making it the largest single party in the chamber.

Remaining in opposition (although welcoming Yeltsin's shift to a more conservative line), the KPRF nominated Zyuganov as its candidate for the mid-1996 presidential election, on a platform condemning the destruction of the Russian Federation's industrial base by **IMF**-dictated policies and promising to restore economic sovereignty. Zyuganov came a close second to Yeltsin in the first round, winning 32% of the vote, and lost the second round run-off, in which his tally was 40.4%. The KPRF then launched the Popular-Patriotic Union of Russia (NPSR) to rally anti-Yeltsin forces, Zyuganov being elected as its leader.

In the late 1990s the KPRF sought to distance itself from the nationalist right, while continuing to articulate a Russian nationalism harking back to the Soviet era. The party urged a return to centralized government and the transfer of presidential powers to the Government and the legislature, as well as the creation of a 'Slavic union' of the Russian Federation, **Ukraine** and **Belarus**, arguing that only a KPRF Government could restore Russia's status as a great power. However, the KPRF's opposition to the war in **Chechnya** cost it some support, so that the party slipped to 113 seats in the December 1999 State Duma elections, although its share of the proportional vote increased to 24.3%, making it still the largest single party.

Yeltsin's unexpected resignation at the end of 1999 presented a new challenge to the KPRF in that his designated successor, Vladimir **Putin**, was popularly perceived as having impeccable nationalist and pro-authority credentials. In presidential elections in March 2000, Zyuganov was again the KPRF candidate but was soundly defeated by Putin in the first round, receiving only 29.2% of the vote. The KPRF subsequently declared its readiness to provide 'constructive opposition' to the new Government, although following the re-election of Zyuganov as Chairman at the seventh party congress in December 2000 the KPRF embarked upon 'active opposition' to what it described as the 'anti-people' Putin administration. In January 2001 Zyuganov was elected Chairman of the Council of Communist Parties in the former Soviet republics.

Opponents of Zyuganov's leadership began to emerge at this time. With the new **United Russia** grouping of Putin's supporters dominating the Duma and its committees, Zyuganov insisted that KPRF members resign from those committees, and ejected from the party anyone who refused to do so. He also shunned the approaches of Sergei Glazyev, who went on to form the **Motherland** party. Zyuganov has since labelled Motherland a government stooge, created solely to divide support for the KPRF.

In the December 2003 legislative elections the Communists sunk to mid-1990s levels, gaining just 12.7% of the vote and 52 seats in the Duma, while Motherland finished a surprise third with 37 seats. The KPRF suffered further defections in 2004, with Vladimir Tikhonov leaving to form the All-Russian Communist Party of the Future, and Gennadii Semigin creating the Patriots of Russia.

The party attempted to confirm its leadership of the left by vocally heading popular discontent at efforts to reform the social benefits system in early 2006, though the protest movement appeared to be largely beyond its actual control.

Leadership: Gennadii Zyuganov (Chair).
Address: M. Sukharevskii per. 3/1, 103051 Moscow.
Telephone: (495) 9287129.
Fax: (495) 2929050.
E-mail: kprf2005@yandex.ru
Internet: www.kprf.ru

Communist Party of the Soviet Union
Kommunisticheskaya Partiya Sovetskogo Soyuza (KPSS)

The former single ruling party of the **Soviet Union** until 1991, from which the **Communist Party of the Russian Federation** (KPRF) claims descent. The KPSS was itself directly descended from Vladimir Lenin's majority (Bolshevik) wing of the Russian Social Democratic Labour Party founded in 1898, which at the party's second congress held in London in 1903 out-voted the minority (Menshevik) wing on Lenin's proposal that the party should become a tightly-disciplined vanguard of professional revolutionaries.

Calling for socialist revolution in **Russia** along Marxist lines, in 1912 the Bolshevik wing became a separate party, which achieved legal status following the overthrow of the Tsar in February 1917. The Bolsheviks then capitalized on mass discontent, and the failure of the new Government to withdraw Russia from the disastrous First World War, to increase their popularity and to agitate for revolution. In October–November 1917 the Bolsheviks seized power in the second Russian Revolution, and instigated a one-party-state system based on Lenin's interpretation of Marxism. Facing opposition from democrats and royalists, as well as from the foreign powers still involved in the war, the Bolsheviks were able to consolidate their control through their victory in the Russian Civil War (1918–20). The Bolsheviks renamed their party the Russian Communist Party (Bolsheviks) in 1918, and the All-Union Communist Party (Bolsheviks) in 1925. Josef Stalin changed its title to the KPSS in 1952.

The KPSS totally dominated Soviet life as the sole political movement, with control over all areas of society. Beneath the Politburo (political bureau) and its leader, the General Secretary, was the Party Secretariat and the Central Committee which ran the party between congresses. At the five-yearly congresses, party members from the regional divisions of the party would meet, theoretically to debate party/government policy. However, under the totalitarian regime they were used merely to endorse the wishes of the General Secretary. At the base of the party were regional cells of at least three party members who would theoretically implement party policy at the local level.

Used by Stalin to promote his own cult of personality, the KPSS was from the beginning entwined with the communist state, in which regard it served as a model for other communist parties around the world. On his climb towards dominance of the party following Lenin's death in 1924, Stalin had opposition groups high up in the party 'liquidated' in various purges, leaving him unassailable by 1929. His paranoia continued, however, into the 1930s culminating in the terrible *Yezovshchina* of 1937, which saw many 'dissident' party members executed or exiled to **Siberia**. The party membership was reduced from a high of 3.5 million in 1933 to just 1.9 million in 1938.

The Second World War, known in the Soviet Union as the Great Patriotic War, galvanized the party's popularity, aided hugely by the Government's propaganda efforts. The death of Stalin in 1953, and the process of 'de-Stalinization' under his successor Nikita Khrushchev, briefly eased the grip of the KPSS in the early 1960s, prompting easier international relations and encouraging low-level liberalization in the Soviet Union. However, Khrushchev was ousted in 1964 by Leonid Brezhnev, who reasserted the party's dominance and increased the control of the state machinery.

After Brezhnev's death in 1982, and short periods of party leadership by Yurii Andropov and Konstantin Chernenko (both of whom died after a year in office), Mikhail **Gorbachev** became in 1985 the last General Secretary of the KPSS. He initiated the reform processes (*see glasnost* and *perestroika*) which ultimately saw the undoing of the Soviet Union in 1991 following attempts by hardline members of the KPSS to halt the changes (*see* **August coup**). Following the defeat of the August coup the new Russian President Boris **Yeltsin** banned the KPSS on 23 August 1991 and seized all of its assets as state property.

Communist Party of Ukraine
Komunistychna Partiya Ukrainy (KPU)

The successor to the **Soviet**-era ruling party in **Ukraine**. The Soviet-era KPU was banned in August 1991, but was revived in mid-1993 under the leadership of Petro Symonenko on a platform calling for the restoration of state control over the economy and a confederative union with the **Russian Federation**. The KPU attracted particular support in the economically-troubled industrial areas of eastern Ukraine, especially in the Donbass mining region, where Symonenko had been a senior party official in the Soviet era. The party gave decisive backing to Leonid **Kuchma** in the mid-1994 presidential elections, while in the 1994 **Supreme Council** elections it emerged as substantially the largest single party, with a total of over 90 seats (nearly all in eastern and southern Ukraine).

The KPU quickly came into conflict with Kuchma, however, and led opposition in 1995–96 to the 'presidential' Constitution favoured by him. Following the final adoption of the new text in June 1996, the party accepted its legitimacy but mounted a campaign for early presidential and parliamentary elections, combined with mass industrial action in protest against the Government's economic policy. The KPU confirmed its position as the largest party in the March 1998 parliamentary elections, advancing to 115 seats on a vote share of 26% and subsequently being joined by some independent deputies.

Standing as the KPU candidate in the autumn 1999 presidential elections, Symonenko came second to the incumbent Kuchma in the first round with 22.2% of the vote, and was defeated in the second round despite increasing his support to 37.8% on the strength of backing from other left-wing parties. The KPU leader complained that the polling had been rigged, as did international observers, and in March 2000 the KPU's headquarters in **Kiev** were briefly occupied by nationalist militants, who accused the party of promoting the colonization of Ukraine by the Russian Federation.

In the major crisis which overtook the Kuchma administration in early 2001, the KPU claimed credit for securing the dismissal of 'pro-US' Prime Minister Viktor **Yushchenko** in April and declared itself ready to form a Government, although it held back from joining moves to impeach Kuchma. However, this marked a high-point in the KPU's fortunes. A split within the party had emerged in 2000 with more moderate members establishing an internal faction known as the KPU-Reformed. Symonenko's anti-Western rhetoric, and his open courting of ever-closer ties with Russia, saw the party's popularity fall off at the 2002 elections: winning just 66 seats and 20% of the vote.

The downward spiral worsened dramatically during the next parliament. A taste of things to come was Symonenko's fourth place position in the first round of presidential elections in October 2004 with just 5% of the popular vote. At the 2006 elections, the KPU appeared to be a spent force. It could claim only 3.7% of the vote, barely keeping its head above the 3% barrier for representation. It was awarded 21 seats. However, the election had been won by the KPU's ally the pro-Russian **Party of Regions**, and after months of negotiations, the KPU found itself as part of the ruling coalition, along with the **Socialist Party of Ukraine** and (initially) the **Our Ukraine** bloc.

Leadership: Petro Symonenko (First Secretary).
Address: vul. Borysohlibska 7, 04070 Kiev.
Telephone: (44) 4255487.
Fax: (44) 4163137.
E-mail: press@kpu.net.ua
Internet: www.kpu.net.ua

Comprehensive Nuclear Test Ban Treaty *see* **Nuclear Test Ban Treaty**.

Contact Group (for the former Yugoslavia)

An unofficial collection of six countries (France, Germany, Italy, **Russian Federation**, UK and USA). It was formed in April 1994 (at which point it comprised five countries—Italy joining in 1996) to co-ordinate US-**European Union**-Russian policy regarding the warring nations of the former Socialist Federal Republic of Yugoslavia. Following the signing of the final Dayton Agreement, which ended the war in Bosnia and Herzegovina in 1995, the Contact Group assumed responsibilities for overseeing the implementation of the Agreement. The Group has continued to apply international pressure in the region to attain security, most notably calling for sanctions and paving the way for air strikes by **North Atlantic Treaty Organization** (NATO) forces against Yugoslavia over the crisis in Kosovo in 1999, and raising concern over the ethnic crisis in Macedonia in 2001. Since then it has been involved in talks to determine the final status of Kosovo.

Conventional Forces in Europe
(or CFE Treaty)

A key disarmament agreement at the end of the **Cold War**, signed in November 1990 by the member states of the **North Atlantic Treaty Organization** (NATO) and of the **Warsaw Pact**. The Treaty limits non-nuclear air and ground armaments in the signatory countries. It was negotiated within the framework of the Conference on Security and Co-operation in Europe (CSCE—*see* **Organization for Security and Co-operation in Europe**) and signed at a CSCE summit meeting in Paris.

Cossacks

A culturally distinct ethnically-mixed **Russian** and **Ukrainian** group of around 140,000 people (2002 estimate) spread across southern **European Russia**. Formed from bands of freed and escapee serfs in the 16th century, the Cossack *hosts* established a fierce reputation as horse-borne warriors. This was put to good use by the Russian Empire which employed them as frontier guards in exchange for land tenure. Cossack military units were thus used effectively throughout the empire, but particularly in the **Don Basin** and the north **Caucasus**.

Following the Russian Revolution of 1917 the Cossacks of the Don region were instrumental in leading the anti-Bolshevik 'White' resistance in the south. Their defeat by the Bolshevik forces led to mass persecution, and deportations under Stalin. Under **Soviet** rule the Cossacks were denied their separate cultural status and officially classed as either Russians or Ukrainians.

A re-emergence of Cossack nationalist sentiment in the late 1980s led to the formation of the Association of Cossacks in 1990. Cossack troops played a key role in the conflict in the breakaway **Moldovan** republic of **Transdnestria** in 1992. Former Russian President Boris **Yeltsin** rehabilitated the Cossacks in 1991 and granted them state support from 1993. These moves strengthened Cossack resolve and have lent weight to calls for an ethnically-based autonomous territory, spearheaded by the Don Cossacks.

Council for Mutual Economic Assistance (CMEA or Comecon)

The now defunct structure (known more colloquially as Comecon) established in 1949 during the Stalin era, within which the centrally-planned economies of the so-called Soviet-bloc countries were co-ordinated. In 1971 the organization moved on from its co-ordination phase to a so-called integration phase, with the adoption of a Comprehensive Programme for the Further Extension and Improvement of Co-operation and the Further Development of Socialist Economic Integration.

Significant growth in mutual trade among member countries was recorded until a generalized slump in the 1980s. Following the collapse of communism in Europe in 1989–91 the CMEA was disbanded, leaving a legacy of problems for member countries. Their economies, having been structured over decades to fulfil specific roles within the CMEA, could suddenly count on neither the resources on which they had come to depend from other member countries (such as gas from the **Soviet Union**, at costs not reflecting the world market) nor the market for their output, particularly in heavy industry.

Members of the CMEA at the time it was disbanded in 1991 were Bulgaria, Cuba, Czechoslovakia, East Germany, Hungary, Mongolia, Poland, Romania, Soviet Union and Viet Nam. A form of associate status in the organization was specified for Yugoslavia in a 1964 agreement. Albania was a member until 1961 (when it ceased participating, although without formally revoking its membership). The People's Republic of China and to some extent North Korea also participated with observer status until 1961.

Council of Europe

A regional organization originally founded in May 1949 with 10 members in western Europe, which has now been expanded continent-wide. Its objectives are promoting regional unity and social progress, and upholding the principles of parliamentary democracy, respect for human rights and the rule of law. It has a Committee of Ministers and a Parliamentary Assembly, which elects its Secretary-General. The European Court of Human Rights, established in 1959 in Strasbourg, is part of the activities of the Council of Europe, overseeing the implementation of the Convention for the Protection of Human Rights and Fundamental Freedoms (usually known as the European Convention on Human Rights). Council member countries are required to adhere to the Convention, which should entail among other things the abolition of the death penalty.

Members: 46 European countries, including **Armenia**, **Azerbaijan**, **Georgia**, **Moldova**, **Russian Federation**, **Ukraine**. No progress has been made on the membership application submitted by **Belarus** on 12 March 1993, owing to its domestic political situation. The 1997 decision to revoke its special guest status was upheld in 2004.

Secretary-General: Terry Davis.
Address: Avenue de l'Europe, 67075 Strasbourg Cédex, France.
Telephone: (3) 88412000.
Fax: (3) 88412745.
E-mail: infopoint@coe.int
Internet: www.coe.int

Council of the Baltic Sea States (CBSS)

A regional forum, meeting usually annually since 1992 at the level of Foreign Ministers (with summit meetings for heads of government on a biennial basis since 1996). It has a broad remit to promote democracy, greater regional unity and economic development. The Council was established in 1992 under the Copenhagen Declaration, the outcome of a meeting held in the Danish capital in March of that year. A permanent International Secretariat was inaugurated on 20 October 1998 and is located in Stockholm, Sweden. Sweden holds the chairmanship of the CBSS from 1 July 2006 to 30 June 2007.

Members: Denmark, Estonia, Finland, Germany, Iceland, Latvia, Lithuania, Norway, Poland, **Russian Federation** and Sweden. The European Commission (of the **European Union**) is also represented in its own right.

Director of the Secretariat: Gabriele Kötschau.

Address: CBSS Secretariat, Strömsborg, POB 2010, 103 11 Stockholm, Sweden.

Telephone: (8) 4401920.

Fax: (8) 4401944.

E-mail: cbss@cbss.org

Internet: www.cbss.st

Council of the Federation
Soviet Federatsii

The upper house of the **Federal Assembly** of the **Russian Federation**.

Council of the Republic
Soviet Respubliki

The upper house of the **National Assembly** of **Belarus**.

Country of Law Party
Orinats Yerkir (OY)

A small right-wing political party in **Armenia** advocating the rule of law. The OY gave important support to the successful presidential candidacy of Robert **Kocharian** (non-party) in March 1998, subsequently forming part of the presidential coalition. The party achieved fifth place in the May 1999 **National Assembly** elections, winning 5.3% of the vote and six out of 131 seats, and dramatically increased its showing in May 2003, finishing second with 13% of the vote and 19 seats. Filled with new confidence, OY leader Artur Bagdasarian has begun to follow an independent line, criticizing the conduct of the constitutional referendum in November 2005 and calling for greater European integration. OY withdrew from the Government in mid-2006 and some observers have suggested Bagdasarian is aligning himself for a possible run at the presidency in 2008.

Leadership: Artur Bagdasarian (Chair).
Address: Arshakuniatis St 2, Yerevan.
Telephone: (10) 527452.
Fax: (10) 548631.
E-mail: oektert@oektert.am
Internet: www.oektert.am

Cour permanente d'arbitrage *see* **Permanent Court of Arbitration**.

CPA *see* **Permanent Court of Arbitration**.

CPC *see* **Centre for the Prevention of Conflict**.

CPSU *see* **Communist Party of the Soviet Union**.

Crimea

An overcrowded and impoverished peninsula and administrative region in the south of **Ukraine**. *Population*: 2m. (2005 estimate). Surrounded by the Black Sea and the Sea of Azov, Crimea is connected to Ukraine proper via the thin Perekop land bridge. Since the arrival of Greek colonists in the 6th century BC, Crimea has had a separate history from Ukraine, but in 1954 it was ceded from the **Russian** to the Ukrainian republic as a 'symbol of friendship between the Russian and Ukrainian peoples'.

The Mongol invasion of **eastern Europe** in the 13th century brought ethnic **Tatars** to the peninsula and in 1443 the khanate of Crimea was established in the wake of the Golden Horde. This state, which gave rise to the ethnically distinct **Crimean Tatars**, was eventually absorbed into the Russian Empire in 1783. Russian suzerainty permanently altered Crimea. The Tatars were persecuted and replaced by ethnic **Russians** and the region was developed as a key base in the Black Sea, its strategic significance attested by the Crimean War in the 1850s. After the Bolshevik Revolution of 1917 the aspirations of the Tatars were to some extent realized when a Crimean Autonomous Republic was created in 1921. The region was heavily developed, particularly the port of **Sevastopol**. This phase in Crimea's history ended abruptly, however, after a three-year period of German occupation during the Second World War (1941–43). Stalin, already responsible for the wholesale suppression of Tatar culture, had the Tatars deported in 1944 (*see* **deported nationalities**). They have not been effectively rehabilitated. In 1945 the region was stripped of its republic status and in 1954 it was ceded to Ukraine, while a determined policy was undertaken to slavicize the region, both culturally and demographically.

Following the collapse of the **Soviet Union** in 1991 Crimea voted in favour of returning to its republic status, this time within Ukraine. The campaign for greater autonomy, led by the majority Russian community, climaxed with a short-lived declaration of independence in May 1992. Since then the Russian nationalist movement has been divided and undermined by the Russian Federation's diplomatic support for Ukraine. Ethnic tensions on the peninsula are high. The returning Crimean Tatars (around 12% of the population by 2001) are marginalized and suffer disproportionately from unemployment. **Ukrainians** (24%) are also disadvantaged by the use of Russian in the peninsula. The general economic situation is of grave concern to the Ukrainian authorities. The regional authorities are frequently stalemated by disagreements between the pro-Ukrainian executive and the pro-autonomy legislature.

Crimean Tatars

An ethnic **Turkic people** originally from the **Crimean** peninsula in **Ukraine** but now scattered throughout the former **Soviet Union**. The Crimean Tatars developed separately from other Russian-based **Tatars** from as early as the 15th century. In 1445 the khanate of Crimea was established on the peninsula from the remnants of the Mongol Golden Horde. The Tatar state was an important regional power for the next 300 years, establishing strong links with ethnically-related Turkey across the Black Sea. However, it was destroyed in 1783 after Crimea was annexed by **Russia** at the conclusion of the latest in a sequence of Russo-Turkish wars.

The Tatars were immediately demoted from the ruling class in Crimea and their language and culture were suppressed amidst attempts to russify the region. During the Crimean War in the 1850s they came under wholesale persecution and even deportation. Ethnic **Russians** were relocated to the region in their stead. Although a Crimean Republic was established under Bolshevik rule in 1921 the Tatars fell foul of Stalin's policy on nationalities from as early as 1928. The Turkic language and culture were again suppressed. However, the worst was yet to come. Following a three-year occupation by German forces between 1941 and 1943, the reinstated Soviet regime identified the Tatars as collaborators. Stalin ordered the deportation of all 183,000 Tatars. Almost half of the Tatars removed to central Asia died during their transportation. Unlike most **deported nationalities** the Tatars were not physically rehabilitated in the 1950s. Their rights were returned in 1956 and they were legally absolved of collusion with the invading Nazis in 1967. However, the failure of the Soviet regime to acknowledge a separate ethnic identity for the Crimean Tatars blocked their repatriation to Crimea. Instead, nominally autonomous regions were created in the central Asian states they now occupied.

Finally in 1987 plans were drawn up to repatriate the Crimean Tatars to Crimea. Since then some 250,000 have returned to the peninsula. Population pressures and institutionalized discrimination have forced many of the returnees to take land in the less fertile south of the peninsula. Tatar groups remain resilient in demanding full compensation and the return of confiscated land and property, but there is little hope of a favourable response. The Crimean Tatar Congress (Kurultai) was constituted in the late 1980s to champion their cause.

CSTO *see* **Collective Security Treaty Organization**.

CTBT *see* **Nuclear Test Ban Treaty**.

Cyrillic alphabet

The script used to transcribe eastern and southern **Slavic** languages as well as some non-Slavic tongues. It was first created in the 9th century by the Byzantine monks St Cyril and St Methodius, when they were dispatched to Moravia to help convert the local Slavic people to Christianity. The monks adapted their native Greek alphabet specifically for the use of the Slavic tribes, enabling the production of a Slavic liturgy. The script was reformed over the centuries with a final deletion of Greek-specific characters in 1918. The adoption of Cyrillic became linked to the **Orthodox Christian** Church, and its use remains a clear point of distinction between the **Roman Catholic** Slavs, who use Latin script, and their Orthodox neighbours. In the most significant cases, the difference has become the focus for nationalists in **Moldova** and has delineated major ethnic divisions in the former Yugoslavia. The alphabet was also exported by the Russian Empire to the conquered non-Slavic peoples. In recent years there have been specific moves to switch from Cyrillic to Latin script by some of these peoples, notably the **Tatars** and the **Azeris**. The reasons are various but include efforts to define non-Russian cultures more clearly and to increase potential trade with the West.

The countries in **eastern Europe** in which the Cyrillic script is used are: **Belarus**, Bosnia and Herzegovina (Serbs), Bulgaria, Macedonia, Moldova, Montenegro, the **Russian Federation**, Serbia and **Ukraine**.

D

Dagestan

A constituent republic of the **Russian Federation** stretching along the western shore of the Caspian Sea down to the **Caucasus** mountains. It is the most ethnically diverse territory in Europe with more than 30 ethnic groups, only four of them numbering more than about 200,000. It is also the centre of Islam in the region. *Population*: 2.6m. (2002 estimate). Russian suzerainty was not officially established over Dagestan until 1877, although contact had been made as early as the 15th century. An autonomous Dagestani **Soviet** republic was created in January 1921. Despite the wide variety of peoples from varying ethnic backgrounds—Caucasians, Iranians, **Slavs** and **Turks**—tensions were kept in check during the Soviet era. Most people are at least bilingual, speaking their own dialect and usually one of the three major languages: Avar, Kumyk and Russian.

Although it was declared a full Soviet republic in May 1991, Dagestan did not become an independent state when the **Soviet Union** collapsed later that year, but instead became a Sovereign Republic within the Russian Federation in March 1992. Adherence to Islam is a major binding force, with **Muslim** brotherhoods regulating social life, but in 1999 an abortive Islamic uprising in the north was swiftly and severely crushed by Russian troops. Clashes over land rights and the campaigns of various nationalist movements have added to the volatility of the situation, as has the occasional overspill of violence from neighbouring **Chechnya**. A series of ethnic nationalist movements, among the mostly Sunni Muslim groups, have made calls ranging from greater ethnic autonomy to full regional separatism. There has been pressure for the establishment of a mini-federal system in the republic to try to reconcile these demands.

The main ethnic groups are the **Avars** (the traditional ruling elite and, at around 25%, the largest single group in the republic), **Dargins** (around 15%), **Kumyks** (whose Turkic language and culture serves as a *lingua franca* across the north **Caucasus region**) (around 14%), **Lezghins** (around 10%) and **Russians** (around 5%). Other groups include the Laks, **Tabasarans**, **Azeris**, Chechens, Nogai, Rutuls, Aguls and Tats. The smallest linguistic group is the c. 200 Hinukhs.

Economic activity is largely agricultural, centring on breeding sheep. Large potential reserves of oil, gas, coal, iron and other minerals have been mostly under-developed, due in part to the mountainous terrain. The republic's capital is at Makhachkala. Mukhu Aliyev was appointed President of Dagestan in February 2006.

Danube Commission

A body set up in 1948 to supervise the implementation of the Convention on the Regime of Navigation on the River Danube. The Commission holds annual sessions, approves projects for river maintenance and supervises a uniform system of traffic regulations on the whole navigable portion of the Danube and on river inspection.

Members: Austria, Bulgaria, Croatia, Germany, Hungary, **Moldova**, Romania, **Russian Federation**, Serbia, Slovakia, **Ukraine**.

President: Milovan Božinovič.

Address: Benczúr utca 25, 1068 Budapest, Hungary.

Telephone: (1) 4618010.

Fax: (1) 3521839.

E-mail: secretariat@danubecom-intern.org

Internet: www.danubecom-intern.org

Dargins

A Caucasian people who make up the second largest group in the **Russian** republic of **Dagestan** after the **Avars**. Known in Dargin as Dargan or Dargwa. Numbering around 425,000 they constitute around one-sixth of the republic's population. They are concentrated in the south and central areas of the republic where they practise agriculture, particularly breeding sheep. Although most Dargins are Sunni **Muslim**, there is a Shi'a minority. Tensions exist between Dargins and **Kumyks**, into which culturally dominant group some Dargins have been assimilated.

Dashnak *see* **Armenian Revolutionary Federation**.

Democratic Moldova Bloc
Blocul Electoral Moldova Democrata (BMD)

A centre-left bloc in **Moldova** formed for the 2005 **Parliament** elections. The BMD was launched in May 2004 with the alliance of three centre-left parties:

Our Moldova Alliance (AMN), the **Democratic Party of Moldova** (PDM) and the **Social Liberal Party** (PSL). It secured a total of 34 seats (with 28.5% of the vote), making it the second largest bloc. Once elected, the alliance effectively fractured with the constituent parties voting independently of each other.

Democratic Party of Armenia
Hayastani Demokratakan Kusaktsutyun (HDK)

A small party established in **Armenia** in late 1991 as the self-proclaimed successor to the former ruling **Communist Party of Armenia** (HKK), but which failed to attract many senior communists who switched allegiance instead to the ruling **Pan-Armenian National Movement** (HHSh). The HDK was also weakened by the revival of the HKK in 1994.

In the 1995 **National Assembly** elections the HDK won only 1.8% of the vote and failed to win representation. The resignation of President Levon Ter-Petrossian (HHSh) in February 1998 triggered a partial recovery for the HDK, whose Chairman became a foreign policy adviser to the new non-party President, Robert **Kocharian**. In the May 1999 Assembly elections the HDK won one seat and 1% of the proportional vote. It has aligned itself behind Ter-Petrossian, and joined the opposition **Justice** bloc in 2003.

Leadership: Aram Sarkissian (Chair).
Address: Koriun St 14, Yerevan.
Telephone and Fax: (10) 525273.
Internet: dem_party.tripod.com

Democratic Party of Moldova
Partidul Democrat din Moldova (PDM)

A centre-left party in **Moldova** which contested the 2005 legislative elections as part of the opposition **Democratic Moldova Bloc** (BMD). The PDM was formed in April 2000 by **Parliament** Speaker Dumitru Diacov in opposition to his former ally, the then President Petru Lucinschi, and as a registration of opposition to the presidential system.

As a member of the BMD alliance, the PDM secured eight seats in **Parliament** in legislative elections held in March 2005.

Leadership: Dumitru Diacov (Chair).
Address: Str. Tighina 32, 2001 Chişinau.
Telephone: (22) 278229.
Fax: (22) 278230.
E-mail: pdm@mtc.md
Internet: www.pdm.md

Department of Privatization

Founded in 1992, the State Property Management Agency was responsible for the divestment of state-owned enterprises in **Georgia**. In 2003 this responsibility passed to the Department of Privatization in the Ministry of Economic Development, with the clear brief to arrange the privatization of all remaining state-owned enterprises. The State Property Management Agency now exists solely to manage existing state property.

Address: Chanturia 12, 0108 Tbilisi.
Telephone: (32) 998980.
Fax: (32) 933575.
E-mail: info@privatization.ge
Internet: www.privatization.ge

Deported nationalities

Ethnic peoples persecuted by Stalin and deported *en masse* to central Asia and **Siberia**. There are two main groups of deported nationalities: those generally targeted by the Soviet regime, and those particularly accused by Stalin of collaborating with the invading Germans during the Second World War and transported across the **Soviet Union** in 1943 and 1944.

The first group consists of strong and traditionally powerful ethnic communities seen to represent an ongoing threat to the regime. These included Adzharians (*see* **Adzharia**), **Cossacks** and **Tatars**. An exception was the **Roma** who suffered simply at the hands of institutionalized racism. For these people their new homes in the extremities of the Soviet Union were essentially permanent.

For the second group the story was different. Following the end of the war and more specifically the death of Stalin, and with him Stalinism, these groups (almost exclusively from the north **Caucasus**) were rehabilitated under Khrushchev in 1956 and 1957. The groups affected included Balkars (*see* **Kabardino-Balkaria**), Chechens (*see* **Chechnya**), Volga **Germans**, Ingush (*see* **Ingushetia**), Kalmyks (*see* **Kalmykia**) and Muslim Ossetes (*see* **Ossetia question**). A special case were the **Meskhetians**, who were never rehabilitated and remain a permanent refugee population, often exposed to severe persecution.

For all groups the experience of being evicted from their homes and land and carted across thousands of miles of barren steppe was horrific and devastating. Up to 20% (some estimates suggest even 50%) of entire ethnic groups died during the decade-long exile, with thousands of people killed during the migration itself.

Dnestr Republic *see* **Transdnestria**.

Don Basin

The heavily-industrialized valley of the Don river in the south of **European Russia**. It first became an economic centre as early as the 2nd century BC and came under the authority of the Turkic **Tatars** in the 13th century AD. Settlements of freed and escapee **Russian** serfs in the Don region developed into the notorious **Cossack** frontier guards. Their descendants, the Don Cossacks, were a renowned military unit used to great effect to guard the borders of the Russian Empire, although they were later persecuted by Stalin. The Don Basin was incorporated into the Russian Empire in the 16th century.

Heavy industrialization came under **Soviet** rule in the 1950s, including the construction of key dams, especially the creation of the Tsimlyansk reservoir. This and other reservoirs were used for irrigation of the surrounding land in a bid to increase its productivity. The Volga-Don Ship Canal connects the navigable Don with its eastern sister and caters for much waterborne traffic. However, the greater use of Don water has severely reduced the usual outflow at the river's mouth and so increased the salinity of the Sea of Azov which has damaged that region's ecosystem. The larger cities along the Don include Rostov and Voronezh.

Donbass Russians

A large ethnic **Russian** community concentrated in the Donbass (Donetsk) industrial region of eastern **Ukraine**, centred on the Luhansk and Donetsk regions (*oblasti*). The majority of the three million Russians in the Donbass are recent migrants, drafted in to carry out the industrial reconstruction of Ukraine after the Second World War. Fears that they might actively seek unification with **Russia** following Ukraine's independence in 1991 proved unfounded during the course of the 1990s. Initial agitation has given way to calls for autonomy within Ukraine. The events of Ukraine's **Orange Revolution** in 2004 highlighted the divide between Ukraine's Russian-dominated eastern provinces and the pro-Western Ukrainian-dominated west of the country.

Duma

The lower house of the **Federal Assembly** of the **Russian Federation**; formally the State Duma (Gossoudarstvennaya Duma).

E

EAEC *see* **Eurasian Economic Community**.

EAPC *see* **Euro-Atlantic Partnership Council**.

Eastern Europe

A term commonly applied to the European region comprising states east of **central Europe**. This region may be regarded as extending south to the **Balkan** states of Albania, Bulgaria, Greece, Romania and the former Yugoslavia (although these countries may also be placed in the separate category of south-eastern Europe), and eastwards to include the **Russian Federation** and the other former Soviet Republics, except those of central Asia (which lie outside Europe's geographical borders). It also can be defined to include Turkey. Following the post-war division of Europe along the 'iron curtain', the term eastern Europe gained a political connotation, denoting all communist (and more recently post-communist) states east of the Oder-Neisse line. In this usage it excluded two Balkan states, Greece and Turkey, and included, on political rather than geographical criteria, the communist states of central Europe.

EBRD *see* **European Bank for Reconstruction and Development**.

ECE *see* **Economic Commission for Europe**.

ECO *see* **Economic Co-operation Organization**.

Economic Commission for Europe (ECE)

The UN Economic Commission for Europe was established in 1947. Representatives of all European countries, the USA, Canada, Israel and the central Asian republics study the economic, environmental and technological problems of the region and recommend courses of action. ECE is also active in the formulation of international legal instruments and the setting of international standards.

Address: Palais des Nations, 1211 Geneva 10, Switzerland.
Telephone: (22) 9171234.
Fax: (22) 9170505.
E-mail: info.ece@unece.org
Internet: www.unece.org

Economic Co-operation Organization (ECO)

The Economic Co-operation Organization was established in 1985 as the successor to the Regional Co-operation for Development. Its focus is on western Asia rather than **eastern Europe**, with member countries from Turkey in the west to Pakistan and the former Soviet central Asian republics. **Azerbaijan**, however, with its traditional and Turkic language links with Turkey, is a member of the ECO, which aims at co-operation in economic, social and cultural affairs.

Members: Afghanistan, Azerbaijan, Iran, Kazakhstan, Kyrgyzstan, Pakistan, Tajikistan, Turkey, Turkmenistan and Uzbekistan.
The 'Turkish Republic of Northern Cyprus' has been granted special guest status.
Secretary-General: Askhat Orazbay.
Address: 1 Golbou Alley, Kamranieh St, POB 14155-6176, Tehran, Iran.
Telephone: (21) 2831733.
Fax: (21) 2831732.
E-mail: registry@ecosecretariat.org
Internet: www.ecosecretariat.org

Equality
Musavat (or New Equality Party, *Yeni Musavat Partiyasi*—YMP)

A moderate Islamic, **pan-Turkic** political formation in **Azerbaijan**. Indirectly descended from the pre-**Soviet** Musavat nationalists, the present-day party was founded in June 1992. It was closely allied with the **Azerbaijan Popular Front Party** (AXCP) under the 1992–93 Government, when Equality leader Isa Gambar was Chairman of the interim National Assembly.

The party came into sharp conflict with the post-1993 Government of Heydar **Aliyev** of the **New Azerbaijan Party** (YAP) and won only one seat in the **National Assembly** elections held in November 1995 and February 1996. Equality boycotted the October 1998 presidential election but participated in local elections in December 1999, winning 618 of some 10,000 seats at issue.

Initially refused registration for the November 2000 Assembly elections, the party was in the event allowed to present candidates and won two constituency seats, having achieved only 4.9% in the proportional section. It subsequently joined with other opposition formations in condemning the ballot as fraudulent.

Gambar, an outspoken critic of the Government, came second in the presidential poll held in October 2003, with an official tally of 14% of the vote. International observers, who roundly condemned the conduct of the election, joined him in dismissing the result. Some observers suggested that had the plebiscite been free and fair, Gambar would have claimed victory outright for himself. As it was, Ilham **Aliyev** was comfortably confirmed in power.

Equality joined with the AXCP and the Azerbaijan Democratic Party to form the **Freedom** (Azadliq) bloc in preparation for legislative elections in November 2005. Internal differences between the electoral partners quickly surfaced after the largely discredited polls, in which none of the bloc's parties fared very well. Equality achieved the best result with five of the bloc's nine seats out of the 115 contested.

Gambar, in a turnaround from his previous aggressive stance, cautioned his allies against prolonged protests over the result of the poll, accurately fearing a harsh clampdown from the Government. He also advised against boycotting re-runs of disputed seats, leading to Equality's withdrawal from the Freedom bloc in February 2006.

Leadership: Isa Gambar (Chair); Vurgun Eyyub (Secretary-General).

Address: Darnagül Qasabasi 30/97, 1025 Baku.

Telephone: (12) 4482382.

Fax: (12) 4482384.

E-mail: info@musavat.org

Internet: www.musavat.org

EU *see* **European Union**.

Eurasian Economic Community (EAEC or EurAsEC)

A grouping which came into existence in 2001 to co-ordinate regional trade. The EAEC's founding agreement was signed in Astana, the capital of Kazakhstan, in October 2000. It grew out of the joint commitment expressed by its original five members to observe the provisions of the **Commonwealth of Independent States'** agreements on economic integration, starting with the Economic Union Treaty in September 1993, which had proven to have little substantive content. The workings of the new organization were to be based on existing customs union agreements, but it was designed as the logical next step in an incremental process of policy harmonization.

The body's decision-making is based on a weighted voting system in which the **Russian Federation** has the largest vote and can block any major policy decision which requires a two-thirds majority. Uzbekistan joined the EAEC in 2006, following agreement by member states on a merger of the EAEC with the Organization of Central Asian Co-operation.

The EAEC consists of an Inter-state Council (presidents, meeting for annual summits, and prime ministers of member governments, meeting twice yearly), an Integration Committee (deputy premiers, meeting every three months) and an Inter-parliamentary Assembly. The chairmanship rotates annually among the presidents of the member states.

Members: **Belarus**, Kazakhstan, Kyrgyzstan, Russian Federation, Tajikistan, Uzbekistan.

Secretary-General: Grigory Rapota.

Euro-Atlantic Partnership Council (EAPC)

A partnership of the **North Atlantic Treaty Organization** (NATO). The EAPC was inaugurated in May 1997 as a successor to the North Atlantic Co-operation Council (NACC), which had itself been established in December 1991 to provide a forum for consultation on political and security matters with the countries of **central** and **eastern Europe**, including the former Soviet republics. It meets on a regular basis to discuss political and security-related issues. As of 2006 there were 46 members: the 26 NATO member countries and 23 partner countries, including **Armenia**, **Azerbaijan**, **Belarus**, **Georgia**, **Moldova**, the **Russian Federation** and **Ukraine**. All non-NATO EAPC members are members of NATO's **Partnership for Peace** programme.

European Bank for Reconstruction and Development (EBRD)

A multilateral financial institution founded in May 1990 and inaugurated in April 1991 with the objective of providing loan capital and project support in **central** and **eastern Europe**, to contribute to the progress and the economic reconstruction of the region. Participant countries must undertake to respect and put into practice the principles of multi-party democracy, pluralism, the rule of law, respect for human rights and a market economy.

Members: 61 countries, including **Armenia, Azerbaijan, Belarus, Georgia, Moldova**, the **Russian Federation** and **Ukraine**.
President: Jean Lemierre.
Address: One Exchange Square, 175 Bishopsgate, London, EC2A 2EH, UK.
Telephone: (20) 73386000.
Fax: (20) 73386100.
Internet: www.ebrd.com

European Court of Human Rights

One of the elements of the **Council of Europe**.
President: Luzius Wildhaber.

European Organization for Nuclear Research
Organisation européenne pour la recherche nucléaire (CERN)

A scientific organization founded in 1954 (initially with 12 member countries) to provide for collaboration among European states in nuclear research of a pure scientific and fundamental character. The work of CERN is for peaceful purposes only and concerns sub-nuclear, high-energy and elementary particle physics. Its membership now amounts to 20 European countries. The six countries with observer status include the **Russian Federation**.
Director-General: Dr Robert Aymar.
Address: European Laboratory for Particle Physics, 1211 Geneva 23, Switzerland.
Telephone: (22) 7676111.
Fax: (22) 7676555.
Internet: www.cern.ch

European Russia

The western portion of the **Russian Federation**, considered to be the eastern edge of Europe. European Russia stretches from the **Kola peninsula** in the north-west to the **Caucasus** mountains to the south, and from the Ural mountains in the far east to the historically mobile political borders of **eastern Europe** in the west. The vast region encompasses Arctic tundra, temperate grassland, boggy marshes, steep mountains, enormous river networks, broad steppe and even desert. It is the traditional home of the **Slavs**. The early Russian state of Muscovy, centred on **Moscow**, was the first political entity that could be described as European Russia.

As Russian power grew, the country took in ever greater swathes of the region and other non-Slavic peoples, including in particular the **Finno-Ugric** peoples now concentrated to the west of the Urals, and the many Caucasian peoples. Although control of European Russia happened in tandem with the conquest of **Siberia**, the former has always been the demographic and economic heart of the Russian state. Its integration with the rest of Europe has been determined by the changing foreign policy aims of Russian Governments. The **pan-Slavic** movement of the early 19th century was tempered by the imperialist expansion towards the century's close. Similarly the revolutionary evangelism of Lenin was toned down by the isolationism of Stalin and the **Cold War**. In the early 21st century the dominance of the 'West' and the expansion of the **North Atlantic Treaty Organization** (NATO) and the **European Union** (EU) have refocused international attention on the relationship between the Russian Federation and Europe.

Soviet-era industrialization and collectivization changed the landscape permanently, giving rise to enormous cities on the **Volga** and **Don** rivers, and forcing nomadic herders into settled communities. With the collapse of the **Soviet Union**, European Russia effectively shrank back as a political entity, with the creation of successor buffer states between it and the rest of Europe and Asia. The integrity of modern European Russia has been tested by nationalist aspirations, particularly in **Chechnya** and **Tatarstan**, but has remained intact. Control from Moscow was reasserted in 2000–01 under the centralizing policies of President Vladimir **Putin**.

European Union (EU)

The principal organization of European integration, which most of the former communist countries of **central** and **eastern Europe** have applied to join. For these countries, EU membership represents a means of cementing the process of transition to free-market economies and pluralist democracies. The EU is also a major source of funding and expertise for their economic reform and development programmes.

The EU developed from the original basis of a 1951 Treaty setting up what was then the six-member European Coal and Steel Community (ECSC), and the 1957 Treaties of Rome setting up the European Economic Community (EEC) and Euratom. Since then it has developed substantially in the economic, monetary, social and (to a lesser extent) political spheres, and also in its membership. Its largest single expansion was on 1 May 2004, from 15 to 25 member countries (Austria, Belgium, Cyprus, Czech Republic, Denmark, Estonia, Finland, France, Germany, Greece, Hungary, Ireland, Italy, Latvia, Lithuania, Luxembourg, Malta, Netherlands, Poland, Portugal, Slovakia, Slovenia, Spain, Sweden and the UK) and it reached a membership of 27 with the admission of Bulgaria and Romania on 1 January 2007. Several other countries are either in the process of accession talks or negotiating stabilization and association agreements.

When the EU enlarged it acquired new neighbours, and it has developed specific policies for each neighbouring region. In eastern Europe this process is known as the Partnership and Co-operation framework for the **Russian Federation**, **Ukraine** and other Newly Independent States (NIS). The EU has Partnership and Co-operation Agreements (PCAs) in place with **Armenia** (entered into force in 1999), **Azerbaijan** (1999), **Georgia** (1999), **Moldova** (1998), Russian Federation (1997) and Ukraine (1998), although not with **Belarus**, relations with that country being limited on account of its poor record on democracy, human rights and the rule of law. At an EU-Russia summit in October 2001 agreement was reached on a High Level Group to develop a concept for a **Common Economic Space**. In May 2003 this was taken a step further with agreement to form four Common Spaces in the zones of economics; freedom, security and justice; external security; and research, education and culture.

Address of European Commission: rue de la Loi 200, B-1049 Brussels,
         Belgium.
Telephone: (2) 2991111.
Fax: (2) 2950138.
Internet: ec.europa.eu

F

Federal Assembly
Federalnoye Sobraniye

The bicameral legislature of the **Russian Federation**, comprising the State Duma (Gossoudarstvennaya Duma) and the Council of the Federation (Soviet Federatsii). The lower State Duma has 450 members, directly elected for a four-year term. The last elections to the State Duma were held on 7 December 2003. The upper Council of the Federation has 172 members (two representatives from each of the constituent federal administrative units of the Russian Federation). The individual members' terms vary according to the electing region.

Address of lower house: Okhotnyi Ryad 1, 103265 Moscow.
Telephone: (495) 2024789.
Fax: (495) 2925358.
E-mail: stateduma@duma.gov.ru
Internet: www.duma.gov.ru
Address of upper house: ul. Bolshaya Dmitrovka 26, 103246 Moscow.
Telephone: (495) 2925969.
Fax: (495) 2925967.
E-mail: post_sf@gov.ru
Internet: www.council.gov.ru

Federal Security Service
Federal'naya Sluzhba Bezopasnosti (FSB)

The secret service and security agency of the **Russian Federation**. The FSB is the direct descendant of the infamous Soviet-era secret service, the KGB (*Komitet Gossoudarstvennoy Bezopasnosti*—Committee for State Security), and was formed from its ashes in 1993—initially as the Federal Counterintelligence Service (*Federal'naya Sluzhba Kontrrazvedky*—FSK) from 1993 to 1995. The FSB continues to be based in the home of the KGB in Lubyanka Square, **Moscow**. The KGB was the result of Soviet efforts to create an all-powerful intelligence-gathering network which began with the creation of the All-Russian

Extraordinary Commission for the Suppression of Counterrevolution and Sabotage (Cheka) in 1917. The Cheka was used to suppress opposition to the newly-formed communist State. Through many transformations and purges the KGB emerged in 1953, with strong links to the Interior Ministry of the **Soviet Union**. The KGB persisted as the main tool of intelligence and counterintelligence work and was closely tied, as were all organs of the communist state, with the **Communist Party of the Soviet Union**. Its workings were demystified by Khrushchev in the late 1950s and the emphasis on the use of terror was somewhat lessened. This process was furthered under Soviet leader Mikhail **Gorbachev** in the late 1980s. In reaction many senior members of the KGB were involved in the hardline **August coup** in 1991, prompting Gorbachev to overhaul the service completely. Internal security matters were initially transferred to a new Security Ministry before the creation of the FSK/FSB. In February 2000 the then acting President Vladimir **Putin** granted the service control over military intelligence, and the Border Guard Service was incorporated into the FSB in 2003. The FSB also had control of operations in the breakaway republic of **Chechnya** from January 2001 until September 2003, and remains heavily involved in the region.

Putin's relationship with the FSB has brought the agency to the forefront of Russian politics in recent years. Putin himself was a former KGB agent and was appointed head of the FSB in July 1998. He relinquished the position on his appointment as Prime Minister in August 1999. Consequently his own past is shrouded in mystery and many of the people he has promoted to positions of authority in his administration have had links with the agency or its predecessors in the past. Former KGB/FSB officer Alexander Litvinenko accused Putin of personally authorizing the assassination of investigative journalist Anna Politkovskaya in October 2006, shortly before his own unexplained murder by polonium-210 radiation poisoning in London in November.

Director: Nikolai Patrushev.
Address: Bolshaya, ul. Lubyanka 1/3, 101000 Moscow.
Telephone: (495) 9142222.
Fax: (495) 6250578.
E-mail: fsb@fsb.ru
Internet: www.fsb.ru

Federalnoye Sobraniye *see* **Federal Assembly**.

Finno-Ugric peoples

An ethnic group, thought to have originated in the west Kazakh steppe but now inhabiting areas from Hungary to the River **Volga**. From the original Uralic group there arose four main descendant groups (in order of separation from original community): the Magyars (Hungarians) in **central Europe** and **Siberia**; the Permians in the centre of **European Russia**—Udmurts (*see* **Udmurtia**) and Komi (*see* **Komi Republic**); the Volga Finns around the River Volga—Mordvin (*see* **Mordovia**) and Mari (*see* **Mari El Republic**); and the Baltic Finns in the Baltic and Scandinavian areas—Estonians, Finns, Karelians (*see* **Karelia question**) and **Sami**.

This wide geographic spread, and the influence of the other European peoples, has emphasized the differences between the various Finno-Ugric peoples. The Volga Finns have largely embraced the **Muslim** faith, while the European Magyars converted to Catholicism (*see* **Roman Catholic Church**) in 1000. Some isolated Finno-Ugric people in the far north still practise a form of the original Uralic animist religion. There are strong linguistic connections between the Finno-Ugric languages, with varying degrees of borrowing from neighbouring tongues.

First Stock Trading System (PFTS)

The larger of **Ukraine**'s two main stock exchanges (the other being the **Ukrainian Stock Exchange**—USE). Founded in July 1996, the PFTS has 220 listed companies and a total market capitalization of almost US $20,000m.

President: Irina O. Zarya
Address: Shchorsa Street 31, 01133 Kiev.
Telephone: (44) 5228808.
Fax: (44) 5228553.
E-mail: pfts@pfts.com
Internet: www.pfts.com

Five Plus *see* **People's Coalition Five Plus**.

Fradkov, Mikhail

Chairman of the Government (Prime Minister) of the **Russian Federation**. Mikhail Fradkov was a surprise appointment as Russian Prime Minister in early 2004, recalled from his post as special envoy to the **European Union** (EU) to be sworn in on 5 March. He was a former Minister of Trade and a Deputy Minister for Foreign Economic Relations, but little was known at that time about his political or economic views. He belonged neither to President Vladimir **Putin**'s inner circle of former security officials, nor to the pro-'**oligarch**' faction that had been dominant under ex-President Boris **Yeltsin**. However, observers speculated that it was just this 'outsider' status that won him Putin's nomination, giving him an aura of independence from any of the factions within the **Kremlin**.

Mikhail Yefimovich Fradkov was born on 1 September 1950 in a small town near the city of Krasnoyarsk in the Kuybyshev region. Fradkov was initially educated at the Moscow Machine-Tool Institute, before going on to the Foreign Trade Academy. His long career as a bureaucrat and diplomat began in 1973, when he worked in the economic section of the Soviet Embassy in India.

From 1975 he served in various executive positions at the Soviet State Committee/Ministry of Foreign Economic Relations, including a stint with the Foreign Trade Agency. From 1991 to 1992 he served as Deputy Resident Representative of the Russian Federation to the General Agreement on Tariffs and Trade (GATT, *see* **World Trade Organization**). In 1992 Fradkov was appointed not only as the senior adviser to Russia's Permanent Mission to the UN, but also as Deputy Minister of Foreign Trade, putting him very close to the helm of the country's growing oil economy.

He was made Director of the Federal Tax Police by President Vladimir Putin in 2001, having previously been Deputy Secretary of the Security Council, and in 2003 he went to Brussels as Russia's envoy to the EU. On 1 March 2004 he was nominated by Putin as the next Prime Minister, and the appointment was approved by the State Duma (lower house of the **Federal Assembly**) on 5 March.

Putin and his allies have praised Fradkov as experienced, professional and honest. When he was named as Prime Minister, much was made in the press of his background as a technocrat and that his appointment represented a change from his predecessor Mikhail Kasyanov, who had often become involved in public disputes with his own Ministers and the Kremlin. Fradkov, however, has turned out to be just as adept at political infighting and well able to defend his own turf.

Fradkov is married with two children.

Address: Office of Government (Prime Minister), ul. Krasnopresnenskaya
          2, Moscow.
Telephone: (495) 2055735.
Fax: (495) 2054219.
Internet: www.government.ru

Freedom
Azadliq

An opposition bloc in **Azerbaijan** formed to contest the 2005 parliamentary election. The Freedom bloc comprised **Equality**, the **Azerbaijan Popular Front Party** and the Azerbaijan Democratic Party. Failing to make much of a dent in the polls on the ruling **New Azerbaijan Party**'s comfortable majority, Freedom quickly ran into internal strife. Differences between Equality and its partners over participation in continued protests after the elections and re-runs of some seats

Freedom

(Equality did not advocate further protests, and wished to stand in the re-run polls), led to crisis talks by early 2006. The alliance fragmented in February 2006.

FSB *see* **Federal Security Service**.

G

G8 *see* **Group of Eight**.

Gagauzia
Gagauz Yeri

An autonomous region in the southernmost tip of **Moldova**. The regional capital is Comrat. *Population*: 155,700 (2006 estimate). The Bashkan, a directly-elected President, answers to the 35-seat Gagauz Popular Assembly (Halk Toplusu). Gagauzia is dominated by the ethnic Gagauzi, a Christian Turkic-language speaking people of either Turkish or Bulgarian ethnicity (*see* **Turkic peoples**) who are popularly thought to have settled in the area during the period of Turkish Ottoman rule in the late 18th–early 19th century; they make up over 80% of the population. Almost three-quarters of Gagauzi consider Russian to be their second language, which tied them closely to the dominant ethnic **Russian** regime established under Soviet rule.

Largely ignored by the Soviet authorities, Gagauzia did not emerge as a defined area until the rise of **Romanian**-centred nationalism in Moldova in the late 1980s. A law designating Moldovan as the country's main official language in 1989 prompted calls for autonomy led by the Gagauz Halki (Gagauz People), the region's most prominent political group. An independent Gagauz Soviet Socialist Republic was declared in 1991 in response to the declaration of Moldovan independence from the **Soviet Union**. The Gagauzi avoided direct involvement in the conflict between the Moldovan authorities and the separatist struggle in **Transdnestria**, but their demands for autonomy gained ground among moderates in **Chişinau**, and in return for dropping their separatist claims they were granted some autonomy within Moldova from December 1994. In 2003 the Moldovan Constitution officially accepted the autonomous status of Gagauzia, although proposals for the federalization of Moldova remained controversial.

Galicia

A historic region stretching from southern Poland into western **Ukraine**. The concept of Galicia was effectively invented by the Habsburg Empire in 1772 when it was awarded the region at the first partition of Poland. It comprised a western and Polish half known as Malopolska (literally 'little Poland'), and an eastern and Ukrainian (or **Ruthenian**) half (*see* **Transcarpathia**) consisting roughly of the ancient duchy of Halychina-Wolyn, from which the name Galicia was derived. Briefly during the Revolutionary–Napoleonic period Galicia stretched to include Warsaw but its reduced borders were finally established when the semi-autonomous Republic of Kraków was added in 1846.

Following the dismemberment of the Habsburg Empire after the First World War, Galicia was included in the new Polish Republic. It was briefly redivided into east and west at the start of the Second World War in 1939 before it was swallowed *en masse* into the Nazi General Government district in 1941. During the Nazi occupation the large **Jewish** population of Galicia, the centre of the Hasidic branch of Orthodox Judaism, was all but wiped out. Under the Polish-Soviet Treaty of 1945 Galicia ceased to exist, with east and west becoming integral parts of Ukraine and Poland respectively. The ethnic **Polish** and **Ukrainian** populations were redistributed to fall within their new states, although traditionally they had been largely restricted to their respective halves in any case.

The main urban centres of the region are Kraków in Poland and Lvov in Ukraine. The area is rich in oil and gas deposits as well as other minerals, and the two halves have become important economic centres in their respective countries.

Gazprom

A partially state-run gas monopoly in the **Russian Federation**, founded in 1989 as part of the **Soviet Union**'s Gas Ministry. Gazprom is now Russia's biggest company and the largest commercial gas producer in the world, accounting for 20% of global gas output and 86% of the Russian Federation's output. Its activities provide 6% of the country's GDP and 8% of tax revenues. It employs over 400,000 people and boasts that 470,000 Russians are shareholders, the company having been part privatized in 1993. Gazprom controls all aspects of gas prospecting, mining, production, refining and supply. In 2005 it bought a 73% share in Russia's fifth largest oil producer Sibneft, now renamed Gazprom Neft. It also has a massive commercial interest in other economic areas, most notably in the country's media industry. Plans were even announced in 2005 for the construction of Gazprom City, a business centre near the heart of **St Petersburg**.

Opponents of President Vladimir **Putin**'s centralizing tendencies view Gazprom as an arm of the state which has been used to mount financial attacks on the **Yeltsin**-era 'oligarchs'. In September 2000 the Chairman of the Media-

MOST press empire, Vladimir Gusinsky, denounced Gazprom's bid to purchase a controlling share in his own company as politically motivated. By January 2001 the seizure of Media-MOST's assets by the state as punishment for Gusinsky's alleged corruption left Gazprom as the single largest shareholder in the country's only private news station, NTV, which had been notably critical of the Putin administration. A matter of months later, the television station was entirely controlled by Gazprom, prompting mass domestic criticism and leading international media watchdogs to warn of the growing threat to press freedom in the Russian Federation. Indeed, in April that year Gazprom helped to close down the Media-MOST-run liberal newspaper *Segodnya*, claiming it was running at a loss. In June 2005 Gazprom Media also acquired *Izvestiya*.

In October 2000 the then Prime Minister Mikhail **Kasyanov** outlined proposals to reform the country's large state monopolies. However, he specifically set Gazprom aside, suggesting that investigations into its reconstruction would wait until late 2001 at the earliest. In May 2001 Deputy Energy Minister Alexei Miller was appointed as Chair of the Management Committee—equivalent of CEO—to oversee the company's reform. The state-owned share in Gazprom was increased to just over 50% in 2005, paving the way for the lifting of foreign ownership restrictions on Gazprom shares in July 2006. That same month Gazprom was granted the exclusive right to export Russia's natural gas.

Gazprom was by now the sole or majority gas supplier to many **eastern** and **central European** countries, with the **European Union** receiving about 25% of its gas supplies from Gazprom. This has given the company considerable influence in foreign affairs. The gas price wars with **Ukraine**, **Georgia**, **Belarus** and other former Soviet states, who have been receiving subsidized gas since the break-up of the Soviet Union, have become known as 'petropolitics'. Temporary cessations of supply to Ukraine and Belarus in the winters of 2006 and 2007 had knock-on effects in European countries that use gas from transit pipes passing through the affected countries. Gazprom has also invested in pipelines connecting to central Asia and the enormous Chinese market.

Chair of the Board of Directors: Dmitry A. Medvedev.
Chair of the Management Committee: Alexei B. Miller.
Address: ul. Nametkina 16, 117997 Moscow, V-420, GSP-7.
Telephone: (495) 7193001.
Fax: (495) 7198333.
E-mail: gazprom@gazprom.ru
Internet: www.gazprom.com

Georgia
Sakartvelos Respublika

An independent republic in the north-western **Caucasus region** of the former **Soviet Union**, bounded by the **Russian Federation** to the north, **Armenia** and Turkey to the south, **Azerbaijan** to the south-east and the Black Sea to the west. The country includes the two autonomous republics of **Abkhazia** and **Adzharia** and the autonomous region of South Ossetia (*see* **Ossetia question**). The rest of the country is divided into nine regions (*mkharebi*) and one municipality.

Area: 69,700 sq km; *capital*: **Tbilisi**; *population*: 4.5m. (2005 estimate), comprising ethnic **Georgians** 83.8%, **Azeris** 6.5%, **Armenians** 5.7%, **Russians** 1.5%, Ossetians 0.9%, others (including **Kurds**, Greeks—*see* **Pontic Greeks**, **Ukrainians**, **Jews** and Abkhaz) 1.6%; *official language*: Georgian (and Abkhaz in Abkhazia); *religion*: **Georgian Orthodox** 65%, **Muslim** 11%, **Russian Orthodox** 10%, **Armenian Apostolic** 8%, other 6%.

Under the 1995 Constitution, the Head of State is the executive President, who is directly elected for a five-year term by universal adult suffrage. In February 2004 the post of Prime Minister was reinstated; the Prime Minister is appointed by the President and is Head of Government. The Council of Ministers is nominated by the Prime Minister, and must be approved by the President. Legislative authority is currently vested in a 235-member unicameral **Parliament**, elected for a four-year term. It comprises 150 deputies returned by a system of proportional representation subject to a 7% threshold, and a further 85 elected from single-member constituencies by majority voting. The Constitution states that the Parliament will be transformed into a bicameral body upon the restoration of Georgia's territorial integrity (see below).

History: Georgia flourished as an independent kingdom in the 12th and early 13th centuries, its territory expanding to encompass the whole of what is now known as the Caucasus region. Subsequently devastated by Mongol and other invasions, Georgia then struggled against Ottoman and Persian incursion, before turning gradually to the Russian Empire (in the 18th century) for protection as a vassal state. After the Russian Revolution of 1917, a nationalist Government came to power in Georgia, declaring independence in 1918. However, occupation by Bolshevik forces in 1921 led the following year to the territory's incorporation in the Transcaucasian Soviet Federative Socialist Republic (with Armenia and Azerbaijan). In 1936 Georgia became a separate republic within the Soviet Union.

Upon the abolition of the communist monopoly on power, the Georgian Soviet Socialist Republic was dissolved in August 1990. Subsequent multi-party elections resulted in the assumption of the presidency by nationalist leader Zviad Gamsakhurdia, following which Georgia declared its independence from the Soviet Union in April 1991. At the same time, the country subsided into serious ethnic and civil strife. Accused of dictatorial tendencies, Gamsakhurdia's regime was confronted by armed opposition and overthrown in January 1992. In March a new State Council was established with Eduard **Shevardnadze** as Chairman. Shevardnadze had long been Georgia's most widely known political figure. He had been First Secretary of the Georgian Communist Party from 1972, gaining prominence on an anti-corruption platform, and had become Soviet Foreign Minister and Politburo member in 1985 as a key player in the reformist **Gorbachev** regime.

Shevardnadze obtained electoral endorsement as Head of State in October 1992. However, by September 1993 rebellion by **Zviadists** (supporters of Gamsakhurdia), separatist military advances in the autonomous republics and general economic chaos had rendered the country seemingly ungovernable. Shevardnadze was forced to seek Russian military support to re-establish his Government's authority.

Separatist tensions in Georgia had revived in 1989 as South Ossetia (seeking reunification with North Ossetia in the Russian Federation) and Abkhazia aspired to independence. Bitter armed conflict with Georgian government forces ensued before ceasefires were declared in South Ossetia (in 1992) and Abkhazia (in 1994), reinforced by the deployment of (largely Russian) peacekeeping forces in both regions and the operation of a UN Observer Mission in Abkhazia. Both territories declared their secession from Georgia, and negotiations on their future status have since continued under UN and other auspices. However, an enduring political settlement remains an elusive goal with continuing low-level hostilities in and around the 'republics'.

In October 1995 Georgia adopted its present Constitution, maintaining the autonomous status under Georgian sovereignty of Abkhazia, South Ossetia and Adzharia (although this provision has been rejected by Abkhazia). Presidential and legislative elections in November 1995 resulted in victory for Shevardnadze and for his new **Citizens' Union of Georgia** (SMK), Shevardnadze being re-elected with around 75% of the votes cast. In the legislative elections, 107 of the 231 seats filled were won by the SMK. In February 1998 there was another in a series of unsuccessful assassination attempts against Shevardnadze, while in May 1999 the authorities foiled a coup plot against the President.

Parliamentary elections in October–November 1999 confirmed the dominance of the SMK, which won an overall majority of 130 of the 227 seats filled. In presidential elections in April 2000 Shevardnadze was re-elected with 78.8% of the vote and he appointed a new SMK Government headed by Giorgi Arsenishvili. A series of variously motivated defections from the SMK parliamentary group later in 2000 highlighted increasing dissatisfaction with the alleged corruption of the Shevardnadze regime.

In May 2001 Shevardnadze floated the idea of reforming the government system with the introduction of a full Council of Ministers under a Prime Minister as Head of Government. However, his proposals were quickly overshadowed by renewed tensions with Abkhazia and by potentially more threatening domestic disturbances. Mass demonstrations in Tbilisi calling for Shevardnadze's resignation in October followed a heavy-handed police raid on the tax-evading television station Rustavi-2. Shevardnadze appeared to regain control of Government through a reshuffle in November while the opposition faction within the SMK was officially sidelined by a Supreme Court order in May 2002.

None the less, the anti-Shevardnadze lobby, now headed by former Justice Minister Mikhail **Saakashvili**, gained significant ground in the build-up to the 2003 parliamentary elections. The newly-formed **New Rights** party gained a majority of seats in municipal elections in June, including all of Tbilisi. Meanwhile, a student movement (Kmara—'Enough'), self-consciously modelled on the successful Otpor movement which had helped to topple President Slobodan Milošević in Serbia in 2000, began organizing widespread anti-government demonstrations. Protests magnified after the elections in November 2003 produced an apparent easy victory for the SMK. On 22 November, Saakashvili led a peaceful protest of 30,000 people in Tbilisi. Marching against the opening of the new Parliament, the protest quickly organized itself into a direct march on the chamber itself. Government troops refused to stop the invaders and Shevardnadze was hustled out by his supporters; he resigned the following day, completing the **Rose Revolution**.

Latest elections: Fresh presidential elections on 4 January 2004 resulted in victory for Saakashvili with 96% of the vote, against five other candidates. The re-run of the November 2003 parliamentary elections for the 150 proportional representation seats on 28 March 2004 was contested by 14 parties and five alliances, but only two groups passed the 7% threshold. Saakashvili's **National Movement-Democrats** (NM-D) took 67% of the vote and was awarded 135 of the proportional representation seats, and the **Rightist Opposition** (MO) took 7.6% and 15 seats. The 75 constituency seats were not rerun.

Including the constituency-seat distribution, the NM-D had a final tally of 152 seats, the MO 23, independents 20, the SMK 19, the Democratic Union of Revival 6 and the Georgian Labour Party (GLP) 4. One single-member constituency remained vacant, while a further 10 seats are held in suspension for representatives from the breakaway republic of Abkhazia.

Recent developments: A new Government, dominated by young and Western-educated ministers, was formed under Saakashvili in February 2004 amidst reforms redefining an empowered Prime Minister. Established statesman and reformist Zurab Zhvania was appointed to lead the Council of Ministers, but he was killed in February 2005 in an explosion blamed on a gas leak. Finance Minister Zurab **Noghaideli** was appointed in his place. Opposition to the new Saakashvili Government has focused on the slow pace of reform, harsh reactions to members of the new opposition and the restructuring of the armed forces (see below).

One notable early success for President Saakashvili was facing down pro-Shevardnadze dissent from the semi-breakaway region of Adzharia. The

Adzharian President, Aslan Abashidze, was toppled by the region's own Rose Revolution in May 2004. Relations with Abkhazia have been characteristically tense on both sides while low-level hostilities broke out along the South Ossetian border in September 2005.

International relations and defence: Georgia was admitted as an independent state to the UN and to the **Organization for Security and Co-operation in Europe** in 1992 and was a founder member of the **Organization of the Black Sea Economic Co-operation**. Full membership of both the **North Atlantic Treaty Organization** (NATO) and the **European Union** (EU) being central foreign policy goals, Georgia became a member of NATO's **Partnership for Peace** programme (launched in 1994) and in 1996 signed a partnership and co-operation agreement with the EU. It was admitted to the **Council of Europe** in February 1999 and to the **World Trade Organization** in June 2000.

From the collapse of the Soviet Union, relations with the **Russian Federation** have been tense. Georgia was effectively forced to join the **Commonwealth of Independent States** (CIS) in 1993 following Russian help in support of the Shevardnadze Government earlier that year. Concern centres around the Russian Federation's ambitions in the region, its maintenance of military bases on Georgian soil, its ambiguous relationships with the breakaway regions of Abkhazia, Adzharia and South Ossetia, and the issue of oil transportation across and to Georgia. A major row between the two countries flared up in September 2006 over alleged espionage, leading to the recall of the Russian Ambassador, who did not return to Tbilisi for four months. Russian troops have been withdrawn piecemeal from their Georgian bases since 2001. Two key military installations in the south are due to be abandoned by 2008.

To counter Russian regional influence, Georgia was a founder member in 1997 of what became the **GUAM group** (with **Ukraine**, Azerbaijan and **Moldova**) within the CIS. Following Georgia's effective withdrawal in May 1999 from the CIS **Collective Security Treaty**, Saakashvili ended co-operation with the policy-forming CIS Council of Defence Ministers in February 2006 and is considering a complete withdrawal from the organization. He has continued to pursue membership of NATO and widened his network of international relations with a prominent visit to the People's Republic of China in April 2006.

Military reforms under Saakashvili have included raising the army's profile in society, ensuring control of the military under the civilian Defence Ministry and reducing its overall size. The high turnover of Defence Ministers (three in 2004 alone) and accusations of militarism creeping into Saakashvili's governing style, has made the issue a key point of public discontent with the Government.

Georgia's defence budget for 2006 amounted to some US $349m., equivalent to about 4.6% of GDP. The size of the armed forces at August 2006 was some 11,320 personnel, including those serving under compulsory conscription of 18 months, while reservists numbered an estimated 250,000.

Georgia, economy

In transition from state control to a free-market system but severely affected by political disorder since independence in 1991.

GNP: US $6,020m. (2005); *GNP per capita*: $1,350 (2005); *GDP at PPP*: $14,217m. (2005); *GDP per capita at PPP*: $3,177 (2005); *exports*: $2,457m. (2005); *imports*: $3,116m. (2005); *currency*: lari (plural: lari; US $1=L1.715 at the end of December 2006).

In 2005 industry accounted for 27.4% of GDP, agriculture for 16.7% and services for 55.9%. Of the workforce of 2.3 million, industry accounts for 9%, agriculture for 54% and services for 37%. Only some 12% of land is arable, 4% under permanent crops, 28% permanent pasture and 40% forests and woodland. The main crops are citrus and other fruit, grapes, tea, flowers, tobacco and grain, and there is a small animal husbandry sector in mountain areas. The principal mineral resources are deposits of manganese ore (although these are becoming increasingly depleted) and of iron ore, together with small quantities of coal and hydrocarbons. The main industries are machine-building, construction of transport and other mechanical equipment, textiles and the production of wine. Georgia's former dependence on tourism on its Black Sea coast has been almost wholly undermined by the loss of central government control in **Abkhazia** and by internal disorder and armed conflict. Georgia's only substantial existing energy source is hydroelectricity; much of the energy requirement is met through imports, but financial constraints have reduced oil imports from the **Russian Federation** and halted imports of natural gas from Turkmenistan, while the continuation of subsidized Russian gas supplies has continually been subject to both financial and political factors.

Georgia's main exports in 2004 by value were rail vehicles, air transport and shipping (15%) and mineral products (11%). Principal imports were mineral products (18%) and machinery and equipment (17%). The main purchasers of Georgian exports in 2004 were Turkey and Turkmenistan (each with 18%), the Russian Federation (16%) and Armenia (8%); the principal sources of Georgia's imports were the Russian Federation (14%), Turkey (11%) and **Azerbaijan** and the UK (each with 9%).

For the first four years after Georgia achieved independence in 1991, the country was riven by armed disturbance, especially in Abkhazia and South Ossetia (*see* **Ossetia question**). When the main conflicts ended the devastated economy had to cope with the repercussions. Moreover, the close economic links which had existed between Georgia and the other Republics of the **Soviet Union** were disrupted after 1991. The resultant deterioration of the Georgian economy was characterized by massive inflation (of some 8,000% in 1993 and 1994), a 70% contraction of GDP in 1990–95 arising from huge falls in agricultural and industrial production, and difficulties in the purchase of oil and natural gas from the Russian Federation and Turkmenistan. A flourishing 'black' market, estimated to account for about 50% of economic activity by the late 1990s, distorted the real economic position and reduced government revenue.

From 1995, however, the Government embarked on a major structural adjustment programme with support from the **International Monetary Fund** (IMF) and **World Bank**, introducing a new currency, the lari, in September 1995 and instituting fiscal and other reforms. As a result, real GDP growth resumed and averaged about 10%–11% in 1996–97, while annual inflation fell to around 7% in 1997 and the fiscal deficit was brought down from 20% of GDP in 1994 to 4.6% in 1997. The Russian financial crisis (*see* **Russian Federation, economy**) in mid-1998 then adversely affected Georgia, where the external value of the lari depreciated sharply, GDP growth fell back to some 2% in 1998 and the budget deficit came in at 5% of GDP. Modest recovery began in 1999, boosted by the opening in April of the Georgian section of the pipeline from **Baku** in Azerbaijan to Supsa on the Georgian Black Sea for the transport of oil from the Azerbaijani Caspian fields; this represented a partial realization of the **EU**-funded Transport Corridor Europe–Caucasus–Asia (**TRACECA**), or the 'Great Silk Road project', initiated in 1993. GDP growth of around 3% was achieved in 1999, 2% in 2000 and 5% in 2001 and 2002. However, budget deficits remained high, as tax evasion and corruption continued, resulting in accumulating wages and pension arrears and the failure of the Government to provide basic services.

Activity in the industrial and communications sectors and construction of the **Baku–Tbilisi–Ceyhan (BTC) pipeline**, to export Caspian oil from Baku via Georgia to the Turkish Mediterranean port of Ceyhan, spurred growth of 11% in 2003, but this was not enough to save the **Shevardnadze** Government from downfall in the **Rose Revolution** in November. The new Government of Mikhail **Saakashvili** embarked on wide-ranging institutional reforms, revising the tax regime and tackling corruption, assisted by US $1,100m. of aid, the resumption of loans from the IMF and World Bank, and the restructuring of $161m. of debt by the 'Paris Club' of creditors. Government revenue rose by a third in 2004, on the back of GDP growth of 6%, enabling the Government to reduce wage and pension arrears and to increase minimum pensions. Growth of 9% was achieved in 2005, one of the fastest rates of growth in **eastern Europe**, and the full opening of the BTC pipeline in 2006 brought in transit revenue that went a long way towards offsetting the rest of the budget deficit. Annual growth of over 5% is expected to continue for the next few years.

Relations with Russia have deteriorated since the election of President Saakashvili: economic issues have often been tools in the disputes, such as the recurring issue of the removal of subsidies on the price of Russian oil and gas, and the banning of Georgian wine exports to Russia in 2006 amidst accusations of Russian interference in separatists struggles in Georgia. Rising foreign investment has helped to offset these trade losses.

The privatization of state-owned enterprises, which was barely on the agenda in the first few years of independence, accelerated from 1995. By 1999 most small and medium-sized enterprises had passed to the private sector. A wide-ranging privatization programme, expected to cover some 400 state enterprises and properties, was announced by the Saakashvili Government in 2004, including the United Telecommunications Company of Georgia, energy-distribution companies and hydroelectric power stations. The State Information Agency, Sakinform, was privatized in 2006.

Georgian National Investment Agency (GNIA)

Set up by the Ministry of Economic Development of Georgia to promote exports of Georgian products and encourage foreign investment.

Director: Merab Iominadze.
Address: Chanturia 12, 0108 Tbilisi.
Telephone: (32) 931028.
Fax: (32) 982755.
E-mail: info@investingeorgia.org
Internet: www.investingeorgia.org

Georgian Orthodox Church

An autocephalous branch of the **Orthodox Christian** Church based in **Georgia**. By tradition Georgia was placed under the spiritual guidance of Mary, the mother of Jesus Christ, and Christianity was first brought to the region on her behalf by the Apostle St Andrew in the 1st century. Christian missionaries succeeded in converting the Georgian princes in 326. From then the religion became closely tied to the concept of an independent Georgian state, bounded as it was by **Muslim** countries to the south and the **Slavs** to the north. After the absorption of Georgia into the **Russian** Empire, the autocephalous Georgian Church was abolished in 1811 and subjugated to the **Russian Orthodox Church**. Its independence was reinstated in 1917 but the Church suffered at the hands of the **Soviet** authorities along with fellow Orthodox Christians in Russia. The autocephalous Georgian Church was recognized by the Ecumenical Patriarch of Constantinople in 1989. Catholicos-Patriarch Illya II was elected in 1977.

Georgian paramilitaries *see* **Mkhedrioni**.

Georgian Stock Exchange (GSE)

The first self-regulated exchange in **Georgia**. Established in January 1999, the GSE was licensed as a stock exchange in January 2000. It was founded by brokerage companies, banks and insurance firms. As at 4 April 2007 there were 17 brokerage companies operating on the exchange.

Chair: George Loladze.

Address: Chavchavadze 74A, 0162 Tbilisi.

Telephone: (32) 220718.

Fax: (32) 251876.

E-mail: info@gse.ge

Internet: www.gse.ge

Georgians

A Caucasian people dominant in **Georgia**. Georgians are considered autochthonous to the **Caucasus region** and constitute a diverse people renowned for their nationalist pride. The Kartli dialect, spoken around the capital **Tbilisi**, is the basis of the literary language, which uses its own unique script. Other distinct dialects exist among the related Mingrelians and Svans (who both live in the region bordering **Abkhazia**), and the Laz who live in Turkey. Almost all Georgians practise **Orthodox Christianity**, and the autocephalous **Georgian Orthodox Church** promotes itself as the final frontier of European Christianity. There are some 1.5 million Georgians resident in Turkey.

Germans

An ethnic group concentrated in **central Europe** but spread in small communities throughout **eastern Europe**, and sharing a common language (although regional variations can be extreme). Thought to have originated on the shores of the Baltic Sea, the Germans spread south to occupy much of the north European plain. Several mini-states flourished in this region in the medieval period, rather than one contiguous German state, with **Prussia** and Austria the most powerful of many German entities. A unified Germany, stretching as far south as Bavaria, did not emerge until the mid-19th century (with Austria even then remaining separate, bound up as it was with the Habsburg Empire).

Meanwhile, steady eastward migration created German communities whose presence in the central European states of the 20th century was to prove a source of conflict. Many Germans were despatched specifically as frontier settlers, notably the Saxons in Northern Transylvania. Penetration of the east by German settlers extended as far as the River Volga where they settled under the invitation of Catherine the Great from 1763. In the Soviet era a German autonomous republic (ASSR) was even created within the **Soviet Union**, although it was disbanded during the Second World War and the so-called 'Volga' Germans deported *en masse* to internment camps in **Siberia**. The survivors were later allowed to return to the **Volga region** where they consider themselves to be among **Russia**'s oppressed peoples.

The irredentist ambitions of Hitler and the Nazi regime were briefly realized in the creation of the so-called Third Reich in the 1930s. Defeat in the Second World War, however, was followed by the forcible movement of thousands of Germans across eastern Europe to the new reduced German state, devastating areas of previous German settlement. A similar, this time voluntary, movement occurred in the 1990s following the collapse of communism in the east. Thousands of ethnic Germans migrated to Germany away from the economic uncertainty of the emerging post-Soviet states.

Officially, the largest ethnic German population in eastern Europe is in Russia, where 600,000 Germans were identified in the 2002 census, mainly in the Volga region. There could be as many as one million Germans living in modern Poland where they are largely considered autochthonous, and where the pursuit of their ethnic identity has only recently been encouraged: only 150,000 people identify themselves as German. The size of this population was greatly affected by the forced post-war migrations (*see* **Yalta Agreements** and **Potsdam Agreements**). The same is true of the once large German population in the Czech Republic which was expelled after 1945. An original community of 750,000 Germans in Transylvania has been cut down to just 60,000 through voluntary and forced migration. Some 75,000 were deported to the Soviet Union after 1945. Representation in Romania is plagued by a lack of resources. Around 120,000 Germans are scattered throughout Hungary, where there is some German-language schooling, but where assimilation has reduced German to a 'grandmother language'. In an attempt to accommodate the many Germans stranded throughout the former Soviet Union, Germany and **Ukraine** agreed in 1992 to assist 400,000 to settle in the south of Ukraine, although many chose to emigrate to Germany instead.

Glasnost

The slogan, meaning 'openness' in Russian, adopted by Soviet leader Mikhail **Gorbachev** in 1985 to cover a package of political reforms improving freedom of speech and information. After the **Chernobyl** disaster of April 1986, which was poorly reported, *glasnost* became more radical, featuring a critical reappraisal of the past, including revelations of repression under Stalin, the toleration of press criticism, the publication of works of literature long banned as subversive and the release of dissidents. *Glasnost* was accompanied by the policy of *perestroika*.

Gorbachev, Mikhail

Last President of the **Soviet Union**, from 1988, and reformist leader of the ruling **Communist Party of the Soviet Union** (KPSS) from 1985. Gorbachev is credited internationally with engineering his country's peaceful retreat from the **Cold War**, and accepting the end of the 'iron curtain' division of Europe. Most Russians resented, however, the economic dislocation and instability they suffered through the demise of Soviet communism itself—the outcome which Gorbachev had unsuccessfully sought to avert by reforming the system.

Mikhail Sergeyevich Gorbachev was born on 2 March 1931 in the Stavropol region of the north **Caucasus**. He was working as a tractor driver at the age of 14, but subsequently gained a place to study law at Moscow University, where he was active in the Communist Youth League (Komsomol) and joined the KPSS in 1952. He also met Raisa Maksimovna Titarenko, a philosophy student, whom he married in 1953; they have one daughter, Irina.

Upon graduation he returned to Stavropol in 1955, working as a Komsomol official, then for the KPSS. He became the party's First Secretary for Stavropol in 1966 and First Secretary of the Regional Party Committee in 1970. He also studied by correspondence for an agriculture degree which he completed in 1967.

A member of the KPSS Central Committee from 1971, Gorbachev moved to **Moscow** in November 1978 to work as its Secretary for Agriculture. He became a candidate member of the Politburo a year later and a full member from October 1980. His chief mentor Yurii Andropov, who also came from the north Caucasus, became KPSS General Secretary after Leonid Brezhnev's death in 1982. Andropov was succeeded in turn by the elderly Konstantin Chernenko as stop-gap leader, but Chernenko's death in March 1985 opened the way for Gorbachev to become General Secretary. The position of Chairman of the Supreme Soviet (Head of State) was given to veteran Foreign Minister Andrei Gromyko, but Gorbachev succeeded to this office too in October 1988.

Once in power, Gorbachev initiated the twin processes of *perestroika* (restructuring) and *glasnost* (openness). The plans to transform the Soviet system into a 'socialist pluralist democracy' resulted in 1989 in competitive elections to a new Congress of People's Deputies. In early 1990 Gorbachev even accepted the recognition of other parties, removing the Constitution's reference to the 'leading role' of the KPSS.

Abroad, he sought relations with the West that would spare the failing economy from the demands of the arms race. A sequence of US-Soviet summits, and the signature in 1987 of the Intermediate Nuclear Forces (INF) treaty, opened the way to strategic arms reductions talks (**START**). The disarmament process ran in parallel with major changes on the diplomatic front, the withdrawal of Soviet troops from Afghanistan and disengagement from **eastern Europe**, as Gorbachev made it known among the leaders of the **Warsaw Pact** member countries in 1989 that there would be no armed intervention to prevent internal change.

The years 1989–90 marked the high water mark of Gorbachev's global popularity. Acclaimed for his statesmanship and honoured by the Nobel Peace Prize judges in 1990, he faced sustained criticism, however, at home. The conservatives saw compromise as fatally weakening the Soviet system, while radicals pressed impatiently for faster change. The Soviet Union itself, in chronic economic crisis, was torn by nationalist and secessionist demands. Gorbachev, having taken on the title of State President in March 1990 as part of a restructuring of Soviet leadership posts, began in April 1991 the so-called 'nine-plus-one' talks with other Soviet Republics on a new Union treaty. He was continually outflanked, however, by demands from the Russian republican leadership and others for more radical reform—and unable to claim the democratic mandate which the popular Russian leader Boris **Yeltsin** was able to evoke as republican President after direct elections in June 1991.

The pace of change, and especially the new draft Union treaty which envisaged a reduction in central powers, provoked leading army generals and their conservative allies to attempt to halt the process by force. Gorbachev, unable to harness to his own reformist objectives the more radical demands which had been unleashed within the Soviet Union, now suffered a double ignominy. His powerlessness was exposed, as the conservatives briefly took over in the **August coup** in Moscow in 1991. Gorbachev, absent from Moscow on an ill-timed holiday, dissociated himself from the coup, but his role was the subject of much speculation, and his position was fatally weakened. Yeltsin, his 'rescuer' in the August coup, called the tune thereafter. Gorbachev, having resigned as General Secretary of the KPSS on 24 August 1991, stepped down as President of the Soviet Union on 25 December 1991, handing over to Yeltsin the command of the armed forces and control of nuclear weapons. By the end of the year the Soviet Union was no more, its successor states more or less loosely associated through a new **Commonwealth of Independent States**.

Gorbachev largely disappeared from domestic view after stepping down. When he stood in the **Russian Federation**'s June 1996 presidential election he came seventh, with a derisory 386,000 votes or 0.51% of the poll. In 2001 he founded the Social Democratic Party of Russia, a merger of several smaller parties, but resigned as its leader in May 2004 after a dispute with the party Chairman.

He does still make occasional appearances in the Western media, giving his perspective on events such as the accession of three former Warsaw Pact member countries to membership of the **North Atlantic Treaty Organization** (NATO) in March 1999. Author of numerous publications, he is also propounding a global environmental charter drawn up by Green Cross International, an organization which he founded in 1993. He heads a Moscow-based International Foundation for Socio-Economic and Political Studies (known as the Gorbachev Foundation), in which he invested some of his own money.

Greater Romania

A nationalist concept of an enlarged Romania covering regions inhabited by ethnic **Romanians** (and **Moldovans**) and lands historically connected to the Romanian state. Ethnically isolated among **Slavic** neighbours, Romanian nationalists held tight to the idea of uniting all Romanian peoples in a single state. This goal was practically achieved following the First World War when Romania was rewarded with the annexation of Transylvania, **Bukovina**, southern Dobruja and all of historic Moldavia (*see* **Bessarabia question**). However, this Greater Romania was short-lived and was greatly reduced after the Second World War, losing Dobruja, northern Bukovina, and most importantly eastern Moldavia.

The possibility of the unification of Moldova and Romania was immediately raised following the collapse of the **Soviet Union**, of which Moldova had been a part, in 1991. However, it was soon rejected in the following years and is now only championed by nationalist Romanian parties and some fringe Moldovan parties.

Greater Russia

A nationalist concept of a dominant **Russian** state which would export Russian language and culture to regions within and near to the modern **Russian Federation**. Unlike other 'Greater' nationalist ideas, Greater Russia has less to do with territorial expansion (Russia is after all the largest country in the world) and more to do with straightforward cultural imperialism. The notion relies on the supposed superiority of Russian culture, including adherence to the doctrine of the **Russian Orthodox Church**. Its champions look to the further centralization of the Russian Federation, the proposed Union with **Belarus** (*see* **Belarus-Russia Union**) and possible future unions with the fellow east **Slavic** State of **Ukraine** and even **Moldova**. On a broader, but less popular, scale the concept of Greater Russia has links with notions of **pan-Slavism**, Russia being the largest and most powerful Slavic state in the world. The imposition of centralized control from **Moscow** and the fearsome response to separatist claimants among the constituent republics could be seen as directed towards the maintenance of such a Greater Russia as already exists, but beyond this the aspiration for a Greater Russia does not have serious political proponents.

Group of Eight (G8)

The grouping created by the decision in the 1990s that the Group of Seven (G7) principal industrialized countries, which had been meeting regularly at summit level since 1976, should also include the **Russian Federation** in their discussions on international affairs. The then Soviet President Mikhail **Gorbachev** attended a meeting in the margins of the London G7 Summit in 1991, and Russian President Boris **Yeltsin** was invited to annual G7 summits from 1992 onwards, initially to discuss the terms of financial assistance to the Russian Federation, and subsequently (beginning in 1994) also to participate in foreign policy discussions. The summit meeting in Denver in 1997 was called the 'Summit of the Eight', in recognition of fuller Russian involvement, while the 1998 Birmingham Summit was the first full G8 Summit.

Members: Canada, France, Germany, Italy, Japan, Russian Federation, UK, USA.

GUAM group

The GUAM (**Georgia**, **Ukraine**, **Azerbaijan** and **Moldova**) group is designed to encourage broad political, economic and strategic co-operation so as to strengthen the independence and sovereignty of these former **Soviet** Republics. Its major focus has been the development of a Europe–Caucasus–Asia transport corridor (**TRACECA**).

The original framework of co-operation first came into being in 1996 at the **Conventional Forces in Europe** (CFE) Treaty Conference in Vienna, followed up by a presidential-level meeting in Strasbourg in October 1997. In April 1999 Uzbekistan joined what then became known as the GUUAM group at a summit meeting held in Washington, DC, on the margin of the **North Atlantic Treaty Organization** (NATO) summit there. They decided the following year to convene regular summits at the level of Heads of State at least once a year, and meetings at the level of Ministers for Foreign Affairs at least twice a year. Uzbekistan withdrew in 2005, leaving the original four members, known again as GUAM.

In May 2006, at a summit in **Kiev** of the four countries' Presidents, the group was transformed into the Organization for Democratic and Economic Development-GUAM. Its headquarters are to be set up in Kiev, and a free trade zone is to be established; until now the dissemination of information about the activities of the GUAM group has been co-ordinated primarily by the embassies of the member countries in Washington, DC.

Internet: www.guam.org

Gypsies *see* **Roma**.

H

Hanrapetutiun *see* **Republic**.

HDK *see* **Democratic Party of Armenia**.

HELCOM *or* **Helsinki Commission** *see* **Baltic Marine Environment Protection Commission**.

Helsinki Final Act

The diplomatic agreement signed in Helsinki on 1 August 1975 at the end of the first Conference on Security and Co-operation in Europe (*see* **Organization for Security and Co-operation in Europe**). The 35 participants, including the members of the **North Atlantic Treaty Organization** and the **Warsaw Pact** and 13 neutral and non-aligned European countries, effectively accepted the post-1945 status quo in Europe. Four 'baskets' of agreement in the Final Act (also known as the Helsinki Accord) covered: security and confidence-building; co-operation on economic, scientific and environmental issues; human rights and freedoms; and the holding of follow-up conferences.

Helsinki process

The continuing round of negotiations and follow-up conferences set in train by the 1973–75 Helsinki conference. The Helsinki process was officially known as the Conference on Security and Co-operation in Europe (CSCE). Over a period of 25 years, the CSCE and its successor the **Organization for Security and Co-operation in Europe** (OSCE) became a significant element in the architecture of European dialogue and ultimately co-operation during and after the **Cold War**. The so-called 'Basket One' of the Helsinki Accord of 1975 set up the process which led ultimately to the conclusion of the landmark multilateral arms reduction treaty on **Conventional Forces in Europe** (CFE) in 1990. 'Basket Two' dealt with co-operation in science, technology and environmental protection. 'Basket Three', in which the participant states made commitments on human rights and freedoms, had a special significance for the emergence of movements pressing for greater respect for civil liberties within communist countries. Notable among these were the Moscow Helsinki Group founded in 1976 by a group including Yuri Orlov, Yelena Bonner and Anatoly Shcharansky; Charter 77 in Czechoslovakia; and the Helsinki Watch group founded in Poland in 1979. These initiatives were supported by 'Helsinki Watch' committees across western Europe, Canada and the USA, leading to the holding of a conference in 1982 and the creation in 1983 of the International Helsinki Federation for Human Rights (IHF).

HHD *see* **Armenian Revolutionary Federation**.

HHK *see* **Republican Party of Armenia**.

HHSh *see* **Pan-Armenian National Movement**.

HIV—human immunodeficiency virus *see* **AIDS**.

HKK *see* **Communist Party of Armenia**.

House of Representatives
Palata Predstaviteley

The lower house of the **National Assembly** of **Belarus**.

HZhK *see* **People's Party of Armenia**.

I

IAEA *see* **International Atomic Energy Agency**.

IBRD

The International Bank for Reconstruction and Development, a constituent part of (and generally known as) the **World Bank**.

Ichkeria *see* **Chechnya**.

ICJ *see* **International Court of Justice**.

Idel-Ural

A collective term for the non-**Russian**, and largely **Muslim**, republics between the River **Volga** (Idel in Tatar) and the southern Ural mountains. The region is inhabited by various **Tatar** and **Finno-Ugric peoples** and came under the dominion of the Russian Empire after the fall of the Kazan khanate in 1552. The connections between the subjugated people led to episodes of collective action against their Russian overlords, culminating in the formation of a Tatar-led Idel-Ural Federation in 1917 in opposition to the Bolsheviks. The success of the Bolsheviks over their adversaries in the Russian Civil War led to the conspicuous division of the Idel-Ural state and the foundation in its place of five ethnically-based successor regions (roughly from west to east, **Mordovia**, **Mari El**, the **Chavash Republic**, **Tatarstan** and **Bashkortostan**) between 1918 and 1930. Today these republics cover the important Volga-Ural oil field and are largely industrialized. There are no serious aims to recreate the Idel-Ural unit.

IDU *see* **International Democrat Union**.

IMF *see* **International Monetary Fund**.

Industry Will Save Georgia (IWSG)
Mretsveloba Gadaarchens Sakartvelos

A pro-business political movement in **Georgia**, known by the initials of its English title. IWSG was launched in advance of the 1999 parliamentary elections by brewery owner Giorgi Topadze. Arguing that the Government's tax policies were damaging Georgian business and forcing dependence on foreign aid, Topadze called for tax breaks and import controls until a stable economy was established. The IWSG, allied in the 1999 elections with the ultra-nationalist Georgia First movement and the Movement for Georgian Statehood, won 15 seats with a 7.1% vote share. Its group of deputies adopted the name Entrepreneurs. It contested the November 2003 legislative elections and the re-run poll in February 2004 as part of the **Rightist Opposition** grouping.

Leadership: Giorgi Topadze (Chair).
Address: Marjvena Sanapiro 7, Tbilisi.
Telephone: (32) 940981.

Information Telegraphic Agency of Russia *see* **ITAR-TASS**.

Infotag News Agency

The main private news agency in **Moldova**. Created in 1993, Infotag rivals the official agency **Moldpres** in providing news about Moldova to domestic and international clients in Romanian, Russian and English.

Director: Alexandru Tanas.
Address: Blvd B. Bodoni 57/114, 2012 Chişinau.
Telephone: (22) 234930.
Fax: (22) 234933.
E-mail: office@infotag.net.md
Internet: www.infotag.md

Ingushetia

A constituent republic of the **Russian Federation** situated in the north **Caucasus region**, which was joined to nearby **Chechnya** from 1934 to 1992. *Population*: 467,300 (2002 est.). The Ingush people (known to themselves as Galgai) are ethnically similar to the Chechens, and were only recognized as a separate ethnic group in the late 19th century after they opposed the Chechens and sided with Russian forces in their war against an Islamic uprising in the north Caucasus. The Ingush only converted to Islam during this period. They were isolated again in the early 20th century when they did join the local resistance to Bolshevik rule. After the success of the Bolsheviks in the Russian Civil War (1918–20) the Ingush were granted a position within the autonomous 'Mountain Republic' and were given their own *oblast* (region) in 1924. In 1934 Ingushetia was joined to Chechnya. During the Second World War the previous loyalty of the Ingush was quickly forgotten and they, the Chechens and many other Caucasian peoples were accused by Stalin of collaborating with the invading German forces and were deported *en masse* to central Asia in 1944 (*see* **deported nationalities**). They were rehabilitated in 1956 and returned to Ingushetia.

Tensions between Chechens and Ingush escalated rapidly in the early 1990s following the declaration of independence by the nationalist regime in Chechnya in 1991. Supported by the Russian authorities, who were opposed to the Chechen regime, Ingushetia declared its sovereignty within the Russian Federation in June 1992. The borders of the new republic in theory followed the 1934 demarcation. However, disputes with neighbouring North **Ossetia** over the Prigorodni region, ceded to the Ossetes in 1944, descended into armed conflict in 1992. Thousands of Ingush fled the fighting and they now constitute a large refugee population, along with Chechens, in Ingushetia. A ceasefire was agreed in 1995 with the help of supervising Russian forces.

A traditionally pastoral economy was converted in the Soviet era into one focused on the petroleum industry. The capital was moved from Nazran, the centre of industrial activity, to the nearby new town of Magas in 2002. The republic was badly hit by the war with North Ossetia and the influx of Chechen refugees from 1994 onwards. It remains impoverished and unproductive, but has been helped by the creation of a free economic zone across the republic to encourage trade. It is also attempting to market its breathtaking Caucasian mountain scenery for tourism, although this is hampered by overspilling violence from the conflict in neighbouring Chechnya. Murat Zyazikov was elected President of Ingushetia in May 2002.

International Atomic Energy Agency (IAEA)

The UN organization founded in 1957 to promote and monitor peaceful use of atomic energy.

Members: 143 countries, including **Armenia**, **Azerbaijan**, **Belarus**, **Georgia**, **Moldova**, the **Russian Federation** and **Ukraine**.

Director-General: Dr Mohammad el-Baradei.

Address: POB 100, Wagramerstrasse 5, 1400 Vienna, Austria.

Telephone: (1) 26000.

Fax: (1) 26007.

E-mail: official.mail@iaea.org

Internet: www.iaea.org

International Bank for Reconstruction and Development (IBRD)

Generally known as the **World Bank**.

International Court of Justice (ICJ)

The principal judicial organ of the UN, founded in 1945.
 President: Rosalyn Higgins.
 Address: Peace Palace, Carnegieplein 2, 2517 KJ The Hague, Netherlands.
 Telephone: (70) 3022323.
 Fax: (70) 3649928.
 E-mail: information@icj-cij.org
 Internet: www.icj-cij.org

International Democrat Union (IDU)

An international grouping of centre-right political parties founded in 1983, which holds conferences every six months. Its membership includes the member parties of the European Democrat Union (EDU) and other political parties in 36 countries.
 Executive Secretary: Eirik Moen.
 Address: POB 1536 Vika, N-0117 Oslo, Norway.
 Telephone: (2) 2829000.
 Fax: (2) 2829080.
 E-mail: emoen@idu.org
 Internet: www.idu.org

International Monetary Fund (IMF)

The principal organization of the international monetary system, founded in December 1945 to promote international monetary co-operation, the balanced growth of trade and exchange rate stability. A critical role of the IMF has been to provide credit resources to members, on condition that specified (and sometimes domestically highly controversial) conditions are met for management of the economy and attainment of monetary targets.

The IMF's 184 member countries now include all the countries of **central** and **eastern Europe**. **Armenia, Azerbaijan, Belarus, Georgia, Moldova**, the **Russian Federation** and **Ukraine** all joined in 1992, after the fall of communism.

Managing Director: Rodrigo de Rato.
Address: 700 19th St, NW, Washington, DC 20431, USA.
Telephone: (202) 6237300.
Fax: (202) 6236278.
Email: publicaffairs@imf.org
Internet: www.imf.org

International Organization for Migration (IOM)

Founded as the International Committee for Migration (ICM) in 1951, the organization changed its name in 1989.
　　Members: 120 countries, including **Armenia**, **Azerbaijan**, **Belarus**, **Georgia**, **Moldova** and **Ukraine**. Observers include the **Russian Federation**.
Director-General: Brunson McKinley.
Address: route des Morillons 17, 1211 Geneva 19, Switzerland.
Telephone: (22) 7179111.
Fax: (22) 7986150.
E-mail: info@iom.int
Internet: www.iom.int

International Space Station (ISS)

A project for a space research unit orbiting the earth, jointly constructed (in orbit) by the space agencies of the USA (NASA), the **Russian Federation** (Roskosmos), Japan (JAXA), Canada (CSA) and Europe (ESA), with additional participation from Brazil (AEB). It is a merger of plans for various national research stations, including **Mir** 2, and was announced in 1993. The first component was sent into orbit in 1998, and the station has been continuously manned since 2000. It will be completed by 2010 for an overall cost estimated at US $130,000m.

International Whaling Commission (IWC)

The organization which reviews the conduct of whaling throughout the world, and co-ordinates and funds whale research. Its 70 member countries include the **Russian Federation**. Traditionally a whaling nation, the Russian Federation observes the international moratorium on commercial whaling introduced by the IWC amidst mounting concern that continued hunting had become unsustainable owing to declining whale numbers.

Chair: Henrik Fischer.
Address: The Red House, 135 Station Road, Impington, Cambridge,
    CB4 9NP, UK.
Telephone: (1223) 233971.
Fax: (1223) 232876.
E-mail: secretariat@iwcoffice.org
Internet: www.iwcoffice.org

IOM *see* **International Organization for Migration**.

Islam *see* **Muslim peoples**.

Islamic fundamentalism

An extreme interpretation of Islam which promotes *jihad* (holy war) against non-Muslims, and aims to implement strict *sharia* (Islamic) law. Since the terrorist attacks in the USA on 11 September 2001 by the fundamentalist al-Qaida group, Islamic fundamentalism has taken on a renewed political importance in **eastern Europe**. Although the small size of **Muslim** communities in the region and their largely peaceful coexistence with Christian neighbours has somewhat negated its threat, the rapid growth of Islamic fundamentalism, fuelled by Arab nationalism and the success of such Islamic states as Iran, has seen it take on an almost evangelic-revolutionary tinge. It is often linked to nationalist causes in separatist regions to further polarize the antagonists. In particular Islamic fundamentalism has influenced separatist struggles in **Chechnya** and **Dagestan**. However, in all cases the major motivation for conflict has been ethno-political, rather than religious.

ISS *see* **International Space Station**.

ITAR-TASS

Informatsionnoye Telegrafnoye Agentstvo Rossii–Telegrafnoye Agentstvo Suverennykh Stran
(Information Telegraphic Agency of Russia–Telegraphic Agency of the Sovereign Countries)

The main state news agency in the **Russian Federation**, focusing originally on the domestic market as opposed to supplying information abroad (*see* **RIA-Novosti**). ITAR-TASS traces its ancestry back to the formation in 1904 of the St Petersburg Telegraph Agency (SPTA), as the Russian Empire's official news service. In 1925 the SPTA was transformed by the Soviet authorities into the Telegraph Agency of the Soviet Union (TASS) and was mobilized in the Government's propaganda efforts. From 1987 it began storing its information electronically in the INFO-TASS department. In 1992, following the collapse of the **Soviet Union**, TASS was reorganized as an open and independent institution, and was renamed as the Information Telegraphic Agency of Russia (ITAR), although it retains the 'TASS' suffix. ITAR now has 74 offices around the Russian Federation and other **Commonwealth of Independent States** countries, and 65 further afield. It has links with most other news agencies around **eastern Europe** and many more beyond. Its photo service is the largest of its kind in the Russian Federation.

Director-General: Vitalii N. Ignatenko.
Address: Tverskoi blvd 10/12, 125993 Moscow.
Telephone: (495) 2022981.
Fax: (495) 2025474.
E-mail: worldmarket@itar-tass.com
Internet: www.itar-tass.com

IWC *see* **International Whaling Commission**.

IWSG *see* **Industry Will Save Georgia**.

J

Jaanilinn question

A border dispute between Estonia and the **Russian Federation** over the division
of the historic town of Narva. The town itself is divided by the River Narva
which, from 1945, came to serve as the border between Estonia and Russia (then
one of the Soviet republics). The incorporation of Estonia into the **Soviet Union**
made this distinction somewhat arbitrary, and the two halves of the town
continued to interact as one, although its eastern district, known as Jaanilinn—in
Russian, Ivangorod—was administered as part of the Leningrad (**St Petersburg**)
oblast. Factories in Narva employed almost half of the residents of Jaanilinn,
which thus acted to draw Russian migrants into eastern Estonia, in line with
Soviet efforts to reduce the ethnic homogeneity of its constituent republics.

With the collapse of the Soviet Union in 1991 and the independence of Estonia
that summer, the question of the sovereignty of Jaanilinn was raised. However,
the fact of its by now overwhelming ethnic **Russian** majority population negated
Estonian claims. The dispute has been muted since initial attempts to redraw the
border were resolved in 1995 with grudging recognition of the Soviet-era
division.

Russia and Estonia signed a border treaty in May 2005, following Estonia's
accession to the **North Atlantic Treaty Organization** and the **European Union**.
However, when during the ratification process Estonia's Parliament amended the
preamble to retain its claim to Jaanilinn with a reference to the 1920 Treaty of
Tartu Russia withdrew from the new treaty.

Javakheti

A predominantly **Armenian** enclave in south-western **Georgia** bordering
Armenia and adjoining **Meskheti**. Situated high up in the Lesser Caucasus
mountains, Javakheti has a harsh climate which has earned it the nickname
'Georgia's **Siberia**'. Tensions between the majority Armenian population (around
113,000) and the Georgian Government have so far not escalated into armed
conflict. The Armenian nationalists (represented by the Javakhk movement) stop

short of separatism, pressing instead for greater autonomy within Georgia. Conflict is also kept at bay by the Georgian authority's fear of sparking another major conflagration (as in **Abkhazia**, where an Armenian minority sided with the separatists, and in South **Ossetia**), and the Armenian Government's reluctance to be drawn into another situation like that in **Nagorno-Karabakh**. The existence of a major **Russian** military base is currently another factor in the security equation. However, the possibility of a future conflict is high, as demands for autonomy remain largely unanswered and Armenian militia such as the Parvents are well armed and experienced from combat in Nagorno-Karabakh.

Javakheti's infrastructure is poor. A lack of Soviet-era investment, along what was then its heavily-restricted border with Turkey, has been exacerbated by economic difficulties in Georgia and the absence of effective Georgian administration. However, unemployment is officially low. Much commerce is generated by the presence of the Russian military base. Russia's agreement to withdraw from its Georgian bases by 2008 sparked fears for the region's economic future. The Georgian Government responded to demonstrations in 2004 and 2005 by promising new jobs and financial assistance to promote small business development, as well as consideration of several cultural demands such as recognition of Armenian as an official language in the region. Construction has also begun on a road to link the region to **Tbilisi** and a rail link into Turkey.

Jehovah's Witnesses

A religion based on Christianity with some 500,000 adherents in **eastern Europe**. Founded in the USA in the late 19th century, it has been spread across the world by 'publishers', who are encouraged to canvass their neighbours door-to-door. The largest communities in eastern Europe are found in the **Russian Federation** (133,000), Poland (130,000) and **Ukraine** (115,000). Jehovah's Witnesses believe in a strict interpretation of the Bible and the essential humanity of Jesus Christ, and they reject the symbol of the cross. Their religion, which isolates its followers from other religious groups, is often vilified by mainstream Christian denominations as a cult. One of its greatest areas of conflict with modern states is its prohibition on members fulfilling military service. In countries where there is no civilian alternative to the draft, Jehovah's Witnesses often end up being prosecuted. The situation is particularly severe in **Belarus**, where prison sentences with hard labour are often passed on Jehovah's Witnesses who conscientiously object to enforced military service, and where the religion has been refused official registration. The situation in **Armenia** improved in 2004 after the religion gained registration there.

Jews

A religious group once found in large communities in many parts of **eastern Europe**, including especially **Belarus**, Poland and regions of **European Russia**, but now greatly reduced in numbers as a result of the Second World War, the Holocaust and large-scale emigration. Eastern Europe was home to the greatest proportion of the world's Jews for many centuries. Sidelined by mainstream society for their religion, Jews often took up industries deemed unfit for Christians, such as money-lending, and promoted their own educational institutions through close-knit communities. Their successes bred resentment and they were the targets of various attacks, early instances of which occurred during the Crusades which began in the 11th century. Anti-Semitism is now officially condemned but low-level discrimination continues across the region, with Jews particularly targeted by far-right nationalist groups.

Most of the Jews from eastern Europe are known as Ashkenazi. The Yiddish language, widely spoken among Ashkenazi Jews, is a hybrid of Hebrew and German. Jewish communities in Bulgaria, however, tend to be Sephardic, i.e. Hispanic, in origin. All of Albania's 300 Sephardic Jews migrated on the invitation of the Israeli Government in 1990–91.

The liberalization of the **Soviet Union** from the 1980s opened up a new mass migration of Jews to Israel. Between 1989 and 1998 over 768,000 Jews made *aliyah* (migration to Israel) from the former Soviet Union, with 375,000 departing in 1990–91 alone. Today the largest populations of Jews in eastern Europe are found in the **Russian Federation** (around 235,000, mainly in urban centres) and among the ethnic **Russian** communities in **Ukraine** (84,000, down from 486,000 in 1989). A couple of thousand remain on Russia's border with the People's Republic of China in the far east of **Siberia**, where a special Jewish Autonomous *Oblast* (AO) was established in the Soviet era, although very few Jews ever migrated there.

Justice

Ardartyun

An electoral alliance of parties in **Armenia** formed in 2003 in opposition to incumbent President Robert **Kocharian**.

Comprising the **People's Party of Armenia** (HZhK), the **National Democratic Alliance Party** (AZhD), the **National Democratic Party** (AZhK), the **Democratic Party of Armenia** (HDK) and the **National Democratic Union** (AZhM), Justice was significant as a leader in opposition protests to Kocharian's re-election in 2003. It suspended its involvement with the **National Assembly** in protest at the election's conduct until September 2003, and withdrew once more during 2004. Since protests against Kocharian and his constitutional referendum in November 2005 have petered out, splits have become apparent within Justice. The HZhK has irked its allies by calling for an end to anti-government protests. Observers consider the shuffling of opinions to have been prompted by the run-up to legislative elections in 2007 and the presidential poll due the following year.

K

Kabardino-Balkaria

A constituent republic of the **Russian Federation**, formed by the amalgamation of the autonomous regions of the Caucasian Kabards and the **Turkic** Balkars. Situated in the centre of the north **Caucasus region**, in the extreme south of **European Russia**, the republic extends from the peaks of the Greater Caucasus mountains down to the Kabardin plain and the Terek river system. *Population*: 901,500 (2002 estimate). Arsen Kanokov was elected President of Kabardino-Balkaria in September 2005.

The Kabards, considered closely related to the **Cherkess** and speaking a language similar to that of the **Abaza** and **Abkhaz**, were one of the last in the north Caucasus to convert to Islam. They allied themselves to the Terek **Cossacks** as early as 1557, which drew their allegiance north to Russia. The Balkars on the other hand, traditionally concentrated in the mountains and more closely related to the neighbouring Karachai, long resisted Russian domination. Both peoples were absorbed into the Russian Empire in the 19th century and were lumped together by the **Soviet** authorities in 1922, first in the Kabardino-Balkar autonomous *oblast* (region), and then in 1936, in a full republic.

The Balkars were persecuted like many other Caucasian peoples during the Second World War after being accused of collaborating with the Germans. Stalin had them deported *en masse* to central Asia and **Siberia** in 1944 (*see* **deported nationalities**). Balkaria was reorganized as part of the **Georgian** republic until the Balkars were politically rehabilitated in 1956 and returned from exile. However, although the Kabardino-Balkar republic was reconstituted the Balkars were prevented from settling in their original homeland and were scattered throughout the republic. This dispersal caused ethnic tensions later when the republic declared its sovereignty within the Russian Federation in March 1992.

The Balkars have pressed for the return of confiscated property and the restitution of a separate Balkar region. A referendum in December 1991 confirmed the desire to form a Balkar republic and for 13 days in November 1996 Balkaria declared itself independent from Kabardinia. Although the move failed there are residual calls to redivide Kabardino-Balkaria and neighbouring

Karachai-Cherkessia into more ethnically homogenous Kabardino-Cherkessian and Karachai-Balkarian entities.

Economic activity is focused on mining of heavy metals and gold. Agriculture is confined mostly to the Kabardin plain and light manufacturing is concentrated in the capital, Nalchik, and the second city, Prokhladny. Nalchik was the scene of fighting between Russian forces and **Chechen** militants in October 2005, when the Chechens briefly seized control of the city.

Kaliningrad

A city and **Russian** exclave adjoining the south-western corner of the Baltic Sea. *Population*: 955,300 (2002 estimate). The Kaliningrad *oblast* (region), roughly rectangular in shape, extends 140 km inland from the city of the same name. It was formed from the northern half of the **German** territory of East **Prussia**, which had been occupied by advancing Soviet troops at the end of the Second World War (1945). Bordering Poland to the south, it is separated from the rest of the Russian Federation by territory belonging to Lithuania (which borders Kaliningrad to the north and east) and by the entire width of **Belarus**.

Germanized since the era of the medieval Teutonic Order, the region around the city of Königsberg (literally 'king's mountain'), the administrative capital of East Prussia, was the centre for the reawakening of German nationalism during the Napoleonic Wars. It was incorporated into the Prussian-dominated unified Germany in 1871. It experienced 20 years as a German exclave from 1919 to 1939, cut off from the rest of Germany by Polish territory under the territorial settlement imposed on defeated Germany at the end of the First World War. Rejoined to Germany by the Nazi military advance eastwards in the Second World War, East Prussia was then split in two by the **Potsdam Agreements** in 1945. The northern half was annexed to Russia and the southern half ceded to the reorganized state of Poland, while the German population left to seek new homes in the rump Germany. For the next 46 years Kaliningrad was merely the edge of the vast **Soviet Union**, abutting only Soviet-dominated **eastern Europe** and repopulated with Russian colonists.

The collapse of the Soviet Union and the emergence of independent **Baltic States** in 1991 turned administrative isolation into a real political distance. With the admission of Poland and Lithuania into the **North Atlantic Treaty Organization** and the **European Union** (EU), Kaliningrad's position has become of even greater diplomatic significance. Civil authorities in the *oblast* have toyed with and ultimately rejected independence from Russia, but have been forced to take a decidedly more Western view than their masters in Moscow, calling for EU investment to help solve their dire socio-economic problems. Kaliningrad was made a free economic zone soon after the fall of the Soviet Union, with the intention of creating a 'Baltic Hong Kong'. However, prosperity proved elusive in the 1990s, as the region's economy fared even worse than that of Russia as a whole; unemployment, violence, poverty and environmental degradation set in. In early 2001 rumours of the Russian Federation's intention of using the *oblast* as a base for nuclear missiles caused uproar among its neighbours. There has also been friction over the freedom of movement from Kaliningrad to Russia proper. The introduction of border checks and visa requirements by Lithuania and Poland seriously strained regional relations, but a system of transit documents is now in place.

Economic growth has returned since the Russian financial crisis of the late 1990s, with the region consistently outperforming the **Russian economy**. Foreign investment is now growing along with EU co-operation, and the Special Economic Zone has been redefined and extended, though Russian accession to the **World Trade Organization** could affect its terms.

The city of Kaliningrad is home to almost half of the *oblast*'s population—426,000 (2002 estimate). Built on the ruined north-western suburbs of Königsberg, Kaliningrad underwent heavy industrialization under Soviet rule and economic activity now centres on engineering and metalworking, although the traditional amber industry is still active. For their size, the city and *oblast* provide a large amount of the Russian Federation's industrial output—around 0.3%—and draw a similar proportion of aid. Georgy Boos has headed the Kaliningrad administration since September 2005.

Kalmykia

A constituent republic in south-western **European Russia**, formally known as Kalmykia-Khalmg-Tangeh, which stretches southwards to a small shoreline on the Caspian Sea. It has an arm of territory that extends west towards Stavropol along the ancient salt beds that once linked the Caspian and Black Seas. It is unique as the only **Buddhist** state in Europe. *Population*: 292,400 (2002 estimate).

Absorbed into the **Russian** Empire after the collapse of the khanate of **Astrakhan** in 1556, the region was inhabited in the early 17th century by the Kalmyks, a nomadic, ethnically Mongolian people who had migrated westwards from what is now Xinjiang province in the People's Republic of China. Welcomed by Peter the Great and given Russian citizenship, they established a Kalmyk khanate in the region under the aegis of the Tsar. This kingdom stretched from Stavropol to Astrakhan. However, incursions on Kalmyk lands by Russian and **German** colonists prompted a mass exodus back to Mongolia in 1771. Some fled west and joined the Don **Cossacks**.

With the fall of the tsarist state a Kalmyk *oblast* (region) was established in 1920 and converted to a full republic in 1936. However, the Kalmyks suffered greatly at the hands of Stalin. They were forced to abandon their nomadic lifestyle for collective farms and industrialized cities, while Buddhist preachers were persecuted and temples destroyed. With the outbreak of the Second World War Stalin accused them of collaborating with their ethnic German neighbours and had all Kalmyks deported *en masse* to **Siberia** in 1943 (*see* **deported nationalities**). A fifth of the deportees are thought to have died on the way and in exile. The end of wholesale Stalinist repression after the dictator's death in 1956 enabled the rehabilitation of the Kalmyks in 1957 and a Kalmyk republic was reinstated. The population did not recover in numbers until 1970.

Perestroika in the late 1980s encouraged Kalmyk political parties to form and a Declaration of Sovereignty was adopted by the authorities in the capital, Elista, in 1990. The modern Republic of Kalmykia-Khalmg-Tangeh was declared on 31 March. Claims have been made for the return of the territory ceded to neighbouring regions after 1943. The charismatic Kirsan Nikolayevich Ilyumzhinov has been President since April 1993. Opposition parties face stiff and often violent action by the state authorities.

The Kalmyks are most closely related to the western, Oyrat Mongols. As well as a Mongolian language, transcribed using the **Cyrillic alphabet** since 1938, the original Kalmyk settlers also brought with them the Buddhist faith. Adherence to the Tibetan creed is widespread and Kalmyk culture remains devoted to the Dalai Lama, who dispatched Telo Rinpoche, a US-educated Kalmyk held to be the reincarnation of an Indian holy man, to serve as the Kalmyk Shaddin (High) Lama.

Karachai-Cherkessia

A constituent republic of the **Russian Federation** situated in the north-west **Caucasus region**. *Population*: 439,500 (2002 estimate). The region came under Russian imperial rule in the 19th century. The republic is dominated by two ethnically dissimilar peoples, the **Turkic** Karachai and the Caucasian **Cherkess**. The Karachai are most closely related to the neighbouring Balkars (*see* **Kabardino-Balkaria**) and suffered deportation at the hands of Stalin in 1944 (*see* **deported nationalities**).

Briefly a part of the abortive Mountain Peoples' Republic in 1921, the Karachai-Cherkess autonomous *oblast* (region) was first created in 1922. The two peoples were given their own administrative regions in 1924, but the whole *oblast* was abolished and incorporated into **Georgia** following the deportation of the Karachai in 1944. It was reconstituted in 1957 when the Karachai were rehabilitated under First Secretary Nikita Khrushchev. In 1990 the *oblast* was upgraded to a full republic and on 31 March 1992 a Sovereign Republic was declared. Mustafa Batdyev has been President since September 2003.

While the Karachai have called for the return of land and property confiscated in 1944, and for possible union with the Balkars, the Cherkess have led the way for calls to reunify the Circassian people (Cherkess, **Adygei** and Kabards). Tensions between Karachai and Cherkess, however, have been kept to a minimum. Relations with the republic's minority **Cossack** community, on the other hand, have been tense. In February 1991 the Zelenchuk-Urup *okrug* (district) was established in the predominantly Cossack areas.

Karelia question

A long-dormant territorial dispute between the **Russian Federation** and Finland, stemming from the annexation of the western half of Karelia by the **Soviet Union** in 1940. Historically Karelia comprises the lands to the east of southern Finland, east of the Gulf of Finland and around the north of Lake Ladoga. As a modern Russian region it also encompasses much of the land to the north of this region as well.

The basis for the Finnish claim to the lands is partly the presence of the Karelians—ethnic Finns (a **Finno-Ugric people**) who converted to **Orthodox Christianity** and have been greatly russified in society and language. There are approximately 65,000 in the Karelian Republic (less than 10% of the total population). The political part of the claim relates to western Karelia and was established from the 14th century. At this time the west fell under Swedish rule and was joined to Finland, while the east came under Russian dominion. The two halves were both under Russian suzerainty from 1721 but remained separate administrative regions, even when the whole of Finland was annexed by the Russian Empire in 1809 and ruled as a Grand Duchy including western Karelia. This political situation was then formalized in 1917 when Finland became an independent country, recognized in 1920 by the new communist authorities in Russia.

Russia's claim to western Karelia was laid down in 1940 when, after the Russo-Finnish 'Winter War', the region was absorbed into the Soviet Union and the border redrawn to reflect the Soviet military victory. A Karelian ASSR was created in 1956. On the collapse of centralized communist rule in the Soviet Union in 1990, Karelia was the first region to declare its sovereignty and is now an integral republic in the Russian Federation. Sergei Katanandov has been Head of the Karelian Republic since May 1998.

Under the firm yoke of Soviet rule and during the nervous diplomacy of the **Cold War**, the Karelia question was effectively buried. However, the post-1991 era released aspirations from sections of the minority Karelian population, and elements of the Finnish right, to return to the pre-1940 border. Some extremists even called for the full annexation by Finland of the whole Karelian Republic. In December 1991, however, the Finnish authorities officially relinquished their claim to any part of Karelia.

Kazakhs

A **Turkic** people dominant in Kazakhstan and forming a small minority of around 650,000 within the **Russian Federation**. The nomadic Kazakhs came under Russian dominion in the 19th century, at the same time that they adopted Islam. Once within the Russian Empire, and particularly the **Soviet Union**, some Kazakhs migrated into Russia in search of work, having been forced to abandon their nomadic lifestyle for collectivization and industrialization.

At the collapse of the Soviet Union in 1991 and the creation of an independent Kazakhstan, the Russian Federation effectively abandoned its Kazakh minority. Leaving it for their own homeland, Kazakhstan, to look after their cultural and linguistic needs, the Russian state has been in no hurry to provide education in Kazakh or support for Kazakh cultural aspirations and the community is expected to fund its own programmes. Caught in this situation many Kazakhs have migrated to Kazakhstan, although this has in no way matched the exodus of ethnic **Russians** from Kazakhstan.

KGB *see* **Federal Security Service**.

Khachatrian, Vartan

Minister of Finance and Economy, **Armenia**. Vartan Khachatrian is a member of the **Republican Party of Armenia** (HHK) and has been a member of the Armenian Government since his appointment as Minister of Finance and Economy on 14 November 2000.

Born on 4 April 1959, in Jermuk in the south of the then Soviet Socialist Republic of Armenia, he attended the Yerevan Polytechnic Institute from 1975 to 1980 before studying as a doctoral student at the Technical University of E. Bauman in **Moscow** between 1982 and 1985. He went on to pursue a career as a manager in the food and water industry in Armenia. Following the country's independence in 1991, he entered the Commission of Privatization and Denationalization. He was first elected to the **National Assembly** in 1995. Until his appointment to the Cabinet in November 2000 he had served on various parliamentary and ministerial budget committees.

Vartan Khachatrian is married and has two children.

Address: Ministry of Finance and Economy, Melik Adamian St 1, 375010
        Yerevan.
Telephone: (10) 595304.
Fax: (10) 545815.
E-mail: mfe@mfe.am
Internet: www.mfe.gov.am

Kiev
(Kyiv)

The capital city of **Ukraine**, situated on the Dnieper river in the northern central region of the country. *Population*: 2.7m. (2005 estimate). The city has, on and off, been an important administrative and commercial centre since the establishment of Kievan Rus, the first **Slavic** state, in the 9th century. Kiev benefited, then as now, from its position on the north–south Dnieper, which serves as part of a transport link between the Black and Baltic Seas. Despite being destroyed by Mongol invaders in 1240, the city regained its importance in the 16th century as a key trading port and the centre of **Orthodox** Slavic resistance to the power of Polish Catholicism. Between 1667 and 1793 Kiev became a ward of the expanding **Russian** Empire.

Under Russian suzerainty Kiev became a flourishing cultural centre and was the focus of aspiring **Ukrainian** nationalists. Russian industrialization in the 19th century connected the city to the rest of the empire and further boosted its economy. During the 1917 revolution Kiev became, briefly, the capital of a self-declared independent Ukraine under the Menshevik rather than the Bolshevik faction. On the front line of, successively, the First World War, the Russian Civil War and the Russo-Polish War, the city was ravaged by sieges, occupation and ultimately by devastating famine. Ukrainian nationalism was then strongly suppressed by the new **Soviet** authorities and between 1920 and 1934 the Ukrainian capital was shifted to Kharkov. However, industrialization continued apace and the city's economy grew substantially under the rolling five-year plans.

During the Second World War Kiev was once again occupied by German forces. Within days of its fall in September 1941 over 30,000 **Jews**, Soviet soldiers and 'partisans' were massacred in the nearby Babi Yar ravine. Thousands more were killed in the following two years. During its capture and liberation by Soviet forces in 1943 much of the city was destroyed, and there was massive industrial reconstruction after the war ended, while Kiev was also politically rehabilitated, receiving the accolade of the Order of Lenin.

Kiev became the capital of an independent Ukraine once again in 1991. As such it is home to the **Supreme Council** and other central administrative institutions, and its squares became the focus of the **Orange Revolution** in 2004. Economic activity is dominated by heavy metal engineering. Other manufacturing includes machinery and engineering parts and tools. Chemical processing is also important.

Kocharian, Robert

President of **Armenia**. Robert Kocharian was once a member of the Soviet-era **Communist Party of Armenia**. In the last years of the **Soviet Union** he became prominent in the pro-independence movement in the **Armenian**-dominated enclave of **Nagorno-Karabakh** (inside **Azerbaijan**), of which he is a native. His term as the enclave's first 'President' (1994–97) was followed by a one-year spell as Prime Minister of Armenia. He was then elected President of Armenia after the incumbent's surprise resignation in early 1998, and was re-elected in 2003.

Robert Sedrakovich Kocharian was born on 31 August 1954 in Stepanakert (now known as Xankändi), Nagorno-Karabakh, and joined the Soviet army in 1972 for three years. He then studied electronics and technology at the Polytechnic Institute in **Yerevan**, the Armenian capital, graduating in 1982. The previous year he had begun a job as an engineer and electrotechnician at the Karabakh silk production factory in Stepanakert. In 1987 he became secretary on the factory's committee of the Communist Party. The following year he began campaigning for the formation of a unified Republic of Armenia, to include Nagorno-Karabakh. He founded Unification (Miatsum), an ostensibly non-political movement which became the leading faction in the Karabakh movement.

In 1989, the year in which he left the Communist Party, Kocharian became a deputy in the Armenian Supreme Council. Towards the end of the year the Council declared an Armenian republic which included Nagorno-Karabakh, although the Soviet government declared this move unconstitutional. On 2 September 1991 Nagorno-Karabakh declared itself a republic, then the Communist Party of Armenia dissolved itself and on 23 September Armenia voted for independence from the Soviet Union. At this time Kocharian was elected a deputy to the Supreme Council of Nagorno-Karabakh. From August 1992, when a state of emergency was declared, he became Chairman of the Defence Committee which effectively governed the region. In December 1994 he was elected the first President of the Republic of Nagorno-Karabakh by the Supreme Council, his position being confirmed in a direct election in the enclave in November 1996.

Kocharian was appointed Prime Minister of Armenia on 19 March 1997 by Armenian President Levon Ter-Petrossian, who hoped to use this nationalistic gesture to relieve popular discontent at the high unemployment and rising poverty brought about by recent economic reforms. Kocharian expressed hopes that his appointment might speed up the resolution of the status of his war-ravaged home territory. In Azerbaijan, however, it was regarded as an insult and as evidence of *de facto* Armenian annexation of the Nagorno-Karabakh enclave.

When Ter-Petrossian unexpectedly resigned as President in February 1998, amidst disagreements with the Government over a proposal from the **Organization for Security and Co-operation in Europe** (OSCE) to end the dispute, Kocharian was successfully elected in his place and was inaugurated on 9 April.

His first term as President was fraught with conflict with the Government. He clashed in particular with Aram Sarkissian, who was Prime Minister for six months after the incumbent, his brother Vazgen Sarkissian, was killed in a shoot-out in the **National Assembly** in October 1999. Sources of friction included the enclave, alleged corruption and Kocharian's authoritarian approach.

There have been several unsuccessful attempts to have Kocharian impeached, including one for his refusal to allow the Military Prosecutor-General to testify in the 1999 National Assembly massacre. Consequently, his rule is frequently protested by large demonstrations in Yerevan, where over 10,000 people rallied in September 2001 against his declared intention to run for a second term in 2003. He won the election in the second round with 67% of the vote, but OSCE observers reported irregularities in the poll, and popular protests demanding Kocharian's resignation for rigging the vote carried on into 2004.

Kocharian is married to Bella Kocharian with two sons and one daughter

Address: Office of the President, Baghramian Avenue 26, 375077 Yerevan.

Telephone: (10) 544052.

Fax: (10) 521551.

E-mail: press@president.am

Internet: www.president.am

Kodori Gorge

A volatile and largely lawless mountain region making up the northern section of the border between **Abkhazia** and **Georgia** proper, and home to the pro-Georgian Svan minority. The Kodori river goes on to flow into the Black Sea via the centre of Abkhaz territory. Officially within the borders of the Abkhaz state, the gorge remained partially under Georgian control after the 1994 ceasefire agreement, although in reality it formed a contiguous lawless zone along the Abkhaz–Georgian border with the southern Gali district.

Brief kidnappings of UN observers in the region raised tensions in 1999 and 2000, and Abkhaz–Georgian relations were pushed to a low ebb in 2001 with the arrival in the gorge of ethnic **Chechen** and renegade Georgian fighters. The destruction of a UN observer helicopter on 8 October 2001 led to a rapid renewal of tensions and precipitated violent clashes between the renegades and Abkhaz forces in the gorge. Georgia sent in 350 special forces troops to safeguard the villages in the upper gorge. In April 2002, the UN observer mission oversaw the withdrawal of these Georgian forces, but two days later Russian troops entered the gorge: the crisis was only defused by the arrival and personal negotiation of Georgian President Eduard **Shevardnadze**. The upper gorge returned to its state as a buffer zone controlled by local militia.

The new regime of President Mikhail **Saakashvili** stripped local militia leader Emzar Kvitsiani of his post as governor in 2004, and called on him to disarm his Monadire paramilitary force the following year. Kvitsiani refused, and in July 2006, in response to his defiant demands for the resignation of the Georgian Interior Minister, Georgian police and security forces launched an offensive which quickly seized control of much of the gorge. The Abkhaz Government accused the Georgians of breaking the terms of the ceasefire (though this only prevented the deployment of soldiers, rather than police) and declared it would respond with force if the offensive continued into Abkhazia proper. Kvitsiani escaped, but many of his militia were captured or surrendered.

The Georgian Government subsequently announced the relocation of the Abkhaz Government-in-exile to the gorge, and pledged substantial investment in infrastructure and reconstruction. A Russian-drafted UN Security Council resolution in October 2006 acknowledged the heightened tensions and called for the Georgians in particular to review their position, but did not go as far as citing a breach in the 1994 accord.

Kola peninsula

A thick finger of land in the far north of **European Russia**, just north of the Arctic Circle, jutting away from **Karelia** and surrounded by the icy waters of the Barents Sea to the north and the White Sea to the south. Kola is sparsely populated owing to its harsh climate, although the sizeable port of Murmansk, home to the Russian Northern Fleet, lies at its western extreme. The rest of the population live mainly in small mining towns, and around 2,000 **Sami** live in the interior. The peninsula, which contains the world's largest known deposit of apatite (used in fertilizers) and considerable quantities of zirconium and columbium, has become a byword for appalling toxic waste pollution.

Komi Republic

The largest non-**Russian** republic of the **Russian Federation** in **European Russia**. *Population*: 1.02m. (2002 estimate). The tundra-covered Komi Republic is situated at the far north of the western Ural mountains. Under the authority of the **Moscow** principality from the 14th century it became a centre for fur-trading until overhunting exhausted supplies. The region's fortunes were restored after the foundation of the capital, Syktyvkar, in the 18th century which prompted a wave of ethnic Russian migration. It was established as an autonomous *oblast* (region) within Bolshevik Russia in 1921, and raised to a Soviet republic in 1936. It gained recognition as a Sovereign Republic within Russia, after the collapse of the **Soviet Union**, in March 1992. Its Government has sought to retain control of the considerable coal deposits and the great natural resource of the Arctic forest. Vladimir Torlopov was elected President of the Komi Republic on 16 December 2001. The republic merged with Komi-Permyak autonomous *okrug* (district) on 1 December 2005, after a referendum had approved the merger the previous year.

The **Finno-Ugric** Komi, who make up only about a quarter of the republic's population (Russians are the majority), profess **Orthodox Christianity**. They are most closely related to the **Mari**, further south. Geographic isolation from the rest of Russia did not prevent russification, especially after the Second World War.

Korbut, Nikolay

Minister of Finance, **Belarus**. Nikolay Petrovich Korbut graduated from the Belarus State Economic University in **Minsk** in 1977. A political independent, he was head of the **National Bank of Belarus** from 15 January 1997 before joining the Council of Ministers as Finance Minister later the same year.

Address: Ministry of Finance, Sovetskaya St 7, 220010 Minsk.
Telephone: (17) 2272726.
Fax: (17) 2224593.
E-mail: web_mf@open.by
Internet: www.ncpi.gov.by/minfin

KPB *see* **Communist Party of Belarus**.

KPRF *see* **Communist Party of the Russian Federation**.

KPSS *see* **Communist Party of the Soviet Union**.

KPU *see* **Communist Party of Ukraine**.

Kremlin

The triangular walled city (literally 'citadel') in **Moscow** which became synonymous with the Government of the **Soviet Union**, and which remains an important office complex and residence for Government Ministers of the **Russian Federation**. It is now also a tourist attraction boasting many fine cathedrals, churches and a theatre. First founded as a fortified settlement overlooking the Moskva and Neglina rivers in the 12th century, it rose to prominence as a political centre distinct from the rest of Moscow in the mid-14th century. Its importance declined after the **Romanov dynasty** switched the Russian capital to **St Petersburg**, but was revived when the Bolsheviks reversed that change and returned central government to Moscow in 1918. From then the Kremlin became a secretive walled citadel, housing all the major organs of the Soviet state machinery, including the infamous secret service, the KGB (*see* **Federal Security Service**). With the collapse of the Soviet Union the Kremlin was opened up once more but retained its links with Government. Since 1992 it has been home to the President of the Russian Federation and his administration.

Kryashen

A sizeable community of **Tatars** who practise **Orthodox Christianity**, having been converted by Russian missionaries in the 18th century. The word Kryashen means 'the baptized'. Found mostly in **Tatarstan** and neighbouring regions of the **Russian Federation**, there are believed to be around 300,000 Kryashen. The community pressed for recognition as a separate ethnic group in time for the Russian census of October 2002—they had last been separately designated in the 1926 Soviet census. The initiative succeeded despite opposition from Tatar nationalists who saw it as an attempt to dilute Tatar unity, but in the event only 24,668 people listed themselves as Kryashens in the census results.

Kuchma, Leonid

Former President of **Ukraine** (1994–2004). Leonid Danilovich Kuchma was constitutionally an independent but received key support from right-of-centre parties in the **Supreme Council**. As a leading advocate of a rapid transition to a free-market economy he was appointed Prime Minister in 1992. He was first elected President in July 1994, and served two five-year terms.

Born on 9 August 1938 in the village of Chaikino, in the Chernihiv region, he graduated as a mechanical engineer from the University of Dnipropetrovsk in 1960. He spent the next 32 years working at the Pivdenmash machine-building factory, the **Soviet Union**'s largest weapons manufacturer, rising to become Managing Director in 1986. From 1966 to 1975 he was also the Technical Manager at Baikonur Cosmodrome in Kazakhstan, the centre of the Soviet space programme. He had joined the **Communist Party of the Soviet Union** (KPSS) in 1960, and was Party Secretary at the Pivdenmash factory from 1975 until 1982. He was a member of the Central Committee of the **Communist Party of Ukraine** from 1981 to 1991 and was elected to the Ukrainian Supreme Soviet in March 1990. He resigned from the party as it went out of existence in the wake of the abortive **August coup** in **Moscow** in 1991 and the ensuing rapid disintegration of the Soviet Union. The following year he retired from his directorship of the Pivdenmash factory, and was appointed as Ukraine's second post-independence Prime Minister on 27 October.

Kuchma resigned as Prime Minister in September 1993 after resistance from leftist parties to his radical economic reforms and use of emergency powers. In December he became President of the pro-market Union of Industrialists and Entrepreneurs (UIE), and the following year won election as Ukraine's President, supported by the centre-right Inter-regional Bloc for Reform (MBR) and, in the second round on 10 July, backed also by the now re-formed Communist Party of Ukraine and ethnic **Russians**.

In his first term he sought to reform the **Ukrainian economy** and increase his own constitutional powers. Obtaining in June 1996 the right to issue legislative decrees, he used his powers to centralize the executive, thus retaining for himself the authority to make both appointments and policy. His authoritarian stance provoked strong opposition from the left but was endorsed by dubious referendums and election results. He was re-elected in October–November 1999. Suggestions of his involvement in the disappearance and murder of outspoken journalist Giorgiy Gongadze in 2000 provoked mass demonstrations against his rule throughout his second term. He also faced stiffening opposition in the Supreme Council, including calls for impeachment over Gongadze's murder and for other crimes including the sale of military technology to Iraq. Kuchma proposed to reduce the powers of the presidency—to only appoint the Prime Minister and two key Ministers, rather than the whole Council of Ministers—and to switch the presidential election to a vote by the Supreme Council rather than the populace. The latter move was viewed by his opponents as an attempt to improve his chances of re-election for a third term, so the Supreme Council rejected that amendment clause.

When opposition presidential candidate Viktor **Yushchenko** was afflicted by dioxin poisoning in the run-up to the 2004 election, the finger was again pointed at Kuchma. He had decided not to stand in the election himself, and was backing his Prime Minister Viktor **Yanukovych**. The central election commission's announcement of Yanukovych's victory in the second round on 21 November, contrary to the exit polls which had clearly favoured Yushchenko, led to mass protests—the **Orange Revolution**—accusing the incumbent regime of vote rigging. Despite Kuchma's politicking and manoeuvring in the ensuing weeks, the eventual re-run a month later resulted in Yushchenko's victory, and in January 2005 Kuchma had to hand power to his former-Prime-Minister-turned-opposition-figurehead. A couple of months later prosecutors questioned Kuchma over the Gongadze murder.

Leonid Kuchma is married to Ludmila Mikolayovna; they have one daughter.

Kudrin, Alexei

Minister of Finance, **Russian Federation**. Alexei Leonidovich Kudrin is a political independent but a key supporter of President Vladimir **Putin**, with whom he served in the Leningrad (now **St Petersburg**) city administration in the early 1990s. He was appointed to President Boris **Yeltsin**'s Office in 1996 and was moved into the Council of Ministers proper under Putin on 18 May 2000.

Born on 12 October 1960 to a military family serving in Dobel, Latvia, he graduated in economics from the Leningrad State University in 1983. For seven years he worked as a researcher at the Soviet Academy of Sciences, where Anatoly Chubais was a lecturer. He followed Chubais into the Leningrad city administration in 1990 and worked under him in the municipal Committee on

Economic Reform. He became First Deputy Mayor of the city under Putin's political mentor, Anatoly Sobchak, in 1994. During his six years in the city's Government he worked with Putin and others to introduce much needed reforms to bring a turnaround in the city's dire finances.

In August 1996 Kudrin was brought into Yeltsin's presidential administration as a Deputy Chief and Head of the Control Department. He was appointed First Deputy Minister of Finance in 1997. He reconnected with Chubais in January 1999 when he was appointed First Deputy Chairman of the Unified Power Grids of Russia (UPGR) under his former colleague. He has tried to distance himself from the '**oligarchic**' image of Chubais since his departure from UPGR in June 1999, when he was reappointed First Deputy Minister of Finance. He was elevated to full Minister in Putin's new Cabinet in May 2000, where he has worked on the revival of the Russian economy. Under Chairman Mikhail Kasyanov (2000–04) he was also a Deputy Chairman of the Government.

Address: Ministry of Finance, ul. Ilinka 9, 109097 Moscow.

Telephone: (495) 2062171.

Fax: (495) 9246989.

Internet: www.minfin.ru

Kumyks

A **Turkic** people whose language and culture has become dominant as a *lingua franca* among the diverse peoples of the north **Caucasus**. Around 366,000 Kumyks live in the interior regions of the **Russian** republic of **Dagestan**, making them the third largest single group (14%) in this ethnically-varied state. Their cultural dominance has led to the assimilation into the Kumyk population of some Caucasian neighbours, particularly from among the **Avars** and **Dargins**. Kumyk nationalists, led by the Equality (Tenglik) movement, have spearheaded calls for greater autonomy within Dagestan, and even for a mini-federal system of ethnic republics. Tensions engendered by these views have led to clashes, particularly with the Dargins. Like most other Dagestanis, the Kumyks are Sunni **Muslim**.

Kurds

A Caucasian people estimated to number around 30 million–35 million spread across the north of the Middle East with sizeable populations in Turkey, Iran, Iraq and Syria, and within **eastern Europe** in **Armenia**, **Azerbaijan** and **Georgia**. The area of Kurdish settlement straddles international borders to an extent which leaves the Kurds unusually vulnerable to cultural fragmentation and political and social discrimination. Thousands attempt to migrate illegally each year to western Europe, especially Germany.

Kurdish is most closely related to Iranian and there are several distinct dialects. Kurds living in the **Caucasus region** have had a separate script based on the **Cyrillic alphabet** since 1944. They arrived in the Caucasus to escape persecution in their homeland (known as Kurdistan) in the 19th century. Economic activity is traditionally agricultural, focusing on livestock, although many Kurds have migrated to urban centres in the 20th century.

While most Kurds are **Muslim** the Yezidis of Armenia, Georgia and Iraq practise a hybrid religion based largely on ancient Persian beliefs with borrowings from Christianity and Judaism. According to this faith the Yezidis are descended from Adam but not from Eve, making them separate from the rest of humanity. They are also prohibited from cultivation, restricting economic activity. Consequently Yezidis are often regarded as a separate ethnic group, especially by Christian and Muslim Kurds.

The largest Kurdish population in eastern Europe—around 150,000—is in the west of Azerbaijan. Azeri attempts to assimilate the country's various ethnic groups prompted a backlash among Kurds who have called for the resurrection of the 1920s autonomous Kurdish region. Almost all the 42,000 Kurds now in Armenia are Yezidis, since many Muslim Kurds were expelled from Armenia along with resident **Azeris** in the early 1990s. The Armenian authorities have been unusually accommodating towards the Kurdish minority, establishing Kurdish-language broadcasts and a Kurdish newspaper as early as 1987. In Georgia the Kurdish minority is small and intermixed with the **Meskhetians**.

Kursk

A **Russian** nuclear submarine, named after the western city, which sank to the bottom of the Barents Sea on 13 August 2000 with the loss of all 118 sailors aboard. Having raised the craft, investigators finally concluded in November 2001 that the explosion of one of its own torpedoes was the main cause of the vessel's sinking, although the reason for this explosion remained unclear. The sinking highlighted endemic weaknesses in the colossal Russian military system, showing the dangers of attempting to retain its capabilities when vital maintenance was impossibly expensive. One consequence of the tragedy was the end of Russian President Vladimir **Putin**'s political honeymoon (although his popularity remains high). His handling of the affair, initially refusing international help and failing to respond in kind to the strong emotional reaction in the country, led to the beginning of popular criticism of his newly-elected regime.

Kyiv *see* **Kiev**.

L

Lapps *see* **Sami**.

Lavrov, Sergei

Minister of Foreign Affairs, **Russian Federation**. Sergei Viktorovich Lavrov, a former Soviet diplomat, was appointed Minister of Foreign Affairs on 9 March 2004 after 10 years as Russia's Permanent Representative (i.e. Ambassador) at the UN.

Born in 1950, he graduated from the Moscow State Institute of International Relations in 1972 and was posted to the Soviet Embassy in Sri Lanka (he can speak Sinhalese, as well as English and French). In 1976 he returned to **Moscow**, working in the Department for International Organizations. He moved to New York in 1981 as a member of the Soviet Permanent Representation to the UN, where he remained for the next seven years. On his return he was appointed deputy head of the Department of International Economic Relations and then Director of his old department, now responsible for International Organizations and Global Problems. This period coincided with the break-up of the **Soviet Union**, and shortly afterwards in 1992 he was appointed Deputy Minister of Foreign Affairs. Two years later he was posted back to New York, this time as Russia's Permanent Representative to the UN—a position he was to hold for a decade. In March 2004, following President **Putin**'s appointment of Mikhail **Fradkov** as Prime Minister, Lavrov was recalled to Moscow and appointed Minister of Foreign Affairs.

Lavrov is married with one daughter.

Address: Ministry of Foreign Affairs, Smolenskaya-Sennaya pl. 32/34,
           119200 Moscow.
Telephone: (495) 2441606.
Fax: (495) 2302130.
E-mail: ministry@mid.ru
Internet: www.mid.ru

LDPB *see* **Liberal Democratic Party of Belarus**.

LDPR *see* **Liberal Democratic Party of Russia**.

Lezghins

A Caucasian and Sunni **Muslim** people found in the north of **Azerbaijan** and in the south of the **Russian** republic of **Dagestan** in a region historically known as Lezghistan. The Caucasian Lezghins were divided between the Russian imperial administrative regions around the cities of **Baku** in Azerbaijan and Derbent in Dagestan. Since the collapse of the **Soviet Union** in 1991 this has meant the first international division of the Lezghin people.

Officially numbering only around 178,000 in Azerbaijan, Lezghins have faced attempts to assimilate them into the **Azeri** population there. Discrimination in the workplace and a lack of education in the Lezghin language is thought to lead many Lezghins to deny their ethnicity in censuses. Estimates suggest that the real number of Lezghins in Azerbaijan may be as high as one million. Tensions with Azeris were fuelled by the conflict with **Armenia**. Azeris evicted from the Armenian enclave of **Nagorno-Karabakh** were resettled in Lezghistan, and the Lezghin community resented conscription to fight in the war. The Unity (Sadual) movement was established to promote Lezghin rights.

The 337,000 Lezghins living in Dagestan have much greater political and cultural freedom. The Unity movement, known in Dagestan as Sadval, has led calls for the reunification of Lezghistan. A Lezghin National Council was created in December 1991 to promote the idea to the regional Governments. The closure of the Russia–Azerbaijan border in 1994 during the war in **Chechnya** provoked strong reactions from the Lezghin community on both sides of the new divide.

Liberal Democratic Party of Belarus
Liberalna-Demokratychnaya Partiya Belarusi (LDPB)

A right-wing **pan-Slavic** formation, the **Belarus** fraternal party to Vladimir Zhirinovskii's **Liberal Democratic Party of Russia**. In September 1998 the LDPB was a founder member of the Belarusian People's Patriotic Union (BNPS), a pro-**Lukashenka** grouping of some 30 conservative parties (including the **Communist Party of Belarus**) which backed the **Belarus-Russia Union** treaty. This did not prevent LDPB leader Syargey Gaydukevich from setting himself up as President Lukashenka's 'decent rival', and refusing to participate in the second round of voting in October 2000 amidst widespread accusations of irregularities. The party has since, however, effectively aligned itself with the Government. The LDPB had shed its apprehensions, and critical members, by the next poll in 2004.

The party won a single seat; it was one of only three parties to win any representation.

Leadership: Syargey Gaydukevich (Chair).

Address: 12th Floor, vul. Platonava 22, 220005 Minsk.

Telephone and Fax: (17) 2316331.

E-mail: ldpb@infonet.by

Internet: www.ldpb.net

Liberal Democratic Party of Russia
Liberalno-Demokraticheskaya Partiya Rossii (LDPR)

A populist ultra-nationalist formation in the **Russian Federation** which rose to prominence in the early 1990s but lost support thereafter. The LDPR was founded in 1990 under the leadership of Vladimir Zhirinovskii, who attracted attention for his xenophobic views tinged with anti-Semitism; his more extravagant proposals including one for a Russian reconquest of Finland. He obtained 7.8% of the vote in the 1991 presidential poll, following which the party was technically banned in August 1992 for falsifying its membership records. It was allowed to contest the December 1993 elections to the State Duma (lower house of the **Federal Assembly**), in which it became the second strongest party with 64 seats and headed the proportional voting with a 22.8% share.

Although forming the main parliamentary opposition to the **Yeltsin** administration in 1993–95, the LDPR gradually lost momentum as Zhirinovskii attracted much international opprobrium for his increasingly controversial statements and conduct. In the December 1995 State Duma elections, the LDPR again took second place with 51 seats, but fell back to 11.4% of the proportional vote. In the 1996 presidential elections, moreover, Zhirinovskii came no better than a poor fifth in the first round, with only 5.7% of the vote.

Having called for the banning of all communist formations, Zhirinovskii led the LDPR to a further major setback in the December 1999 State Duma elections, in which the party slumped to 17 seats and 6% of the proportional vote. Even worse followed in the March 2000 presidential elections, in which the LDPR leader obtained only 2.7% of the vote.

Dissatisfaction over the country's mediocre economic performance in the succeeding years, resentments over the Government's centralization drive and concerns over increased terrorist attacks worldwide served to rescue the LDPR's fortunes as a strident opposition voice at the legislative elections in December 2003. Receiving 11.6% of the vote, it won 36 seats, making it the fourth largest party within the Duma. In the 2004 presidential elections Zhirinovskii effectively acknowledged President Vladimir **Putin**'s insurmountable position by refusing to accept the LDPR candidacy himself, and the party's eventual choice came fifth, polling just 2% of the vote.

The LDPR remains to the far right with calls for the return of imperial borders, capital punishment and economic protectionism.
Leadership: Vladimir Zhirinovskii (Chair).
Address: Lukov per. 9, Moscow 103045.
Telephone: (495) 6921195.
Fax: (495) 6929242.
E-mail: pressldpr@list.ru
Internet: www.ldpr.ru

Liberal International

The world union of 83 liberal parties in 58 countries, founded in 1947.
President: Lord Alderdice.
Address: 1 Whitehall Place, London, SW1A 2HD, UK.
Telephone: (20) 78395905.
Fax: (20) 79252685.
E-mail: all@liberal-international.org
Internet: www.liberal-international.org

Livonia

A historic term for an area in the hinterland of the Baltic coast comprising territory now in modern Estonia, Latvia and the **Russian Federation**. After the conquest of the region by the German Teutonic Knights in the early 13th century it was given the name Livland (Livonia in Latin) after the Livs, a **Finno-Ugric** tribe native to the area but later replaced by Latvians and Estonians. After centuries of rule the area was divided and redivided by conquest and war until the 18th century when Livonia was occupied by Russia and split into the administrative districts of Estonia (to the north), Livonia (in the centre: modern-day southern Estonia and northern Latvia) and Courland (modern-day southern Latvia). The concept of Livonia was effectively lost in 1917 when Estonia and Latvia claimed their independence, dividing historic Livonia once again. These territorial boundaries were passed down to the present day.

Lukashenka, Alyaksandr

President of **Belarus** since 1994. Alyaksandr Lukashenka was manager of a collective farm in the **Soviet** and immediate post-Soviet era. At the international level he has made close relations with **Russia** the centrepiece of his presidency, but has become increasingly isolated within Europe as the head of a regime which lacks convincing democratic credentials. He continues to favour a considerable degree of state regulation of the economy.

Alyaksandr Grigorjevich Lukashenka was born on 30 August 1954 in the village of Kopys in north-eastern Belarus. He graduated from the history faculty of the Mogilev Pedagogical Institute in 1975. He also has a degree in agricultural and industrial economics from the Belarusian Agricultural Academy (1985).

During his military service in 1975 and 1977, he worked as a political propagandist with the Soviet border troops in Brest and then in 1977–78 in the Communist Youth League (Komsomol). From 1980 to 1982 he rejoined the army as a deputy company commander but then moved to various positions within the command economy. He rose to the post of Deputy Chairman of the collective farm in Shklov and then Deputy Manager of a construction materials factory in the same town. In 1987 he became head of the Harazdiec farm in the Mogilev region, a post he held until 1994.

In July 1990 Lukashenka was elected as a deputy to the Supreme Council of the Belarusian Soviet Socialist Republic and founded a Communists for Democracy group of deputies. At the time of the short-lived **August coup** against Soviet President Mikhail **Gorbachev** in 1991 he supported the 'national emergency committee' which briefly seized power in the **Kremlin**. In December of the same year he was the only deputy in the Belarus Supreme Council to vote against the formation of the **Commonwealth of Independent States** (CIS).

Lukashenka subsequently built up his popularity as Chairman of the Supreme Council's Commission for the Struggle against Corruption, a post to which he was appointed in April 1993. The Commission's allegations played a key role in ousting the reformist Stanislau Shushkevich as Chairman of the Supreme Council in January the following year. A new Constitution providing for a presidential form of government opened the way for direct presidential elections held in two rounds in June and July 1994. In an unexpected result, Lukashenka was elected President for a five-year term, polling 44.8% of the vote in the first round and 80.1% in the second.

Working with the then Russian president Boris **Yeltsin**, Lukashenka oversaw the drafting of a full Union treaty in December 1999, setting 2005 as the deadline for full integration of the political and economic structures of Belarus and Russia. However, the election of President Vladimir **Putin** in Russia in 2000 put a brake on the pace of unification and strained relations, weakening Lukashenka's position. A draft agreement on the adoption of the Russian rouble as the common currency was signed in June 2003, but Lukashenka stalled the process later that year as relations deteriorated.

Domestically Lukashenka has come increasingly into conflict with the legislature, the judiciary, the media and the wider public, as he has strengthened his hold on power. A referendum on 24 November 1996 received a 70.4% 'yes' vote for establishing a bicameral **National Assembly** and extending Lukashenka's term of office to the year 2001. The opposition denounced the vote as a 'farce' designed to legitimize a dictatorship and strongly denounced the later extension of Lukashenka's term to 2002.

Nevertheless, Lukashenka was re-elected in 'early' presidential elections on 9 September 2001, with 75% of the vote. The opposition candidate Vladimir Goncharik was backed by the international community in claiming large-scale fraud and intimidation during the election. In 2002 the **European Union** (EU) responded to Lukashenka's authoritarian regime by banning him and his Government from travelling to EU member states. He replied by allegedly threatening to help illegal immigrants across the border into Poland in protest at the EU's refusal to compensate Belarus for maintaining its border security.

A crackdown on dissenting media outlets in August 2004 preceded a referendum (held alongside Assembly elections) in October whereby Lukashenka got 80% backing for the removal of the constitutional limit of two presidential terms in office. The opposition decried the referendum as a move that gave Lukashenka the presidency for life, while US and EU election observers said that the poll fell 'significantly' short of being free and fair; the USA imposed sanctions and the EU reinstated and broadened its visa ban.

In 2005 US Secretary of State Condoleezza Rice labelled Belarus as Europe's 'last true dictatorship' and one of the world's six 'outposts of tyranny'. Many in the West openly hoped for a '**colour revolution**' mirroring those that had recently ousted repressive leaders in **Georgia**, **Ukraine** and Kyrgyzstan. Lukashenka warned that any such attempt would be doomed to failure. Opposition activists were arrested in the run-up to the 2006 presidential poll, which Lukashenka won with a landslide 82.6% of the vote. Thousands of demonstrators took to the streets to protest the result; around 500 were arrested, including opposition candidate Alyaksandr Milinkevich. Observers declared the vote had not been free and fair, and the international community again condemned the autocratic regime, extending sanctions further. Nevertheless Lukashenka was inaugurated for a third term on 31 March.

Lukashenka is married to Galina Rodionovna, and they have two sons.

Address: Office of the President, Dom Urada, vul. Karl Marksa 38, 220016
       Minsk.
Telephone: (17) 2223217.
Fax: (17) 2260610.
E-mail: contact@president.gov.by
Internet: www.president.gov.by

LUKoil

The largest private oil-producing, refining and exporting company in the **Russian Federation**. LUKoil was founded in 1991 through the merger of three of the biggest oil concerns in western **Siberia**: Langepasneftegaz, Uraineftegaz and Kogalymneftegaz. Since then it has expanded operations to other areas of the

Russian Federation and particularly oil fields in Kazakhstan. In 1999 LUKoil absorbed the KomiTEK company, Russia's largest merger by a private company. LUKoil operates in 30 different countries and controls one of the biggest oil reserves in private hands, accounting for 18% of all oil produced in the Russian Federation and employing 150,000 people worldwide.

President: Vagit Yusufovich Alekperov.
Address: Sretenski blvd 11, 101000 Moscow.
Telephone: (495) 6274444.
Fax: (495) 6257016.
E-mail: pr@lukoil.com
Internet: www.lukoil.com

M

MAK *see* **United Labour Party**.

Mammadyarov, Elmar

Minister of Foreign Affairs, **Azerbaijan**. Elmar Maharram oglu Mammadyarov is a career diplomat and was Azerbaijan's Ambassador to Italy prior to his appointment as Foreign Minister on 2 April 2004.

Born on 2 July 1960 in **Baku**, he graduated from the School of International Relations and International Law at Kiev State University in 1982. He spent the next six years working at the Ministry of Foreign Affairs, before entering the Diplomatic Academy of the Ministry of Foreign Affairs of the **Soviet Union** in 1988 where he gained a doctorate in history. During this time he spent a year in the USA as an exchange scholar at the Center for Foreign Policy Development at Brown University. In 1991 he returned to the Ministry of Foreign Affairs as Director of the Division of State Protocol, and a year later was appointed as First Secretary at the Permanent Mission of the newly independent Republic of Azerbaijan to the UN.

In 1995 he became Deputy Director of the Department of International Organizations in the Ministry of Foreign Affairs. Three years later he was appointed back to the USA as Counsellor at the Embassy in Washington, DC. In 2003 he rose to the rank of Ambassador, with a transfer to the Italian Embassy. His tenure in this post was very short as in April 2004 he was appointed Foreign Minister.

Elmar Mammadyarov is married and has two sons; he speaks Russian, Turkish and English.

Address: Ministry of Foreign Affairs, Shikhali Gurbanov St 4, 1009 Baku.
Telephone: (12) 4929692.
Fax: (12) 4988480.
E-mail: secretariat@mfa.gov.az
Internet: www.mfa.gov.az

Mari El Republic

A republic in the **Volga region** of the **Russian Federation**, some 500 km east of **Moscow**. Absorbed into the Russian Empire in the 15th–16th centuries, the **Finno-Ugric** Mari people (formerly Cheremis) were granted an Autonomous Soviet Socialist Republic (ASSR) in December 1936. Today they constitute around 42% of the 728,000-strong Mari El population. Long contact with the **Russians** brought the Mari to an urban lifestyle and they adopted the **Cyrillic alphabet** to transcribe their language. However, the Mari are unusual among the regional Finns for resisting the spread of **Orthodox Christianity** and still retain elements of the original Finnish animist religion and culture. A crackdown on Mari identity under the **Soviet Union** served to strengthen the connection between Mari nationalism and efforts to preserve the Mari language and culture.

Situated on marshy land extending north from the River Volga, the republic is heavily forested and has a continental climate. Economic activity is centred on the forest and associated products. Raw wood is floated down the Volga to processing plants in the capital Ioshkar-Ola and other cities. Only a third of the republic's population live in rural areas. Mari El receives little in the way of foreign investment or aid. Leonid Igorevich Markelov has been President of Mari El since January 2001.

Markarian, Andranik

Prime Minister of **Armenia**. A computer specialist and career politician who was briefly detained for seditious nationalism under **Soviet** rule, Andranik Markarian is seen as a close ally of President Robert **Kocharian**. Markarian heads the **Republican Party of Armenia** (HHK) and was appointed Prime Minister on 13 May 2000.

Andranik Naapetovich Markarian was born on 12 June 1951 in what was then the Soviet Socialist Republic of Armenia. From an early age he became involved with nationalist activists. In the early 1970s he joined the banned National Unity Party and was arrested by the Soviet authorities in 1974. After two years in a penitential gulag he returned to Armenia. His prisoner-of-conscience past is renowned in Armenia where he insists it does not equate with modern-day anti-Russian sentiment.

Following the assassination of Prime Minister Vazgen Sarkissian in a shoot-out in the **National Assembly** building in October 1999, and the dismissal in May 2000 of his brother and successor Aram Sarkissian, the President filled the vacuum with Markarian, who had become the new Chair of the HHK, which was the leading member of the powerful Unity (Miasnutiun) parliamentary bloc.

Upon his appointment Markarian faced hostility from large factions of the Unity bloc and promptly relieved himself of dissident ministers mostly from the

Yerkrapah Union of Veterans of the Karabakh War. Despite resistance from the National Assembly, Markarian pledged to continue the policies of his immediate predecessors and to rule a Government of accord. A major part of his new policy revolved around an ending of conflict between the Government and Kocharian, a position that led to the break-up of the Unity alliance.

Pro-presidential parties dominated the National Assembly after the May 2003 elections and Markarian remained in post heading a coalition of the HHK, the **Country of Law Party** (OY) and the **Armenian Revolutionary Federation** (Dashnak). OY withdrew in mid-2006 after its leaders had begun pushing for greater European integration.

Markarian is married with two daughters and one son.

Address: Office of the Prime Minister, Government House, Republic Sq., 375010 Yerevan.
Telephone and Fax: (10) 528712.
E-mail: press@arminco.com
Internet: www.gov.am

Martynov, Sergei

Minister of Foreign Affairs, **Belarus**. Sergei N. Martynov is a career diplomat who has been Foreign Minister since 21 March 2003.

Born on 22 February 1953, he graduated from the Moscow State Institute of International Relations in 1975 and worked in the Department of International Economic Organizations until 1991 when he was posted as Deputy Permanent Representative of the Republic of Belarus to the UN. A year later he moved to the US Embassy, initially as Chargé d'Affaires, but then promoted to Ambassador in 1993. In 1997 he was recalled to Belarus to become First Deputy Minister of Foreign Affairs. Four years later he headed to Brussels, as Ambassador to Belgium and Head of the Belarusian Missions to the **European Union** and the **North Atlantic Treaty Organization**. In 2003 he returned again to Belarus on his appointment as Foreign Minister.

Sergei Martynov is married and has two sons. He speaks English, French and Swahili.

Address: Ministry of Foreign Affairs, Lenin St 19, 220030 Minsk.
Telephone: (17) 2272922.
Fax: (17) 2274521.
E-mail: mail@mfabelar.gov.by
Internet: www.mfa.gov.by

MEP *see* **Baku–Tbilisi–Ceyhan pipeline**.

Meskhetians

A people of undetermined **Turkic/Kurdish** origin who were deported *en masse* from their homeland in southern **Georgia** in 1944. During the final stages of the Second World War, Stalin's paranoia reached such heights that whole ethnic groups around the **Soviet Union** were uprooted and exiled to **Siberia** and central Asia. The Meskhetians were one such unfortunate group and in 1944 around 120,000 were relocated to the steppes of central Asia. Many thousands died on the way. The Meskhetians are significant among the **deported nationalities** as for them the 1950s did not bring rehabilitation and they have largely remained a refugee population ever since. Some 20,000 managed to return to the **Caucasus region**, settling in Georgia and **Azerbaijan**, but the rest were barred from re-entry. Demands for their repatriation to Meskheti increased after bloody attacks on the Meskhetians in the Fergana Valley region of Uzbekistan in 1989.

The collapse of the Soviet Union in 1991 transferred the Meskhetian refugee problem from Moscow to Tbilisi. The Georgian authorities, soon occupied with ethnic separatism themselves, were not keen to establish a new non-Georgian region, especially next to the (so far peaceful) **Armenian** enclave of **Javakheti**. Arguing that the Meskhetian homeland was not in Georgia but ultimately in Turkey, they finally agreed in 1996 to accept 5,000 Meskhetians (of a total population now numbering up to 300,000) over the following four years. However, very few have arrived in Meskheti and some have faced immediate deportation from Georgia despite the decree.

In 2004 the **International Organization for Migration** began overseeing the resettlement of Meskhetians from the Russian region of Krasnodar to the USA. By mid-2006, around 20,000 had applied to the programme and about half had been approved and moved.

Milli Majlis

Common term used in Islamic states for a representative assembly, as used in **Azerbaijan** for the **National Assembly**.

Minsk

The historic capital city of **Belarus**. *Population*: 1.7m. (2003 estimate). The settlement was first mentioned in 1067. The centre of a **White Russian** principality, the city with its surrounding territory was absorbed by Lithuania in the 14th century and later by Poland. In the second partition of Poland in 1793 Minsk was made a regional administrative centre of the **Russian** Empire. Economic activity increased after the completion of a rail link from the Baltic coast to **Ukraine** via Minsk in the 1870s, and its regional importance made it the capital of the emergent Belarusian republic in 1919. However, its position between **eastern Europe** and **European Russia** has led to repeated and damaging military occupation during major campaigns. The city was destroyed by French troops in 1812, by German soldiers in 1918, by Polish conquerors between 1919 and 1920, and by the Germans again in 1941, but the greatest damage occurred during the **Soviet** advance in 1944. The city's large **Jewish** population of around 80,000 had been almost entirely wiped out during the Nazi occupation.

Post-war development produced wide streets and large apartment blocks. The population grew faster than any other Soviet city, tripling from 500,000 in 1959 to 1.6 million by 1989. Minsk became the capital of Belarus and the administrative centre of the **Commonwealth of Independent States** (CIS) in 1991. Its main economic activity today is the production of heavy machinery. As the Belarusian capital it is also home to the **National Assembly** and other government offices.

Minsk Group

A group established in 1992 as an offshoot of the **Organization for Security and Co-operation in Europe** (OSCE) to oversee the peace process in **Nagorno-Karabakh**. The intention was to convene a peace conference on Nagorno-Karabakh, to take place in **Minsk**. Although it has not to this date been possible to hold the conference, the so-called Minsk Group spearheads the OSCE effort to find a political solution to this conflict. In December 1994 the OSCE decided to establish a co-chairmanship for the process, and expressed the political will to deploy multinational peacekeeping forces as an essential part of the overall settlement of the conflict.

> *Members*: **Armenia**, Austria, **Azerbaijan**, **Belarus**, France, Germany, Italy, Portugal, Romania, **Russian Federation**, Sweden, Turkey and the USA.
>
> *Co-Chairs*: Matthew Bryza (USA), Bernard Fassier (France) and Yuri Merzlyakov (Russian Federation).

Mir space station

The world's first permanently-manned space station. Mir (literally 'commune' or 'village', from the Russian word for peace) was launched by the **Soviet Union** in February 1986 and finally brought back to Earth on 23 March 2001, crashing into the Pacific Ocean. Its 15-year history coincided with the end of the **Cold War** and the transition of Russia from communism to democracy. Its launch demonstrated the Soviet Union's ability to out-perform the USA, in a year that the US Space Shuttle programme saw its darkest hour with the *Challenger* disaster. However, the station was not fully completed until 1996, having been given an extension to its original seven-year lifespan, and the final module was attached at a time when US-Russian relations had entered a new co-operative phase. The joint Shuttle-Mir programme saw Russian cosmonauts and US astronauts take part in the two countries' space programmes from 1995 onwards. Cosmonauts aboard Mir performed experiments on the effects of long-term weightlessness, and made many scientific observations of Earth. The increasing cost of maintaining Mir proved too great for the economically-weakened **Russian Federation**, and the station was commercialized in 2000. However, despite the insistence of MirCorp, the new operators, that the station should be maintained as a potential tourist attraction, the Russian Government agreed to destroy the spacecraft to clear the scientific budget for its involvement in the new **International Space Station**, for which Mir had acted as an important base for construction.

Mkhedrioni

A right-wing political faction in **Georgia** formed in September 1998 from the remains of the outlawed paramilitary group of the same name (literally 'warriors'). The original Mkhedrioni was set up in 1988 by bank-robber-turned-playwright Dzhaba Ioseliani as a nationalist pro-democracy group. Its violent activities in 1992 against supporters of the former President Zviad Gamsakhurdia (the **Zviadists**) are well documented, including beatings and torture. By the time of the war with **Abkhazia** in 1993 the group had been legalized by the Georgian Government and had attracted around 3,000 young volunteers, many of whom fought with the regular Georgian forces in the conflict. Relations between the Mkhedrioni and the Georgian Government deteriorated thereafter, however, and the group was banned in 1995. Ioseliani, who at his height had been described by visiting journalists as the second most powerful man in Georgia, was sentenced to 11 years in prison in November 1998 for the group's various crimes, and more specifically, for his involvement in the August 1995 assassination attempt on Georgian President Eduard **Shevardnadze**. Ioseliani was released in May 2000, and elected Chairman of the Mkhedrioni, which had been reformed as a non-violent right-wing political movement calling among other things for an end to the present presidential system. The Mkhedrioni merged with a group of Zviadists, their former opponents, headed by Badri Zarandia, in 2002 to form the Union of Patriots, but Zarandia was assassinated in January 2003 and Ioseliani suffered a heart attack two months later.

MO *see* **Rightist Opposition**.

Moldova
Republica Moldova

A landlocked independent republic in **eastern Europe**, bounded to the north, east and south by **Ukraine**, and to the west by Romania. Administratively, the country is divided into 33 districts, two municipalities and two autonomous entities.

Area: 33,700 sq km; *capital*: **Chişinau**; *population*: 4.2m. (2005 estimate), comprising ethnic **Moldovans** 64.5%, **Ukrainians** 13.8%, **Russians** 13%, Gagauz (*see* **Gagauzia**) 3.5%, **Jews** 1.5%, **Bulgarians** 2%, others 1.7%; *official language*: Moldovan (very close to Romanian); *religion*: Eastern **Orthodox** 98.5%, **Jewish** 1.5%.

Under amendments to the 1994 Constitution adopted in 2000, Moldova is a 'Parliamentary Republic' in which supreme authority is vested in the unicameral **Parliament** (Parlamentul), which has 101 members directly elected for a four-year term by proportional representation of parties which obtain at least 6% of the national vote. The Head of State is the President, who is elected by the Parliament for a four-year term (having before 2000 been directly elected). Executive authority is vested in the Prime Minister and Council of Ministers, subject to approval by the Parliament.

History: Once a Roman province, Moldova became an independent principality in the mid-14th century and was a powerful state under Stefan the Great. A period of decline followed his death, and by the mid-16th century Moldova had become an Ottoman principality. It was then caught up in the struggles between the **Russian** and Ottoman Empires before being partitioned under the Treaty of Bucharest in 1812, by which tsarist Russia annexed the territory, east of the River Prut and stretching to the River Dnester, naming it **Bessarabia**, and the Ottoman Turks retained the region west of the River Prut. The latter region became part of the independent state of Romania under the 1878 Treaty of Berlin, while Bessarabia was incorporated into a **greater Romania** following the First World War.

In 1924 the new Bolshevik regime in Moscow established the Moldovan Autonomous Soviet Socialist Republic (ASSR) on the eastern bank of the Dnestr to signify its non-acceptance of the post-1918 territorial settlement. Soon after the start of the Second World War, Romania was forced to cede Bessarabia to the **Soviet Union**, as agreed under the 1939 **Nazi-Soviet Pact**. The major part of the province was united with the ASSR to form the Moldovan Soviet Socialist Republic, while the southernmost parts were joined to Soviet **Ukraine**. Allied with Nazi Germany, Romanian forces occupied the lost territory from 1941 until the Red Army regained control in 1944, Soviet sovereignty being confirmed by the 1947 Treaty of Paris. The subsequent 'Sovietization' of Moldova included the collectivization of agriculture, the imposition of a **Cyrillic alphabet** to separate the Moldovan and Romanian languages, and immigration of ethnic Russians and Ukrainians.

In the late 1980s the influence of the ***glasnost*** (openness) initiative in the Soviet Union encouraged the growth of a pro-Romanian popular movement in Moldova, whose demands focused on the language issue. A law was passed in 1989 returning Moldovan from the Cyrillic to the Latin alphabet. The following year the communist monopoly of power ceased, the nationalist Moldovan Popular Front securing a majority of seats in the February 1990 elections to the Moldovan Supreme Soviet. The Government declared the sovereignty of the republic and denounced the 1940 Soviet annexation of Bessarabia as illegal. Following the failure of the attempted **August coup** in the Soviet Union to remove President **Gorbachev**, Moldova declared its independence in August 1991. In December, in the first popular presidential election, Mircea Snegur (formerly the Supreme Soviet Presidium Chairman) was elected unopposed.

In parallel developments among Moldova's ethnic minorities, the **Slavs** of **Transdnestria** in the east and the Turkish-speaking people in Gagauzia in the south declared breakaway republics in September 1990, with their capitals in Tiraspol and Komrat respectively. Fearing a resurgence of Romanian nationalism, Slav guerrillas waged war with government forces in Transdnestria, before a Russian-Moldovan peacekeeping force was deployed in July 1992 and a ceasefire declared in August.

The Moldovan Popular Front Government fell in July 1992 and was replaced by a Government of national consensus. In Moldova's first multi-party parliamentary elections in February 1994, the Agrarian Democratic Party of Moldova (PDAM) led by Andrei Sangheli won an overall majority of seats in the new Parliament, the defeat of parties advocating union with Romania being followed by a referendum in March which returned a 95% vote in favour of Moldova's independence. The new Constitution adopted in July 1994 proclaimed the country's neutrality and granted special autonomous status to Gagauzia and Transdnestria within Moldova. However, Transdnestria's leader, Igor Smirnov, called a number of referendums which favoured ultimate independence. A memorandum of understanding was initialled in July 1996 and signed in May 1997 defining Transdnestria as a 'republic within Moldova' and committing the two sides to further negotiations, pending which Russian troops remained deployed in the breakaway republic (see below).

In the second round of presidential elections in December 1996, Petru Lucinschi, the PDAM-backed Speaker of the Parliament, defeated Snegur, who had earlier launched the rival Party of Revival and Accord of Moldova (PRCM) with a cautious leaning towards unification with Romania. In January 1997 President Lucinschi appointed free-market reformer Ion Ciubuc as Prime Minister.

In the March 1998 parliamentary elections the revived **Communist Party of the Moldovan Republic** (PCRM) led by Vladimir **Voronin** became the largest party but failed to win a majority. The various centre-right formations, headed by Snegur's right-wing Democratic Convention of Moldova (CDM) alliance and including pan-Romanian parties, were therefore able to form a majority coalition under the continued premiership of Ciubuc. He was replaced in February 1999 by Ion Sturza, previously Deputy Prime Minister and a member of the Movement for a Democratic and Prosperous Moldova. Before the year was out, however, Sturza had lost a vote of confidence and had been succeeded by Dumitru Braghis (then non-party), who formed a mainly technocratic Government backed by most of the centre-right parties.

Changes secured by the Braghis Government in 2000 included the abolition of the death penalty and the adoption by Parliament of constitutional amendments which curtailed the executive powers of the President, who would henceforth be elected by Parliament rather than by the people (see above). Unsuccessfully resisted by President Lucinschi, the changes meant that Parliament was called upon to elect a new Head of State in December. Amidst increasing disarray on the centre-right, the deputies failed to produce the required majority for any candidate, so that Lucinschi was able to dissolve Parliament and call early elections. Following the dissolution, Prime Minister Braghis launched the Braghis Alliance (AB) electoral bloc of assorted centrist and left-wing parties.

The February 2001 parliamentary elections yielded a landslide victory for the PCRM, which won 71 of the 101 seats. Only two other formations gained representation. In early April 2001 Moldova became the first former communist country to democratically elect a communist as Head of State, when Voronin was elected President by the new Parliament, while later that month Vasile **Tarlev** became Prime Minister of a PCRM Government committed to a strong state role in the economy and the re-establishment of close ties with the Russian Federation.

Pro-Russian policies, including the compulsory teaching of Russian language and history in schools, prompted three months of mass protests in Chişinau in early 2002. In 2003 Voronin announced his support for the Russian-backed plan for a federalized constitution, with Transdnestria becoming a fully autonomous region. Popular protests in Moldova, arguing that the plans aimed to cement Moldova in the Russian sphere of influence, forced him to backtrack in December in favour of a more vague US-sponsored plan involving the deployment of international—rather than just Russian—peacekeepers ahead of a political reorganization of the country. During 2004 he attempted to crack down on smuggling in Transdnestria, and a dispute over the Transdnestrian closure of schools using the Latin script spiralled into mutual recriminations and an economic blockade.

Latest elections: The 6 March 2005 parliamentary elections were won again by the PCRM, but with a reduced majority of 56 of the 101 seats, with 46% of the vote. Again only two other formations gained representation, namely the **Democratic Moldova Bloc** (BMD) with 34 seats (28.5% of the vote) and the **Christian Democratic People's Party** (PPCD) with 11 seats (9.1%). This left the PCRM five seats short of the number required to guarantee the re-election of

Voronin. However, with support from the PPCD Voronin received 75 votes in the ballot and was sworn in for a second and final term on 7 April. He renominated Tarlev as Prime Minister.

Recent developments: In July 2005 the Moldovan Government established Transdnestria as an 'autonomous territorial unit'. Transdnestria responded with a referendum in September 2006 overwhelmingly backing independence.

International relations and defence: Independent Moldova joined the **Commonwealth of Independent States** (CIS) in 1991 and was admitted to the **Organization for Security and Co-operation in Europe** (OSCE) and the UN in 1992. It became a member of NATO's **Partnership for Peace** programme in 1994 and of the **Council of Europe** in 1995. It is also a member of the **Organization of the Black Sea Economic Co-operation** and the **Central European Initiative**. In August 1998 Moldova concluded a border delineation agreement with Ukraine (to allow for the construction of a Moldovan oil terminal on the Danube river). Moldova was a founder member in 1997 of what became the **GUAM group** (with **Georgia**, Ukraine and **Azerbaijan**), set up to counter Russian regional influence. However, Moldova has opted out of GUAM military co-operation, on grounds of its neutrality. Although it effectively abstained from the CIS Collective Security Treaty on these same grounds, a military co-operation agreement signed with the Russian Federation in 1997 was nevertheless speedily ratified by the Moldovan Parliament following the PCRM's election victory in 2001. Relations with Russia subsequently soured, however, over tensions regarding the Transdnestrian breakaway republic. Russian soldiers had begun to pull out of the region on time, under an OSCE timetable for their withdrawal in January 2002, but they were repeatedly delayed—by Transdnestrian non-co-operation according to the Russian authorities. President Voronin declared the continued presence of Russian troops in the region 'illegal' in March 2006. Tensions increased as Ukraine introduced more stringent border controls on Transdnestrian goods, in agreement with the Moldovan Government; the Russian Government responded by openly backing the Transdnestrian separatist cause.

Moldova's defence budget for 2006 amounted to some US \$9.5m., equivalent to about 0.3% of GDP. The size of the armed forces at August 2006 was 6,750 personnel, including those serving under compulsory conscription of 12 months, while reservists numbered an estimated 66,000.

Moldova, economy

The poorest country in Europe, Moldova has faced a slow and difficult transition from Soviet-era central control; steady growth since 2000 has not yet restored the economy to its pre-independence levels. One of the smallest former Soviet republics, Moldova is landlocked but has river access to the Black Sea, and the land is very fertile.

GNP: US $3,172m. (2005); *GNP per capita*: $880 (2005); *GDP at PPP*: $8,026m. (2005); *GDP per capita at PPP*: $1,908 (2005); *exports*: $1,502m. (2005); *imports*: $2,422m. (2005); *currency*: leu (plural: lei; US $1=L12.95 at the end of December 2006).

In 2005 agriculture accounted for 21.3% of GDP, industry for 24.2% and services for 54.5%. Of the workforce of 2.2 million, agriculture accounts for 41%, industry for 16% and services for 43%. Some 56% of the land is arable, 9% under permanent crops, 11% permanent pasture and 10% forests and woodland. The main crops are fruit (notably grapes for wine), tobacco, vegetables and grain, and there is animal husbandry and dairy farming. There are few substantial mineral reserves, although some oil and natural gas fields have been identified. The industrial sector is dominated by food processing, wine and tobacco production, machine-building and metalworking, and light industry. As there is no domestic exploitation of fuel reserves, all energy sources are imported, notably as oil and natural gas from the **Russian Federation**, Romania and **Ukraine**.

Moldova's main exports are foodstuffs, wine, other beverages and tobacco (36% of the total in 2005), textiles and textile articles (18%) and vegetable products (12%). The principal imports are mineral products (22%), machinery and mechanical appliances (14%) and chemical products (10%). The Russian Federation was the principal purchaser of Moldovan exports in 2005 (32% of the total), followed by Italy (12%) and Romania (10%). The principal suppliers of Moldova's imports were Ukraine (21%), the Russian Federation (12%) and Romania (11%).

Within the **Soviet Union**, Moldova had been an important supplier of industrial goods to the other republics, but such activity is concentrated in the eastern **Transdnestria** region, which declared a breakaway republic in 1990. Since then the economies of the two parts of Moldova have functioned largely separately and economic restructuring efforts by the Moldovan Government have been concerned principally with small and medium-sized industries. Independence and the security situation, as well as a severe drought in 1992, combined to cause huge inflation (of some 1,800% in 1993), until the introduction of a new currency in 1993 and a tightening of monetary and fiscal policy resulted in a progressive reduction to about 11% in 1997. However, financial stabilization did not result in improved living standards, as GDP fell sharply following independence, before showing modest growth of 1.6% in 1997. Officially registered unemployment remained low at around 2% in 1997–98, but underemployment was believed to be very high.

Moldova was particularly hard hit by the financial crisis in the Russian Federation (*see* **Russian Federation, economy**) in mid-1998, the sudden collapse of its main export market resulting in a contraction in real GDP of 8.6% in 1998, while the inflation rate rose to over 18% and the national currency lost some 60% of its external value between July 1998 and May 1999. Further GDP contraction of 4.4% was experienced in 1999, in which inflation climbed to over 40%, and

Moldova continued to suffer difficulties in its trade position, notably in paying for its large imports of natural gas from the Russian Federation. Some signs of recovery were apparent in 2000, in which GDP growth of 1.9% was provisionally recorded and inflation was reduced to around 20%.

The successful conclusion in February 2001 of negotiations for Moldova to join the **World Trade Organization** (WTO) boosted confidence in longer-term economic prospects. On the other hand, major doubts about Moldova's commitment to a free-market economy were raised by the election the same month of a communist Government pledged to maintaining a strong state role and even to reintroducing state monopolies in some sectors.

Steady growth of around 6% per annum was achieved from 2001 to 2005, through structural reforms, the increased provision of social services, and rising remittances from Moldovans abroad, particularly from Russia; however, this economic recovery started from a small base because of the contraction of the economy during the 1990s. Inflation dropped to a low of 5% in 2003 and then hovered just over 10% in 2004–05. The poverty rate dropped dramatically from its 1999-level of 73%, though by 2004 26% of the population were still living in poverty, and this figure actually rose in 2005. GDP growth slowed in 2006 to 3%, both as a consequence of rising global energy prices (and the reduction in subsidies on Russian gas imports) and due to a nine-month export ban on Moldovan wine imposed by Russia as part of the ongoing political confrontation over Transdnestria. These issues also increased the Government's budget deficit and threatened to send inflation upwards again.

An economic reform plan adopted in 1991 anticipated a programme of privatization, largely through the issue of vouchers (*see* **voucher privatization**), but this was slow in taking off and was replaced by a new scheme in 1994. By 1996 privatized enterprises were estimated to account for some two-thirds of Moldova's industrial base. In December 1998 parliamentary approval was given to the privatization of the monopoly provider of telecommunications services and the sale of certain power companies, while in 2000 the privatization of agricultural land was accelerated. In April 2000, however, the **Parliament** rejected proposals for the privatization of the state-owned wine and tobacco industries, and the communist Government elected in 2001 cancelled several more privatization agreements, raising concerns among foreign investors of possible plans for renationalization. President **Voronin**'s first term in office saw relations with Russia sour and an increasing reorientation towards the West; the Government pledged in 2004 to reorganize companies in which the Government had more than a 50% stake into 'people's enterprises', 75% owned by the workers. By 2005 the privatization process was relaunched, and measures were being taken to combat smuggling and arms-trading on the Transdnestrian–Ukrainian border.

Moldovan Export Promotion Organization (MEPO)
Organisaţia de Promovare a Exportului din Moldova

A specialized agency of the Ministry of Economics and Commerce of **Moldova** facilitating foreign investment and trade.

Address: Trade Information Centre, Str. Alexei Mateevici 65, 2009
        Chişinau.
Telephone: (22) 273654.
Fax: (22) 224310.
E-mail : office@mepo.net
Internet: www.mepo.net

Moldovan Stock Exchange (MSE)
Bursa de Valori a Moldovei SA

The stock exchange in **Chişinau**, **Moldova**, established in December 1994. Trading began in June 1995 and with US assistance the MSE was upgraded to a 'modern exchange' by October that year. By 31 January 2007, 20 joint-stock companies were listed on the MSE and trading was conducted in shares of around 1000 unlisted firms. Trade volume in 2006 reached US $26.8m.

Chair: Corneliu Dodu.
Address: Blvd Ştefan cel Mare 73, 2001 Chişinau.
Telephone: (22) 277594.
Fax: (22) 277368.
E-mail: dodu@moldse.md
Internet: www.moldse.md

Moldovans

A Romance people dominant in **Moldova** and ethnically identical to the neighbouring **Romanians**. Like the Romanians they are descended from ancient **Vlach** communities, and largely follow the Eastern **Orthodox Christian** faith. Moldovans can be distinguished from Romanians by the use of the **Cyrillic alphabet** to transcribe their form of the shared Romanian language. Separated from the rest of Romania by imperial **Russian** occupation in 1812 the Moldovans have since been strongly russified, particularly during the Soviet era.

Calls for reunification with Romania followed the collapse of the **Soviet Union** in 1991. Any chance of realizing this idea was dispelled, however, by regional separatism in Moldova's non-Moldovan enclaves, particularly the struggle of the mixed Moldovan/Russian population of **Transdnestria**. The dire economic plight of Moldova has forced a great many Moldovans to seek seasonal employment in neighbouring countries.

Moldpres–State Information Agency

The state news agency of **Moldova**. Separated from the state broadcasting monopoly in 1997, Moldpres continues to provide news from Moldova to other regional news agencies, chiefly **ITAR-TASS**. As the state agency it also specializes in official statements and releases.

Director: Valeriu Renita.
Address: Str. Puşkin 22, 2012 Chişinau.
Telephone: (22) 232629.
Fax: (22) 232698.
E-mail: director@moldpres.md
Internet: www.moldpres.md

Molotov-Ribbentrop Pact *see* **Nazi-Soviet Pact**.

Mordovia

A constituent and impoverished republic of the **Russian Federation** situated in the centre of **European Russia**. *Population*: 888,800 (2002 estimate). The **Finno-Ugric** Mordvin constitute a third of the republic's population and are divided into two distinct groups—the Erzya and the Moksha—with mutually unintelligible languages. They first encountered ethnic **Russians** as early as the 12th century and came under direct Russian rule after the fall of the Kazan khanate in 1552. This long contact with Russian culture has somewhat diluted Mordvin identity, a process speeded up during the **Soviet** era. Mordovia (also known as Mordvinia) was made an autonomous *oblast* (region) in 1930 and a full republic from 1934. Nikolay Ivanovich Merkushkin has been President of the Republic since September 1995.

Unlike the other **Volga**-Ural republics Mordovia was not heavily industrialized and agriculture remains the main economic activity. Most crops are grains, but some tobacco and hemp are also harvested. The Mordvin are renowned as expert beekeepers, and also raise livestock including horses. Light industries focus on agricultural and timber products. Peat is burned as fuel at the capital Saransk.

Moscow

The capital and largest city of the **Russian Federation**, situated in the west of **European Russia** on the Moskva river. *Population*: 10.1m. (2002 estimate). The foundation of the city is generally ascribed to the Russian Prince, Yuri Dolgoruky, who held a feast in Moscow in 1147. The site of the contemporary wooden settlement corresponds to the modern citadel, or **Kremlin**. The location of the town, near important riverine trade routes, led to its growing importance under the suzerainty of the **Tatar** Golden Horde from 1237. Having become a separate principality in its own right, Moscow ceased paying tribute to the Horde under the reign of Ivan III ('the Great') in the 15th century. Despite being briefly captured by Polish forces in the 1570s, the Muscovite state spread rapidly into the surrounding Russian lands and formed the basis of the future Russian Empire over the course of the following centuries and under the rule of the **Romanov dynasty** from 1613. At this time it was one of the largest cities in the world with over 200,000 occupants. Its international importance was founded on its position as the foremost **Slavic** state in Europe and the home of the **Orthodox Christian** Church—earning it the title 'the Third Rome'.

Despite the removal of the Russian capital from Moscow to **St Petersburg** in 1712, the city remained an important political, cultural and economic centre, situated as it was near to the geographic middle of the Empire. All Russian Tsars continued to be crowned in the city and the invading armies of Napoleon Bonaparte sought its capture as the key to taking the entire Empire. Following the defeat of Russian forces at the 1812 Battle of Borodino, Napoleon's army entered a deserted city which was burned to the ground that night, forcing the invading army to begin its disastrous retreat from Russian territory. The city was rapidly rebuilt as the heart of the modernizing state. In 1851 it was connected to the capital by one of the country's first railways and became the terminus of the famous **Trans-Siberian Railway** in 1891. By the opening of the 20th century the city's population passed one million. During the October Revolution of 1917, Moscow was the scene of some of the worst street violence across the country. It was restored to its status as the capital of Russia in 1918 as German forces encroached on St Petersburg (which had recently been renamed Petrograd).

As capital of the **Soviet Union**, Moscow was developed as the centre of the vast bureaucracy and remodelled along Stalinist lines in a comprehensive and ambitious development plan. The underground rail system was completed in 1935. Unlike St Petersburg (by now renamed Leningrad), Moscow did not suffer direct attack during the Second World War, although German forces came within 40 km of the capital in December 1941. Development continued after the war with many high-rise buildings and housing developments spreading across the old city. The urban sprawl advanced on the surrounding region and the earlier charm of the city was overshadowed by concrete and glass. As the political heart of the Soviet Union, Moscow was also home to the pro-democracy movement in the 1980s. Boris **Yeltsin**, the head of the city's municipal branch of the **Communist Party of the Soviet Union**, purged the city administration of the **nomenklatura** and gave permission for open demonstrations on the streets. His personal popularity in the city secured mass support for his stand against communist hardliners during the 1991 **August coup**, and ultimately his election as President. Moscow remained the Russian capital after the collapse of the Soviet Union in December 1991. The post-Soviet city has faced similar problems to other urban areas in the Russian Federation: economic instability and rising crime. Its fortunes have reflected those of the country at large.

Moscow is home to a variety of industries and is the main transport hub for the entire country. The Federal Government is based there, in the Kremlin and the **White House**, as are the headquarters of major financial and cultural institutions.

Moscow Stock Exchange (MSE)

The main stock exchange of the **Russian Federation**, established in March 1997. There are in addition a number of regional exchanges and an active electronic trading system, the **Russian Trading System** (RTS).

President: Victor Utkin.
Address: ul. Vsevoloda Vishnyevek, dom 4, 127422 Moscow.
Telephone: (495) 7713580.
Fax: (495) 7713581.
E-mail: mse@mse.ru
Internet: www.mse.ru

Moscow theatre siege

A hostage crisis in the House of Culture of the State Ball-Bearing Plant Number 1 in the **Russian Federation**'s capital. On 23 October 2002, during the second act of *Nord-Ost*, 42 **Chechen** militants (including 18 women) seized the packed theatre, armed with guns, grenades and explosives. The 850 hostages—audience and performers—were held for two and a half days before Russian special forces stormed the building after pumping an anaesthetic aerosol in through the air-conditioning system to incapacitate the hostage-takers. All the militants were killed, along with a total of 128 hostages: most of the fatalities were due to the effects of the gas. Chechen rebel leader Shamil Basayev claimed responsibility for the attack: his group were also later to carry out the **Beslan school siege** in 2004.

Efforts to treat the surviving hostages were hampered by the Russian authorities' refusal to reveal the type of gas used. After intense domestic and international pressure, it was described as a fentanyl derivative, and is now generally thought to have been Kolokol-1 developed by the KGB (*see* **Federal Security Service**).

President Vladimir **Putin** used the heightened sense of fear in Russia following the crisis to push forward his plans for centralization of power and increase his control of the media. The Duma (lower house of the **Federal Assembly**) refused to hold an official inquiry into the handling of the siege.

Motherland
Rodina

A leading left-wing bloc in the **Russian Federation** which has eaten into the traditional support base of the **Communist Party of the Russian Federation** (KPRF). Motherland is a union of left-wing, patriotic parties and was created under the guidance of leading left-wing activists Sergei Glazyev and Dmitrii Rogozin. The two came together after Glazyev, an economist and head of the Party of Russian Regions, had been rejected in his advances towards an alliance with the KPRF. Rogozin, the Chairman of the nationalist Congress of Russian Communities, had abandoned his membership of the **People's Party of the Russian Federation** (NPRF) in mid-2003 and made the unexpected move towards Glazyev rather than the pro-Putin **United Russia** (YR) party. (Many other erstwhile NPRF deputies pledged their allegiance to YR.)

Motherland scored a notable success in the December 2003 legislative elections, winning 9.1% of the vote and 37 seats in the Duma (lower house of the **Federal Assembly**). The KPRF was the first to accuse the Government of engineering the creation of Motherland in order to undermine its own support.

Almost immediately, tensions between Rogozin and Glazyev became apparent. Glazyev announced his intention to run against President Vladimir **Putin** in 2004, and was promptly pushed from the leadership of Motherland. Running as an independent candidate he came third in the poll with 4% of the vote. Rogozin attempted to unite leftist parties under the Motherland banner, and had some success when the People's Will–Party of National Rebirth joined with it in 2004. His own increasingly anti-Putin stance, however, led to his replacement as party Chairman at the 2006 congress by Aleksandr Babakov.

Leadership: Aleksandr Babakov (Chair).
Address: ul. Bolshaya Dmitrovka 32/1, 107031 Moscow.
Telephone: (495) 2211515.
E-mail: info@rodina-nps.ru
Internet: www.rodina-nps.ru

Musavat *see* **Equality**.

Muslim peoples

People who have embraced Islam, including over 20 ethnic groups in **eastern Europe**. Islam is the second largest religion in the world with around 1,400 million adherents. It is divided into two main denominations, the majority Sunni and the smaller Shi'a sect. The biggest populations of Muslims in Europe can be found in the **Balkans**, in southern **European Russia** and the **Caucasus**. Islam was brought to these regions by the invading **Turkic peoples** in the 14th century and, although their political power was shattered by the early 20th century, their religious legacy has been the source of ethnic tensions into the 21st century, and a significant element in conflicts in Bosnia and Herzegovina, **Chechnya**, **Dagestan** and Macedonia. The wide variety of languages, and intermingling of Muslim with non-Muslim peoples, particularly in the **Russian Federation**, dilutes pan-Islamic sentiment among European Muslims, but such sentiment is nevertheless significant, notably in the Caucasus, where it has heightened since the commencement of the war in Afghanistan in 2001 and the 2003 US-led invasion of Iraq.

The only majority Muslim independent states in Europe (not including Turkey which lies mostly in Asia) are **Azerbaijan** (93% Muslim) and Albania (70%). Other majority Muslim republics lie within the Russian Federation. Ethnic groups in eastern Europe with a majority of Muslim followers are the **Abaza**, Abkhaz (*see* **Abkhazia**), Adygei (*see* **Adygeya**), Adzharians (*see* **Adzharia**), Albanians, **Azeris**, Balkars (*see* **Kabardino-Balkaria**), Bashkirs (*see* **Bashkortostan**), Bosniaks, Bulgarian Turks, Chechens, **Cherkess**, Ingush (*see* **Ingushetia**), Kabards, Karachai (*see* **Karachai-Cherkessia**), **Kazakhs**, **Kumyks**, **Kurds**, **Meskhetians**, Ossetes (*see* **Ossetia question**), Pomaks and the **Tatars**, together with the majority of peoples in the ethnically-mixed republic of Dagestan.

N

NACC (North Atlantic Co-operation Council) *see* Euro-Atlantic Partnership Council.

Nagorno-Karabakh

An effectively autonomous **Armenian**-populated enclave in western **Azerbaijan**. *Population*: 145,000 (2002 estimate). *Capital*: Xankändi (formerly Stepanakert). Tensions between the predominantly Armenian (and Christian) population and the **Azeri** (**Muslim**) authorities led to a protracted war between **Armenia** and Azerbaijan in 1988–94, and a final peace accord remains elusive.

Between 1920 and 1923 Nagorno-Karabakh was officially an autonomous Armenian region within the Transcaucasian Republic, but this status was revoked by Stalin in his role as the then **Soviet** Commissar for nationalities, and it was instead ceded to the Azeri republic. Both Armenia and Azerbaijan now lay claim to the mountainous district, centred on Xankändi. Attempts by the 75% Armenian community to assert Nagorno-Karabakh's independence from Azerbaijan in 1988 led to a series of armed clashes with Azeri forces. The move was popularly supported in Armenia although the Government there has never officially admitted any military involvement in the ensuing war.

The Soviet military was deployed in the region but failed to calm tensions. A period of direct rule from Moscow was dropped in November 1989 and the Armenian Government declared that Nagorno-Karabakh should become a part of the Armenian republic, which became independent in 1991. The situation escalated into all-out war in 1992, when a Karabakh legislature was created and independence for the 'Nagorno-Karabakh Republic' (NKR) was approved through referendum. In the following two years Karabakh forces successfully beat back their Azeri opponents. They claimed control both of the enclave and of the Lechin corridor joining it to neighbouring Armenia—a total area equal to about 15% of Azeri territory. Ethnic Armenians living in the rest of Azerbaijan, facing a series of bloody pogroms, migrated to the enclave and Armenia proper in their thousands.

For Azeris in the NKR the situation was similar the other way around. The land of evicted Azeris was given over to arriving Armenians. An effective Azeri counter-offensive in early 1994 prompted moves to secure a ceasefire, which has held ever since. Peace talks, however, have been mired in nationalist rhetoric, unable to deal with the intractable problem of evicted nationals from both sides, while the Karabakh authorities became increasingly resistant to any form of accommodation which would leave the enclave still part of Azerbaijan. Renewed efforts to bring the two sides together in Key West, Florida, in 2001 proved fruitless, with an outline proposal being rejected on closer inspection.

Some suggestions for a compromise included territory-swaps involving the Lechin corridor and land in southern Armenia adjacent to the Azeri **Nakhichevan** exclave. Hopes of a renewed effort in the peace process rose briefly in December 2003 when the new President of Azerbaijan, Ilham **Aliyev**, held preliminary talks with his Armenian counterpart Robert **Kocharian**. Since then, however, both countries have increased their defence spending and further presidential summits have failed to reach any agreements, leaving the international community exasperated over both sides' intransigence.

The NKR effectively administers itself as an independent republic, even issuing its own car licence plates. It uses the Armenian dram as currency. Its army, largely funded by covert donations from Armenia and the Armenian diaspora, is considered one of the most efficient in the **Commonwealth of Independent States**. Arkadii Ghukasian has been President of the NKR since September 1997.

Nakhichevan
(Naxçivan)

An autonomous **Azeri** exclave sandwiched between **Armenia**, Iran and Turkey on the north bank of the Aras river. It is 30 km at nearest approach to the rest of **Azerbaijan**, of which it is part. *Population*: 367,100 (2003 estimate). Like the rest of Azerbaijan, Nakhichevan and its similarly-titled capital city, has had a long history of conquest and reconquest. It finally passed to the **Russian** Empire in 1828. Having a predominantly Azeri population it became an autonomous region under the **Soviet** authorities from 1924, and maintained strong links with Azerbaijan. When the Soviet Union collapsed in 1991 Nakhichevan became a part of independent Azerbaijan.

The conflict in 1992–94 with Armenia over the **Armenian**-dominated **Nagorno-Karabakh** enclave in Azerbaijan raised tensions in Nakhichevan. With Armenian troops making successful gains across the border in the main part of Azerbaijan, it was feared that the exclave could be targeted next. However, the proximity of Azerbaijan's ally Turkey effectively guaranteed the area's security. Ongoing discussions on the Nagorno-Karabakh issue have included Armenian claims to the area of Nakhichevan, and some have even suggested a 'population swap' for the two regions, with Azerbaijan ceding its sovereignty over Nakhichevan.

NAM *see* **Non-Aligned Movement**.

National Assembly (Armenia)
Azgayin Joghov

The unicameral legislature of **Armenia**. It has 131 members, directly elected for a four-year term. The last elections were held on 25 May 2003 (with three seats contested on 14–15 June). Under the new Constitution approved by referendum in 2005, the National Assembly will have a five-year term from the 2007 elections.
  Address: Baghramian Avenue 19, 375095 Yerevan.
  Telephone: (10) 588225.
  Fax: (10) 529826.
  E-mail: info@parliament.am
  Internet: www.parliament.am

National Assembly (Azerbaijan)
Milli Majlis

The unicameral legislature of **Azerbaijan**. It has 125 members, directly elected for a five-year term. The last elections were held on 6 November 2005.
  Address: Parliamentary Avenue 1, 1152 Baku.
  Telephone: (12) 4399750.
  Fax: (12) 4934943.
  E-mail: azmm@meclis.gov.az
  Internet: www.meclis.gov.az

National Assembly (Belarus)
Natsionalnoye Sobranie

The bicameral legislature of **Belarus**, comprising the House of Representatives (Palata Predstaviteley) and the Council of the Republic (Soviet Respubliki). The lower House of Representatives has 110 members, directly elected for a maximum of four years. It met for the first time on 17 December 1996, and consisted of members of the previous legislature, the Supreme Council. The upper Council of the Republic has 56 members elected by regional Soviets, and eight members appointed by the President, all for four-year terms. It first met on 13 January 1997. The last elections were held on 17–18 and 27 October 2004 and

20 March 2005 (House of Representatives) and 15 October and 21 November 2004 (Council of the Republic).

Address of lower house: ul. Sovetskaya 11, 220010 Minsk.
Telephone: (17) 2273784.
Fax: (17) 2223178.
E-mail: admin@house.gov.by
Internet: www.house.gov.by
Address of upper house: ul. Krasnoarmeiskaya 4, 220016 Minsk.
Telephone: (17) 2891181.
Fax: (17) 2272318.
E-mail: cr@sovrep.gov.by
Internet: www.sovrep.gov.by

National Bank of Azerbaijan

The central bank of **Azerbaijan**. Established in 1992, the Bank is an arm of the state which attempts to regulate the national currency, the manat (which replaced the rouble and became sole legal tender in 1994). The Bank also regulates banking in Azerbaijan and deals in the securities market as well as foreign currencies. As at December 2003 the Bank held reserves of 397,413m. manats.

Chair: Elman Roustamov.
Address: R. Bebutov küç 32, 1014 Baku.
Telephone: (12) 4931122.
Fax: (12) 4935541.
E-mail: mail@nba.az
Internet: www.nba.az

National Bank of Georgia (NBG)

The central bank of **Georgia**. The NBG was founded in 1991 from the Georgian branches of the State Bank of the **Soviet Union**. It is the 'bank of banks', overseeing currency policy and supervising and regulating the banking industry. Although it is independent it is the banker of the Government. The NBG has issued the lari from December 1995, although the notes are printed in France. As at December 2002 the NBG had reserves of 46.2m. lari.

President and Chair of Board: Irakli Managadze.
Address: Leonidze 3/5, 0105 Tbilisi.
Telephone: (32) 996505.
Fax: (32) 999346.
E-mail: nbg@access.sunet.ge
Internet: www.nbg.gov.ge

National Bank of Moldova
Banca Naţionala a Moldovei (BNM)

The central bank of **Moldova**. A two-tier banking system was established in 1991 creating the BNM from the remains of the Soviet State Bank. Its main concern is overseeing monetary policy. The Moldovan leu was introduced by the Bank in November 1993 and helped to control rampant inflation, bringing it down from 2705.7% in that year to just 11.2% in 1998. Although the Bank is independent of the Government it is answerable to **Parliament**. From 1995 the BNM has also been responsible for regulating the country's banking system. As at December 2004 the BNM had reserves of 352.4m. lei.

Governor: Leonid Talmaci.
Address: Blvd Renaşterii 7, 2006 Chişinau.
Telephone: (22) 406006.
Fax: (22) 220591.
E-mail: official@bnm.org
Internet: www.bnm.org

National Bank of the Republic of Belarus (NBRB)

The central bank of **Belarus**. A Belarusian branch of the Soviet State Bank was established in **Minsk** in 1922 and acted as a central bank for the Belarusian republic within the **Soviet Union**. It was temporarily rehoused during the Nazi invasion of the Soviet Union in the Second World War, and at one time was based in Kazakhstan. The Bank returned to Minsk in 1944. It was transformed into the National Bank of Belarus in December 1990 and took on the role of regulating the country's currency and banking industry. The Belarusian rouble was introduced in 1992 and suffered massive hyperinflation until 1994, the year in which it fully replaced the old Soviet rouble. The planned reintroduction of the Russian rouble as a precursor to the introduction of a joint currency in 2008 has been postponed. The Belarusian rouble was readjusted in December 2000. As of January 2004 the Bank had reserves of 483,958m. readjusted Belarusian roubles.

Chair: Pyotr P. Prakapovich.
Address: pr. Nezavisimosti 20, 220008 Minsk.
Telephone: (17) 2192303.
Fax: (17) 2274879.
E-mail: email@nbrb.by
Internet: www.nbrb.by

National Bank of Ukraine

The central bank of **Ukraine**. An office of the **Russian** imperial State Bank in

Kiev was first opened in 1839 and the building remains the home of the National Bank which emerged in March 1991. The Bank controls monetary policy and regulates the banking sector. It began issuing the karbovanets in November 1992 to replace the Russian rouble but was forced to supersede the currency with the hryvna in September 1996 as part of widespread banking reforms. As at December 2003 the Bank had reserves of 4,575m. hryvnas.

Governor: Volodymyr Stelmach.
Address: vul. Institutska 9, 01008 Kiev.
Telephone: (44) 2534478.
Fax: (44) 2302033.
E-mail: postmaster@bank.gov.ua
Internet: www.bank.gov.ua

National Democratic Alliance Party
Azgayin Zhoghovordakan Dashink (AZhD)

A minor party in **Armenia** formed in 2001 following a split in the **National Democratic Union**. It contested the May 2003 election as part of the **Justice** (Ardartyun) bloc, alongside its former ally.

Leadership: Arshak Sadoian (Chair).
Address: Yerevan.

National Democratic Party
Azgayin Zhoghovordavarutuyan Kusaktsutuyun (AZhK)

A minor party in **Armenia** formed in 2001 following a split in the **National Democratic Union**. It contested the May 2003 election as part of the **Justice** (Ardartyun) bloc, alongside its former ally.

Leadership: Shavarsh Kocharian (Chair).
Address: Abovian St 12, Yerevan.
Telephone and Fax: (10) 563188.
E-mail: adjm@arminco.com

National Democratic Union
Azgayin Zhoghovrdavarakan Miutyun (AZhM)

A centre-right political party in **Armenia** formed by Vazgen Manukian following his resignation as Prime Minister in September 1991, when he left the then ruling **Pan-Armenian National Movement** (HHSh).

Having staged demonstrations against the HHSh Government, the party won 7.5% of the vote and five seats in the 1995 **National Assembly** elections. In the

September 1996 presidential contest Manukian was runner-up with 41.3% of the vote; he subsequently claimed that the result had been rigged.

Manukian stood again in the March 1998 presidential elections, but was eliminated in the first round with 12.2% of the vote. Having failed to find alliance partners for the May 1999 Assembly elections, the AZhM slipped to 5.2% of the vote but increased its representation to six seats. Although critical of the presidency of Robert **Kocharian** (non-party), the party accepted a ministerial post in February 2000. Manukian ruled out an alliance with the main ruling **Republican Party of Armenia** (HHK), or any other formation, at an AZhM congress in December, but favoured qualified co-operation with the Kocharian presidency. He was therefore attacked by party members who advocated a return to outright opposition, and several members broke away, forming the **National Democratic Alliance Party** and the **National Democratic Party**. Bowing to this groundswell, Manukian led the AZhM into the opposition **Justice** bloc in the run-up to general elections in May 2003. Since the group's failure to break the stranglehold of the Government in the polls, the AZhM has been a leading force in anti-government demonstrations.

Leadership: Vazgen Manukian (Chair).

National Investment Agency
Natsionalnoe Investitsionnoe Agentstvo (NIA)

Set up by the Government of **Belarus** to facilitate foreign investment.
Director: Oleg Zinoviev.
Telephone and Fax: (17) 2679184.
E-mail: agency@invest.belarus.by
Internet: www.invest.belarus.by

National Movement–Democrats (NM-D)

The ruling party of **Georgia**, formed (as the United National Movement—UNM) as a right-of-centre, pro-market and anti-government party led by former Justice Minister Mikhail **Saakashvili**. The party rose to prominence as the main opposition to the then President Eduard **Shevardnadze** in the lead up to parliamentary elections in November 2003. It brought together other opposition factions, including Zurab Zhvania's United Democrats and the youth group Kmara in the umbrella United People's Alliance in 2003.

Following the **Rose Revolution** in November 2003, the alliance coalesced as a unified party, under the direct leadership of the UNM. The NM-D was officially formed in February 2004. In the re-run of the party-list seats from the 2003 elections, held in March 2004, it secured a massive majority, with 67% of the vote. Of the 150 seats at stake in the re-run, it was allocated 135, adding these to the 17 seats it had already won as single-seat constituencies in November 2003. It dominates the **Parliament of Georgia**, though it is still a few seats short of the two-thirds majority necessary to change the Constitution without support from other groups.

Leadership: Mikhail Saakashvili (Chair).
Address: Vukol Beridze 9, 0118 Tbilisi.
Telephone: (32) 938969.
Fax: (32) 921231.
E-mail: i_kvartaradze@hotmail.com

National Unity Party
Azgayin Miabanutiun (AzM)

A small nationalist party in **Armenia** formed in 1997. Led by Artashes Geghamian, a former Mayor of **Yerevan**, the AzM calls for closer ties with the **Russian Federation** along with a pro-European foreign policy. Geghamian polled third in the first round of presidential elections in February 2003, claiming 16.9% of the vote. The AzM went on to win nine seats in parliamentary elections in May.

Leadership: Artashes Geghamian (Chair).
Address: c/o Azgayin Joghov, Baghramian Avenue 19, 375095 Yerevan.
Telephone: (10) 580137.

NATO *see* **North Atlantic Treaty Organization**.

NATO-Russia Council

A forum for co-operation between the North Atlantic Treaty Organization (NATO) and the Russian Federation. Established in May 2002, following the September 2001 terrorist attacks in the USA, it reflected the growing need for co-ordinated action against common threats. Russia had forged relations with NATO in 1991, joined its Partnership for Peace programme in 1994 and signed the NATO-Russia Founding Act in 1997.

Natsionalnoye Sobranie *see* **National Assembly (Belarus)**.

Nazi-Soviet Pact

A non-aggression pact signed between Nazi Germany and the **Soviet Union** on 23 August 1939 which enabled Germany to invade Poland unopposed on 1 September, effectively beginning the Second World War. Red Army troops crossed the Polish border on 17 September, dividing the briefly independent state between the two aggressors. The pact also included the division of the **Baltic States** into German and Soviet zones of influence, with the Soviet Union gaining access to Finland, Estonia and Latvia and leaving Germany with proposed control of Lithuania. Also known as the Molotov-Ribbentrop Pact, after the Foreign Ministers of the Soviet Union and Germany respectively, it came as a severe shock to the international community which had hitherto witnessed the two countries engaging in a vicious war of rhetoric against one another. Collaboration with Germany ended abruptly in June 1941 when Adolf Hitler tore up the non-aggression pact and launched Operation Barbarossa—the Nazi invasion of the Soviet Union.

Naxçivan *see* **Nakhichevan**.

NCP *see* **New Rights**.

Near abroad

A phrase used in **Russia** to denote neighbouring states of the former **Soviet Union** in which Russia retains a special interest (for economic, military-strategic or nationalistic reasons). The phrase has been criticized as implying that these states are somehow less than fully sovereign and are liable to be included within a newly-imposed Russian sphere of influence, particularly through the institution of the **Commonwealth of Independent States** (CIS).

Neman question

A question of the border between southern Lithuania and the Russian enclave of **Kaliningrad** along the River Neman (Nemunas in Lithuanian). At the end of the Second World War the borders of the **Baltic States** were redrawn by the Soviet authorities to create ethnic republics and guarantee direct Russian access to an ice-free port on the Baltic Sea at Kaliningrad. Following the disintegration of the **Soviet Union** in 1991 and the resurrection of an independent Lithuania the issue of this somewhat arbitrary border was raised. Elements on the far right of Lithuanian politics called for the total annexation of the Kaliningrad enclave (home to a mixed **Russian-German** population) in light of its geographic separation from the rest of the **Russian Federation** by around 750 km. However, Lithuania and Russia signed a border treaty in 1997, ratified by Lithuania two years later and by Russia in 2003. It came into force in August 2003, making Lithuania the first ex-Soviet state to secure a border agreement with Russia.

New Azerbaijan Party
Yeni Azarbaycan Partiyasi (YAP)

Azerbaijan's ruling party from 1993 onwards. Founded by Heydar **Aliyev** in September 1992 as an alternative to the then ruling **Azerbaijan Popular Front Party** (AXCP), the YAP continues to be the power base of the Aliyev dynasty, with Ilham Aliyev's taking the helm two months ahead of his father's death in 2003.

Heydar Aliyev's initiative in founding the YAP followed his exclusion from the June 1992 presidential election because he was over a newly-decreed age limit of 65. A former Politburo member of the Soviet Communist Party, and First Secretary of the party in Azerbaijan from 1969, Aliyev was at this time President of the Azerbaijani enclave of **Nakhichevan**, and had conducted an independent foreign policy for the enclave, signing a ceasefire with **Armenia** and developing relations with the **Russian Federation**, Turkey and Iran.

Aliyev used the YAP to rally opposition to the AXCP Government of Abulfaz Elchibey, who was deposed in June 1993. Taking over as interim Head of State, Aliyev was officially credited with 98.8% of the vote in a presidential election in October 1993 (for which the 65-year age limit was rescinded). Meanwhile, at his urging, in September long-delayed parliamentary approval had been given to Azerbaijan's membership of the **Commonwealth of Independent States**. The new Government launched a crackdown against the AXCP, while Aliyev moved to improve Azerbaijan's regional relations and sought a settlement of the **Nagorno-Karabakh** conflict with Armenia, involving the return of a limited Russian military presence to Azerbaijan proper.

In the November 1995 **National Assembly** elections (completed in February 1996), the YAP formed a front with three minor parties and was credited with 62% of the national vote in its own right. It therefore held an overwhelming majority of Assembly seats when pro-government independents were included in the tally. Firmly entrenched in power, Aliyev secured a predictable victory in the October 1998 presidential elections as the YAP candidate, winning 76.1% of the vote against five other contenders. International bodies criticized widespread irregularities in the polling, the official result of which was rejected by the opposition parties. Aliyev nevertheless reappointed Artur **Rasizade** as Prime Minister of a YAP-dominated Government.

In December 1999 Aliyev was re-elected YAP Chairman at the party's first congress, which also elected the President's son, Ilham Aliyev, as one of five

Deputy Chairmen. Ilham Aliyev headed the YAP list for the proportional section of Assembly elections held in November 2000. Amidst opposition claims of widespread fraud, the ruling party won another overwhelming victory, taking 75 seats out of 124 filled and also having the backing of most of the 29 'independents' elected.

In November 2001 the party voted to give its backing to Ilham Aliyev as his father's eventual successor, and he smoothly took over the chairmanship of the party as Heydar Aliyev's health declined over the course of 2003. Ilham Aliyev successfully ran as YAP presidential candidate in the October 2003 elections and his father died in December.

In parliamentary elections in November 2005, the YAP won a convincing 56 of the 115 seats being contested. The result was roundly condemned, with opposition parties launching a series of protests against apparent electoral irregularities.

Leadership: Ilham Aliyev (Chair).
Address: Bül-Bül pr. 13, 1000 Baku.
Telephone: (12) 4934276.
Fax: (12) 4980322.
E-mail: yap@bakinter.net
Internet: www.yap.org.az

New Conservative Party *see* **New Rights**.

New Equality Party *see* **Equality**.

New Policy
Yeni Siyaset (YeS)

An opposition bloc in **Azerbaijan** formed to contest the 2005 parliamentary election. New Policy comprised the Azerbaijan National Independence Party, the Azerbaijan Social Democratic Party, the For Azerbaijan public forum, the Intelligentsia movement and various public figures and NGOs. The bloc won no seats in the election on 6 November 2005.

New Rights (or New Conservative Party)
Axale Memarjveneebi (Axlebi or NCP)

A conservative political party in **Georgia**, which was formed in 2000 by former members of the **Citizens' Union of Georgia**. It gained a majority of seats in the June 2003 municipal elections, including all of Tbilisi. It contested the November 2003 as part of the New Rights bloc, and joined with **Industry will Save Georgia** as the **Rightist Opposition** grouping ahead of the re-run poll in March 2004.

In August 2005 New Rights signed a co-operation agreement with other opposition parties to field united candidates in future elections.

Leadership: David Gamkhrelidze (Chair).
Address: Bevreti 3, 0114 Tbilisi.
Telephone: (32) 920313.
Fax: (32) 923858.
E-mail: ncp@ncp.ge
Internet: www.ncp.ge

NFB-A *see* **Belarusian Popular Front-Renaissance**.

NM-D *see* **National Movement–Democrats**.

Noghaideli, Zurab

Prime Minister, **Georgia**. Zurab Noghaideli was first elected to the **Parliament of Georgia** in 1992 after the overthrow of President Zviad Gamsakhurdia. Like most politicians in the current Government, he initially served under Eduard **Shevardnadze** before the **Rose Revolution** of 2003. He is a technocrat with a background in natural sciences, Noghaideli's appointment as Prime Minister in February 2005 following the death of Zurab Zhvania came as a surprise to some; Zhvania was regarded as one of Georgia's few statesmen, and many doubted that Noghaideli would be able to fill the gap.

Zurab Noghaideli was born on 22 October 1964 in the coastal town of Kobuleti in **Adzharia**, south-west Georgia. He was educated at the Moscow State University, where he graduated in physics in 1987, and worked at the Geography Institute of the Georgian Academy of Sciences until 1989, when he moved to the Geology Institute at the Estonian Academy of Sciences.

In 1991 Noghaideli joined the Green Party led by Zurab Zhvania. He was elected as a Deputy to the **Parliament of Georgia** for the first time in 1992, after the overthrow of President Gamsakhurdia, and he became Chairman of the Parliamentary Committee on Environmental Protection and Natural Resources. Along with Zhvania and current President Mikhail **Saakashvili**, Noghaideli joined President Eduard Shevardnadze's **Citizens' Union of Georgia**. He was re-elected as a deputy in 1995, and in 1996 served as a member of the Adzharian Supreme Court. In 1999 Noghaideli chaired the Parliamentary Tax and Income Committee. He joined the Government for the first time in May 2000 as Minister of Finance, but was dismissed without explanation two years later. He joined Zhvania's United Democrats (UD), an opposition party founded the same year.

Following the Rose Revolution of November 2003 which ousted Shevardnadze, Noghaideli became economic adviser to acting President Nino

Burdzhanadze. He was reappointed Finance Minister in February 2004 by Prime Minister Zhvania, in a Government of the **National Movement-Democrats** (NM-D), formed by a merger of the UD with President Saakashvili's United National Movement.

Zhvania died of carbon monoxide poisoning in February 2005, and Noghaideli was nominated to replace him on 11 February; he was confirmed by Parliament on 17 February. Many analysts and commentators found the choice of Noghaideli puzzling. He is known as a technocrat with little political experience, and lacks the charisma of his predecessor. Others, however, see his appointment as partly a nod to Zhvania's supporters, and partly a desire on the part of Saakashvili to balance his own spontaneous and rather disorganized temperament with a premier known for strictness and organization.

Noghaideli is married with one child.

Address: Office of the Government, Ingorovka 7, 380007 Tbilisi.

Telephone: (32) 935907.

Fax: (32) 982354.

Internet: www.government.gov.ge

Nomenklatura

(Russian, 'list of names and offices'.) The system of appointments in the **Soviet Union**, co-ordinated by the security police (the KGB or its precursor the NKVD—*see* **Federal Security Service**) and the Cadres Department of the Central Committee of the **Communist Party of the Soviet Union**, which together assigned 'suitable' candidates to a range of state offices. The nomenklatura system ensured discipline and deference to the party. Those rewarded by the nomenklatura came to be regarded as an elite and were treated preferentially in the distribution of resources such as apartments, cars and holidays. In the early post-communist period, well-placed officials were sometimes able to reinvent themselves as business leaders and secure the choicest assets when state industries were being sold—a process described derisively as 'nomenklatura privatization'.

Non-Aligned Movement (NAM)

An international grouping of countries professing not to be aligned with either side in the **Cold War**, and therefore not including any of the socialist states of **eastern Europe** which were part of the **Warsaw Pact** military structure. Yugoslavia, however, was an active member of the Non-Aligned Movement, which was founded as an organized entity in 1961 when it held its first summit conference in Belgrade. Yugoslavia's membership was suspended in 1992. The only other eastern European country among the 115 members is **Belarus**, which joined as a mark of its independence (having previously been part of the **Soviet Union**) after 1991.

Address: c/o Permanent Representative of South Africa to the UN, 333 East 38th St, 9th Floor, New York, NY 10016, USA.
Telephone: (212) 2135583.
Fax: (212) 6922498.
Internet: www.nam.gov.za

North Atlantic Co-operation Council (NACC)

Replaced in 1997 by the **Euro-Atlantic Partnership Council**.

North Atlantic Treaty Organization (NATO)

The key institution of the Atlantic Alliance, which after the end of the **Cold War** underwent a reappraisal of its identity and purpose, seeking ways of co-operating with, instead of confronting, the countries of **eastern Europe** which had hitherto been members of the **Warsaw Pact**. The original 1949 North Atlantic Treaty was a defensive and political military alliance of a group of European states (then numbering 10) and the USA and Canada. Its objectives were (and remain) to provide common security for its members through co-operation and consultation in political, military and economic fields, as well as scientific, environmental and other non-military aspects. Since January 1994, NATO's **Partnership for Peace** programme has provided a loose framework for wider co-operation.

A Founding Act on Mutual Relations, Co-operation and Security was signed between the **Russian Federation** and NATO in May 1997 (*see also* **NATO-Russia Council**). This addressed some Russian concerns about the implications of an eastward expansion of NATO itself, for which a number of countries were pressing. The Czech Republic, Hungary and Poland were the first three such countries to join NATO, on 12 March 1999, with a further wave of expansion in March 2004 to include Bulgaria, Estonia, Latvia, Lithuania, Romania, Slovakia and Slovenia. Albania, Croatia and Macedonia could be invited to join in 2008, while **Armenia**, **Azerbaijan**, Bosnia and Herzegovina, **Georgia**, Montenegro, Serbia and **Ukraine** have expressed their desire to join. Georgia, Montenegro, Serbia are expected to embark on the Membership Action Plan in 2007, with possible accession for Georgia in 2009 and Montenegro in 2010. In Ukraine, a majority of the population are currently against membership, and pro-Russian Prime Minister Viktor **Yanukovych** is not anxious to push the matter.

> *Members*: Belgium, Bulgaria, Canada, Czech Republic, Denmark, Estonia, France, Germany, Greece, Hungary, Iceland, Italy, Latvia, Lithuania, Luxembourg, Netherlands, Norway, Poland, Portugal, Romania, Slovakia, Slovenia, Spain, Turkey, UK, USA.
> *Secretary-General*: Jaap de Hoop Scheffer.
> *Address*: blvd Léopold III, B-1110 Brussels, Belgium.
> *Telephone*: (2) 7074111.
> *Fax*: (2) 7074579.
> *E-mail*: nato-doc@hq.nato.int
> *Internet*: www.nato.int

North Ossetia *see* **Ossetia question**.

Northern Bukovina *see* **Bukovina question**.

Novosti *see* **RIA–Novosti**.

NPRF *see* **People's Party of the Russian Federation**.

NPT *see* **Nuclear Non-Proliferation Treaty**.

NU *see* **Our Ukraine**.

Nuclear Non-Proliferation Treaty (NPT)

The 1968 Treaty on the Non-Proliferation of Nuclear Weapons (known as the Non-Proliferation Treaty—NPT), which entered into force in 1970, attempts to maintain a clear distinction between countries which have nuclear weapons, and the wider group which have nuclear power. All non-nuclear-weapon states party to the treaty (i.e. states which had not manufactured and exploded a nuclear weapon or other nuclear explosive device prior to 1 January 1967) were required to conclude an agreement with the **International Atomic Energy Agency** (IAEA) undertaking to accept IAEA safeguards on all nuclear material in all their peaceful nuclear activities for the purpose of verifying that such material is not diverted to nuclear weapons or other nuclear explosive devices. The five nuclear-weapon states at the time the treaty was concluded—the People's Republic of China, France, the **Soviet Union**, the UK and the USA—concluded safeguards agreements with the IAEA permitting the application of IAEA safeguards to all their nuclear activities, excluding those with 'direct national significance'.

At the break-up of the Soviet Union in 1991, the successor states of the **Russian Federation**, **Belarus**, Kazakhstan and **Ukraine** inherited nuclear weapons. Russia agreed to honour the commitments of the Soviet Union, while the other three signed up to the NPT as non-nuclear-weapon states and agreed to transfer the weapons to Russia, a process which was completed by 1996.

India and Pakistan (known to have developed nuclear weapons after 1967) and Israel (believed to have developed nuclear weapons) have not acceded to the treaty. North Korea withdrew in January 2003 and carried out a nuclear test in 2006.

Nuclear Suppliers' Group (NSG)

A group formed in the 1970s, at US instigation and spurred by India's nuclear test in 1974, to create common guidelines among the countries supplying nuclear material and technology so as to prevent their being used by non-nuclear-weapon states for weapons development. The NSG included France, which was then not party to the 1968 **Nuclear Non-Proliferation Treaty** (NPT), and had 15 member countries by early 1978 when its guidelines and control list were published.

The NSG did not meet throughout the 1980s, but resumed annual meetings beginning in The Hague in March 1991, its membership expanding to 45 (including **Belarus**, the **Russian Federation** and **Ukraine**). It also holds two consultations annually on its arrangement to control nuclear-related 'dual-use' exports, of material and technology which could be used both for nuclear weapons and fuel-cycle activities and for other, non-nuclear purposes.

Nuclear Test Ban Treaty

A term usually referring to the Partial Test Ban Treaty (PTBT) of 1963, signed by the USA, the **Soviet Union** and the UK but not by the other two known nuclear-weapon states of that time, France and the People's Republic of China. It banned nuclear tests in the atmosphere, under water and in space, but not underground. The treaty was intended to address concern both about the nuclear arms race and about nuclear fallout from atmospheric testing. On the former issue it was reinforced by the **Nuclear Non-Proliferation Treaty** (NPT) in 1968, prohibiting non-nuclear-weapon states from possessing, manufacturing or acquiring nuclear weapons.

In 1991 the parties to the PTBT met to discuss converting it into a ban on all nuclear-weapon tests. Negotiations for a Comprehensive Nuclear Test Ban Treaty (CTBT) began in 1993 and culminated in the treaty's conclusion on 10 September 1996 by the UN General Assembly in New York. Opened for signature on 24 September, it was signed immediately by 71 states, including the five declared nuclear-weapon states of that time, but not by India or Pakistan.

By January 2007 the treaty had 177 signatories, and 138 countries had ratified it, though this included only 34 of the prescribed 44 countries whose ratification is required for the treaty to come into force. The People's Republic of China, Iran, Israel and the USA are among those that have signed but not ratified the treaty, while India and Pakistan (which carried out underground tests in 1998) and North Korea (which carried out an underground test in 2006) have not signed the treaty.

O

OECD *see* **Organization for Economic Co-operation and Development**.

Ohryzko, Volodymyr

A career diplomat who in January 2007 became acting Minister of Foreign Affairs in **Ukraine**.

Volodymyr Ohryzko was born on 1 April 1956 in **Kiev**. He graduated in 1978 in international relations from Taras Shevchenko Kiev State University and joined the Foreign Ministry. Initially in the press department, he moved in 1988 to the Principal Counsellor's Department, where he became a Counsellor himself three years later. He spent the early years of Ukraine's independence in the Ukrainian Embassies in Germany and Austria before returning to Kiev in 1996 to head President **Kuchma**'s Foreign Policy Department. In 1999 he received his first posting as Ambassador, sending him back to Austria. After five years in Vienna, he was moved to become Ambassador-at-large in the Department of Euro-Atlantic Co-operation at the Ministry of Foreign Affairs.

In February 2005 he was appointed First Deputy Minister of Foreign Affairs, and it was in this capacity that he took over the full ministerial role on the resignation of Boris Tarasyuk in January 2007. The foreign minister's post had become a pawn in the power struggle between President Viktor **Yushchenko** and Prime Minister Viktor **Yanukovych**. The 2005 constitutional amendments had switched responsibility for the majority of Cabinet appointments from the President to the Prime Minister, but the post of Foreign Minister was one of the three (along with the post of Prime Minister and Defence Minister) retained by the President. The enforced Yushchenko–Yanukovych cohabitation had led by late 2006 to a **Party of Regions**-dominated Government containing a pair of beleaguered **Our Ukraine** ministers. Even Yushchenko's nomination in February 2007 of the independent Ohryzko to the vacated Foreign Minister post was not deemed acceptable by the Party of Regions, and he was rejected by the **Supreme Council** at successive votes on his nomination, therefore continuing in the post only in an acting capacity.

Ohryzko speaks German and English. He is married with a son and two daughters.

> *Address*: Ministry of Foreign Affairs, Mykhaylivska pl. 1, 01018 Kiev.
> *Telephone*: (44) 2381513.
> *Fax*: (44) 2263169.
> *E-mail*: zs@mfa.gov.ua
> *Internet*: www.mfa.gov.ua

OIC *see* **Organization of the Islamic Conference**.

Oligarchs

Term used in post-**Soviet** countries to refer to tycoons whose vast business empires gave them great wealth and political influence. In the **Russian Federation** market liberalization began in the 1980s under President Mikhail **Gorbachev**, but it was not until the **Yeltsin** era that the rapid economic transition to a market economy allowed entrepreneurs to amass vast fortunes by profiting from underpriced 'shock therapy' privatization, corruption in Government and the 'black' economy. The oligarchs backed Yeltsin's re-election in 1996, and their political influence grew, but some suffered major losses in the 1998 financial crisis (*see* **Russian Federation, economy**). After Vladimir **Putin** succeeded as President in 2000, he reined in on tax evasion and other irregularities, targeting the oligarchs in particular. Some left Russia to avoid prosecution, including Vladimir Gusinsky, who headed the Media-MOST empire, and Boris Berezovsky, while Mikhail Khodorkovsky, Chairman of **Yukos** oil company, was jailed for nine years in 2005 for tax evasion.

Oligarchs also profited from the market transition in **Ukraine**, where Viktor Pinchuk, son-in-law of former President Leonid **Kuchma**, heads a media empire and is the second wealthiest man in Ukraine behind Rinat Akhmetov. Former Prime Minister Yuliya Tymoshenko, leader of the opposition **Yuliya Tymoshenko bloc**, amassed a large fortune from the gas sector.

Orange Revolution

The peaceful '**colour revolution**' in **Ukraine** that led to the re-run of the second round of the 2004 presidential election and the ultimate defeat of Viktor **Yanukovych**, the chosen successor to President Leonid **Kuchma**.

Official results from the first round of the presidential elections on 31 October 2004 put opposition leader Viktor **Yushchenko** ahead with just under 40% of the vote to Yanukovych's 39%. Allegations of fraud and voter intimidation from government supporters increased after the run-off poll on 21 November. The initially-declared victory of Yanukovych, contradicting the exit polls which had given Yushchenko an 11% lead, was roundly rejected. Mass rallies held in Kiev, inspired by the previous year's **Rose Revolution** in **Georgia** and adorned with the orange colour of the **Our Ukraine** bloc, received general support from the international community, with the notable exception of the **Russian Federation**. Local administrations, particularly in the western part of the country where Yushchenko's support was concentrated, refused to accept the result, and 'Oranges' (Yushchenko supporters) took to the streets in these cities as well. Meanwhile in pro-Russian industrial cities in the east where Yanukovych had his support base, groups of demonstrators adopted the colour blue as their symbol.

The day after the election hundreds of thousands of supporters gathered to demonstrate in favour of Yushchenko outside the parliament building. On 23 November they marched in front of the **Supreme Council**, and Yushchenko took a presidential oath within the chamber—though the lack of quorum made it a purely symbolic gesture. Negotiations between Yushchenko and Kuchma for a peaceful resolution of the situation quickly collapsed, and the election commission went ahead and confirmed Yanukovych's victory on 24 November. In response Yushchenko called publicly for mass protests, a general strike and sit-ins.

On 3 December, faced with the popular strength of this so-called Orange Revolution, the Supreme Court decided to annul the second round of the vote. In the re-run held on 26 December, Yushchenko's victory was finally recognized with 52% of the vote. He was inaugurated on 23 January 2005.

Organization for Democratic and Economic Development-GUAM *see* **GUAM group**.

Organization for Economic Co-operation and Development
(OECD)

An influential grouping within which the governments of industrialized countries discuss, develop and attempt to co-ordinate their economic and social policies. Founded in 1961, it replaced the Organization for European Economic Co-operation (OEEC) which had been established in 1948 in connection with the Marshall Plan for post-war reconstruction. The OECD's officially-stated aims are to promote policies designed to achieve the highest level of sustainable economic growth, employment and increase in the standard of living while maintaining financial stability, and to contribute to economic expansion in member and non-member states and to the expansion of world trade.

Members: 30.
Secretary-General: Angel Gurría.
Address: 2 rue André-Pascal, 75775 Paris Cédex 16, France.

Organization for Security and Co-operation in Europe (OSCE)

Telephone: (1) 45248200.
Fax: (1) 45248500.
E-mail: webmaster@oecd.org
Internet: www.oecd.org

Organization for Security and Co-operation in Europe (OSCE)

The Organization for Security and Co-operation in Europe was established in 1972 as the Conference on Security and Co-operation in Europe (CSCE), providing a multilateral forum for dialogue and negotiation. The areas of competence of the CSCE were expanded by the **Charter of Paris for a New Europe** (1990)—which transformed the CSCE from an *ad hoc* forum to an organization with permanent institutions—and the Helsinki Document 1992. CSCE membership had reached 52 by 1994, as it sought to encompass all recognized states in Europe and the former **Soviet Union**, together with Canada and the USA.

The CSCE's role included securing the observance of human rights, and providing a forum for settling disputes among member countries. Some member countries, notably the **Russian Federation**, advocated its development as the principal organization for managing the responses of European countries on a range of continent-wide concerns. Its initial impact, however, was principally in promoting East-West détente, bringing together 35 countries including the rival **North Atlantic Treaty Organization** and **Warsaw Pact** alliances for the Helsinki CSCE conference which began in July 1973 and culminated in the 1975 **Helsinki Final Act**.

In December 1994 the summit conference adopted the new name of OSCE, in order to reflect the organization's changing political role and strengthened Secretariat. The OSCE's main decision-making body, the Permanent Council, convenes weekly in Vienna to discuss and make decisions on current developments in the OSCE area. Also meeting weekly in Vienna is the Forum for Security Co-operation, which is concerned with military aspects of security in the OSCE area, in particular confidence- and security-building measures. The OSCE's Senior Council/Economic Forum convenes once a year in Prague to focus on economic and environmental issues.

The OSCE also has: a Parliamentary Assembly; an Office for Democratic Institutions and Human Rights (ODIHR), based in Warsaw and originally created (in 1990) as the Office for Free Elections, concerned to promote human rights and democracy; a High Commissioner on National Minorities and a Representative on Freedom of the Media; and a Court of Conciliation and Arbitration overseeing its disputes settlement procedures.

190

Members: 56 participating states, comprising all the recognized countries of Europe and the former Soviet republics, Canada and the USA.

The position of Chairman-in-Office is held by a Minister of Foreign Affairs of a member state for a one-year term; the post was held in 2007 by Miguel Ángel Moratinos when Spain held the one-year chairmanship of the organization.

Secretary-General: Marc Perrin de Brichambaut.
Address: Kärntner Ring 5–7, 1010 Vienna, Austria.
Telephone: (1) 514360.
Fax: (1) 51436105.
E-mail: info@osce.org
Internet: www.osce.org

Organization of the Black Sea Economic Co-operation (BSEC)

An organization derived from the Black Sea Economic Co-operation (BSEC) grouping formed in 1992 to strengthen regional co-operation, particularly on economic development. In June 1998, at a summit meeting held in Yalta, **Ukraine**, participating countries signed the BSEC Charter, thereby officially elevating the BSEC to regional organization status. The Charter entered into force on 1 May 1999, at which time the BSEC formally became the Organization of the Black Sea Economic Co-operation, retaining the same acronym.

Members: Albania, **Armenia**, **Azerbaijan**, Bulgaria, **Georgia**, Greece, **Moldova**, Romania, **Russian Federation**, Serbia, Turkey and **Ukraine**.

Secretary-General: Leonidas Chrysanthopoulos.
Address: Sakıp Sabancı Caddesi, Müşir Fuad Paşa Yalısı, Eski Tersane 34460, Istanbul, Turkey.
Telephone: (212) 2296330.
Fax: (212) 2296336.
E-mail: info@bsec-organization.org
Internet: www.bsec-organization.org

Organization of the Islamic Conference (OIC)

An organization which groups 57 countries, principally in the Middle East, Africa and Asia, to promote Islamic solidarity and co-operation. **Azerbaijan** and Albania, its only **eastern European** members, joined in 1991 and 1992 respectively. The organization had formally been established in May 1971, when its Secretariat became operational. The impetus for the creation of the organization had come from the summit meeting of **Muslim** Heads of State at Rabat, Morocco, in September 1969, followed up by conferences at foreign ministerial level in Jeddah and Karachi during 1970.

Secretary-General: Prof. Dr Ekmeleddin İhsanoğlu.
Address: Kilo 6, Mecca Road, POB 178, Jeddah 21411, Saudi Arabia.
Telephone: (2) 6900001.
Fax: (2) 2751953.
E-mail: info@oic-oci.org
Internet: www.oic-oci.org

Orthodox Christianity

The form of Christianity most widespread in south-eastern and **eastern Europe**. Its formal separation from western Christianity (**Roman Catholicism**) was completed by the Great Schism in 1054. The eastern Orthodox Catholic Church was championed by the Eastern Roman (Byzantine) Empire centred on Constantinople, and was spread to the pagan tribes north and east of that city. This geographical spread, and conversely the success of Roman Catholicism in the western world, has given Orthodox Christianity a distinctly 'eastern' feel. Its practices are dominated by the belief that the form of worship has not changed since the days of Jesus Christ. The tradition of iconic art is strong.

Unlike the Roman Catholic Church with its Pope, the Orthodox Church does not have a single head, but rather is divided into separate *autocephalous* (independent) Churches or Patriarchates. These Churches are headed by a local Patriarch or Metropolitan. The original branch, the Greek-speaking Autocephalous Church of Constantinople (Istanbul), is deemed the 'first among equals' and the Patriarch of Constantinople is considered 'ecumenical', but theoretically does not have any actual powers over the other Churches. Ecumenical Patriarch Bartholomew I ascended the throne of the Constantinople See on 2 November 1991. The **Russian Orthodox Church** also carries great weight within the religion, having by far the largest single congregation (see below).

Estimates of the number of Orthodox Christians worldwide range from 200 million to 300 million. The biggest congregations are in the **Russian Federation** (up to 125 million) and Romania (c. 20 million). Orthodox Christians were persecuted by the communist authorities; 98% of churches in the **Soviet Union** were closed and many priests executed. However, a general revival in religious activity since the late 1980s has seen a resurgence in the size of congregations and the social influence of the Church hierarchy.

Eastern European countries with autocephalous Churches are: Albania, Bulgaria, **Georgia**, Poland, Romania, Russian Federation and Serbia. The autonomous Churches of **Moldova** (*see also* **Bessarabian Church**) and **Ukraine** are subordinated to the Russian Church. Small congregations in other countries are subordinate to various neighbouring Churches. The symbol of the Orthodox

Church is the three-barred cross (representing the crucifix upon which Jesus Christ was executed, and including the nameplate above his head and the footplate).

OSCE *see* **Organization for Security and Co-operation in Europe**.

Oskanian, Vardan

Minister of Foreign Affairs, **Armenia**. Vardan Oskanian is an Armenian-American who came to prominence as Armenia's chief negotiator after the 1994 ceasefire in the **Nagorno-Karabakh** conflict while he was Deputy Foreign Minister. He has been full Foreign Minister since the inauguration of President Robert **Kocharian** in April 1998.

Born on 7 February 1955 in Syria, he was educated there and at the Yerevan Polytechnic Institute before travelling to the USA where he studied at Tufts University and at Harvard. He became actively involved in the Armenian-American community, editing the *Armenian International Magazine*, and became a naturalized citizen of the USA. He returned to Armenia in 1992 after independence and began work at the Ministry of Foreign Affairs. As the Azeri-Armenian conflict over Nagorno-Karabakh came to a tentative ceasefire in 1994, Oskanian was appointed principal negotiator at the **OSCE** dialogue in **Minsk**. His promotion to full Minister was assured in April 1998 on the election of President Kocharian and represented a key continuity with the previous peace process.

Vartan Oskanian is married and has two sons.

Address: Ministry of Foreign Affairs, Government House 2, Republic Sq. 1, 375010 Yerevan.

Telephone: (10) 544041.

Fax: (10) 543925.

E-mail: info@armeniaforeignministry.com

Internet: www.armeniaforeignministry.com

Ossetia question

A territorial dispute arising from the division of the territory of the ethnic Iranian Ossetes between the **Russian Federation** and **Georgia**. The region first came under the Russian Empire in 1774 and control from Moscow was confirmed with the establishment of a fortress at Vladikavkaz (literally 'rule of the **Caucasus**') in 1784. It was briefly united in a single ethnic territory from 1905, but was ultimately divided into the present two halves by the **Soviet** Commissar for Nationalities, Josef Stalin, in the 1920s. North Ossetia, now known locally as Alania, was expanded slightly during the Soviet era at the expense of neighbouring **Ingushetia**, leading to ethnic tensions which were further exacerbated by the influx of southern Ossetes after 1990. Russian troops were deployed there in 1993.

In the face of growing Georgian nationalism, the *oblast* (region) of South Ossetia in Georgia pressed in 1989 for an upgrade to full autonomous republic status (as enjoyed by **Adzharia**) as a precursor to unification with North Ossetia. The calls were led by the nationalist South Ossetia Popular Front (Adaemon Nykhas). In response the Georgian authorities voted in 1990 to abolish South Ossetia's regional autonomy altogether. This vote in turn prompted the South Ossetian authorities to proclaim the region's independence from Georgia in September. The ensuing tensions quickly spilled over into clashes between Ossete and Georgian paramilitaries and prompted the migration of nearly two-thirds of South Ossetia's 60,000 Ossetes into North Ossetia.

A concerted effort in 1992 by newly-appointed Georgian leader Eduard **Shevardnadze** and Russian President Boris **Yeltsin** brought a joint Russian-Georgian peacekeeping force into the region and calmed the violence. However, no final solution to the Ossetia question was reached and the South Ossetian Republic, declared in 1990, remains essentially a separate state (with its capital at Tskhinvali), reliant on aid donations from the Russian Federation and the lucrative oil smuggling industry. The economic inability/unwillingness of Georgia to uphold its pledges to invest in the region has turned South Ossetia even further towards its northern neighbour. However, unpaid power bills led to the temporary termination of energy supplies from the Russian Federation and from Georgia in 1999 and calls for the resignation of South Ossetian President Lyudvig Chibirov. Although this particular problem was overcome it highlighted the economic vulnerability of the Republic.

North Ossetian President Aleksandr Dzasokhov, elected in January 1998, pressed for a rapprochement between all sides in the dispute. In 2001 he added calls for the eventual unification of the Ossetias. He was particularly keen to repatriate the 40,000 South Ossetian refugees and to develop the economic potential of the poorer southern neighbour. He facilitated talks in late 2000 on increasing Georgia's actual financial commitment to South Ossetia.

Russian citizen Eduard Kokoyev was elected President of South Ossetia in November–December 2001. He declared during the campaign that he would insist on the region becoming a part of the Russian Federation. Following the ousting of Shevardnadze in 2003, tensions rose as Georgia's new President Mikhail **Saakashvili** pledged to bring all Georgia's breakaway republics 'to heel'. After several armed confrontations between troops in the region, Georgia, Russia and the South Ossetian authorities signed a deal in July 2004 promising not to use force to end the dispute, though this did little to end the war of words between the Governments, and sporadic clashes continued. Georgian troops began to withdraw in August, to be replaced by a tripartite joint peacekeeping force.

On 1 September 2004 North Ossetia hit global headlines during the **Beslan**

school siege. Ingush and **Chechen** militants held up to 1,200 children, teachers and parents hostage for two days until Russian special forces forcibly ended the crisis, at a cost of 362 lives, over half of whom were children. The Russian authorities were blamed for the chaotic denouement and for the fact that the siege had happened at all, and President Dzasokhov resigned in June 2005, to be replaced by Taimuraz Mamsurov.

As relations between Georgia and Russia sank to a new low in 2006, Georgia accused Russia of trying to annex South Ossetia. The South Ossetian authorities responded with a referendum on independence held in November, in which over 90% voted for independence. The vote was not recognized by the international community, with the **European Union**, the **Council of Europe** and the **Organization for Security and Co-operation in Europe** (OSCE) condemning the referendum as unhelpful and unproductive.

Our Moldova Alliance
Alianţa Moldova Noastra (AMN)

The largest single opposition party in **Moldova** and the biggest component of the **Democratic Moldova Bloc** (BMD). Formed in July 2003, the AMN itself comprised three separate parties: the main member, the Social Democratic Alliance, the centrist Liberal Party and the Alliance of Independents.

The Social Democratic Alliance had itself been formed from an earlier merger of centre-left parties and had initially been known as the Braghis Alliance after its leader, former Prime Minister Dumitru Braghis. In the February 2001 elections the party had become one of only two opposition parties to be elected to **Parliament** with 19 of the 101 seats available.

Within the BMD coalition, the AMN secured 22 seats for itself in the March 2005 elections.

Leadership: Dumitru Braghis (Co-Chair), Serafim Urecheanu (Co-Chair) and Veaceslav Untila (Co-Chair).

Address: Str. Puşkin 62A, Chişinau.

Telephone: (22) 548538.

E-mail: alianta@amn.md

Internet: www.amn.md

Our Ukraine
Nasha Ukraina (NU)

A political alliance in **Ukraine** formed to support former Prime Minister Viktor **Yushchenko** in his bid to become President, which was achieved through the so-called **Orange Revolution** of 2004. The NU traces its origins to the anti-

Communist Popular Movement of the Ukraine for Reconstructuring (Rukh) of the pre-independence period. It is now a centre-right alliance dominated by the Popular Movement of Ukraine (Narodnyi Rukh Ukrainy—NRU).

The NRU itself was divided by factionalism in the late 1990s, but its various contending elements nevertheless came together to contest the 2002 elections under the banner of Our Ukraine (NU), also widely known as the Viktor Yushchenko bloc after its leading figure (who had been Prime Minister from December 1999 to May 2001). Its success in gaining 112 seats, and thus becoming the largest single party in the **Supreme Council**, made it the spearhead of the opposition to the then President, Leonid **Kuchma**.

Seen as a moderate of the rightist opposition, Yushchenko became the focus of efforts to unify parties against Kuchma. The orange colours of the NU alliance became a running theme in anti-Kuchma demonstrations. Yushchenko was considered both less controversial and less charismatic than his leading political contemporary, Yuliya Tymoshenko, but his public profile was raised in the lead up to the 2004 presidential election when, as the opposition's candidate, he fell suddenly ill with suspected poisoning. Images of his scarred face achieved iconic status alongside the orange banners in protests to the rigged second-round poll held in November 2004. The so-called Orange Revolution saw the elections annulled and another round called which finally secured Yushchenko's (and by extension NU's) rise to power. As a nod to Tymoshenko's vital support for his bid, she was nominated Prime Minister ahead of any NU candidate.

The first year of office, however, proved less dramatic. Public perceptions were that the revolution had lost steam amidst internal bickering between Yushchenko and the supporters of Tymoshenko, thereby compromising efforts to reach parliamentary consensus. Tymoshenko was sacked as Prime Minister in September 2005 and replaced by Yuriy Yekhanurov of the NU.

The NU received a mauling at the polls in March 2006, finishing third to the opposition **Party of Regions** (PR) and the **Yuliya Tymoshenko bloc** (BYT) with 14% of the vote and 81 seats in the Supreme Council. Many suggested that the alliance's continued personal tie to Yushchenko has increased the image of partisan politics. Months of negotiations followed as the former allies of the Orange Revolution attempted to re-form their coalition to keep the PR out of power. When the **Socialist Party of Ukraine** switched its support to the PR, the NU was faced with leaving government. It negotiated a deal with the PR to join the new coalition which took office in August, but the uneasy partnership only lasted just over two months, with the NU withdrawing its ministers in late October. The presidentially-appointed Foreign and Defence Ministers remained initially in the Council of Ministers, but soon their posts became pawns in the ongoing battle between Yushchenko and Prime Minister Viktor **Yanukovych**.

Leadership: Viktor Yushchenko (Chair).
Address: vul. Borychiv Tik 22A, 04070 Kiev.
Telephone: (44) 2066095.
E-mail: tak@ua.org.ua
Internet: www.razom.org.ua

OY *see* **Country of Law Party**.

P

Palata Predstaviteley
(House of Representatives)

The lower house of the **National Assembly** of **Belarus**.

Pamyat—National Patriotic Front

An extremist anti-Semitic group in the **Russian Federation** which aims to return the country to an autocratic **Orthodox Christian** monarchy. Formed from a collection of far-right groups in the 1970s, Pamyat (literally 'memory') was one of the founding parties of the far-right political movement in Russia. However, its electoral popularity was minimal and it was undermined by continual discord and new splinter movements. The long-time leader of Pamyat, Dmitri Vasiliev, died in 2003, since when the group has lost significance.

Pan-Armenian National Movement
Haiots Hamazgaien Sharjoum (HHSh)

The political formation established in late 1989 which led **Armenia** to independence in 1990–91 but gradually lost influence thereafter.

The HHSh originally brought together the pro-independence elements of the then ruling **Communist Party of Armenia** (HKK). It won a landslide victory in the May 1990 legislative elections. Following the temporary dissolution of the HKK, the then HHSh leader Levon Ter-Petrossian was directly elected President in October 1991 with 83% of the vote. In the 1995 **National Assembly** elections the HHSh headed the victorious Republican Bloc (Hanrapetutiun), which also included the **Republican Party of Armenia**, the Armenian Christian Democratic Union and the Social Democratic Hunchakian Party. As the governing party, the HHSh sought a successful outcome of the **Nagorno-Karabakh** conflict with **Azerbaijan** involving territorial adjustments to make it contiguous with Armenia proper.

The election of Mayor of **Yerevan** and former Interior Minister Vano Siradeghian as HHSh Chairman in July 1997 precipitated internal divisions culminating in the formation in September 1997 of the breakaway Homeland movement. The resignation of Ter-Petrossian as President in February 1998 increased the party's difficulties. Although it backed the successful candidacy of Robert **Kocharian** (non-party) in the March 1998 presidential elections and was included in the new Government, by the end of 1998 the HHSh had become an opposition party. It was also damaged by strong criticism of Siradeghian's record as Interior Minister in 1992–96. Accused of instigating political assassinations in that period, Siradeghian fled abroad in January 1999 two weeks before the Assembly voted to strip him of parliamentary immunity from prosecution.

Siradeghian was nevertheless re-elected as HHSh Chairman in March 1999 at the party's 11th congress, which launched a fierce attack on the creation of a 'military-police system' by the Kocharian presidency. Siradeghian returned to Armenia shortly before the May 1999 Assembly elections and was promptly arrested. The elections demonstrated the marginalization of the HHSh, which was reduced to a single seat (won by Siradeghian in a constituency contest) and only 1.2% of the proportional vote. Siradeghian again fled abroad in April 2000 and was replaced as HHSh Chairman by former Foreign Minister Aleksandr Arzumanian, who was confirmed in the leadership by the party's 12th congress in December 2000.

The HHSh absorbed the smaller National Democratic Party–21st Century in 2002. It won no seats at the 2003 election.

Leadership: Aleksandr Arzumanian (Chair);
          Levon Ter-Petrossian (President).
Address: Khanjian St 27, 375019 Yerevan.
Telephone: (10) 570470.

Pan-Germanism

An internationalist concept promoting the closer integration and unity of ethnic **German** people across Europe. Significant numbers of ethnic Germans have been spread across **eastern Europe** since medieval times, but are now only loosely connected. The notion of unifying them under a single state was partially realized with the unification of Germany in 1871 under the dominance of **Prussia**, although this did not include other German communities more widely distributed across the region, mostly under the suzerainty of the German-speaking Austrian Empire. Later 20th-century attempts to press ideas of pan-Germanism were of course hijacked by Nazism and the expansion of Hitler's Third Reich. The failure of the Nazi German Empire prompted mass movements of German people into the rump German state (*see* **Yalta** and **Potsdam Agreements**). Another mass migration followed the collapse of the **Soviet Union** and other communist states in eastern Europe in 1989–91. The resettlement of ethnic Germans in Germany has consequently stripped pan-Germanism of much of its potency.

Pan-Slavism

The idea that promotes the closer integration and possible unification of all **Slavic peoples** based on their shared ethnic and linguistic background. In practice, the creation of Yugoslavia was the main, partial and ultimately unsuccessful implementation of this idea. The agitation of Croat and Slovene pan-Slavists for a union of south Slavs, or Yugoslavs, was the basis for the creation in 1918 of the Kingdom of Serbs, Croats and Slovenes, but the deep religious divides and historical animosities among south Slavs violently undid the Yugoslav experiment in the 1990s. More recently, the close ethnic similarities of the east Slavs were the foundation for initiatives towards a **Belarus-Russia Union** and for closer links between these two countries and **Ukraine**.

Pan-Turkism

The idea that promotes the closer integration and possible unification of all **Turkic peoples** based on their shared ethnic and linguistic background. The Turks are spread across the far east of Europe, mostly in constituent republics of the **Russian Federation**, and in Asia. Their language and culture are similar, although regional differences can be great. The concept of uniting these territories under a single Turkish state has had little strength and is often viewed with suspicion by Turkic people outside modern Turkey who are wary of Turkey's own international ambitions. However, the idea of pan-Turkism does encourage greater co-operation between these states, for example Turkey's support for **Azerbaijan** during its conflict with neighbouring **Armenia**. Within the Russian Federation the **Tatars** of **Tatarstan** have led efforts to increase pan-Turkic ties (*see* **Idel-Ural**).

Pankisi Gorge

An area of north-eastern **Georgia** bordering the Russian federal republic of **Chechnya** and with an estimated 3,000 Chechen minority population (known as Kists) and several thousand Chechen refugees.

The open conflict since 1994 between Chechen separatists and the Russian army across the border has made the gorge a diplomatic tinderbox. The Georgian authorities attempted to clamp down on the movement of ethnic Chechens in the region and prevent the trafficking of troops and arms. However, around 7,500 Chechens arrived in Pankisi after the renewed Russian offensive in 1999 and 2000.

The Georgian Government steadfastly refused requests to allow the Russian army into the gorge, and maintained that the migrating Chechens were merely refugees and not militants. However, the arrival in the region in late 2001 of Islamic extremists fleeing the US bombing campaign in Afghanistan turned the region into a new focus of the global 'war on terror'. As many as 200 US special forces arrived in Georgia in late February 2002 to train the Georgian army on how to tackle 'terrorists'. US authorities assured that their forces would not be directly involved in any combat, but the deployment angered the Russian Government as a further intrusion into its sphere of influence.

By mid-2002 the Georgian authorities announced that it had regained full control of the region and flushed out all terrorists: the levels of kidnapping, drug-trafficking and lawlessness have declined. Russia still claims that Chechen militants are taking refuge in the valley, and has been accused of launching air attacks over the region.

The possibility of the destabilization of the area and its already-troubled neighbour South **Ossetia**, and suggestions in some circles of proclaiming an autonomous Chechen republic in the gorge have led to Georgian calls to repatriate the refugees. Many have moved on to **Moldova**, Poland and elsewhere in Europe and the world, while a few hundred have returned to Chechnya: an official repatriation scheme began in 2005.

Paris Charter *see* **Charter of Paris for a New Europe**.

Parliament
Parlamentul

The unicameral legislature of **Moldova**. It has 101 members, directly elected for a four-year term. The last elections were held on 6 March 2005.
Address: Blvd Ştefan cel Mare 105, 2073 Chişinau.
Telephone: (22) 237009.
Fax: (22) 233210.
E-mail: info@parlament.md
Internet: www.parlament.md

Parliament of Georgia
Sakartvelos Parlamenti

The unicameral legislature of **Georgia**, which is to become bicameral 'following the creation of appropriate conditions', according to the 1995 Constitution. The Parliament has 235 members, 85 elected in single-member constituencies and the rest from party lists, for a four-year term. The last elections were held on 2 November 2003. Repeat elections for the 150 party-list seats were held on 28 March 2004.

Address: Rustaveli Ave 8, 380018 Tbilisi.
Telephone: (32) 935113.
Fax: (32) 999594.
E-mail: hdstaff@parliament.ge
Internet: www.parliament.ge

Partial Test Ban Treaty *see* **Nuclear Test Ban Treaty**.

Partnership for Peace (PfP)

The **North Atlantic Treaty Organization**'s Partnership for Peace programme was established in January 1994 within the framework of the North Atlantic Co-operation Council (NACC—*see* **Euro-Atlantic Partnership Council**). It provided a mechanism for a rapprochement between NATO and the countries of **central** and **eastern Europe** after the end of the **Cold War**. The PfP incorporated practical military and defence-related co-operation activities that had originally been part of the NACC Work Plan. Participation in the PfP requires an initial signature of a framework agreement, establishing the common principles and objectives of the partnership, the submission of a presentation document, indicating the political and military aspects of the partnership and the nature of the future co-operation activities, and finally, the development of individual partnership programmes establishing country-specific objectives.

Participating states: 23 countries. Albania, **Armenia**, Austria, **Azerbaijan**, **Belarus**, Bosnia and Herzegovina, Croatia, Finland, **Georgia**, Ireland, Kazakhstan, Kyrgyzstan, Macedonia, **Moldova**, Montenegro, **Russian Federation**, Serbia, Sweden, Switzerland, Tajikistan, Turkmenistan, **Ukraine** and Uzbekistan.

Party of Regions
Partiya Regioniv (PR)

A powerful political party in **Ukraine**, loyal to Prime Minister Viktor **Yanukovych**. Founded in March 2001 as a pro-government bloc in the **Supreme Council**, the PR was formed from a parliamentary alliance of centrist parties with a strong regional power base in the eastern Donetsk region. In opposition after the 2004 **Orange Revolution**, its unexpectedly strong showing in the 2006 parliamentary elections brought Yanukovych back to office.

The PR grew out of an agreement between five parties in July 2000 to work together in the Supreme Council on a platform of supporting the interests of Ukraine's regions in Government. The Labour Party of Ukraine was the longest-established of these five, having been formed in 1992; the four others were the Party of Regional Revival of Ukraine (headed by Donetsk Mayor Volodymyr Rybak), the Party for a Beautiful Ukraine, the All-Ukrainian Party of Pensioners and the Party of Solidarity of Ukraine. In November 2000 the group adopted the title Party of Regional Revival/Labour Solidarity of Ukraine. It reconstituted as the PR at its opening congress in March 2001. It joined the pro-government For a United Ukraine alliance for the 2002 elections, giving its backing to the then President Leonid **Kuchma**.

Once Yanukovych had become Prime Minister (in 2002) and Kuchma's chosen candidate for succession to the presidency, the PR manoeuvred itself firmly into the populist sphere. It also consciously took steps towards courting left-wing support as the presidential election approached in October 2004.

The claimed victory of Yanukovych in the second round of that poll was heavily disputed by the opposition and international observers, and eventually annulled by the Supreme Court as fraudulent—an outcome hailed as the triumph of the so-called Orange Revolution. The re-run in December saw Yanukovych defeated, with 44% of the vote behind Viktor **Yushchenko**'s 52%. Finding itself in opposition, the PR struggled to provide a unifying voice against the Yushchenko Government, and claimed to be the victim of official repression. It alleged that the jailing of a senior regional leader in April 2005 was politically motivated, whereas the Government claimed that the arrest was a simple matter of investigating allegations of extortion.

In the March 2006 elections, the PR benefited greatly from lack of solidarity among the bickering government parties, and growing discontent over the perceived loss of momentum of the Orange Revolutionaries. It claimed the greatest single share of the vote (33.1%) and the largest number of seats in the Supreme Council (186). Its electoral base is in the east of the country, primarily among the Russian-speaking community there, while it has little support among the Ukrainian-speaking population of western Ukraine.

The former allies of the Orange Revolution attempted to re-form their coalition to keep the PR from power, but after months of negotiations the small but pivotal **Socialist Party of Ukraine** (SPU) switched its support to the PR. In August 2006 President Yushchenko reluctantly put forward the nomination of Yanukovych as Prime Minister, heading a PR-dominated Government that also included the **Communist Party of Ukraine**, the SPU and members of Yushchenko's **Our Ukraine** bloc. Divisions had emerged by October 2006 and Our Ukraine withdrew its ministers, though the presidentially-appointed Foreign and Defence Ministers remained initially in the Council of Ministers; soon, however, their posts became pawns in the ongoing battle between Yushchenko and Yanukovych.

People's Coalition Five Plus

Leadership: Viktor Yanukovych (Chair).
Address: vul. Kudryavska 3/5, 04053 Kiev.
Telephone: (44) 2542920.
Fax: (44) 2125583.
E-mail: PressCenter@partyofregions.org.ua
Internet: www.partyofregions.org.ua

PCA *see* **Permanent Court of Arbitration.**

PCRM *see* **Communist Party of the Moldovan Republic.**

PDM *see* **Democratic Party of Moldova.**

Pechenga *see* **Petsamo question.**

Pechory *see* **Petseri question.**

People's Coalition Five Plus
Narodnaya Kaalicyja Piaciorka Plus (V-Plus)

The main opposition coalition in **Belarus**, organized ahead of parliamentary elections in 2004. The alliance comprised the major opposition parties: the **Belarusian Popular Front-Renaissance** (NFB-A), the Belarusian Social Democratic Assembly (which later voted to merge with the Belarusian Social Democratic Party-People's Assembly), the Party of Communists of Belarus (which splintered from the ruling **Communist Party of Belarus** in 1996 in opposition to President **Lukashenka**), the United Civic Party of Belarus (a pro-market party, and the main driving force in V-Plus alongside the NFB-A) and the Belarusian Labour Party (which was officially deregistered by the Supreme Court in August 2004). The grouping also welcomed the support of the Belarusian Ecological Party of the Greens. Amidst widespread domestic and international accusations of voting fraud, none of the V-Plus parties managed to win any seats in the poll.

The V-Plus backed the candidacy of independent presidential hopeful, Alyaksandr Milinkevich in the widely condemned election of March 2006. Milinkevich, nominated by the NFB-A, officially received less than 4% of the vote, in the face of Lukashenka's overwhelming, 90% victory. Calls for Milinkevich to take personal control of the opposition movement have met stiff resistance from the well-established parties within it.

People's Party of Armenia
Hayastani Zhoghovrdakan Kusaktsutyun (HZhK)

A party in **Armenia** founded in February 1999 on a platform of 'democratic and popular socialism' and calling for the reversal of post-**Soviet** 'deindustrialization'.

The first HZhK leader was Karen Demirchian, the runner-up to Robert **Kocharian** (non-party) in the March 1998 presidential elections, and a former First Secretary between 1974 and 1988 of the then ruling **Communist Party of Armenia**.

The HZhK contested the May 1999 **National Assembly** elections in an alliance with the **Republican Party of Armenia** (HHK) called the Unity (Miasnutiun) bloc, which dominated the contest by winning 55 of the 131 seats and 41.7% of the proportional vote. While the then HHK leader became Prime Minister, Karen Demirchian was elected Speaker of the new Assembly. However, in October 1999 he was one of eight political leaders, including the Prime Minister, shot dead by gunmen during an Assembly debate. He was succeeded as HZhK Chairman in December by his younger son, Stepan Demirchian, while Armen Khachatrian of the HZhK became Speaker.

Although Stepan Demirchian initially pledged the HZhK's continued participation in the Unity bloc, his criticism of the Government's policies intensified following the appointment of HHK Chairman Andranik **Markarian** as Prime Minister in May 2000. The divisions sharpened in September when HHK deputies led an attempt to oust Khachatrian from the speakership. The following month, Demirchian refused to commit the HZhK to supporting the Markarian Government; he withdrew the party from Unity altogether in September 2001. Instead it formed the core of the **Justice** (Ardartyun) opposition bloc in the run-up to elections in 2003.

Demirchian gained 27.4% in the first round of presidential elections in February 2003. He squared up to President Kocharian and was beaten in the March run-off, receiving only 32.5% of the vote. As part of Justice, the HZhK was at the forefront of anti-government demonstrations in 2003–05. Demirchian, however, has begun to soften his party's stance since late 2005. Insisting that there is little remaining point in pursuing the unsuccessful protests, he has pulled the HZhK away from its Justice partners, prompting speculation of an imminent split. Demirchian insists that the HZhK is sufficiently popular to function alone.

Leadership: Stepan Demirchian (Chair).
Address: Moskovian St 24, Yerevan.
Telephone: (10) 581577.

People's Party of the Russian Federation
Narodnaya Partiya Rossiiskoi Federatsii (NPRF)

A party in the **Russian Federation** founded in 2001 from the People's Deputy Movement. It supports President Vladimir **Putin** and **United Russia**.

At the December 2003 election it only polled 1.2% of the party-list vote, but won 16 majority seats. Gennadii Gudkov replaced Gennadii Raikov as party Chair in April 2004.

Leadership: Gennadii V. Gudkov (Chair of the Central Committee).
Address: ul. Nizhnyaya Krasnoselskaya 39/2, 107066 Moscow.
Telephone: (495) 7999340.
Fax: (495) 2922932.
E-mail: press@narod-party.ru
Internet: www.narod-party.ru

Perestroika

The slogan, meaning 'restructuring' in Russian, adopted by Soviet leader Mikhail **Gorbachev** in late 1986 to denote his policies of pragmatic reform, particularly in the economic sphere. *Perestroika*'s themes were efficiency (as reflected in decentralization, the limited introduction of market mechanisms and campaigns against alcohol abuse) and equality of opportunity (an emphasis on ending corruption, nepotism and excessive party privilege). *Perestroika*, however, failed to galvanize a moribund command economy, and Gorbachev's liberal critics attacked it as timid and directionless.

Permanent Court of Arbitration (PCA)
(also known as *Cour permanente d'arbitrage*, CPA)

An international court based in The Hague, Netherlands, designed to provide a peaceful forum for the solution of international disputes. The PCA was established by the Convention on Pacific Settlement of International Disputes, which was signed in 1899 during the first Hague Peace Conference—convened by Russian Tsar Nicholas II as an attempt to prevent future international conflict and to de-escalate the arms race of the time.

The Convention was revised at the second Conference in 1907 and 106 countries had, as of 28 April 2006, signed up to either one or both of the conventions, giving them access to the PCA. These included **Belarus**, the **Russian Federation** and **Ukraine**. The court also now hears cases of international commercial arbitration in a specially-convened Council. The court uses two official languages, English and French.

Secretary-General: Tjaco van den Hout.
Address: International Bureau, Peace Palace, Camegieplein 2, 2517 KJ, The
      Hague, Netherlands.
Telephone: (70) 3024165.
Fax: (70) 3024167. ·
Email: bureau@pca-cpa.org
Internet: pca-cpa.org

Petsamo question

A dispute between Finland and the **Russian Federation** over the far northern
Petsamo border district (known in Russian as Pechenga). The district with its
mainly ethnically Finnish population was incorporated, along with southern
Karelia, into the newly independent Finland in 1920 under the second Treaty of
Tartu. Hostilities between the two countries during the Second World War saw
the region occupied by Soviet forces in 1944 and permanently absorbed into the
Soviet Union. Until the collapse of communist power in 1991 the question of
sovereignty over the Petsamo region was firmly locked away with both sides
claiming the new border inviolable. However, in the early 1990s the
disintegration of the Soviet Union sparked calls among irredentist Finns for the
recovery of the ceded territories as the basis for better cross-border relations. The
Finnish Government has not supported these calls.

Petseri question

A dormant territorial dispute between Estonia and the **Russian Federation** over
the Petseri county area (known in Russian as Pechory), which lies south-east of
Narva. The county was ceded to Estonia under the first Treaty of **Tartu** in 1920
along with other **Russian**-dominated areas, but the Soviet authorities reannexed
Petseri in 1944. The collapse of the **Soviet Union** in 1991 and the creation of an
independent Estonia raised calls for a return to the borders agreed in 1920.
However, Petseri has a predominantly Russian community, a fact which did not
leave the Estonian claim with much weight, and in November 1995 Estonia
agreed to drop its claims to the county.

    Russia and Estonia signed a border treaty, which confirmed the Petseri area as
part of Russia, in May 2005, following Estonia's accession to the **North Atlantic
Treaty Organization** and the **European Union**. However, when during the
ratification process Estonia's Parliament amended the preamble with a reference
to the 1920 Treaty of Tartu, Russia withdrew from the new treaty.

PfP *see* **Partnership for Peace**.

Poles

A west **Slavic people** overwhelmingly dominant in modern Poland with sizeable minority populations in **Belarus**, Germany and Lithuania. The Polish language is very similar to Czech and Slovak. The ancestors of the Poles were dominant in the east of the north European plain by the 10th century when the northern Polanie united with the southern Wislanie to create a single Polish state. Despite their proximity to their east Slavic relations the Poles followed a westward-leaning path through history after accepting **Roman Catholicism** and the Latin script from the Czechs of Bohemia in 966. In the modern period the decline of Polish power was mirrored by the growing importance of **Prussia** (originally based on Königsberg, now called **Kaliningrad**), as a focal point of German unification, and by the westward extension of **Russian** power. The Poles' ethnic homogeneity was greatly challenged as their territory was swallowed up by the neighbouring powers, the Polish state disappearing entirely in the late 18th century. The influx of non-Polish people was accompanied by attempts to germanize and russify the population, with most Poles reduced to little better than the status of serfs. However, the preservation throughout this period of a sense of Polish identity, enhanced by the brief existence of the Napoleonic Duchy of Warsaw, provided a basis for nationalism in the independent state established in 1918. The devastation of the country under Nazi domination after 1939, the obliteration of its minority population of **Jews**, the mass deportations, and then the displacement of ethnic **Germans** (and redrawing of boundaries) in 1945, left modern Poland with an almost entirely ethnic Polish population.

Pontic Greeks

An ethnic Greek minority found in **Georgia** and originally concentrated in the breakaway republic of **Abkhazia**. The Pontic Greeks are ultimately descended from Greek colonists of the **Caucasus region** (who named the Black Sea the Pontic Sea). Practising **Orthodox Christianity**, they were easily assimilated into the mixed-faith Abkhaz population despite a prevalence of Islam. However, the Greeks felt a stronger kinship with the **Georgian** majority in Abkhazia and were exiled along with them after the Abkhaz victory in the 1992–94 separatist war in the region. Most of the 15,000 Pontic Greeks were forced to seek refuge in Greece or Georgia proper and their homes and land were confiscated by the Abkhaz authorities. In the early 21st century the Pontic Greek community expressed concern that efforts to repatriate war migrants were focusing almost exclusively on ethnic Georgians.

Pop, Mihail

Minister of Finance, **Moldova**. Mihail (or Mihai) Pop trained as an economist and worked initially in industry. He rose up through the Ministry of Finance, heading the State Fiscal Inspectorate before joining the Government as Deputy Minister of Finance in 2005. He was appointed full Finance Minister on 12 October 2005.

Pop was born on 31 October 1955 in the village of Apsa de Mijloc in **Transcarpathia, Ukraine**. He studied economics at the Chişinau Polytechnic Institute, specializing in the economics and management of the food industry. Graduating in 1977, he became head of economic planning at the fermented tobacco factory in Falesti, in north Moldova. After nine years there, he was appointed industry co-ordinator economist at Falesti's Agricultural and Industrial Agency. In 1989 he moved away from industry, becoming instructor at the Organizational Agency of the Falesti District Party committee. A year later he was appointed Head of the Finance Agency, and then Deputy Head of the Finance and Economics Department of the Falesti district Executive Committee. From 1994 he was in charge of the State Fiscal Inspectorate for Balti Municipality, and was promoted after five years to head the Main Inspectorate. In May 2005 he was appointed Deputy Finance Minister, and five months later was promoted to full Minister.

Mihail Pop is married and has two children.

Address: Ministry of Finance, Cosmonauţilor 7, 277005 Chişinau.
Telephone: (22) 233575.
Fax: (22) 228610.
Internet: www.fisk.md

Potsdam Agreements

The conclusion of the Potsdam Conference on 17 July 1945 between the Heads of Government of the UK, the USA and the **Soviet Union**, held at Potsdam in Germany following the conclusion of the war in Europe. The Potsdam meeting essentially endorsed the conclusions of the previous summit held in **Yalta**, placing **eastern Europe** effectively within the Soviet sphere of influence. It also established the principle of an international tribunal for war criminals (which became the basis for the Nuremburg trials, and more recently the International Criminal Tribunal for the former Yugoslavia), and agreed a framework for the mass repatriation of ethnic **Germans** from all over eastern Europe.

PPCD *see* **Christian Democratic People's Party**.

PR *see* **Party of Regions**.

Pridnestrovie *see* **Transdnestria.**

Pripet Marshes

Europe's largest marshland, lying across some 270,000 sq km of north-western **Ukraine** and southern **Belarus**. The heavily-wooded and impenetrable region is filled by water from the Pripet and Dnieper rivers and from heavy rainfall. Since 1872 reclamation projects have provided a vast amount of land for agricultural use. The process has been accelerated owing to economic pressures since the late 20th century.

Protestantism

Any Christian denomination founded on the principles of the 16th-century reformers who rejected the hierarchy and supremacy of the **Roman Catholic Church**. Started in Germany by Martin Luther, the Reformation, the adherents of which 'protested' against the authority of the Pope and the decay of the Church, spread across western and northern Europe. Protestantism represented a two-pronged attack on medieval society, on the one hand affirming the political independence of European states from Rome, and on the other attempting to democratize and personalize Christianity for the laity. It served as both a revolutionary movement for greater democracy and at the same time as a means to increase the power of local rulers. The establishment of Protestant states in northern Europe and the rationalist development of the enlightenment stripped mainstream Protestantism of its antagonistic vein and pushed it firmly into the religious mainstream. It is now represented by many different denominations, the major ones of which in **eastern Europe** are Lutheranism and Calvinism. However, it is greatly overshadowed in the region by Roman Catholicism and **Orthodox Christianity**.

Prussia

Historically, the ethnically **German** state whose original centre was around Königsberg (now **Kaliningrad**) and the southern Baltic coast. The Kingdom of Prussia was a key player in European and **pan-German** politics from the 17th century and a key driving force in shaping the German unification process, culminating in 1870–71. Prussia's growth during this period saw it stretch across the economically important regions of Pomerania (along the Baltic coast) and Silesia, both of which are now integral parts of modern Poland. Prussia was effectively reintroduced into the European story in 1919 with the territorial changes imposed on Germany under the Treaty of Versailles. Parts of Pomerania were ceded to Poland, leaving the isolated German exclave of East Prussia as a focus for German nationalism and regional tensions. Following the mass resettlement of populations after the Second World War, most of what was Prussia is now indisputably Polish, with the remainder forming the **Russian** enclave of Kaliningrad.

PSL *see* **Social Liberal Party**.

PTBT *see* **Nuclear Test Ban Treaty**.

Putin, Vladimir

President of the **Russian Federation**. Vladimir Putin was little known when Boris **Yeltsin** made him Prime Minister in 1999; he was then propelled into the presidency by Yeltsin's unexpected resignation that December. He had spent the majority of his career working as a KGB agent, and had no political affiliation in the post-Soviet era. As acting Head of State he pursued the war in **Chechnya** with determined ferocity, and with the **Russian economy** in an apparent state of recovery he won a convincing first-round victory in presidential elections in March 2000. Despite criticism of his behaviour at the time of the sinking of the *Kursk* submarine and draconian security measures following the **Beslan school siege**, Putin has retained his popularity—and his grip on the Russian media—and he won his second election in 2004 with 71% of the vote. He has pushed for greater centralization of power from the regions to **Moscow**.

Vladimir Vladimirovich Putin was born on 7 October 1952 in Leningrad (now **St Petersburg**). His grandfather was Lenin's cook and from a young age Putin expressed a desire to serve the state by working as a spy. In 1975 he graduated from the law department of Leningrad's State University and was immediately recruited by the Committee for State Security (KGB). Little is known of the details of his secret service career other than that he spent most of his time in East Germany following his transfer there in 1984. By the time he left active service in 1990 he had reached the rank of colonel.

Returning to Leningrad (renamed St Petersburg the following year), Putin began work as an adviser on international affairs to the State University and the city council in 1990 and quickly made his name in city politics under his old law professor and mentor, the reformist Mayor Anatoly Sobchak. Putin became a Deputy Mayor and worked as the Chairman of the Committee on Foreign Relations from 1994 to 1996. He instigated a series of successful export quotas designed to generate funds to tackle the city's acute shortages, which had followed hard on the heels of the **Soviet Union**'s collapse in 1991. After Sobchak was defeated in mayoral elections in 1996, Putin moved to Moscow to pursue a governmental career in the **Kremlin**. In 1997 he was appointed as Head of the Control Department, Deputy Manager of Property and Deputy Administrator for the Presidential Department; in the latter role he was an influential adviser to President Yeltsin on matters concerning Russia's regional policy.

In July 1998 Yeltsin promoted Putin to be head of the KGB's successor, the **Federal Security Service** (FSB). In this role his main mandate was economic espionage and cracking down on illegal foreign trading. By March 1999 he had added the role of Secretary of Yeltsin's Security Council and was heavily involved in the dispute with the **North Atlantic Treaty Organization** (NATO) over Kosovo.

On 9 August 1999 Yeltsin named Putin as his new Prime Minister and endorsed him as his preferred presidential heir. Putin's lack of high-powered political experience made him an unusual choice for the role of Prime Minister, the fourth since March 1998. From his first day Putin showed what his approach would be, taking a hard line on separatism in the **Caucasus**, no matter the international response, while leaving the economic policies of his predecessor largely unchanged to minimize domestic upheaval. Rebels in **Dagestan** were crushed with remorseless swiftness, and in October Putin masterminded an invasion of Chechnya. Despite initial media cynicism, this soon won him the rating of Russia's most popular politician, as Russian troops made steady advances on the Chechen capital Grozny. He was also building an impressive base of support in the Duma (lower house of the **Federal Assembly**), with the newly formed pro-Putin grouping Unity Inter-regional Movement (Medved) making sizeable gains in legislative elections in December.

The drama climaxed on 31 December 1999 when Yeltsin publicly announced his resignation and personally nominated Putin as his interim replacement. As acting President, Putin became solely responsible in the public's eye for the continuing Chechen war which persistently overran its 'imminent' end, and he quickly sought to soften his authoritarian image. A hastily drawn together collection of interviews was published as an autobiography, and much was made of his concerns for animal welfare with the release of his e-mail correspondence with the famous ex-film-star activist Brigitte Bardot. Despite mounting international criticism of the war, Putin retained his lead over other Russian politicians and clinched the presidency in the first round of elections in March 2000 with 52.9% of the vote. His nearest rival, Gennadii **Zyuganov**, leader of the **Communist Party of the Russian Federation**, received less than 30%.

One of his first acts as President-elect was to talk of the 'dictatorship of the law' while recommitting his administration to the Chechen war. While some Russian writers talked of a 'modernized Stalinism', others suggested that in Russia 'dictatorship' was not seen as inherently bad. Fears abroad were allayed when Putin assembled an economic think tank comprising the four men considered the most liberal and pro-market on the Russian scene. He also rejected outright the Communist Party's demand that it be included in the new Council of

Ministers in proportion to its size in the Duma. Confirming his non-party style of politics, Putin made it clear that his chosen Ministers would have to leave their party affiliations at the door when they entered his Government. Putin was inaugurated on 7 May.

Domestically, Putin consolidated his power, beginning with a fierce assault on the '**oligarchs**' of the Yeltsin era and a concerted attempt to centralize control over the country's vast infrastructure. In the Duma he enabled the growth of Medved into a full political party which, through mergers and defections, became a rival in size to the Communists. In April 2001 Medved merged with the Fatherland-All Russia party to form **United Russia** (YR).

Putin's political popularity was jolted in August 2000 by the sinking of the *Kursk* nuclear-powered submarine with the loss of all 118 sailors aboard. His hesitation over whether to involve foreign countries in the ultimately doomed rescue effort, and his failure to cancel a vacation on hearing the news, severely damaged his personal standing in Russian eyes. Despite this setback, however, a noticeable cult of personality began forming around the President.

Internationally, Putin's position was revolutionized by the 11 September 2001 terrorist attacks on the USA. Where once he was openly criticized by the West over the war in Chechnya (which he grandly and somewhat disingenuously declared to be 'over' in April 2002), Putin was suddenly welcomed by US President George W. Bush and his allies as a fellow combatant against terrorism. Putin quickly capitalized on this change, toning down previous criticism of the USA's controversial National Missile Defence system, and shelving suspicion of NATO expansion in the **Baltic States** to move instead to participation, through the **NATO-Russia Council**, from May 2002. His publicly cordial relations with Bush became less convincing towards the end of 2002, however, as Putin joined a chorus of doubters over the justification for a US-led war on Iraq.

The YR won a landslide victory in the 2003 parliamentary elections, helped by a media that barely acknowledged other contenders. Putin increased the pressure on the Yeltsin-era 'oligarchs', with such former luminaries as Boris Berezovsky, Mikhail Khodorkovsky and Vladimir Gusinsky subject to government investigations into their business interests. On 24 February 2004, just ahead of presidential elections, Putin sacked his entire Council of Ministers and appointed Viktor Khristenko as Prime Minister.

Putin won the presidential poll on 14 March 2004 with 71% of the vote—his nearest rival, Nikolay Kharitonov, could muster just 14%. His political opponents again claimed media bias, and indeed most Russian television channels were by this stage owned or controlled by Putin and his supporters, and they made little attempt at even-handedness. Nevertheless, the **Organization for Security and Co-operation in Europe** (OSCE) declared the election and the balloting as free and fair. Putin appointed a technocrat, Mikhail **Fradkov**, as Prime Minister.

In September 2004 the Putin presidency faced its second major shock after armed terrorists took hundreds of schoolchildren and their families hostage in

Beslan in North **Ossetia**. In the bloody resolution of the siege, more than 300 people were killed, most of them children. Controversy raged over whether government special forces precipitated the storming of the school and caused booby-trapped explosives to be detonated, and why the number of hostages being held was consistently underestimated by official sources.

Putin responded to the crisis by suggesting a series of draconian reforms of the country's political and security systems. A crackdown on people without identity papers was ordered, while plans were announced to replace directly elected regional governors with appointees from the **Kremlin**. Reintroduction of the death penalty was mooted. These suggestions were generally received well within Russia, with some opinion polls suggesting that they did not go far enough. In response to international criticisms of his proposals, Putin told Western leaders to sit down and negotiate with Osama bin Laden before they told him to negotiate with child-killers.

In November 2004 Putin caused some controversy by endorsing US President George W. Bush ahead of that country's parliamentary elections, though in the event he picked a winner. However, he was not so successful in personally backing Ukrainian presidential candidate Viktor **Yanukovych**. It was even suggested that his unconditional support for Yanukovych in the face of allegations of electoral fraud contributed to provoking **Ukraine**'s **Orange Revolution**. Putin was subsequently more circumspect in offering his endorsements during political upheaval in Kyrgyzstan in 2005.

Putin is constitutionally barred from seeking a third consecutive term in office after March 2008; he has promised to respect the limit, but has announced that he will 'retain influence' after leaving the post. There is much speculation over who he will endorse as his successor; the promotion of Defence Minister Sergei Ivanov to joint First Deputy Chair of the Council of Ministers alongside Dmitry Medvedev in February 2007 was widely viewed as the positioning of Putin's two favourites for the succession.

Vladimir Putin is married to the media-shy Lyudmila; they have two children.

Address: Office of the President, Staraya pl. 42, 103132 Moscow.
Telephone: (495) 9253581.
Fax: (495) 2065173.
E-mail: president@gov.ru
Internet: president.kremlin.ru

Pytalovo *see* **Abrene question**.

R

Rasizade, Artur

Prime Minister of **Azerbaijan**. Artur Rasizade is an engineer by training who worked in machine construction for the oil industry before becoming involved in the State Planning Committee. For the last five years of the Communist era (1986–91) and the first year of independence he was a Deputy Prime Minister at republican level. He is a member of the **New Azerbaijan Party** (YAP), a party of former Communists founded in September 1992 by the country's dominant political figure and long-term president, Heydar **Aliyev**.

Artur Tahir oglu Rasizade was born on 26 February 1935 in Gyandja. He trained as an engineer at the Azerbaijan Institute of Industry and joined the Azerbaijan Institute of Oil Machine Construction when he was 22. He worked there for 21 years, rising to the post of Director in 1973. From 1973 to 1977 he was also chief engineer of Trust Soyuzneftemash. In 1978 he left the engineering sector to become Deputy Head of the Azerbaijan State Planning Committee for three years. Then he joined the Central Committee of the Azerbaijan Communist Party as a head of section from 1981 until 1986, before his appointment as First Deputy Prime Minister. He retained this position until 1992, the year after the independence of Azerbaijan.

When the former Communists were defeated in presidential elections in 1992 by the **Azerbaijan Popular Front Party** (AXCP), Rasizade had to resign and became an adviser to the Foundation of Economic Reforms. Meanwhile Aliyev broke away from the AXCP, which had declared a new age limit for presidential candidates which disqualified him from contesting elections. He formed the YAP (which Rasizade subsequently joined), ousted the AXCP regime, rescinded the age limit and was elected President in 1993.

In February 1996 Rasizade became Aliyev's assistant, before being appointed First Deputy Prime Minister again in May. After the resignation of the Prime Minister on 19 July, following accusations from Aliyev of bad management of the economy, Rasizade became acting Prime Minister. He was confirmed in this position on 26 November 1996, and remained in office following the November 2000 legislative elections.

In August 2003, as part of the manoeuvring around the succession to the ailing veteran President, the **National Assembly** approved the appointment of Aliyev's son Ilham **Aliyev** as Prime Minister, but two days later he took leave to contest the October presidential elections and Rasizade took control again in an acting capacity. Ilham Aliyev reappointed Rasizade as Prime Minister on 4 November 2003, after his own inauguration as President. Rasizade was confirmed in office again following the 2005 legislative polls.

Artur Rasizade is married with one child.

Address: Office of the Prime Minister, Lermontov St 63, 370066 Baku.

Telephone: (12) 4957528.

Fax: (12) 4980822.

Republic
Hanrapetutiun

A small party in **Armenia** formed in 2001 as a splinter of the governing **Republican Party of Armenia** (HHK). Under the leadership of Albert Bazeian, Republic stood in opposition to the HHK in elections in May 2003, winning one seat. Its current leader, former Prime Minister Aram Sarkissian, has steered the party towards a pro-Western stance, calling for Armenia's membership of the **North Atlantic Treaty Organization** (NATO). Bazeian led a faction away from the party in September 2005 in response.

Leadership: Aram Sarkissian (Chair).

Address: Mashtotsi Ave 30-37, 375002 Yerevan.

Telephone: (10) 538634.

E-mail: republic@arminco.com

Republican Party of Armenia
Hayastani Hanrapetakan Kusaktsutyun (HHK)

A centre-right formation which became the main ruling party in **Armenia** in 1999.

The current HHK party was launched in mid-1998 as the result of a merger between the Yerkrapah Union of Veterans (of the **Nagorno-Karabakh** war) and the original HHK, which had been founded in May 1991 and had been part of the victorious Republican Bloc in the 1995 **National Assembly** elections. The Yerkrapah leader and then Defence Minister Vazgen Sarkissian was elected Chairman of the new HHK, which espoused free-market economic policies.

The HHK stood in the May 1999 Assembly elections in an alliance with the left-leaning **People's Party of Armenia** (HZhK) called the Unity (Miasnutiun) bloc, which won 55 of the 131 seats and 41.7% of the proportional vote. As leader of the stronger partner, the HHK's Vazgen Sarkissian became Prime Minister of a Government in which smaller parties were also represented. However, in October 1999 he was one of eight political leaders assassinated by gunmen who invaded an Assembly debate. He was succeeded as Prime Minister by his younger brother, Aram Sarkissian, and as HHK Chairman by Andranik **Markarian**.

In May 2000 Aram Sarkissian was dismissed by President **Kocharian** and replaced by Markarian, who quickly faced opposition from the HHK's Yerkrapah wing, which formed a separate Assembly group strongly critical of the President. Soon afterwards Aram Sarkissian announced his intention to form a new party with Yerkrapah members as its nucleus.

The Miasnutiun alliance was finally dissolved in 2001 as the HZhK declared its partners a 'stooge' for President Kocharian. Shed of its dissenting ally, the HHK went on to cement its ties to the President, and was subsequently retained in Government following its dominance in the May 2003 elections, winning the largest share (33) of the 131 seats and 23.7% of the vote. Markarian was reappointed Prime Minister.

Leadership: Andranik Markarian (Chair).
Address: Melik Adamian St 2, 375010 Yerevan.
Telephone: (10) 580031.
Fax: (10) 581259.
E-mail: hhk@hhk.am
Internet: www.hhk.am

Republican Party of Georgia (RPG)

A small opposition party in **Georgia**. Formed in 1990 as a right-of-centre opposition party, the RPG was temporarily a part of the unsuccessful United Republican Party in 1995. RPG leader David Berdzenishvili was a strong supporter of Mikhail **Saakashvili**'s 2003 **Rose Revolution**, but broke with the new Government in June 2004 complaining of ballot rigging in his home territory of Adzharia. Long opposed to the ousted Adzharian leader Aslan Abashidze, Berdzenishvili claimed that the RPG, which contested new elections in the autonomous area, had been the victim of irregularities perpetrated by the ultimately successful pro-Saakashvili bloc. The RPG immediately announced that its two parliamentarians would join the opposition groups in the **Parliament of Georgia**. David Usupashvili replaced Berdzenishvili as Chairman at the 2005 party congress.

Leadership: David Usupashvili (Chair).
Address: Antoneli 31/2, Tbilisi.
Telephone and Fax: (32) 932536.

E-mail: cdc@access.sanet.ge
Internet: www.republic.org.ge

RIA-Novosti
Rossiiskoye Informatsionnoye Agentstvo-Novosti/Vesti
(Russian Information Agency-News/Guide)

The main state news agency in the **Russian Federation**, focusing originally on supplying information to foreign countries, as opposed to handling domestic markets (*see* **ITAR-TASS**). Novosti was created in 1991 but dates back to the creation in 1941 of the Soviet Information Bureau (Sovinformburo), which was transformed into the Novosti Press Agency (APN) in 1961. APN acted as a tool to spread the Soviet authorities' official line on life in Russia to the outside world, and to keep the Russian people 'informed' about life beyond the **Soviet Union**. Over 120 APN offices were established abroad. It launched the *Moscow News*, which became independent in 1990, and was responsible for publishing more than 200 books. The agency branched into television in 1989 with the launch of TV Novosti. APN was transformed into the RIA in 1991 and was subordinated to the Foreign Ministry in the newly democratic Russian Federation. In 1998 RIA was officially renamed RIA-Vesti (guide), but retained the 'Novosti' suffix in general use.

Chair: Svetlana Mironyuk.
Address: Zubovskii blvd 4, 103786 Moscow.
Telephone: (495) 2018209.
Fax: (495) 2014545.
E-mail: marketing@rian.ru
Internet: www.rian.ru

Riga, Treaties of

Two peace treaties signed by the **Soviet Union** with neighbouring countries. The first, signed with Latvia on 11 August 1920 at the conclusion of the brief war between the two countries, included the recognition of Latvian independence by the Soviet Government (later revoked) and the cession of the **Abrene** region to Latvia. The second was signed with Poland on 18 March 1921 after the defeat of a Polish invasion of **Russia**. It fixed the two countries' border mid-way between the medieval Polish border far to the east and its modern edge to the west. The second treaty was revoked with the division of Poland between Soviet and Nazi forces in 1939 (*see* **Nazi-Soviet Pact**). *See also* Treaties of **Tartu**.

Rightist Opposition
Memarjvene Opozitsia (MO)

An opposition grouping in **Georgia**. Formed in early 2004 from a union of two parties, the **New Rights** (Conservative) party and **Industry Will Save Georgia**. The grouping claimed 7.6% of the vote in the March 2004 re-run election, when it was one of only two groupings to pass the 7% barrier to receive seats. It was allocated 15 of the 150 party-list seats at stake in the re-run (adding to the eight seats that its constituent parties had won as single-seat constituencies in November 2003) and is consequently dwarfed by the ruling **National Movement-Democrats**.

The Rightist Opposition, as its name suggests, steers a political path to the right of the Government. Efforts to galvanize opposition to the **Saakashvili** Government have been slow to gain momentum. Criticism of the Government has hinged around an apparent adoption of authoritarian attitudes, following the suspicious beating of an opposition activist in July 2005.

Leadership: David Gamkhrelidze (Joint Chair, New Rights), Giorgi Topadze (Joint Chair, Industry Will Save Georgia).

Rodina *see* **Motherland**.

Roma

A nomadic people of traditionally-mixed ethnicity who arrived in Europe from the Indian sub-continent in waves of migration beginning in the 9th century. There are around 10 million–12 million worldwide, and are also known in English as the Gypsies, a name generally considered to be derogatory and which is derived from the misconception that they originated in Egypt. As a nomadic people they spread across the European continent and have been subject to serious discrimination and outright abuse ever since.

They were often enslaved in feudal societies. Following the end of Romani slavery in the mid-19th century, great numbers joined other disfavoured groups of European society in emigrating to the New World. One of the most systematic persecutions of Roma was in the Nazi Holocaust when an estimated half a million were liquidated in death camps across occupied territories.

Persecution continued after the Second World War on a local level, with many regional authorities reflecting popular prejudice in open discrimination. Often Roma have been forced to take on a settled lifestyle so as to participate in the industrialization of the European economies. To this day the Roma are seriously maligned as a minority across **eastern Europe**, with poor access to education and employment, and are targeted in violent attacks by the extreme right. However, the division of Romani society into sub-tribes has greatly hindered collective action to press for greater rights.

Roman Catholic Church

The dominant Christian denomination centred on the Vatican City in Rome. Roman Catholicism (often just called Catholicism, taking its name from catholic, meaning 'universal') is the largest single religious denomination in the world and is prevalent over much of Europe, particularly in western and **central Europe**. It chiefly differs from other Christian Churches in its belief in the primacy of the Bishop of Rome (Pope) as the 'Vicar of Christ'. It was divided from **Orthodox Christianity** in the Great Schism of 1054 (a split which, more than 900 years later, formed the basis of one of the principal divisions in Yugoslavia), and from **Protestantism** during the 16th-century Reformation. The cult of the saints and particularly the Virgin Mary are very strong. The role of priests is central to the religion. Unlike in most other Christian denominations, Roman Catholic priests (only men) take a vow of celibacy. The election of the Polish Cardinal Karol Wojtyła as Pope John Paul II in 1978 (the first Polish Pope ever, and the first non-Italian pontiff for over 400 years) brought Catholicism closer to the communist-dominated east and helped link it to pro-democracy movements such as Poland's Solidarity. Pope John Paul II also attempted to breach the divide between Catholicism and Orthodoxy, making historic visits to Greece and **Ukraine** in 2001. Pope John Paul II died in April 2005 and was succeeded by Pope Benedict XVI.

The connection between spiritual and temporal power and the Church's inherent conservatism have led to the formation of Catholic-orientated right-of-centre political parties in many central European countries, often called Christian Democrats or People's parties. Catholic political activity and influence often attracted repression under communist rule, although the Church's popularity in some countries led to efforts to integrate it into the political mainstream.

Despite the close association of much of **eastern Europe** with Orthodoxy, there are some 70 million Catholics in the region with the largest congregations in Poland (37 million—96% of the population), Hungary (7.4 million—77%) and the Czech Republic (4 million—43%). Countries with majority Catholic populations are Croatia, Hungary, Lithuania, Poland, Slovakia and Slovenia. All Roman Catholic Churches are subordinate to the papacy, as is the **Uniate Church**.

Romanians

An Indo-European people indigenous to the fertile banks of the eastern end of the Danube and now comprising around 90% of people in the modern state of

Romania. A growing number of Romanians live abroad, with around 150,000 in **Ukraine**. Romanians are ethnically and linguistically identical to the neighbouring **Moldovans**, differing only in that they use the Latin alphabet rather than the **Cyrillic alphabet**. Both are descended from ancient **Vlach** communities. At the 2004 Moldovan census, there were 75,000 Romanians in Moldova, but a further two million Moldovans (out of a total population of 4.2 million) identified Romanian as their main language.

The Romanian language is derived ultimately from Latin and has strong similarities with modern Italian. The region converted to Christianity at the time of the Roman Empire. A majority of modern Romanians practise **Orthodox Christianity**. Despite their shared creed the Romanians foster a sense of cultural isolation amidst the predominantly Slavic countries around them (*see* **Slavic peoples**).

Romanov dynasty

The royal dynasty which ruled **Russia** from 1613 until the first Russian Revolution of February 1917. Key members of the dynasty include: its founder Michael Romanov, Peter the Great who transformed the Kingdom into an Empire in 1721, Alexander II who abolished serfdom in 1861 and the final Tsar, Nicholas II, who abdicated in 1917 and was infamously murdered, along with his entire family and retinue, in Yekaterinburg on 17 July 1918. The Bolshevik Government maintained that the execution had never been officially sanctioned, and was treated as a crime. Remains which were generally accepted to be the bones of the Romanov family, exhumed from their unmarked forest grave in 1991, were reinterred in July 1998 in St Petersburg, though scientific debate continues over the accuracy of the identification. The remains of the Tsar's mother Empress Maria Feodorovna were moved from Denmark to share the same imperial crypt in 2006.

Nicholas II and his family were elevated to sainthood in 2000 by the **Russian Orthodox Church**. He became the fourth Russian monarch to be canonized, although the Church stressed that it was for his execution that he had been sanctified and not for his much-criticized reign. The move reflected the growing popular cult of the Tsar, adopted by nationalists and royalists.

Rose Revolution

The peaceful 'colour revolution' in **Georgia** that ousted President Eduard **Shevardnadze** in November 2003.

In the run-up to the November 2003 parliamentary elections, the anti-Shevardnadze lobby, headed by former Justice Minister Mikhail **Saakashvili**, gained significant ground. Meanwhile, a student movement (Kmara—'Enough'), self-consciously modelled on the successful Otpor movement which had helped to topple President Slobodan Milošević in Serbia in 2000, began organizing widespread anti-government demonstrations. The elections produced an apparent easy victory for the ruling **Citizens' Union of Georgia** (SMK), but international observers found many irregularities in the poll; independent exit polls supported Saakashvili's claim that his United National Movement (*see* **National Movement-Democrats—NM-D**) had in fact won the election. Thousands of people took to the streets of **Tbilisi**, mainly under the organization of the Kmara movement, to demand the holding of a new, free poll. Counter-demonstrations also marched through the capital, their numbers boosted by **Adzharians** sent to support the Shevardnadze Government by Adzharian President Aslan Abashidze. On 22 November Saakashvili led a peaceful protest of 30,000 people with roses in their hands (hence the name Rose Revolution) against the opening of the new **Parliament**; it quickly organized itself into a direct march on the chamber itself. Government troops refused to stop the invaders—the protesters placed roses in their gun barrels—and Shevardnadze was hustled out of the chamber by his supporters. The next day, following a meeting with Saakashvili and another opposition leader Nino Burdzhanadze, arranged by the **Russian** Foreign Minister, Shevardnadze announced his resignation. Burjanadze became acting President until presidential and partial legislative elections were held in March 2004, won by Saakashvili and his NM-D.

Tensions continued between the new Government in Tbilisi and Abashidze's regime in Adzharia. Under organization from the NM-D and Kmara, thousands of Adzharians launched the second Rose Revolution on the streets of Batumi, the Adzharian capital, and Kobuleti in early May 2004, protesting against Abashidze's dictatorial and confrontational policies. Troops were sent in to disperse the crowds, but the people returned to the streets in the following days in greater numbers. On 6 May Abashidze announced his resignation, and fled to **Moscow**.

Rosoboronexport

The state-run arms-exporting monopoly which accounts for almost 90% of defence-related exports from the **Russian Federation**. Rosoboronexport was created from the amalgamation of the two leading state-run arms exporters, Rosvooruzenie and Promexport, in November 2000. It has built on previous experience in marketing and selling complete defence systems around the world. Exports include everything from tanks and warships, to fighter planes and space rockets and even general purpose vehicles and handheld weapons.

In August 2006 the US Government imposed sanctions on Rosoboronexport for supplying anti-aircraft defences to Iran, in contravention of the USA's Iran Non-Proliferation Act of 2000.

Director-General: Sergey V. Chemezov.
Address: ul. Stromynka 27/3, 107076 Moscow.
Telephone: (495) 9646140.
Fax: (495) 9632613.
Internet: www.roe.ru

Rosspirtprom

The state-run brewery and management company established to centralize and regulate the production of alcohol, principally vodka, in the **Russian Federation**. Rosspirtprom, often referred to as the 'alcohol ministry', was created within months of President Vladimir **Putin**'s inauguration in mid-2000, and by December 2001 had taken control of many regional distilleries and vodka producers. However, a majority of producers remain independent and the entire industry has become riddled with illegal producers.
Director-General: Igor Chuyan.
Address: Kutuzovsky pr. 34, 21A, 121170 Moscow.
Telephone and Fax: (495) 7853825.
E-mail: rsp@rosspirtprom.ru
Internet: www.rosspirtprom.ru

Rouble zone

The zone, originally comprising all 15 countries of the former **Soviet Union**, within which the rouble continued to operate as a single currency for the initial period after the break-up of the Soviet Union in December 1991. This was initially a *de facto* arrangement, there being no other currency arrangements in place in the countries concerned. The **Central Bank of the Russian Federation** was the sole issuer of cash roubles, and the central banks of the new states issued money substitutes tied to the rouble's value at 1:1 parity. All countries were also entitled to issue credit within prescribed limits, and in practice did so without observing those limits.

Fundamental disagreements between the 15 countries about the desirable pace of economic reform, together with their need to make radical changes in the pattern of economic activity, undermined the case for retaining a single currency. Payments and settlements in roubles effectively meant that large price increases for fuel and raw materials fed through directly in the form of cost inflation in the various post-Soviet economies. The **Baltic States**, led by Estonia in June 1992, were the first to leave the rouble zone and establish their own currencies. In October 1992, eight **Commonwealth of Independent States** (CIS) participants—**Armenia**, **Belarus**, Kazakhstan, Kyrgyzstan, **Moldova**, **Russian**

Federation, Uzbekistan and **Ukraine**—signed an agreement on a single currency system and co-ordinated monetary policy. However, this idea was not implemented, and more countries issued their own national currencies. Ukraine in November 1992 took this step by way of the intermediate stage of issuing coupons, moving subsequently to a full national currency, a route also followed by others such as **Georgia** and Uzbekistan. Also, by mid-1993, the Russian Federation was increasingly concerned that its own ability to control monetary policy was weakened by the fact that the rouble remained the currency of other CIS states.

The rouble zone had thus become to a large extent defunct by mid-1993. In July of that year, following the Russian Federation's own currency reform, six countries—Armenia, Belarus, Kazakhstan, Russian Federation, Tajikistan and Uzbekistan—signed an agreement on setting up a new-style rouble zone, but this also was never implemented, the Russians alienating the other potential participants by insisting that all gold and convertible currency reserves from rouble zone countries should be held in **Moscow**.

Attempts to use the CIS structure as a route to monetary union, with a central bank set up in 1993 and a payments union created nominally in 1994, have flown in the face of the increasing insistence on national-level control of the economy. Tajikistan, the last country to introduce its own currency, used the Tajik rouble from May 1995 until 30 October 2000 when its new currency, the somoni, was introduced. The rouble remained legal tender until 1 April 2001.

In Belarus, however, President **Lukashenka** promoted a trend in the other direction, towards reunification with the Russian Federation. A draft agreement on the creation of a rouble zone involving the two countries was signed in May 2003, but the scheduled date for the introduction of the combined currency has repeatedly been postponed as enthusiasm for the **Belarus-Russia Union** has waned in recent years.

RPG *see* **Republican Party of Georgia**.

Russia *see* **Russian Federation**.

Russian Aluminium (RusAl)

A large private company based in the **Russian Federation** which produces and exports aluminium products.

Founded in March 2000 through the merger of Sibirsky Aluminium and Sibneft, RusAl has operations across the world. It is now the world's third largest producer of primary aluminium products (and the largest privately-owned producer). In October 2006 it announced a merger with its main Russian competitor Siberian Ural Aluminium (SUAL), to proceed in 2007 if approved by the Russian Government.

Chair of the Board of Directors: Oleg V. Deripaska.
Chief Executive Officer: Alexander Bulygin.
Address: ul. Nikoloyamskaya 13/1, 109240 Moscow.
Telephone: (495) 7205170.
Fax: (495) 7457046.
E-mail: press-center@rusal.ru
Internet: www.rusal.com

Russian Federal Property Fund

Founded in 1992 to ensure consistency in the privatization process and to implement privatization legislation. It operates under the aegis of the Council of Ministers, carrying out legislation passed by the Russian Federation.

Chair: Igor Ivanovich Shuvalov.
Address: Leninskii pr. 9, 119049 Moscow.
Telephone: (495) 9167030.
Fax: (495) 9167164.
E-mail: info@fpf.ru
Internet: www.fpf.ru

Russian Federation
Rossiyskaya Federatsiya

The Russian federal state, an independent sovereign state since the demise in 1991 of the **Soviet Union**, which had included the Russian Soviet Federative Socialist Republic (RSFSR) as its largest element.

The territory of the Russian Federation is identical with that of the former RSFSR, spanning north-eastern Europe and stretching beyond the Ural mountains across northern Asia to the Pacific Ocean. The area commonly considered to constitute **European Russia** is bounded in the north by the Barents Sea, in the east by the Urals, and in the south by the **Caucasus** mountains. It has outlets to the Caspian Sea and the Black Sea in the south, and to the Baltic Sea in the north-west along a short coastline near **St Petersburg**. It also includes the enclave of **Kaliningrad** (former German Königsberg) further to the west, which has its own Baltic coastline but is separated from the rest of the Russian Federation by Lithuania and **Belarus**. The Kaliningrad enclave has borders with Lithuania and Poland, while the main territory of the Russian Federation has borders with another 12 countries: Norway in the far north-west, Finland, Estonia, Latvia, Belarus, **Ukraine**, **Georgia**, **Azerbaijan**, Kazakhstan, Mongolia, China and

North Korea.

Administratively, the country consists of 86 federal units, which were grouped into seven federal districts under a presidential decree of May 2000.

Area: 17,075,200 sq km; capital: **Moscow** (Moskva); *population*: 143m. (2005 estimate), comprising **Russians** 79.8%, **Tatars** 3.8%, **Ukrainians** 2%, Bashkirs (*see* **Bashkortostan**) 1.2%, **Chavash** 1.1%, Chechens (*see* **Chechnya**) 0.9%, **Armenians** 0.8%, Mordvin (*see* **Mordovia**) 0.6%, **Belarusians** 0.6%, others 9.2%; *official language*: Russian; *religion*: **Russian Orthodox** (75%), **Muslim** (10%) and others (15%).

Under the Constitution approved in 1993, executive authority is vested in the President, who is directly elected for a maximum of two four-year terms. The President appoints the Chair of the Council of Ministers (who takes over from the President in the event that he cannot carry out his duties), subject to approval by the legislature. Legislative authority rests with the bicameral **Federal Assembly** (Federalnoye Sobraniye), consisting of (i) the upper 172-member Council of the Federation (Soviet Federatsii), to which each of the 86 federal administrative units returns two representatives; and (ii) the lower State Duma (Gossoudarstvennaya Duma), half of whose 450 members are directly elected for a four-year term from single-member constituencies and half by proportional representation from party lists. If the State Duma rejects three presidential nominations to the office of Chair of the Council of Ministers (Prime Minister), the President is required to dissolve the Duma and order fresh elections.

History: The first unified state of Eastern **Slavs**, Kievan Rus, was founded around **Kiev** (Kyiv) in the late 9th century, converting to Orthodox Christianity in about 988. Invaded by the Mongol Tatars in the 13th century, Russia was ruled by the khanate of the Golden Horde until the Muscovite prince Ivan III ('the Great') unified the Russian principalities in the late 15th century and formed a centralized independent state. In the 16th century Ivan IV ('the Terrible'), who was crowned 'Tsar of Muscovy and all Russia' in 1547 and ruled until 1584, began the eastern expansion of Russian territory. Peter the Great, who reigned from 1682 to 1725, established Russia as a European power, modernizing the civil and military institutions of the state and founding St Petersburg as the new capital and centre for Russia's first navy. By the end of his reign Sweden had ceded the Baltic territories of present-day Estonia and Latvia to Russia. Catherine the Great, who ruled in 1762–96, continued to expand the Russian Empire, southwards in wars with the Ottoman Turks and westwards as a result of the partitions of Poland, in which Russia absorbed what are now Belarus, Lithuania and Ukraine.

During the reign of Alexander I (1801–25), Russia seized Finland from Sweden and **Bessarabia** from Turkey, and repelled the invading French forces of Napoleon Bonaparte. Under Tsars Nicholas I (1825–55) and Alexander II (1855–81), Russia's frontiers were extended into the **Caucasus**, central Asia and the Far East. Meanwhile, British and French mistrust of Russian territorial ambitions led to the Crimean War of 1853–56. Having abolished serfdom in 1861, Alexander II was assassinated in 1881, as internal opposition mounted to autocratic rule and general economic deprivation. Russia's humiliating defeat in its 1904–05 war with Japan provoked insurrection at home, the last Tsar, Nicholas II, being forced to introduce limited political reforms, including elections to a parliament (Duma).

Russian military reverses in the First World War, coupled with domestic economic and social chaos, left the tsarist regime so weakened and vulnerable that it was overthrown in 1917. The first of the two revolutions of that year, the February Revolution, forced the Tsar to abdicate in favour of a provisional Government, which forfeited popular support by opting to remain in the war. In the October Revolution the anti-war Bolsheviks (the communist majority wing of the Russian Social Democratic Labour Party) led by Vladimir Ilyich Lenin seized power and proclaimed the Russian Soviet Federative Socialist Republic (RSFSR) with **Moscow** as its capital. The Treaty of Brest-Litovsk of March 1918 ended the war with Germany and the other Central Powers on draconian territorial terms for Russia. The Tsar and his family were executed in July, as civil war erupted between the Bolshevik Red Army and 'White' anti-communist forces supported by the UK and France. By 1922 the Red Army had defeated the 'White' challenge and regained control of Belarus, eastern Ukraine, **Transcaucasia** and the central Asian republics. These territories were united with the RSFSR to form the Union of Soviet Socialist Republics (USSR or **Soviet Union**).

Following Lenin's death in 1924, power passed to Josef Stalin as General Secretary of what became the All-Union Communist Party (Bolsheviks) in 1925. Creating a highly-centralized regime, Stalin instituted a programme of accelerated industrialization under a series of five-year plans, as well as the forcible collectivization of agriculture (at the cost of widespread famine). To maintain his leadership position, Stalin initiated a campaign of internal repression and political purges, resulting in mass arrests and executions in the 1930s.

Despite the signing of the **Nazi-Soviet Pact** shortly before the outbreak of the Second World War in 1939 and consequent Russian territorial gains, collaboration with Hitler's regime ended abruptly in June 1941 when German forces invaded the Soviet Union. An estimated 20 million Soviet citizens died in the subsequent Great Patriotic War before Germany surrendered to the Allied Powers (principally the Soviet Union, UK and USA) in 1945, with the Red Army in control of most of **central** and **eastern Europe**. Under the post-war settlement, the Soviet Union not only recovered all the Russian territories lost in 1918 but also annexed eastern Poland, eastern **Prussia** (from Germany), substantial Finnish territory, Ruthenia (from Czechoslovakia—*see* **Transcarpathia**) and northern **Bukovina** (from Romania), as well as the southern Kurile Islands (from Japan). Stalin proceeded to install communist regimes in the countries of what became known as the Soviet bloc, bringing down a so-called 'iron curtain' across Europe. Tensions with the Western powers deteriorated into the **Cold War** after the Soviet Union became a nuclear power in 1949.

After Stalin's death in 1953, Nikita Khrushchev eventually established undisputed power as leader of what had become the **Communist Party of the Soviet Union** (KPSS). At the 20th KPSS congress in 1956 Khrushchev stunned the world by denouncing Stalin's dictatorship and cult of personality, but his domestic bombshell had little effect on East–West tensions. Having formed the **Warsaw Pact** military alliance with its satellite states in 1955, the Soviet Union developed an inter-continental ballistic missile capability (by 1956) and inaugurated manned space flight (in 1961). Ideological differences with communist-ruled China led to an open rift in 1960, while in 1962 the Soviet Union came to the brink of nuclear war with the USA in the Cuban missile crisis.

The increasingly erratic Khrushchev was deposed in 1964 and replaced by Leonid Brezhnev, who maintained rigid communist orthodoxy. During the Brezhnev era the Soviet Union appeared to have established itself as a military and political superpower, recognition of which status facilitated an improvement in Soviet–US relations in the 1970s. However, East–West détente and disarmament initiatives were undermined by the Soviet invasion of Afghanistan in 1979, while the ultimate failure of that intervention not only revealed the serious limitations of Soviet military power but also stimulated the first popular criticism of the KPSS regime.

Brezhnev's death in November 1982 was followed by a 30-month interregnum, during which first Yurii Andropov and then Konstantin Chernenko died in office as Soviet leader. In March 1985 the 54-year-old Mikhail **Gorbachev**, a reformist, became KPSS leader (and in 1988 also Head of State), initiating radical economic and political change under the *glasnost* (openness) and *perestroika* (restructuring) initiatives and a new détente in international relations. The major nuclear accident at **Chernobyl** in 1986 heightened awareness of the need for fundamental reform in the Soviet polity. Events accelerated in 1989 as the European satellite communist regimes collapsed one after another, while some of the Soviet Union republics declared independence. Seeking to preserve the Soviet Union, Gorbachev proposed a new voluntary Union federation, before an attempted coup in Moscow in August 1991 (*see* **August coup**) sought to reinstate hardline communist government. The failure of the coup attempt was due in large measure to determined resistance by democratic forces led by Boris **Yeltsin**, the recently-elected President of the Russian Federation.

The failed coup accelerated the break-up of the Soviet system, in that most of the republican parties withdrew from the KPSS while it was in progress, and were subsequently banned or suspended as the republics asserted their independence. In the Russian Federation itself both the KPSS and its Russian wing were banned in November 1991 by presidential decree, their assets being declared state property. On 21 December 1991 the Russian Federation and 10 other Soviet republics signed up to the **Commonwealth of Independent States** (CIS), thereby effectively dissolving the Soviet Union, of which Gorbachev resigned as President four days later.

In the newly independent Russian Federation, a power struggle ensued between President Yeltsin, backed by reformist political groups, and the legislative structure left over from the Soviet era. In September 1993 Yeltsin dissolved the Congress of People's Deputies and announced elections to a new bicameral Federal Assembly. At an emergency session of the Congress on the night of 21–22 September, however, Vice-President Aleksandr Rutskoi was appointed acting President and led a revolt against Yeltsin. A siege of the **White House** (the parliament building) followed, until troops loyal to Yeltsin stormed it on 4 October, with over 100 fatalities and the arrest of the leaders of the revolt.

A referendum on a new constitution granting the President substantial authority to govern by decree was held in December 1993, together with the first post-Soviet parliamentary elections. The approval of the Constitution by 58.4% of the vote was a victory for Yeltsin. However, the Federal Assembly elections, while resulting in the emergence of the pro-reform Russia's Democratic Choice (DVR) as the largest bloc in the State Duma, also saw the unexpected rise of the right-wing nationalist **Liberal Democratic Party of Russia** (LDPR) and the achievement of significant representation by the revived **Communist Party of the Russian Federation** (KPRF).

In 1994 civil war broke out in predominantly Muslim **Chechnya**, which had declared its independence in 1991 after a nationalist coup and had refused to sign the Russian Federation Treaty the following year. Russian military intervention in the face of fierce Chechen resistance resulted in a high civilian death toll and increasing international concern. Opposition to the Government's handling of the crisis and concerns about Yeltsin's faltering health were reflected in the results of further State Duma elections in December 1995, when the KPRF became substantially the largest parliamentary group with 157 seats and the DVR retained only nine deputies.

Yeltsin responded to the conservative left's electoral advance by dropping prominent reformists from the Government. He nevertheless faced a strong challenge in presidential elections in mid-1996, obtaining only a marginal first-round lead over KPRF leader Gennadii **Zyuganov**. Yeltsin therefore speedily appointed the third-placed candidate, ex-Gen. Aleksandr Lebed of the nationalist Congress of Russian Communities, as National Security Adviser, this alliance enabling him to win the second ballot against Zyuganov with 54% of the vote. Lebed resumed negotiations with the Chechen rebel leadership in August 1996, concluding a ceasefire and withdrawal agreement which deferred a final decision on Chechen sovereignty for five years.

Facing the opposition of a KPRF-dominated State Duma, Yeltsin used his strong presidential powers to make frequent and increasingly unpredictable government changes, dismissing four Prime Ministers (Viktor Chernomyrdin, Sergei Kiriyenko, Yevgenii Primakov and Sergei Stepashin) between March 1998 and August 1999, as his deteriorating health and drinking habits gave increasing cause for concern. Stepashin's successor was Vladimir **Putin**, a former official of the KGB (*see* **Federal Security Service**) and then politically unknown, who was also nominated as Yeltsin's preferred candidate for the next presidential elections due in 2000.

Concurrently with the political turmoil in Moscow, Muslim insurgents declared an independent Islamic state in the southern republic of **Dagestan** in August 1999, while the following month further political violence linked to Chechen Islamic separatism led to renewed Russian military intervention in the republic. Russian forces besieged the rebel-held Chechen capital of Grozny, finally capturing it in February 2000 after a ferocious assault which, although popular with the Russian public, attracted widespread international criticism.

Elections to the State Duma in December 1999 resulted in the conservative left and the ultra-nationalists losing ground to more liberal formations. The KPRF declined to 113 seats while the new pro-Putin Unity Inter-regional Movement (Medved) won 72 seats.

In a surprise announcement on 31 December 1999, President Yeltsin resigned from office, Putin becoming acting President pending fresh presidential elections. These were held in March 2000 and resulted in Putin, running without party affiliation but backed by most of the centre-right formations, achieving a comfortable first-round victory.

On being inaugurated in May, President Putin appointed Mikhail Kasyanov (First Deputy Prime Minister and Finance Minister under Yeltsin) as Prime Minister, heading a Government which included some reformists in economic ministries but showed continuity with the previous administration in the 'power' ministries covering national security. Putin's first legislative initiative was aimed at curtailing the powers of the elected governors of the Russian Federation's constituent regions, who had often resisted central policy decisions. Seven 'super-regions' were created to encompass the federal units, numbering at that time 89, with presidential envoys being appointed to each to ensure compliance with federal legislation.

Putin also ended the automatic right of leaders of the federal units to sit in the Council of the Federation (the upper chamber of the federal legislature), creating as an alternative a new advisory State Council as a forum in which the Presidents and Governors of the federal entities would advise on regional issues. In the State Duma, Putin could normally rely on majority support from the groups of the centre-right led by Medved, although these continued in apparently endless flux, in contrast to the constancy of the KPRF on the conservative left.

Putin's high post-election standing was badly dented in August 2000 when the Russian nuclear submarine *Kursk* sank in the Barents Sea with the loss of all 118 personnel on board. The President was strongly criticized for being slow to react to the disaster, which was seen as highlighting the deterioration in Russian capabilities and the unchanged official inclination to withhold information.

At the end of 2000 the Russian Federation adopted a new national anthem restoring the Soviet-era tune (with new words), as well as state insignia based on those of the tsarist era. In March 2001 the Interior and Defence Ministers were replaced in changes described by Putin as 'the demilitarization of public life'. Later in the year proposals to formalize the party system were finalized with a law on party formation passed on 29 June: parties now had to pass a certain threshold of support across the country to be officially registered. In April 2001 the union of Medved and Fatherland-All Russia (OVR) into the **United Russia** (YR) consolidated parliamentary support for Putin with its *de facto* emergence as the largest single party in the Duma.

A key policy in Putin's first term was the pursuit of the so-called '**oligarchs**'; the new super-rich who had amassed fortunes and economic influence under Yeltsin. Chasing down alleged tax evasion, Putin rounded on Vladimir Gusinsky (head of telecommunications firm Media-MOST), Boris Berezovsky (leading shareholder in television firm ORT) and Mikhail Khodorkovsky (Chairman of the petroleum giant **Yukos**). All were forced into exile or arrested in the course of 2000–03. Meanwhile, state companies, principally the gas concern **Gazprom**, were manoeuvred to hold a majority stake in the abandoned companies, prompting accusations of overt state control of the economy. None the less, Putin's strict approach to the 'oligarchs' won him continued domestic support, as did his strong hand against Islamic terrorists. High-profile attacks in a Moscow theatre (*see* **Moscow theatre siege**) in October 2002 and in the city's Metro in February 2004, and a number of smaller-scale incidents throughout European Russia, kept the Islamic terrorist threat to the forefront of public consciousness.

Latest elections: Elections to the State Duma on 7 December 2003 resulted in victory for YR with 120 of the 225 proportional representation seats (with 37.1% of the vote) and 102 of the 225 majority seats. The KPRF declined to a total of 52 seats (with a party-list vote share of 12.7%), while the **Motherland** (Rodina) bloc won 37 seats (9.1%), the LDPR 36 (11.6%), the **People's Party of the Russian Federation** (NPRF) 16 (1.2%), Yavlinskii-Boldyrev-Lukin Bloc (**Yabloko**) 4 (4.3%), the **Union of Right Forces** (SPS) 3 (4%), the **Agrarian Party of Russia** (APR) 2 (3.8%), others 9 and independents 69.

In the 14 March 2004 presidential election Putin again achieved a comfortable first-round victory with 71% of the vote against 14% for Nikolay Kharitonov of the KPRF; four other candidates contested the election.

Recent developments: In a growing atmosphere of conflict with Kasyanov, Putin had sacked his entire Council of Ministers in February 2004 and appointed Viktor Kristenko as the new Prime Minister, but after the March elections he in turn was replaced by unknown technocrat Mikhail **Fradkov** as Prime Minister. The failure of opposition forces to come together during the 2003–04 elections meant that they posed no credible alternative to Putin, leaving him with an undeniably convincing mandate in a YR-dominated Duma. Learning from the *Kursk* disaster, Putin was quick to show sympathy for the families of victims in the aftermath of the bloody attack by Islamists on a school in **Beslan**, North Ossetia, in September 2004. He also used it as a pretext for pushing through further centralization of the regions in December, with a law ending the election of all regional governors in favour of presidential appointment. The last gubernatorial election was held in Nenets Autonomous *Okrug*, in January 2005 and more than a third of regional governors have been replaced by the central Government since then. New electoral laws, passed in April 2005, have outlawed the formation of electoral blocs in an another effort to further the process of 'vertical centralization' which tightens the political control of Putin's backers.

The KPRF did manage to force a rethink on social welfare reforms in January 2005 with an unsuccessful, but noted, vote of no-confidence in the Government. Concerns continue over the stretch of state-controlled organ Gazprom: it bought the leading newspaper *Izvestiya* in June 2005 and a controlling share in oil company Sibneft in October.

Putin has declared that he will not seek to amend the Constitution to allow himself to run for a third term in office in 2008, though there is continuing pressure from his political backers for him to do so. In September 2005, Putin suggested he might take up an advisory role after 2008, amidst a growing number of candidacy declarations, including one from former Prime Minister Kasyanov. The promotion of Defence Minister Sergei Ivanov to joint First Deputy Chair of the Council of Ministers alongside Dmitry Medvedev in February 2007 was widely viewed as the positioning of Putin's two favourites for the succession.

International support for NGOs working in the field of human rights and political accountability, has riled the Putin administration. A high-profile 'spy ring', involving British diplomats feeding information and funds to NGOs, was broken in January 2006, leading anti-Putin critics to warn of an impending crackdown on the work of such organizations in the lead up to presidential elections in 2008. Former KGB/FSB officer Alexander Litvinenko accused Putin of personally authorizing the assassination of investigative journalist Anna Politkovskaya in October 2006, shortly before his own unexplained murder by polonium-210 radiation poisoning in London in November. There is also particular concern over the rapidly growing number of racist killings in Russia, mostly in Moscow where they are an almost daily occurrence.

International relations and defence: The Russian Federation succeeded to the Soviet Union's seat on the UN Security Council in 1991, and its membership of the **Organization for Security and Co-operation in Europe**, also assuming the Soviet Union's obligations under international and bilateral arms control treaties. It subsequently became a member of the **Council of Europe**, the **Organization of the Black Sea Economic Co-operation** and the **Arctic Council**.

A partnership and co-operation agreement with the **European Union** (EU) entered into force in 1997, since when Russian Presidents have regularly conferred with EU leaders during EU summits. The Russian Federation is also a member of the **Group of Eight** (whose other members are the Group of Seven leading industrialized countries). Russia is actively seeking final approval of its bid for membership of the **World Trade Organization**, expected in 2007.

A participant in NATO's **Partnership for Peace** programme since 1994, the Russian Federation signed a further important co-operation agreement with the alliance in May 1997. However, relations cooled during 1999 over Russian opposition to NATO's enlargement into eastern Europe and the alliance's bombing campaign against **Serbia** over the conflict in Kosovo. Russian troops joined the subsequent UN-approved peacekeeping force in Kosovo, however, and relations with the USA in particular received a major boost as a consequence of the Russian Federation's supportive stance in the immediate aftermath of the September 2001 terrorist attacks on New York and Washington, DC. In May 2002 the **NATO-Russia Council** was formed.

Since then, however, as President Putin's administration has steadily reasserted Russia's independent stance in the international arena, the West has become increasingly critical of the degradation of media freedoms, the rise of racially motivated violence in Moscow and the continued war of attrition in Chechnya.

Relations with the USA chilled noticeably as Russia opposed the 2003 US-led invasion of Iraq and resented the open US courting of new alliances among Russia's traditional sphere of influence in central Asia. The Russian Federation's dealings with Iran, over that country's desire to pursue a nuclear energy programme, has been another bone of contention between Putin and the West. Offering to take the Iranian programme in hand, and forcefully rejecting US and EU-based moves to present a unified stance through the UN in September 2005, the Putin Government again set out its independent stance over the geopolitical situation in the Middle East.

A lengthy dispute with Ukraine over ownership of the **Black Sea Fleet** was officially resolved under a framework agreement concluded in 1997 (with final resolution due in 2017). An unrelated dispute, however, over control of the shared Sea of Azov, prompted the despatch of Ukrainian border guards to the region in late 2003. An agreement delineating maritime boundaries was eventually reached in December 2003, but relations were severely strained when Putin openly backed Viktor **Yanukovych** at the time of the 2004 **Orange Revolution**.

Despite signing the **Belarus-Russia Union** in 1999, the Putin Government has edged away from its rhetoric of reunification of the two countries, especially as Belarusian President **Lukashenka**'s autocratic tendencies continue to draw international condemnation. Putin's revised plan which would incorporate Belarus as a constituent part of the existing Russian Federation was rejected by Lukashenka in August 2002.

The Russian Federation and China definitively settled their immense land border and signed a raft of economic pacts in 1999, followed by an agreement to end riverine disputes in October 2004. In August 2005 the two countries held their first joint military exercise, Peace Mission 2005, in a significant show of strategic support.

An unresolved territorial dispute with Japan over the southern Kurile Islands, annexed by the Soviet Union at the end of the Second World War, has prevented the two sides from signing a formal peace treaty.

The Russian Federation's defence budget for 2006 amounted to some US $24,900m., equivalent to about 2.6% of GDP. The size of the armed forces at August 2006 was some 1.2 million personnel, including those serving under compulsory conscription of 18–24 months. Since 2004 an alternative, civilian service of 36–42 months has been available. A bill passed by the State Duma in 2006 will reduce conscription to 12 months from 2008. Reservists number an estimated 20 million. The Russian Federation's large strategic defence capability is believed to include over 2,000 nuclear warheads.

Under a new military doctrine approved by Putin in April 2000, the existing stipulation that the Russian Federation would not initiate a nuclear war was supplemented by a clause permitting first use of nuclear weapons in the event of a threat to the 'very existence' of the country. The size of the military has been drastically reduced due to financial cuts, although efforts to move from conscription to a fully volunteer force have been unsuccessful. The parlous state of morale in the armed forces, where violent 'hazing' has made regular news bulletins, is a major cause of public discontent with the otherwise popular Putin administration.

Russian Federation, economy

A huge economy with diverse resources, which was vastly the largest economic component of the former **Soviet Union**, but has since been engaged in a difficult and contentious transition from a centrally-planned to a market-orientated system. Economic recovery from 1999 has been driven by high global prices for oil and gas. The Russian Federation is in geographical size more than three times the combined area of the other 14 former Soviet republics, and it has about the same aggregate population as those 14. As of 2005 its GNP was more than double that of the other 14 republics combined.

GNP: US $639,080m. (2005); *GNP per capita*: $4,460 (2005); *GDP at PPP*: $1,559,934m. (2005); *GDP per capita at PPP*: $10,897 (2005); *exports*: $269,760m. (2005); *imports*: $164,042m. (2005); *currency*: rouble (plural: roubles; US $1=R26.33 at the end of December 2006).

In 2005 industry accounted for 38% of GDP, agriculture for 5.6% and services for 56.4%. Of the 73 million workforce, about 31% are engaged in industry, 10% in agriculture and 59% in services. Some 7% of the land is arable, 5% permanent pasture and 49% forests and woodland, while 41% is described as 'other'. The main crops are grain, potatoes and other vegetables, and animal husbandry is an important agricultural sector. The Russian Federation has huge reserves of oil, natural gas (one-third of the world's total) and coal (both hard coal and lignite). There are large amounts of many strategic minerals, including palladium, platinum and rhodium, but climatic and other conditions make some of these reserves difficult to exploit. There is a wide range of industrial activity, including mining and extractive industries, machine-building and transport equipment, textiles and foodstuffs. The Russian Federation's electricity requirements are met from coal-, gas- and oil-fuelled stations (66%), hydroelectricity (17%) and nuclear power plants (17%).

The Russian Federation's main exports by value in 2003 were mineral fuels and lubricants (53%), basic manufactures (14%) and machinery and transport equipment (7%). Principal imports that year were machinery and transport equipment (32%), foodstuffs and live animals (15%), basic manufactures (13%) and chemical products (12%). The largest markets for Russian exports in 2003 were the Netherlands, China and **Belarus** (6% each), while the principal suppliers of imports were Germany (14%), Belarus (9%), **Ukraine** (8%) and China (6%). The Russian Federation has consistently recorded substantial trade surpluses, achieved principally from its exports of petroleum and gas.

The dissolution of the Soviet Union at the end of 1991 brought to the forefront many of the economic problems of the unified state, including significant uncompetitiveness in the industrial sector. With the development of *perestroika* and *glasnost* in the 1980s and the effective end of the **Cold War**, it became clear that much of Soviet industry had become obsolete and this weakness was in fact hindering these initiatives. The emergence of an independent Russian Federation paved the way for dramatic moves to liberalize the economy, to reduce the prime role of state ownership, to cut central government expenditure and to end the remaining aspects of the command economy. However, as in other post-communist states, there was initially very high inflation (especially in 1992–93) and declining GDP in the first few years. Over the period from 1989 to 1997 industrial output fell by about a half, with even higher reductions in sectors such as light industry and engineering, while agricultural output dropped by 40%. In terms of GDP there was in 1990–96 an annual average fall of 9.0% compared with an annual average growth of 2.8% in 1980–90.

From 1995 the Russian Federation's economy was assisted by a series of measures agreed with the **International Monetary Fund** (IMF), which it had joined in June 1992. In April 1995 the IMF agreed a 12-month US $6,800m. standby loan for the Russian Federation to assist the current 'bold and imaginative' economic and stabilization programme. This was followed in March 1996 by a three-year $10,200m. extended fund facility credit to support the Government's medium-term macroeconomic programme. As a result, the economic situation appeared to stabilize in 1997: real GDP growth (of 1%) was achieved for the first time since independence and inflation fell to around 15%.

In July 1998 the IMF increased the extended fund facility credit by US $8,300m. to support the Government's economic programme for 1998 and also agreed a $2,900m. compensatory and contingency funding facility in respect of an export shortfall related mainly to lower prices of crude oil in 1998. However, the situation was thrown into turmoil in August 1998 when a banking and financial crisis hit the country and led to a huge devaluation of the rouble and a moratorium on certain categories of debt service. As a result the IMF suspended further releases of credit. The economic crisis was aggravated by political turmoil, with President Boris **Yeltsin** making constant appointments to ministerial and other posts amidst a seeming inability on the part of the authorities to institute necessary economic changes. The result was a contraction in GDP of 4.9% in 1998, during which the rouble depreciated from 5.96 to the US dollar to 20.65 and the year-on-year inflation rate spiralled to 85% by December 1998.

A new US $4,500m. IMF standby credit granted in July 1999 underpinned a return to relative financial stability in 1999, assisted by the tripling of world oil prices in the second half of the year. Real GDP expanded by 3.2% in 1999 (and industrial production by 8%), while the year-on-year inflation rate was brought down to under 40% by December 1999. Vladimir **Putin**, who came to power early in 2000, focused on restoring economic stability and applying economic reforms consistently, in order to raise investor confidence. The recovery gathered strength, inflation fell to 20% and real GDP grew by 8.3% (and industrial production by 9%), so that overall output was officially stated to have returned to its 1994 level. At the same time, official figures showed that over 25% of incomes were below the official 'survival minimum' in the last quarter of 2000, real unemployment was estimated at over 10% of the active population, the 'black' economy was believed to account for some 45% of activity and large sectors of industry remained essentially uncompetitive. There was also increasing evidence that much of the financial assistance received by the Russian Federation was being siphoned off by profiteers and criminals and laundered into foreign bank accounts.

Growth slowed in 2001–02 to around 5% a year, as the rouble strengthened and oil prices stabilized, but from 2003 oil, gas and other commodity prices shot up again, driving economic growth of around 7% a year over the next four years. Strong budget surpluses were achieved each year, as tax revenue from the oil sector in particular increased, and incomes rose, allowing poverty to fall below 20% for the first time ever. Internal consumer demand also continued to increase by over 12% a year between 2000 and 2005. However, the income disparities between regions remains a major challenge to continuing growth—the **Moscow** region, with 10% of the Russian population, generates one-third of the total GDP.

Recent strong economic performance has allowed Russia to repay much of its Soviet-era debt, and in 2004 it set up a Stabilization Fund to use revenue from the oil and gas sectors to offset future commodity price volatility. Industrial military hardware is now the largest non-commodity export. Investment in small and medium-sized enterprises will be key to reducing dependency on raw commodities, but investors are wary of the state's intervention in business: Putin's drive against the power of the **'oligarchs'**, and in particular the gradual suffocation of the **Yukos** oil company, were the most visible examples of increased harassment. Corruption also remains a major deterrent, and the 'black' economy still accounts for around 40% of GDP. However, Russia was removed in 2003 from the list of 'non-compliant' countries on money 'laundering', following the introduction of various measures to combat the problem.

Accession to the **World Trade Organization** is expected to be achieved finally in 2007, and will require the removal of several protective import barriers; this will greatly ease the access of foreign firms to the Russian market.

Privatization of state and municipal assets started in 1992 with the issue of **vouchers**, while from July 1994 provision was made for the auction of state companies. Disposal of state farms was instituted, so by mid-1996 some 60% of the Russian Federation's agricultural land was in private ownership, although most field crops such as grain and sugar beet were produced on unreconstructed former state and collective farms. By 1997 some 125,000 enterprises had been privatized, of which a third were in manufacturing, construction, transport and communications, just over 2% in agriculture and the rest in services and other sectors. Around 70% of the Russian Federation's GDP was generated in the private sector in 1998, while restrictions limiting foreign participation in petroleum companies were lifted.

In the last period of the Yeltsin presidency, however, the privatization process stagnated and foreign investors were scared off by the unstable financial situation, widespread corruption among officials and endemic organized crime. Also of concern was the increasing economic and political influence exercised by the 'oligarchs', the prominent businessmen who now controlled major former state enterprises, some of them with criminal connections. In co-operation with the IMF, the Putin administration from 2000 included a new commitment to privatization in its economic reform programme, especially in the area of land ownership. The effective renationalization of Yukos's production unit in 2004, and other moves to ensure that control of certain natural resources could not be lost to foreign investors, raised fears (refuted by Putin) that he was planning to reverse some of the privatizations of the 1990s. Foreigners were even permitted to control up to 49% of **Gazprom** shares from 2006, though the majority 51% shareholding remained firmly under state control.

Russian Information Agency–Novosti *see* **RIA–Novosti**.

Russian nationalist group *see* **Pamyat—National Patriotic Front**.

Russian Orthodox Church

An autocephalous branch of the **Orthodox Christian** Church based in the **Russian Federation**. By tradition Christianity was first brought to modern

Russian territory by the Apostle St Andrew in the 1st century, but it was not until 988 that a Russian ruler, Prince Vladimir of **Kiev**, officially adopted the religion. From then until 1448 the Russian Church was subordinated to the Constantinople Patriarchate, but achieved full independence just before the collapse of the Eastern Roman (Byzantine) Empire. The Patriarchate of **Moscow** then took on the mantle as the champion of Orthodox Christianity, adopting the unofficial title of the 'Third Rome' (Constantinople being the 'Second Rome'). Under the reforms of Peter the Great, the Russian Church abandoned its traditional hierarchical model in 1721 and switched from a single Patriarch to a collective Holy Synod. However, the primacy of the Moscow Patriarch was restored in 1917. For the first three decades of communist rule the Church was pitted as a direct enemy of the atheist state. Thousands of priests, monks and nuns were imprisoned or even executed and 98% of churches were closed down across the country. A convenient rapprochement between Church and State was encouraged by the needs of the latter during the Second World War, and the Church even sponsored a tank and a naval division. Relations remained tense, however, into the late 20th century until the collapse of the **Soviet Union** in 1991. Since then the Church has grown rapidly, with churches and monasteries restored across the country. Patriarch Aleksiy II was elected in 1990. A division in Russian Orthodoxy was expected to end in 2007 with an agreement between the Moscow Patriarchate and the Russian Orthodox Church Abroad, which had rejected communist rule.

Russian Trading System (RTS)

An active electronic trading system set up in the **Russian Federation** in October 1995, and which acquired a stock exchange licence in January 2000.

Address: ul. Dolgorukovskaya 38, bld. 1, 127006 Moscow.
Telephone: (495) 7059031.
Fax: (495) 7339515.
E-mail: ttat@rtsnet.ru
Internet: www.rts.ru

Russians

An east **Slavic people** dominant throughout the constituent republics of the **Russian Federation** and with sizeable minorities in most of the former **Soviet** states. Arriving in **European Russia** in the 5th century the Russians established themselves in the thick forests of the north. Political and economic power was brought to the Slavic tribes by the Viking Rus (from whom the name Russian is derived) who developed the riverine trade routes between the Baltic and Black

Seas. The first ever ethnic Slavic state was thus created around the modern Ukrainian capital of **Kiev** in the 9th century. A century later the Russians adopted Christianity from the west, adhering to **Orthodox Christianity** (*see also* **Russian Orthodox Church**) and thereby acquiring the **Cyrillic alphabet**.

During the steady expansion of the emerging Russian Empire, from the 15th to the 20th century, Russians colonized the farthest reaches of modern Russia, soon coming to outnumber the resident populations. Russian language and culture became the *lingua franca* of the Empire. A strong sense of nationalism built on these beginnings survives today.

Russians account for around 80% of the Russian Federation's population, totalling around 116 million. Russian migrations to the former Soviet states fall into two distinct phases: pre-20th century (historic) migrations and the larger Soviet-era movement of workers. These migrations have been greatly countered by post-1991 repatriations to Russia owing to economic conditions and social discrimination. Despite this growing trend a large number of Russians—around 22 million—live outside the Federation.

The largest of these Russian minorities is the eight-million-strong community in **Ukraine**. In some areas, notably the **Crimea**, Russians form a majority and a large number of Ukrainians consider themselves bilingual, with Russian often dominating business. Fears of separatist movements arising after independence in 1991 proved largely unfounded, and Ukrainian Russians have pushed instead for regional autonomy and protection of their language. The east–west divide within Ukraine between ethnic Russians and ethnic Ukrainians has been highlighted in the recent fractious elections.

The second largest group of Russians in **eastern Europe**, outside the Federation—1.1 million—reside in **Belarus**, where their strong east Slavic affiliation with the local Belarusians has mitigated any major tension. Relations between ethnic Russians and their hosts are not so cordial in the **Baltic States** where the influx of over 1.5 million Russians in the Soviet era greatly undermined the countries' ethnic balances, particularly in Estonia and Latvia where they formed almost a third of the populations. In this region Russians are almost exclusively urbanized and generally live in regions close to the Russian Federation or Belarus. The question of language has dominated these countries with Russian downgraded in the latter two to an unofficial tongue. This discrimination has encouraged a large exodus of Russians back across the border since 1991.

A similar story is also true for the six million Russians living in the five central Asian states (4.5 million live in Kazakhstan). Smaller communities range from 202,000 in **Moldova** (particularly in **Transdnestria**) and 144,000 in **Azerbaijan** to 68,000 in **Georgia** and smaller numbers in **Armenia**. In all cases, voluntary returns to the Russian Federation after 1991 have reduced these communities considerably, although levels of discrimination vary greatly. Modern migrations are also to be found within the Federation, with the north **Caucasus region** suffering particularly badly from a loss of ethnic Russians.

Ruthenia *see* **Transcarpathia**.

Ruthenians

An east **Slavic people**, dominant in western **Ukraine** (*see* **Transcarpathia**). Historically, the term Ruthenian was applied to all ethnic **Ukrainians**. A distinction arose in the 16th and 17th centuries when the **Orthodox** Church of western 'Ruthenia' recognized the supremacy of the **Roman Catholic Church**, while under Polish sovereignty (*see* **Uniate Church**). These people, who were later brought into the Austro-Hungarian Empire, are the inheritors of the designation 'Ruthenian'.

S

Saakashvili, Mikhail

President of **Georgia** since January 2004, and previously the leading figure in the **Rose Revolution**. A multilingual, Western-educated human rights lawyer, Mikhail Saakashvili (known to most as Misha) rode a wave of popular discontent to a landslide electoral victory and was sworn in as President of Georgia on 25 January 2004. A long-time campaigner against corruption, he had first served in government as Justice Minister in 2000 under President Eduard **Shevardnadze**, but resigned in 2001 claiming that it would have been immoral to remain.

Mikhail Saakashvili was born on 21 December 1967 in **Tbilisi**. He studied at Kiev University in **Ukraine** and the International Institute of Human Rights in Strasbourg, before moving to the USA. He attended Columbia University in New York, where he gained his Master's degree in law in 1994, and the following year he gained a doctorate in juridical science from the George Washington National Law Center in Washington, DC. After a year as an intern for the New York-based law firm Patterson, Belknap, Webb & Tyler he was offered a lucrative job with the firm, but he declined, choosing instead to return to Georgia to take up a political career.

Saakashvili's friend Zurab Zhvania, whose Green Party had been one of a number of opposition groups striving for Georgia's independence, recruited Saakashvili in the mid-1990s to join the Government of Eduard Shevardnadze. He stood in the December 1995 elections along with Zhvania, and both men won seats in **Parliament**, standing for Shevardnadze's **Citizens' Union of Georgia** (SMK). Saakashvili soon made a name for himself as Chairman of the parliamentary committee charged with creating a new electoral system, an independent judiciary and a non-political police force. He achieved a high degree of public recognition, with opinion surveys finding him to be the second most popular person in Georgia, behind Shevardnadze.

On 12 October 2000 Shevardnadze appointed Saakashvili to the post of Minister of Justice. He immediately moved to reform the decrepit, corrupt and highly politicized Georgian criminal justice and prisons system, winning plaudits from human rights activists and the international community. However, in a

Council of Ministers meeting in August 2001, Saakashvili accused Economics Minister Vano Chkhartishvili, State Security Minister Vakhtang Kutateladze and Tbilisi police chief Soso Alavidze of profiting from corrupt business deals and displayed photos of their opulent houses in Tbilisi to support his claims. On 5 September 2001 Saakashvili resigned, declaring that corruption had penetrated to the very centre of the Government and that Shevardnadze lacked the will to deal with it.

In October 2001 Saakashvili founded the opposition United National Movement (UNM), a left-of-centre political party akin to the social democrats in Europe with a touch of nationalism. In June 2002 he was elected as Chairman of the Tbilisi Assembly—in effect, the city's Mayor—following an agreement between the UNM and the Georgian Labour Party. This gave him a powerful new platform from which to criticize the Government. It made him enemies as well; even his great friend and ally Zurab Zhvania was reluctant to align closely with him at this time, and Zhvania was quoted as criticizing what he termed Saakashvili's 'excessive radicalism'.

Elections were held on 2 November 2003, and the election bloc forged together by Shevardnadze around the SMK set about manipulating the election returns. Denouncing the results as a fraud, Saakashvili was prominent as a leader of massive political demonstrations (the so-called Rose Revolution) in Tbilisi, with over 30,000 people participating. As pressure built up on Shevardnadze to resign, Saakashvili 'stormed' Parliament on live national television as his supporters placed roses in the gun barrels of the soldiers outside. The events were described by one journalist as 'a coup masked as a street party'. Shevardnadze resigned as President on 23 November. On 4 January 2004 Saakashvili won a landslide victory with 96% of the vote to become President of Georgia; he was sworn in three weeks later. In February the UNM and Zhvania's United Democrats finally amalgamated and the new political movement was named the **National Movement-Democrats** (NM-D).

Saakashvili positioned himself and his country firmly facing West, and has announced his intention to see Georgia become a member of both the **North Atlantic Treaty Organization** (NATO) and the **European Union** (EU)—even going so far as to hoist an EU flag over the **Parliament of Georgia**. He reined in the ambitions of long-term **Adzharian** leader Aslan Abashidze, forcing him to resign and flee to **Russia**. His actions in Adzharia and in the disputes with the other breakaway republics of South **Ossetia** and **Abkhazia** have greatly strained relations with the Russian Government.

Saakashvili is married to Dutch national Sandra Roelof who used to work at the Dutch consulate in Tbilisi; they have one son.

Address: Office of the President, Ingorovka 7, 380007 Tbilisi.
Telephone: (32) 999653.
Fax: (32) 990879.
E-mail: media@president.gov.ge
Internet: www.president.gov.ge

St Petersburg

The second city of the **Russian Federation** and formerly the imperial capital, situated in the far west of the country at the confluence of the River Neva and the Gulf of Finland. *Population*: 4.7m. (2002 estimate). The Neva region, an integral part of Russian states from the 9th century, was annexed to the Swedish Empire in 1617 but won back in the early stages of the Northern War (1700–21) under the **Romanov** Tsar Peter the Great. Despite the widely-acknowledged unsuitability of the site, with its damp climate and persistent flooding, its strategic significance led Peter to found the city of St Petersburg there in May 1703. Construction of the fortified encampment was hazardous in the extreme and scores of soldiers and peasants were killed. Peter employed European architects to create a distinctly European city. By 1712 his 'Venice of the North' had become sufficiently prosperous and important to become the new capital of the Russian Empire, indicating its westward orientation.

St Petersburg was to be the economic and cultural heart of the expanding Empire. In 1837 it became one terminus of the country's first railway and in 1851 it was connected by track to **Moscow** deep in the interior. As the centre of political life, it was also the focus of popular dissent. The emancipation of the serfs in 1861 prompted an influx of migrant labour, creating overcrowding and the basis for mass unrest. The 'Bloody Sunday' massacre of pro-reform supporters in the city's Palace Square in January 1905 launched a revolution leading to the introduction of broad, if poorly-backed, political liberalization. The legislative **State Duma** was based in the city from 1906.

Following the outbreak of war with Germany in 1914 the city's name was changed in a gesture of Russian patriotism to the less Germanic form Petrograd. The severe impact of the First World War on the city and the country at large prompted further discontent. The scene in early 1917 of the February Revolution, Petrograd then became the base for the meetings of the Soviets and the cradle for the burgeoning Bolshevik party, which organized the celebrated siege of the governmental headquarters in the Winter Palace—the start of the October Revolution. The establishment of a Bolshevik state prompted a Civil War and saw the city once again threatened by hostile forces. In early 1918 the new authorities removed their capital to Moscow. This loss of status was compounded by the massive loss of population inflicted by the war. From a 1917 high of 2.3 million, the city's population had fallen to 722,000 at the end of 1920. In 1924, on the death of Lenin, the city was renamed once again, as Leningrad to honour the founding father of the **Soviet Union**.

Reconstruction and the renewed expansion of the city began under Stalin. By 1939 it had a population of three million and was the source of 11% of the Soviet Union's industrial output. Progress was devastatingly interrupted in 1941, however, when the invading Nazi forces began the 900-day Siege of Leningrad. From 8 September 1941 until 27 January 1944 the city was blockaded, leaving 641,000 people dead. Most of the victims were buried in mass graves. After the conclusion of the siege, and later of the Second World War itself, Leningrad quickly returned to relative prosperity. Cheap housing became a central issue, but unlike other war-ravaged Soviet cities, Leningrad was reconstructed largely along its pre-war lines, rather than rebuilt in Stalinist sobriety. The city gathered momentum as an economic dynamo into the second half of the 20th century, regaining its pre-war population level in the 1960s.

In 1991 a referendum popularly endorsed the reversion to the original name of St Petersburg and the city faced the collapse of the Soviet Union with falling wages and a sudden rise in crime levels. Nevertheless, foreign investment flooded in and the city once again became Russia's main portal to the West. As the country's economy wobbled towards stability at the turn of the century, so the city took on a renewed sense of calm and prosperity. The election of Vladimir **Putin** as President in May 2000 did much to bring St Petersburg back into the political limelight. Putin had spent the first five years after the collapse of the Soviet Union in the city's administration and continues to promote the careers of fellow former members of the city's Government. Valentina Matvienko has been Governor (Mayor) of St Petersburg since 15 October 2003.

St Petersburg's economic importance is based on its large size and its position as the country's only Baltic port, giving it unique access to northern and western European markets. It is also a hub for the regional transport network, particularly for the many waterways of northern **European Russia**, making it the centre of systems linking the Baltic and White Seas with the **Volga** river, and the Caspian and Black Seas beyond. Its Soviet legacy is a preponderance of heavy engineering.

Sakartvelos Parlamenti *see* **Parliament of Georgia**.

SALT

The Strategic Arms Limitation Talks, held between the USA and the **Soviet Union** between 1969 and 1979. The first round, SALT I, in 1969–72, produced the important 1972 treaty limiting anti-ballistic missile systems (known as the ABM Treaty), and another accord on limiting each side's overall number of ballistic missiles. The second phase, SALT II, began with the Washington, DC, summit of 1973, when the two sides set out an agenda for moving from arms control—the stage involving weapons classifications and ceilings—on to the actual **START** arms reduction process. Although the talks became bogged down in complexities over multiple warheads, the climate of détente was restored by the new US President Jimmy Carter in 1977 and his decision to halt development of the neutron bomb and long-range B-1 bomber. A SALT II treaty was concluded and signed in Vienna on 18 June 1979 (after which the SALT talks were renamed START), but the Soviet intervention in the Afghan War destroyed any prospect of its being ratified by the US Senate. Carter's successor Ronald Reagan never resubmitted it for ratification, although both the USA and the Soviet Union agreed informally to comply with its provisions.

The US plan for a National Missile Defence system, pursued from 2001 by new President George W. Bush, led to US withdrawal from the ABM Treaty on 13 June 2002, six months after written notice to the **Russian Federation** of this intention. In May 2002 Presidents Bush and **Putin** had signed the **SORT** treaty, though this was criticized for its lack of definition, flexible system for counting warheads and failure to encourage destruction of warheads.

Sami

A **Finno-Ugric people** (formerly widely called Lapps) living across the Arctic tundra of Scandinavia and the **Kola peninsula**. Present in the region from 1500 BC, the nomadic Sami developed separately from the Finns. Until very recently the herding of reindeer was central to their way of life. Only a small number of Sami now live in their traditional manner, however, as there has been great pressure for them to adopt a more sedentary lifestyle and so contribute to the economic dynamics of their respective countries.

The language of the Sami divided from Finnish around 3,000 years ago and bears little real relation to modern Finnish. Indeed the isolation of their traditional nomadic lifestyle has created several strongly distinct, and sometimes mutually unintelligible, dialects.

Around 2,000 Sami live in northern **Russia**. Their small number means that they have not been represented as a distinct group in the Russian Federation, but since 1992 they have sent representatives to the Sami Council. They are joined on the council by members from the much larger communities living in Norway (approximately 50,000), Sweden (approximately 20,000) and Finland (approximately 10,000).

Savings Bank of the Russian Federation (Sberbank)
Sberbank Rossii

Founded in 1841 as a deposit institution, and reformed in 1991 as a joint-stock commercial bank. It is 60.6% owned by the **Central Bank of the Russian Federation**. As of January 2004 the Bank held reserves of 44,600m. roubles.

Chair and Chief Executive: Andrei I. Kazmin.
Address: ul. Vavilova 19, 117997 Moscow.
Telephone: (495) 9575758.
Fax: (495) 7473758.
E-mail: sbrf@sbrf.ru
Internet: www.sbrf.ru

SBS-Agro

A large bank in the **Russian Federation** which collapsed with disastrous effects on the **Russian economy** in 1998. The former Stolichny Savings Bank merged with the remnants of the Soviet-era Agroprombank in 1995 to create SBS-Agro, which soon became the main agent of the Ministry of Agriculture and built up a network of investments in the Russian media under the stewardship of Russian 'oligarch' Aleksandr Smolensky. As the global financial crisis of 1998 began to impact on the Russian Federation, SBS-Agro was quickly proved to have very few actual financial reserves, prompting its rapid descent into bankruptcy. It had the inglorious commendation of being the first Russian bank to have its licence revoked by the new **Central Bank**. Its assets, and debts, were redivided, but not before the Russian economy had faltered, prompting a devaluation of the rouble.

SCO *see* **Shanghai Co-operation Organization**.

Serpents' Island

A small island (or cliff) opposite the delta of the Danube river in the Black Sea, which is the subject of a territorial dispute between Romania and **Ukraine**. The island was ceded to Romania in 1878 but control was handed to the authorities of the **Soviet Union** in 1948 in a clandestine agreement. It remains unclear who has the legal claim to the island. The matter is of significance, not only because of the question of the movement and stationing of the post-Soviet **Black Sea Fleet**, but also because of the sea's deposits of oil and natural gas. In 2004 Romania submitted its claim to the **International Court of Justice**; a ruling is expected in 2008.

Sevastopol

A strategically important port on the **Crimean** peninsula in southern **Ukraine**. *Population*: 378,441 (2005 estimate). The impressive natural harbour has served the people of the peninsula since the Greeks established the colony of Chersonesus at the site. Despite years of neglect under the Turkish Ottoman Empire the city was rapidly developed as a major strategic port by **Russia** after it annexed the Crimea in 1783. Severe damage sustained during the crucial Crimean War siege of Sevastopol between 1854 and 1855 was repaired in the late 19th century. However, commercial activity was shifted to the port of Feodosiya, while Sevastopol took on its present role as a principal naval base for the imperial **Black Sea Fleet**. Further destruction during the Second World War was again repaired, by the **Soviet** authorities. The Russian navy still maintains a significant presence in the city.

Shanghai Co-operation Organization (SCO)

An organization founded in June 2001 to promote regional security and co-operation between the People's Republic of China, the **Russian Federation** and four of the former Soviet central Asian Republics—Kazakhstan, Kyrgyzstan, Tajikistan and Uzbekistan. The SCO has specifically pledged to work to combat terrorism and to promote regional stability. Its Declaration to this effect was signed on 15 June 2001 by the Presidents of its six member states. The SCO is based on the 'Shanghai Five' group (not at that time including Uzbekistan) brought together at the invitation of the Chinese in Shanghai in 1996.

Economic co-operation between the member states has increased since 2003, as China has focused on enhancing its links with its central Asian neighbours. China has proposed that a free trade area should eventually be formed.

India, Iran, Mongolia and Pakistan are observers at the SCO, with all but India also applying for full membership.

Secretary-General: Zhang Deguang.
Address: No 41, Liangmaqiao Road, Chaoyang District, Beijing 100600,
　　　　China.
Telephone: (10) 65329806.
Fax: (10) 65329808.
E-mail: sco@sectsco.org
Internet: www.sectsco.org

Sharifov, Samir

Minister of Finance, **Azerbaijan**. Samir Rauf oglu Sharifov is a trained economist who worked within the Foreign Economic Relations Department of the former Soviet Azeri apparatus. He was appointed Minister of Finance on 18 April 2006.

Born on 7 September 1961, he graduated in economics from the Department of International Economic Relations of the Faculty of International Relations and International Law in the Azeri capital **Baku** in 1983. For the rest of the Soviet era he worked as a state economist in Baku and abroad in South Yemen. Following Azeri independence in 1991 he was appointed Deputy Chief of the Department of International Economic Relations of the Azeri Ministry of Foreign Affairs. Four years later he became head of the Office of Currency Regulation and Control at the **National Bank**. In 2001 he was appointed Executive Director of the State Oil Fund of the Azerbaijan Republic, and subsequently represented Azerbaijan as Director at the Black Sea Trade and Development Bank. While still in post at the State Oil Fund he also was appointed Chairman of the Government Commission on the Extractive Industries Transparency Initiative in 2003. On 18 April 2006 President Ilham **Aliyev** dismissed the incumbent Finance Minister Avaz Alekperov and appointed Sharifov to the Council of Ministers in his place.

Sharifov is married and has one son.

Address: Ministry of Finance, Samed Vurghun St 83, 1022 Baku.
Telephone: (12) 4933012.
Fax: (12) 4930652.
E-mail: info@maliyye.gov.az
Internet: www.maliyye.gov.az

Shevardnadze, Eduard

Dominant political figure of post-independence **Georgia** until the 2003 **Rose Revolution**, and Head of State from 1992 to November 2003. He was formerly high-ranking communist who, as Soviet Foreign Minister under Mikhail **Gorbachev** in 1985–90, helped to engineer the **Soviet Union**'s withdrawal from the **Cold War** arms race and from regional hegemony in **eastern Europe**.

Eduard Amvrosiyevich Shevardnadze was born on 25 January 1928, the son of a teacher in the Georgian village of Mamat. Heavily involved as a teacher and activist in the Communist Youth League (Komsomol), he became its First Secretary in Georgia in 1957. Two years later he was elected to the Supreme Soviet in the Republic, and also in 1959 completed a correspondence degree in history. Drafted into the civilian police (MVD), Shevardnadze began to make a name for himself as Head of Georgia's Ministry of Public Order from 1965 onwards, tackling both unrest and corruption, and clamping down on self-enrichment by government and party officials. He was promoted to be the Republic's Minister of the Interior and, from 1972, First Secretary of the Communist Party of Georgia. His sudden emergence within the top leadership at Soviet level in 1985, when he became a member of the Politburo of the

Communist Party of the Soviet Union (KPSS) and simultaneously Soviet Foreign Minister, was mainly owing to his political association and growing personal friendship with new KPSS General Secretary Gorbachev. The crowds who welcomed the collapse of communism across the countries of central and eastern Europe in 1989 hailed Shevardnadze, like Gorbachev, as a hero of democratization.

Shevardnadze felt the growing danger, however, of a Soviet military and hardline backlash. Resigning as Foreign Minister in December 1990, he warned that 'dictatorship is coming', a fear which was later vindicated by the 1991 **August coup** attempt in **Moscow**. Joining in efforts to rally support for Gorbachev, he returned briefly to the post of Soviet Foreign Minister as the Soviet Union was disintegrating in 1991.

He returned in March 1992 to a newly independent Georgia, where open conflict between nationalist factions was threatening to destroy a country already in serious economic disarray. Appointed within four days as Chairman of a military-dominated State Council, he was pitched into a period of overt conflict with the ousted former President Zviad Gamsakhurdia and more seriously with secessionists in **Abkhazia**. On 11 October 1992, he was elected Chairman of the **Parliament of Georgia**, and a referendum endorsed him as Head of State and Commander-in-Chief of the Armed Forces. Following Russian military support against the **Zviadists**, he took Georgia into the Russian-dominated **Commonwealth of Independent States** (CIS), recognizing how vulnerable Georgia's isolated position had become, especially after rebel forces gained the upper hand in Abkhazia (where he himself came under heavy shelling during one visit). In February 1994 he and **Russian** President Boris **Yeltsin** signed a treaty of friendship and co-operation, controversially allowing the extended presence of Russian military bases on Georgian soil.

The country faced economic problems so severe that Shevardnadze was forced to announce unpopular food-rationing measures. Over the next few years, however, he began to be able to claim some success in tackling chronic instability, although there were renewed flare-ups in the conflict with Abkhazia, and other separatist struggles in different parts of the country. Shevardnadze's own life came under threat, his regime having struggled to control the private armies of various nationalist leaders. He survived a car bombing in **Tbilisi** in August 1995, and another assassination attempt in February 1998.

Under a new Constitution in 1995, the office of President was reintroduced, with executive powers, and Shevardnadze was elected for a five-year term in a nationwide ballot on 5 November 1995, winning more than three-quarters of the votes cast. He was re-elected overwhelmingly in April 2000 for a further five-year term commencing on 1 May. Shevardnadze also chaired the **Citizens' Union of Georgia** (SMK), which he founded in 1993 as a pro-democracy and free-market-orientated alliance and which was the leading party in the 1995 and 1999 legislative elections.

The November 2003 parliamentary elections were marred by widespread irregularities. Official results gave victory to the pro-Shevardnadze For a New Georgia bloc, centred around the SMK. Protests broke out, which became known as the **Rose Revolution**, and 30,000 people marched against the opening of the new Parliament on 22 November. Government troops refused to stop the invaders and Shevardnadze was hustled out by his supporters; he resigned the following day.

Shevardnadze published his memoirs *Thoughts about the Past and the Future* in 2006.

Siberia

The vast, empty steppe and tundra stretching to the east of the Ural mountains. Siberia constitutes the major part of Asiatic **Russia**. It is perhaps most famous as the final destination of many of Stalin's **deported nationalities** and the setting for the many gulag prison camps. The Arctic Circle passes across almost half of Siberia and the climate is unforgiving all year round. A particularly harsh winter struck the region in 2000/01, but there are also real concerns about the effect of global warming on the permafrost of the north. Heavy industry is concentrated in cities such as Magnitogorsk at the south-western edge near the Ural mountains and in equally isolated settlements scattered throughout. Industrial output (mainly oil and gas production) from Siberia accounts for around 25% of the country's total output.

The indigenous people of Siberia were first conquered by the Mongols in the 13th century under the rule of the Golden Horde. Russian dominance came quickly between the 1590s and the 1640s and has remained ever since. Annexation by the Russian Empire brought waves of ethnic **Russian** colonists and permanently altered the ethnic make-up of Siberia. Population is most dense along the region's southern edge. Industrialization supplemented fur trading in the Arctic wastes and was speeded up greatly following the construction of the celebrated **Trans-Siberian Railway** (TSR), which eventually linked **Moscow** with Vladivostok (literally 'rule of the east') on the Amur Valley's Sea of Japan coast.

The principal non-Russian republics and regions of Siberia include Yakutia in the north-east, Buryatia on the eastern shores of Lake Baikal in the south-east and the Jewish Autonomous *Oblast* (region) on the border with China.

Sidorsky, Sergei

Prime Minister, **Belarus**. Sergei Sidorsky was appointed acting Prime Minister of Belarus on 10 July 2003, and confirmed on 19 December. He trained as an electrical engineer in **Soviet**-era Belarus. Like his predecessor Gennadz Novitski, Sidorsky is very much in the shadow of the more constitutionally powerful President. Indeed, it could be argued that he was appointed precisely because he poses little threat to President Alyaksandr **Lukashenka**: Sidorsky is unpopular with the **Russian** leadership due to his previous role as a tough negotiator over oil and gas transhipments and would be unlikely to gain any backing from that vital quarter should he have any ambitions for the presidency.

Sergei Sidorsky was born on 13 March 1954 in the town of Gomel. In 1976 he graduated from the Belarusian Institute of Railroad Engineers (Faculty of Electrical Engineering), and began his working life as an electrician. He speaks three languages—Belarusian, Russian and German—and has more than 40 scientific articles to his name.

Sidorsky's career began in the Gomel Radio Equipment Plant, where he worked his way up from foreman to Director over a 25-year span. By 1992, he had moved to become the General Manager of the Gomel Scientific Production Association (RATON). In 1998 Sidorsky became a serious regional political player, as the First Deputy Chairman of the Gomel Regional Administration, but it was not until 2001 that he was appointed Deputy Prime Minister of Belarus.

In July 2003 Lukashenka dismissed Prime Minister Gennadz Novitski and three senior members of the Council of Ministers, accusing them of massaging statistics relating to an outstanding debt owed to the agricultural sector for cattle and milk deliveries to the state. Observers initially questioned the appointment of Sidorsky as replacement; as one of the leaders of negotiations with giant neighbour Russia on oil and gas supplies, he was hardly a favourite of Russia, the major power broker in Belarus.

However, Lukashenka had determined to hold a referendum to extend his own rule, for which he needed Russian backing. Were he to step down instead, then traditionally the serving Prime Minister—Sidorsky—would stand for President in his place. By appointing Sidorsky as Prime Minister, he weighted Russian elite opinion in favour of a referendum—which passed in 2004—allowing the extension of his own rule by re-election.

Sidorsky is married with two daughters.

Address: Office of the Prime Minister, House of Government, Independence Square, 220010 Minsk.
Telephone: (17) 2226905.
Fax: (17) 2226665.
E-mail: contact@government.by
Internet: www.government.by

Single Economic Space

An agreement on a supranational commission to govern trade and tariffs between

Belarus, Kazakhstan, the **Russian Federation** and **Ukraine**, proposed in February 2003. The first three took the initial step of forming a customs union in August 2006; Ukraine's participation is dependent on approval by anti-Russian President Viktor **Yushchenko** and the pro-Russian Government of Prime Minister Viktor **Yanukovych**.

See alternatively **Common Economic Spaces**.

Slavic peoples

The largest single ethnic family in Europe. The Slavs are an Indo-European ethnic group whose area of settlement spreads from the far-eastern shores of Asiatic **Russia** to the heart of **central Europe** and across the **Balkans**. Slavs are divided into three main branches: the east Slavs (**Belarusians**, **Russians** and **Ukrainians**), west Slavs (Czechs, **Poles**, Slovaks and the minority Sorbs, or Wends, in eastern Germany) and south Slavs (Bosniaks, Croatians, Montenegrins, Serbs and Slovenes—Yugoslavs). The **Bulgarians** and Macedonians are also considered south Slavs and they speak a Slavic language, although their origin is generally accepted to have been from a mixing of Slavs and **Tatars**.

Arising from Asian origins in the 3rd or 2nd millennium BC, the Slavs historically settled north of the Carpathian mountains. The divide into the three major groups occurred from the 5th century AD as **German** tribes migrated westward into central Europe. The resultant geographic division encouraged separate linguistic and cultural differences.

The most potent of these differences is the split between **Roman Catholicism** (west Slavs, Croats, Slovenes, and some Belarusians and Ukrainians) and **Orthodox Christianity** (remaining east Slavs, Bulgarians, Macedonians, Montenegrins and Serbs). Along this fault line can also be found the use of the Latin and **Cyrillic alphabets** respectively (although all Belarusians and Ukrainians use Cyrillic). Pan-Slavic movements, usually inspired by Russian imperialism, have generally failed owing to this religious/cultural difference, among others. The most recent experiment, uniting the majority of south Slavs in Yugoslavia, proved a notable disaster—the religious differences there being further complicated by the existence of two groups of south Slavs which follow the Islamic faith, the Bosniaks (who use the Latin script) and the Pomaks in Macedonia (who use Cyrillic).

Slavic languages are similar enough for rudimentary understanding between all Slavic peoples. In some cases, particularly within the former Yugoslav states, the differences between languages are small and distinctions are inspired more by nationalism than by linguistics.

The development of the various Slavic countries today has been largely due to the political divisions of the 20th century. The west and the south Slavs now generally aspire to greater integration with western Europe whereas the east

Slavs, the most homogenous group, tentatively seek closer regional integration between themselves, based around the economic dominance of the **Russian Federation**.

SMK *see* **Citizens' Union of Georgia**.

Social Liberal Party
Partidul Social Liberal (PSL)

A centrist pro-Western party in **Moldova** formed in 2001, and the smallest member of the opposition **Democratic Moldova Bloc** (BMD) at the March 2005 elections, when it took four of the BMD's 34 seats in **Parliament**.
    Leadership: Oleg Serebrean (Chair).
    Address: Str. Bulgara 24в, Chişinau.
    Telephone: (22) 276620.
    Fax: (22) 222503.
    E-mail: secretariat@psl.md
    Internet: www.psl.md

Socialist International

The world's oldest and largest association of political parties, founded in 1864 and grouping democratic socialist, labour and social democratic parties from 86 countries, including many of the countries of **central** and **eastern Europe**. The Socialist International provides a forum for political action, policy discussion and the exchange of ideas.
    Members: 104 full member parties, 30 consultative and 14 observer parties.
    President: George Papandreou.
    Address: Maritime House, Clapham, London, SW4 0JW, UK.
    Telephone: (20) 76274449.
    Fax: (20) 77204448.
    E-mail: secretariat@socialistinternational.org
    Internet: www.socialistinternational.org

Socialist Party of Ukraine
Sotsialistychna Partiya Ukrainy (SPU)

A small but influential political formation in **Ukraine**, directly descended from the **Soviet**-era ruling party. The first self-proclaimed successor to the **Communist Party of Ukraine** (KPU), the SPU was launched two months after the **August**

coup attempt by hardliners in **Moscow** in 1991. Under the leadership of Oleksandr Moroz, who had been Chairman of the Soviet-era Ukrainian legislature, the party attacked the growth of 'national-fascism' and called for the reintroduction of state direction of the economy, price controls, 'socially just privatization' and closer economic and political ties with the **Russian Federation** and the other members of the **Commonwealth of Independent States** (CIS).

In June 1993 the SPU formed an alliance called 'Working Ukraine' with the Peasants' Party of Ukraine (SelPU) and smaller left-wing groups, in close co-operation with the KPU, although the latter did not join and quickly superseded the SPU as the leading left-wing formation. The SPU emerged from the 1994 elections with a parliamentary group of only 27 members, although Moroz was elected President of the **Supreme Council** with KPU and other left-wing support. In early 1996 the SPU was weakened by a split resulting in the formation of the breakaway Progressive Socialist Party (PSP).

The SPU contested the 1998 parliamentary elections in an alliance with the SelPU called 'For the Truth, For the People, For Ukraine' ('Za Pravdu, Za Narod, Za Ukrainu'), their joint list winning 44 seats with 8.5% of the proportional vote. Plans for a joint presidential candidate of the alliance and other left-leaning parties foundered in the run-up to the 1999 contest, with the result that Moroz stood for the SPU and received 11.3% of the first-round vote. In the second round the SPU supported KPU leader Petro Symonenko, who was defeated by incumbent Leonid **Kuchma**. In early 2000 the SPU was prominent in left-wing attempts to prevent the ousting of Supreme Council President Oleksandr Tkachenko (SelPU) by the centre-majority, whose action was described by Moroz as tantamount to a *coup d'état*.

Moroz and the SPU were also prominent in the further political crisis which developed from late 2000 over President Kuchma's alleged role in the murder of the journalist Giorgiy Gongadze. After being sued for slander by Kuchma's chief of staff for revealing apparent presidential involvement in the affair, Moroz described the crisis as 'a turning point' in Ukraine's national history. Kuchma, however, managed to evade censure and ultimately escaped relatively unscathed from what proved to be a long drawn out scandal.

In the 2002 legislative elections the SPU stood alone and garnered 7% of the vote to secure 23 seats. While standing separately from both the Yushchenko- and Tymoshenko-led opposition blocs, the SPU firmly supported their efforts to derail Kuchma in the lead up to the 2004 presidential elections, with a particular focus on the unresolved Gongadze case. In a notable turnaround of fortune, Moroz did better than KPU presidential candidate Petro Symonenko in the poll, finishing third with 6% of the total vote in the first round. The SPU threw its weight behind Viktor Yushchenko in the second ballot and in the **Orange Revolution** that followed.

Now aligned with the new Government, the SPU was welcomed into the Cabinet in 2005 and expanded its parliamentary base in the 2006 elections with

33 seats—the fourth largest total—despite a drop in its overall share of the vote to 5.7%. Months of protracted coalition negotiations followed these polls, which had been won by the pro-Russian **Party of Regions** (PR). In July the SPU switched sides, providing the PR and KPU with enough support to form a majority. The new Government was sworn in in August, with two SPU ministers.

Leadership: Oleksandr Moroz (Chair).
Address: vul. Bankova 12, Kiev 02100.
Telephone and Fax: (44) 5735897.
E-mail: pravozahist2003@scinfo.kiev.ua
Internet: www.spu.org.ua

SORT

The Strategic Offensive Reductions Treaty, signed by the **Russian Federation** and the USA in Moscow on 24 May 2002, committing both sides to reducing the levels of their strategic nuclear warheads to 1,700–2,200, a level nearly two-thirds below the current levels at the time of the treaty. It came into force on 1 June 2003 and the deadline for implementation is 31 December 2012.

SORT was criticized for its lack of definition, its flexible system for counting warheads and its failure to encourage destruction of warheads, allowing storage or repair of delivery devices to equate to non-deployment. It was signed a month before the USA's withdrawal from the ABM Treaty (*see* **SALT**), of which Russia had been forewarned in December 2001.

South Ossetia *see* **Ossetia question**.

Southern Bukovina *see* **Bukovina question**.

Soviet Federatsii
(Council of the Federation)

The upper house of the **Federal Assembly** of the **Russian Federation**.

Soviet Respubliki
(Council of the Republic)

The upper house of the **National Assembly** of **Belarus**.

Soviet Union
(Union of Soviet Socialist Republics, USSR)

The historic communist state of 1922–91, which at its height was one of two global superpowers, and stretched from the Pacific coast of **Siberia** in the east to the borders of **eastern Europe** in the west, and from the Arctic Circle in the north to the edges of the Middle East in the south. The Soviet Union (known in Russian by its **Cyrillic** acronym *CCCP* [SSSR]) was the largest country in the world, and adhered closely to the borders of the old Russian Empire (the **Baltic States** and modern **Moldova** being added to the Union through military conquest in the Second World War). Its disintegration in 1991 left 15 independent successor states: **Armenia**, **Azerbaijan**, **Belarus**, Estonia, **Georgia**, Kazakhstan, Kyrgyzstan, Latvia, Lithuania, **Moldova**, the **Russian Federation**, Tajikistan, Turkmenistan, **Ukraine** and Uzbekistan. All but the three Baltic States then joined together to form the loose **Commonwealth of Independent States** (CIS).

Following the Bolshevik (communist) victory in the Russian Civil War (1918–20) the new authorities sought to spread socialist revolution but also to recentralize control of the far-flung Russian dominions. At first these were given the right to national determination, but very soon the 'ideal' of a communist revolution was enforced everywhere. Communist governments were set up in the constituent republics, and the structure for the Soviet Union was drawn up under the guidance of the then Commissar for Nationalities, Josef Stalin. The new socialist state was based on the principle of rule by the soviets (essentially councils representing trades unions and other collective groups). It was formally established on 30 December 1922.

The USSR brought together at the top level the Soviet Socialist Republics (SSRs), of which the Russian Soviet Federative Socialist Republic (RSFSR) was by far the largest. Within the SSRs were Autonomous Soviet Socialist Republics (ASSRs), based on smaller ethnic groups. (Within the Russian Federation of the post-Soviet era the ASSRs survive, for the most part, in the form of the various Republics. In the non-Russian successor states, however, the ASSRs have largely been subsumed into unitary structures, which has created tensions particularly in Georgia and Moldova.) Smaller subdivisions of SSRs and ASSRs were the *krai* (province), *oblast* (region) and *okrug* (district), as well as city, administrations.

Mikhail **Gorbachev** was the last President of the Soviet Union, from which post he formally resigned on 25 December 1991 thereby dissolving a Union that had been made effectively redundant through the declarations of independence of the SSRs and the formation of the CIS.

Spitzbergen *see* **Svalbard**.

SPS *see* **Union of Right Forces**.

SPU *see* **Socialist Party of Ukraine**.

START

The Strategic Arms Reduction Talks between the USA and the **Soviet Union**, which began in June 1982 despite the deadlock over ratification of **SALT** II. The US side began by pressing for major cuts in inter-continental ballistic missiles (land-based strategic missiles being much less significant in the US arsenal than in the Soviet one). The **NATO** decision, however, to go ahead with deployment of cruise and Pershing II missiles in Europe, prompted a Soviet walkout from the START talks in November 1982. When they reconvened in 1985 it was under an 'umbrella' framework linking strategic, intermediate and space-based systems. The talks, held in Geneva, moved towards separating the agenda on strategic weapons, creating a potential START I agreement and deferring more complex areas to START II. In the event, whereas START I took nearly a decade (and was signed in **Moscow** in July 1991), START II was agreed in principle in Washington, DC, in a completely different global context in June 1992, and signed only six months later by the **Russian Federation** and the USA in January 1993. START II went far beyond the cuts agreed in START I, committing both sides to cut two-thirds of their strategic arsenals.

The collapse of the Soviet Union created complexities in the START I ratification process, particularly with **Ukraine**, but the promise of large-scale US aid eventually cleared the way for the accession by early 1994 of all four post-Soviet nuclear weapons states. The agreement involved three of them, **Belarus**, Kazakhstan and Ukraine, transferring ownership of all remaining weapons to the fourth, the Russian Federation. The reductions were completed by 5 December 2001, according to the terms of the treaty, limiting the USA and Russia to a maximum of 6,000 deployed warheads, with a maximum of 1,600 deployed delivery vehicles.

START II was ratified by the USA in 1996, but the process stalled in the Russian Duma (lower house of the **Federal Assembly**) until 2000. It was then passed, subject to US ratification of a 1997 amendment that linked the START II agreement to the ABM Treaty (which had been signed at the conclusion of SALT I). However, the USA was already considering withdrawing from the ABM Treaty, in order to pursue its planned missile defence system. The USA abrogated the ABM Treaty in June 2002, and in response Russia withdrew from its START II commitment. The previous month Presidents Bush and **Putin** had signed the **SORT** treaty.

State Department for Privatization of the Republic of Moldova
Departamentul Privatizarii al Republicii Moldova

Government department set up in 1991 to carry out the State Privatization Plan.
Director-General: Alexandr Bannicov.
Address: Str. Puşkin 26, 2012 Chişinau.
Telephone: (22) 234350.
Fax: (22) 234336.
E-mail: dep.priv@moldtelecom.md
Internet: www.privatization.md

State Duma
Gossoudarstvennaya Duma

The lower house of the **Federal Assembly** of the **Russian Federation**.

State Export-Import Bank of Ukraine (UkrExImBank)

Founded as an independent entity in Ukraine in 1992, formerly a branch of the **Soviet Union** External Trade Bank. As of December 2003 the Bank held assets of US $ 2,937m. and had 29 branches.
Chair: Oleksandr Sorokin.
Address: vul. Horkoho 127, 03150 Kiev.
Telephone: (44) 2478070.
Fax: (44) 2478082.
E-mail: bank@eximb.com
Internet: www.eximb.com

State Property Fund of Ukraine
Fond Dezhavnoho Maina Ukrainy

Government agency in **Ukraine** responsible for the state's holdings in business.
Manager: Valentyna P. Semenyuk.
Address: vul. Kutuzova 18/9, 01133 Kiev.
Telephone: (44) 2003333.
Fax: (44) 2867985.
E-mail: marketing@spfu.kiev.ua
Internet: www.spfu.gov.ua

State Property Management Agency *see* **Department of Privatization**.

State Telegraph Agency of Azerbaijan *see* **AzarTAc**.

Stratan, Andrei

Deputy Prime Minister and Minister of Foreign Affairs and European Integration, **Moldova**. Andrei Stratan worked for the Customs Department for many years before becoming an Ambassador and then rising to the top of the Ministry of Foreign Affairs. He joined the Council of Ministers in February 2004 and was made Deputy Prime Minister 10 months later.

Born on 3 September 1966 in **Chişinau**, he graduated with a doctorate in economics from the Chişinau Polytechnic Institute in 1991. He got a job initially at the General Department of the Customs Control of the Council of Ministers of the **Soviet Union**, before moving the following year to the Moldovan Customs Department where he was to work for a decade, rising to Director-General in 1999. During this time he also studied law at Moldova's State University. In 2002 he was appointed Ambassador with special missions at the Ministry of Foreign Affairs, co-ordinating Moldova's involvement in the Stability Pact for South-eastern Europe. On 11 June 2003 he became Deputy Minister of Foreign Affairs and was promoted to full Minister on 4 February 2004. By December he had also been made a Deputy Prime Minister.

Andrei Stratan is married and has one child. He speaks Russian and English.
Address: Ministry of Foreign Affairs, 31 August 80, 227012 Chişinau.
Telephone: (22) 578207.
Fax: (22) 232302.
E-mail: secdep@mfa.un.md
Internet: www.mfa.md

Subcarpathia *see* **Transcarpathia**.

Supreme Council
Verkhovna Rada

The unicameral legislature of **Ukraine**. It has 450 directly elected members. Following the electoral reform of 2004, the 2006 election used an entirely proportional representation system, and members now serve a five-year term (rather than four years). The last elections were held on 26 March 2006.
Address: M. Grushevskogo St 5, 01008 Kiev.
Telephone: (44) 2930486.
Fax: (44) 2933217.
E-mail: portal@rada.kiev.ua
Internet: www.rada.gov.ua

Svalbard

A group of islands deep in the Arctic Circle directly north of Norway. Its population of around 2,400 (2005 estimate) has had a Norwegian majority since 1998. The once majority ethnic **Russian** community formed the bulk of those leaving the islands in the 1990s, and now accounts for less than a third of the population. The Svalbard islands were ceded to Norway under the 1920 Spitsbergen Treaty which gave **Russia** access to the region's resources. A dispute between the two countries over the maritime border flared in 1977 when Norway declared an exclusive economic zone around its coast. The status of the Russian population of the islands was questioned in the late 1990s when the Russian Federation withdrew its state subsidies to the islanders.

T

Tabasarans

A Caucasian people largely resident in the southern **Russian** republic of **Dagestan**. Along with the closely-related **Lezghins** the Tabasarans are among the oldest-recorded inhabitants of the **Caucasus region**, first mentioned in the 5th century. Like most other Dagestanis they abandoned their animist beliefs and adopted Islam in the 8th and 9th centuries, although traditional practices are still widespread. The 110,000-strong Tabasaran community remains largely agriculturally based, with activity following the general Dagestani pattern— livestock in the highlands, cultivation in the few lower areas. Tabasaran is one of Dagestan's nine indigenous languages to have a literary tradition. It has been transcribed in **Cyrillic** since 1938.

Taraclia

A semi-autonomous district in southern **Moldova** with a 66% majority **Bulgarian** population of some 43,100 (2005 estimate). Attempts by the Moldovan authorities to strip Taraclia of its distinct status in 1998–99 met stiff resistance from the Bulgarian community, which was supported by the Government of Bulgaria. Legislation drawn up in November 1998 proposed the incorporation of Taraclia into the greater Cahul County. Fearing loss of cultural rights in the new entity, where Bulgarians would have become merely 16% of the population, an illegal referendum in Taraclia rejected the move by a sweeping 92% in January 1999. Eventually the Moldovan Government accepted their opposition and restored the district status of Taraclia in October 1999. Plans were announced in 2003 to establish a Bulgarian-language university.

Tarlev, Vasile

Prime Minister of **Moldova**. Vasile Tarlev was inaugurated as Prime Minister of Moldova on 19 April 2001. Five times the **Chişinau** 'businessman of the year' at the head of the sweet and chocolate giant Bucuria, he had no affiliation to any political party, and his appointment signalled the new **Communist Party** Government's intention to maintain a free-market economy after its sweeping electoral victory in early 2001 (*see* **Communist Party of the Moldovan Republic**—PCRM). His position is somewhat undermined by the efforts of President Vladimir **Voronin** to strengthen his own role.

Vasile Petru Tarlev was born into the ethnic **Bulgarian** community in Bascalia in the extreme south of **Soviet**-controlled Moldova on 9 October 1963, and worked in the village as a tractor and goods vehicle driver before being conscripted into the Soviet army in 1981. He returned to work as a driver, moving in this capacity to the Pushkin Theatre in the capital Chişinau, until 1985 when he enrolled with the technology faculty of the Chişinau Polytechnic Institute.

On graduation Tarlev found employment in the capital with the Bucuria confectionery firm as a mechanic, and steadily worked his way up the company. By the time of Moldovan independence in 1991 he was chief engineer, and within a further four years he had become Director-General of Bucuria and been elected Chairman of the National Producers' Association. He was first awarded the accolade of 'businessman of the year' by the Chişinau city authorities in 1996 and held the title for four successive years.

In 1998 Tarlev was awarded a doctorate in technical studies and entered government as a member of President Petru Lucinschi's Supreme Economic Council. This experience, along with his prominent role at the head of Bucuria, made Tarlev an attractive choice for Prime Minister in April 2001 for the newly elected President Voronin, eager to convince foreign donors that his PCRM Government would not derail the country's post-Soviet economic reforms. Tarlev's lack of political affiliation also helped counter the concern that the Communists' parliamentary majority would be used to swamp the Government with party apparatchiks. His lack of a power base in the party was another reason for Voronin to favour him, avoiding the emergence of a powerful party rival.

As Prime Minister, Tarlev has continued the free-market policies of his predecessors but did criticize the method of previous privatizations. Under his stewardship the country has been welcomed into the **World Trade Organization** (WTO) and the Balkan Security Pact. Tarlev was re-elected to **Parliament** in the March 2005 elections on the PCRM list, and Voronin reappointed him as Prime Minister, giving him a mandate to form a Council of Ministers that would focus on modernizing the country, rooting out corruption, reforming education and paving the way towards European integration.

Tarlev is married with two children.

Address: Office of the Prime Minister, Piaţa Marii Adunari Nationale 1,
     227033 Chişinau.
Telephone: (22) 233092.
Fax: (22) 242696.
Internet: www.gov.md

Tartu, Treaties of

Treaties signed in 1920 by Soviet **Russia** securing peaceful relations and common borders with Estonia (2 February) and Finland (14 October). The first treaty guaranteed Russia's recognition of Estonia's independence (later revoked), while the second significantly included the cession of the **Petsamo** district to Finland.

See also Treaties of **Riga**.

Tatars

A **Turkic** and **Muslim** people numbering over 10 million worldwide, mostly spread across the south of **European Russia** and into **Ukraine**. Tatars arrived in **eastern Europe** in the 13th century at the head of the Mongol invasion of Genghis Khan. From 1237 to 1552 the Tatar Golden Horde and its successor khanates dominated the **Russians**. With the collapse of the Kazan and **Astrakhan** khanates in 1552 these former masters fell under the dominion of the growing Russian Empire and have remained the second largest ethnic group in Russia after the Russians. The Tatars were used as an administrative class to help subjugate the **Muslim peoples** of the north **Caucasus** and central Asia. However, the majority Tatar population fell victim to intense efforts to russify them and break links between the main communities in the southern Urals, **Crimea** and the **Volga region**.

Tatar nationalism has long been a centre for anti-Russian protest. Stalin, and later Soviet leaders, crushed Tatar protests with characteristic severity. Many Tatars were deported to **Siberia** and central Asia to break up their communities. Since the end of the **Soviet Union** the Tatars of **Tatarstan** have pushed for high levels of autonomy within the **Russian Federation** and Tatar language and culture have flourished. The Tatars are most closely related to the **Bashkirs**.

Today just over a third of Russia's estimated 5.6 million Tatars live in Tatarstan, the only ethnic Tatar state in the world. The Volga and **Crimean Tatars** do not have autonomous representation.

Tatarstan

A heavily-industrialized constituent republic of the **Russian Federation** situated in the centre of the **Volga**-Ural region of **European Russia**. *Population*: 3.8m. (2002 estimate). **Tatar** nationalism flourished in the late 19th and early 20th centuries, centred in the main Tatar city of Kazan. During the Russian Civil War (1918–20) the Tatars sided with the anti-Bolshevik 'White' Russians and pressed for a Tatar-dominated **Idel-Ural** state. This aspiration was defeated, and when the Tatar-based republic of Tatarstan (known as Tataria in Russian) was formed in

1920 its borders were redrawn to place three-quarters of Russia's Tatars outside the republic.

During the **Soviet** era Tatarstan was heavily developed as an industrial centre. The first oil well opened in 1943. The main centre for oil is at Almetyevsk and natural gas production is based in Nizhnyaya Maktama. The petroleum chemical industry is based in the republic's capital, Kazan. The Volga river, which forms the republic's western border, is the main channel for the transport of exports to the rest of the Russian Federation. In 2003 Tatarstan accounted for around 4% of the Federation's industrial output. Industrialization has brought high real wages and higher than average levels of crime.

Perestroika (restructuring) encouraged a resurgence in Tatar nationalism in the late 1980s and Tatarstan was at the forefront of calls for greater regional autonomy. A Sovereign Republic was declared on 30 August 1990. The new authorities refused at first to sign the 1992 Federation Treaty and actually declared independence after a successful referendum. However, complete separation from the Russian Federation was not internationally recognized and was never a tenable position, surrounded as the republic is by the Federation, and with a 40% **Russian** minority. A power-sharing agreement was concluded with the Russian authorities on 15 February 1994 and Tatarstan joined the Federation fully. Regional autonomy flourished under the *laissez faire* presidency of Boris **Yeltsin**. However, the efforts of Yeltsin's successor Vladimir **Putin** to recentralize the Federation brought Tatarstan into dispute with his administration. In April 2001 it was included in a list of four republics which maintained laws seriously contradicting the federal Constitution. In December 2002 the Russian Duma (lower house of the **Federal Assembly**) passed a law to enforce the use of the **Cyrillic** script across the Russian Federation, after Tatarstan (and other republics) had attempted to introduce the Latin script in an effort to promote their own non-Russian cultures and international links.

In October 2005 Putin did renew Tatarstan's power-sharing agreement, albeit with tighter restrictions on some aspects of governance, but retaining the Tatar language's dominance over Russian. The Duma passed the bill in February 2007, but it was rejected by the Council of the Federation (the Russian upper house) later that month fearing it would create an unwanted precedent.

Mintimer Sharipovich Shaimiev has been Tatar President since April 1990.

Tbilisi

The capital city and main urban centre of **Georgia**, situated in the south-east of the country. Also known as Tiflis. *Population*: 1.1m. (2002 estimate). Originally established as the capital of a Georgian kingdom in 458, the city has fallen to numerous conquerors throughout its history—the Persians, Arabs, Turks and finally, in 1801, the **Russians**. As a frontier of the Russian Empire the city was developed as an administrative centre and military garrison. It was linked to Russia via the direct trans-Caucasian Georgian Military Highway from Vladikavkaz. East–west links were improved at the end of the 19th century with rail lines to Poti on the Black Sea coast and **Baku** (in **Azerbaijan**) on the Caspian. Tbilisi has since become a centre for railway products. It also has a diverse range of lighter industries including textiles and consumer goods.

TRACECA
(Transport Corridor Europe–Caucasus–Asia)

A project assisted by the **European Union** to promote, co-ordinate and plan alternative transport links between **eastern Europe** and central Asia, via the **Caucasus**. Established in May 1993 as an extension of the existing transport corridor, TRACECA aims to increase regional trade and political ties. A Permanent Secretariat of the Inter-governmental Commission TRACECA is based in **Baku, Azerbaijan**.

Members: **Armenia**, Azerbaijan, Bulgaria, **Georgia**, Kazakhstan, Kyrgyzstan, **Moldova**, Romania, Tajikistan, Turkey, Turkmenistan, **Ukraine** and Uzbekistan.
Secretary-General: Rustan Jenalinov.
Address: Gen. Aliyarbekov St 8/2, 1005 Baku.
Telephone: (12) 5982718.
Fax: (12) 4986426.
E-mail: r.jenalinov@ps.traceca-org.org
Internet: www.traceca-org.org

Trans-Siberian Railway

The famous railway connecting **Moscow** in **European Russia** with Vladivostok on the Pacific Ocean. Construction of the railway began in 1891 at the behest of Tsar Alexander III and his industrialist-reformist Government, keen to exploit the vast mineral resources of **Siberia** and to definitively stamp **Russia**'s sovereignty on the far-eastern provinces of the Amur Valley. It was finally completed in 1905, and a new route bypassing Chinese-administered Manchuria made it conform to its present course from 1916. Since then the Trans-Siberian Railway (TSR or Transsib) has served as the main source of on-land shipment between the mines and factories of Siberia and the **Volga region**, the industrial heart of European Russia. Electrification was completed in 2002. It is also now used as a lucrative tourist attraction. The complete 9,310-km journey can take between five and seven days passing through the industrial cities of Yekaterinburg and Irkutsk and skimming past the scenic region around Lake Baikal.

Transcarpathia

A sliver of western **Ukraine** in the northern Carpathian mountains. The region forms the central edge of the historic region of Ruthenia ('Little Russia', or more accurately, west Ukraine). Since its return to Ukraine in 1945 the territory has been known as the Zakarpatskaya *oblast* (region). It forms the modern border between Ukraine and (from north to south) Poland, Slovakia, Hungary and Romania. The ethnic **Ruthenian** peasantry was traditionally allowed access to its **Uniate Church** and developed a strongly pro-Russian culture after the 19th century.

The region was part of Hungary from 1015 until 1918, firmly establishing Hungarian claims to the region. However, with the collapse of the Habsburg Empire at the end of the First World War, the Hungarian lands were divided and Transcarpathia was incorporated into the new Czechoslovak state under the 1920 Treaty of Trianon. Between 1938 and 1945 Hungary reoccupied Transcarpathia under the supervision of the Nazi state. With the defeat of the Axis powers all of historic Ruthenia was absorbed as part of the victorious **Soviet Union** and ceded to the Ukrainian republic, including Transcarpathia. Although Transcarpathia is now accepted as an integral part of Ukraine, on the basis of its majority **Ukrainian** population, irredentist Hungarian nationalists still lay claim to the province and aim to revise the borders set out by the Treaty of Trianon.

Economic activity is distinctly rural with the region's mountainous terrain precluding major industrial development. Timber and wood products dominate along with intensive agriculture on the small plains. Wine is produced in the Tisza valley area. The town of Chop in the western corner serves as the main entry point to Ukraine for traffic from Hungary and the surrounding region.

Transcaucasia or Transcaucasus

A geographical expression for the region and countries to the immediate south of the Greater **Caucasus** mountains which effectively form the south-eastern border of Europe. The countries in question are **Armenia**, **Azerbaijan** and **Georgia**. These three countries were briefly united between 1922 and 1936 in the Transcaucasian Soviet Federal Socialist Republic before being divided into today's modern states.

Transdnestria
(Transdnester Moldovan Republic/Pridnestrovie Moldovan Republic, PMR)

A small breakaway republic situated on the industrialized east bank of the Dnester river in **Moldova**, known in Moldovan as Transdnestria and in Russian as Pridnestrovie. *Population*: 601,088 (2003 estimate). Designated the PMR in

October 1991 it is ethnically divided between **Moldovans**, the largest group at around 32%, **Ukrainians** and **Russians**, but the Russian language is dominant. Open conflict with Moldovan forces in 1992 led to the intervention of Russian peacekeepers and was seemingly resolved in July 1996 when Transdnestria was designated 'a republic within Moldova'. The unicameral regional government is based in Tiraspol and headed by self-styled President Igor Smirnov.

Politically dominated by **Russia** since absorption into the Russian Empire in 1791, Transdnestria was only briefly occupied by enemy forces during the two world wars. Its 200-year connection has led to a high degree of russification. Under Soviet rule the **Cyrillic alphabet** was introduced into the Moldovan Soviet Socialist Republic and Transdnestria in particular was developed as a regional centre for heavy industry, resulting in an influx of ethnic Russians. The Russian minority in Transdnestria and the Moldovan capital **Chişinau** came to dominate the Soviet bureaucracy. Calls for the unification of Moldova with Romania following the collapse of the **Soviet Union** spurred the declaration of sovereignty for the PMR through a referendum. Clashes between paramilitaries and the Moldovan army escalated into full conflict in the summer of 1992, leaving hundreds dead and leading to the intervention of the Russian army as peacekeepers. Despite the definitive failure in Moldova of the movement for unification with Romania, and the constitutional accommodation reached with the moderate pan-Moldovan Government in 1996, Transdnestria continued to demand more autonomy.

Moldova's newly-elected pro-Russian President Vladimir **Voronin** launched renewed peace talks in 2001, although these talks achieved few tangible results to match their many headlines. Meanwhile, the Russians repeatedly missed deadlines set by the **Organization for Security and Co-operation in Europe** (OSCE) for the withdrawal of troops, claiming that the Transdnestrian authorities were delaying their departure. In 2003 Voronin announced his support for the Russian-backed plan for a federalized constitution, with Transdnestria becoming a fully autonomous region with its own national symbols and budget, and with Russian as an equal official language. Popular protests in Moldova, arguing that the plans aimed to cement Moldova in the Russian sphere of influence, forced him to backtrack in December in favour of a more vague US-sponsored plan involving the deployment of international—rather than just Russian— peacekeepers ahead of a political reorganization of the country.

Relations between the Moldovan and Transdnestrian Governments soured during 2004. Smuggling was rife in the breakaway region, and Voronin labelled the Transdnestrian authorities a 'transnational criminal group'. A dispute over the Transdnestrian closure of schools using the Latin script spiralled into mutual recriminations and an economic blockade. Customs restrictions introduced by **Ukraine** in 2005, requiring all Transdnestrian exports to bear Moldovan documentation, caused an economic crisis in Transdnestria; humanitarian aid was supplied to the region by Russia and the **European Union**. In July the Moldovan

Government, without consultation with the Transdnestrian authorities, passed the Law on Basic Provisions of the Special Legal Status of Localities from the Left Bank of the Dnester, which established Transdnestria as an autonomous territorial unit within Moldova.

By 2006, Russia was openly backing the separatist cause in Transdnestria, as relations between the Russian and Moldovan Governments hit an all-time low. In September a referendum was held in Transdnestria in which 97% of voters supported continuing the course towards independence and subsequent free association with the Russian Federation, and 94% rejected the possibility of renouncing Transdnestria's independent status and subsequently becoming part of Moldova. The poll was viewed as illegitimate by the international community, except for Russia.

Turkic peoples

A large ethnic group encompassing nationalities spread across **eastern Europe** (particularly in **European Russia**) and central Asia. Historically the Turks are thought to have originated among the nomadic T'u-chüeh of western Mongolia. Through their 6th-century empire the Turks spread across the Russian steppe and established the first of their European colonies.

Turkic nationality groups in eastern Europe are the **Azeris**, Balkars (*see* **Kabardino-Balkaria**), Bashkirs (*see* **Bashkortostan**), Bulgarian Turks, **Chavash, Karachai, Kazakhs, Kumyks, Meskhetians** and **Tatars** (*see also* **Crimean Tatars**). All have mixed with local peoples over the centuries, often retaining only their language—which is of the Altaic group—by which they can be identified as Turkic, although they share similarities in culture and, apart from the Chavash and **Kryashens**, all embrace Islam. **Pan-Turkic** sentiment is strongest in **Tatarstan** but has found little popular support elsewhere within the **Russian Federation**.

Tymoshenko, Yuliya *see* **Yuliya Tymoshenko bloc**.

U

Udmurtia

A heavily-industrialized constituent republic of the **Russian Federation** situated in the east of **European Russia**. *Population*: 1.6m. (2002 estimate).

Inhabited by the **Finno-Ugric** Udmurt people, the region came under the suzerainty of the Kazan khanate in the 14th century before being absorbed into the Russian Empire in 1552. Under the **Soviet Union**, Udmurtia was granted the status of an autonomous *oblast* (region) in 1920 (known as Votskaya until 1932) and became an autonomous republic in 1934. It was developed as a major industrial centre and now supplies around 1% of the Russian Federation's annual output. The republic declared its sovereignty on the collapse of the centralized Soviet state in September 1990.

The geography of Udmurtia displays strong differences between the largely marshy north and the drier, more fertile, south. Following these differences the republic's main industrial centres are in the north and produce a wide variety of goods including building materials, metal products, heavy industrial machines and textiles. The oil and gas industry is also important for the region. The capital, Izhevsk, focuses on the construction of machinery and armaments.

Udmurts are most closely related to the neighbouring **Mari** and **Komi** and constitute around 30% of Udmurtia and minority communities in the neighbouring republics; there are approximately 637,000 Udmurts in total. Aleksandr Volkov has been President of Udmurtia since 19 April 1995.

Ukraine
Ukraina

An independent republic in **eastern Europe** since 1991, formerly part of the **Soviet Union**. Ukraine is bounded to the west by Poland, Slovakia and Hungary, to the north by **Belarus**, to the north and east by the **Russian Federation** and to the south by Romania, **Moldova** and the Black Sea. Administratively, the country is divided into 24 provinces (*oblasti*), one autonomous republic (**Crimea**) and two municipalities.

Area: 603,700 sq km; *capital*: **Kiev** (Kyiv); *population*: 46.5m. (2005 estimate), comprising **Ukrainians** 78.1%, **Russians** 17.3%, others 4.6%; *official language*: Ukrainian; *religion*: **Orthodox, Roman Catholic**.

Under the Constitution adopted in June 1996, executive authority is vested in the President, who is directly elected for a five-year term. Under constitutional amendments adopted in December 2004, the President nominates the Prime Minister, Defence Minister and Foreign Minister, for approval by the legislature. The Prime Minister nominates other members of the Government, for approval by the legislature. Legislative authority is vested in the unicameral **Supreme Council** (Verkhovna Rada), which has 450 members serving for a five-year term. Under a 1997 constitutional amendment, the 1998 elections used a system where half of the members were elected by proportional representation from party lists, subject to a 4% threshold, while the other half were elected from single-seat constituencies. A legislative move to introduce proportional representation for all seats in the 2002 elections was vetoed by the President early in 2001, but approved in 2004 ahead of the 2006 elections. The 2004 amendments also extended the Supreme Council's term from four to five years.

History: The first unified state of Eastern **Slavs**, Kievan Rus, was founded in the late 9th century with Kiev at its centre. Christianity was adopted in 988. The Kievan state disintegrated into warring principalities and was destroyed by invading Mongol **Tatars** in the 13th century. By the mid-15th century most of Ukraine was ruled by Lithuania, subsequently coming under Polish influence in 1569. A **Cossack** revolt in 1648, fuelled by the imposition of serfdom and religious persecution, drove the **Poles** from central Ukraine. The eastern part of the territory became a Russian protectorate in 1654, and Ukraine was partitioned east–west between Russia and the Polish-Lithuanian confederation in 1667. The subsequent partitions of Poland, however, in the late 18th century, brought western Ukraine too under Russian rule except for the regions of **Galicia** and **Bukovina** (and the Crimea, which had been ruled by the **Crimean Tatars**, as the Crimean khanate, since 1475). The country was then subject to intense 'russification', including the banning of the use of the Ukrainian language.

In the wake of the Russian Revolution of 1917 and the final defeat of German forces at the end of the First World War, a briefly independent Ukraine was embroiled in the Russian Civil War and in conflict with newly independent Poland. The eastern part was incorporated into the **Soviet Union** as a constituent republic in 1922, while western Ukraine became part of Poland. In the 1930s, forced collectivization of agriculture led to a severe famine which, coupled with the political purges under Stalinist rule, accounted for millions of deaths in Ukraine.

After the start of the Second World War, Soviet forces annexed western Ukraine from Poland and northern Bukovina from Romania (as agreed under the terms of the 1939 **Nazi-Soviet Pact**). German forces then occupied Ukraine from 1941 until 1944 (during which time millions more died) before the Soviet Union regained control of the territory. The post-war Ukrainian Soviet Socialist Republic, which (although part of the Soviet Union) was accorded membership of the UN in its own right, included not only former Polish territory but also Czechoslovak **Transcarpathia**, southern **Bessarabia** (a Romanian territory between the world wars) and parts of Moldova, while the Crimea was transferred from Russia in 1954. Although nationalist sentiment began to reassert itself among Ukrainians after Stalin's death in 1953, in the early 1970s an arch-conservative, Vladimir Shcherbitsky, assumed the leadership of the **Communist Party of Ukraine** (KPU) and initiated a widespread crackdown on political dissent.

In the late 1980s, encouraged by the *glasnost* (openness) initiative in the Soviet Union, opposition activity re-emerged, led by the Popular Movement of Ukraine (Rukh—*see* **Our Ukraine**). In elections to the Ukrainian Supreme Soviet in March 1990, the Democratic Bloc (an electoral coalition including Rukh candidates) won about a quarter of the seats. The following July the new legislature declared Ukrainian sovereignty and elected Leonid Kravchuk as its Chairman.

In the aftermath of the abortive **August coup** by hardliners in **Moscow** in 1991, Ukraine declared full independence and outlawed the KPU (although the party was allowed to re-form in 1993). In December 1991 independence was approved by referendum (with 90% of the vote), Kravchuk was elected President and Ukraine joined the **Commonwealth of Independent States** (CIS). In May 1992 Ukraine granted the mainly Russian-speaking Crimea full autonomy, having revoked Crimea's earlier declaration of sovereignty.

The pursuit of market-led economic policies, the declared objective of post-independence Ukrainian Governments, was obstructed by a Supreme Council dominated by parties associated with the Soviet era. Leonid **Kuchma** was appointed Prime Minister in October 1992, entering into a long power struggle with President Kravchuk, who assumed Cabinet leadership in 1993. The following year the revived KPU, in alliance with the **Socialist Party of Ukraine** (SPU) and the Peasants' Party of Ukraine (SelPU), won the largest share of the seats in parliamentary elections. In the 1994 presidential elections, Kravchuk was defeated by Kuchma, who then appointed himself executive head of a reformist Government. In June 1995, having lost a no-confidence vote in the Supreme Council, Kuchma secured a constitutional agreement strengthening presidential powers, the changes being incorporated in the new Constitution adopted in 1996. Nevertheless, persistent conflict between Kuchma and the left-dominated legislature severely impeded the process of government, as Ukraine sank further into economic and social decline (*see* **Ukraine, economy**). A parallel crisis over Crimea, where a pro-Russian bloc in its own Supreme Council had voted through a demand for Crimean sovereignty in 1994, led eventually to the introduction of a new Crimean Constitution in 1999 giving the autonomous republic greater budgetary powers.

Elections to the Supreme Council in March 1998 confirmed the dominance of the KPU, which won 115 of the 442 seats validly filled; Rukh came a poor second with 42. Most of the independents joined parliamentary groups set up by the main parties, with the result that the centre-right factions commanded an overall majority of seats, although their precise composition was subject to a Byzantine process of endless flux.

Despite his unpopularity over Ukraine's economic difficulties, Kuchma retained office in presidential elections in October–November 1999, defeating KPU candidate Petro Symonenko by 56.3% to 37.8% in the second round. International observers reported that the polling had been flawed by many irregularities to the advantage of the incumbent.

President Kuchma's rediscovered commitment to economic reform was signalled by the appointment of the Governor of the **National Bank of Ukraine**, Viktor **Yushchenko**, as Prime Minister in December 1999. In another move welcomed in the West, in March 2000 the death penalty was formally abolished. However, the political process was again paralysed in early 2000 by the determination of the centre-right parties to oust Oleksandr Tkachenko (SelPU) as Chairman of the Supreme Council, which they achieved only after a protracted crisis in which two alternative legislatures were sitting at one stage.

President Kuchma then launched a campaign to correct the perceived deficiencies of the Supreme Council, securing overwhelming approval in a national referendum in April 2000 for proposed constitutional amendments providing for a bicameral legislature, a reduction in the size of the lower house from 450 to 300 members, reduced parliamentary immunity from prosecution and enhanced presidential powers of dissolution. None of these proposed changes secured the necessary parliamentary approval, however. Conversely, a new electoral law adopted by the Supreme Council in January 2001, under which all seats would henceforth be allocated by proportional representation, was vetoed by Kuchma in March, and in May the Supreme Council failed to muster the two-thirds majority needed to override the veto.

Meanwhile, another major political crisis had developed over the discovery in November 2000 of a headless body believed to be that of an opposition journalist, Giorgiy Gongadze, and the publication of tape transcripts appearing to show that Kuchma had been implicated in the murder. Amidst growing popular demands for his resignation, Kuchma persisted with his denials of the authenticity of the tapes and resisted parliamentary moves to impeach him. His position was strengthened by the unwillingness of the KPU and its allies to support impeachment proceedings. In return, Kuchma in April 2001 bowed to a KPU-inspired vote of no confidence in the Government by dismissing Yushchenko as Prime Minister, to the general dismay of Western Governments.

Although Kuchma himself retained office, his parliamentary supporters were pushed to second place in elections held in March 2002. Yushchenko's Our Ukraine (NU) bloc of won 112 of the 450 seats, against 102 for the pro-Kuchma bloc For a United Ukraine.

With continuing criticism of Kuchma over the Gongadze murder case, his apparent arms dealing with the pariah state of Iraq and the administration's perceived corruption, Kuchma eventually bowed to pressure and pledged not to seek re-election in 2004. Instead his Prime Minister Viktor **Yanukovych**, who had been appointed in November 2002, was nominated by the pro-government parties.

The opposition, united behind Yushchenko's candidacy, claimed a series of efforts at government intimidation, including arrests of activists and a dramatic accusation that government agents had attempted to poison Yushchenko. Rushed to hospital in Austria, Yushchenko still bears the facial scarring he claimed was a result of this attempt on his life. The first round of presidential elections held on 31 October 2004 ended with Yushchenko leading the field with 39.9% of the vote, followed closely by Yanukovych with 39.3%. The next closest contender won just 5.8% of the vote. Allegations of fraud and violence by government supporters increased at the run-off poll on 21 November and the initially-declared victory of Yanukovych with 49.5%, ahead of Yushchenko's 46.6% was roundly rejected. Mass rallies held in Kiev and adorned with the orange colour of the Our Ukraine bloc received general support from the international community, with the notable exception of Russia. Local administrations, particularly in the western part of the country where Yushchenko's support was concentrated, refused to accept the result. Hundreds of thousands of supporters gathered to demonstrate in favour of Yushchenko outside the Supreme Council building. Faced with the popular strength of this so-called **Orange Revolution**, the Supreme Court decided to annul the vote. In the re-run held on 26 December, Yushchenko's victory was finally recognized with 52% of the vote. He was inaugurated on 23 January 2005.

Yushchenko immediately sought to reduce his own constitutional powers by raising the profile of the Prime Minister, and turned to veteran opposition leader Yuliya **Tymoshenko** to form a Government. Tymoshenko presented Parliament with a new, overtly pro-EU agenda seeking to create a civil society. Differences in political style between President and Prime Minister, however, became apparent from an early stage. By September 2005, members of Tymoshenko's Government had begun to resign amidst allegations of corruption. Yushchenko then dismissed the whole Cabinet and replaced Tymoshenko with economist Yuriy Yekhanurov. To win parliamentary confirmation of the appointment of Yekhanurov, Yushchenko was forced to agree with opposition leader Yanukovych to declare an amnesty for those accused of electoral fraud. These moves saw the popularity of the administration plunge.

For his part, Yekhanurov made Ukraine's hope to join the **World Trade Organization** his main priority in the few months remaining before legislative elections due in March 2006.

Latest elections: Elections to the Supreme Council on 26 March 2006 resulted in the pro-Yanukovych **Party of Regions** (PR) becoming the largest single party with 186 of the 450 seats available, having won 32.1% of the vote. The **Yuliya Tymoshenko bloc** (BYT) came second with 129 seats and 22.3% of the vote. Yushchenko's NU came third with 81 seats (14.0% of the vote). The SPU won 33 seats (5.7%) and the KPU 21 (3.7%). No other party broke the new 3% barrier for representation.

Recent developments: In the months following the elections, Yushchenko and Tymoshenko attempted to rebuild their old coalition, in order to keep the PR out of power. However, when the SPU announced in July that it would switch its support to a PR-KPU coalition, cohabitation between Yushchenko and Yanukovych appeared to be inevitable. Yushchenko held out against this solution for several more weeks, but after the deadline passed for dissolving the Supreme Council he finally agreed on 3 August to nominate Yanukovych as Prime Minister. Yanukovych was approved as Prime Minister by the Supreme Council on 4 August, in the absence of most members of the BYT. As per the new constitutional arrangements, the President chose the Defence and Interior Ministers, while Yanukovych appointed the remainder of his Council of Ministers from his coalition: the PR, the KPU, the SPU and some members of Yushchenko's NU. Divisions swiftly became evident, unsurprisingly over the direction of foreign policy and NATO membership. By October the NU had withdrawn its support, and the President and Council of Ministers were soon at loggerheads over approval of the two presidentially-appointed ministerial positions.

International relations and defence: Following independence in 1991 and accession to the CIS, Ukraine became a member of the **Organization for Security and Co-operation in Europe**, the **Council of Europe**, the **Central European Initiative**, the **Organization of the Black Sea Economic Co-operation** and the **Danube Commission**. Its long-standing application for membership of the **World Trade Organization** remains under discussion. Ukraine was also a founder member in 1997 of what became the **GUAM group** (with **Georgia**, **Azerbaijan** and Moldova) within the CIS.

Having acceded in 1994 to the **Partnership for Peace** programme of the **North Atlantic Treaty Organization** (NATO), Ukraine in 1997 signed an important co-operation agreement with NATO. A partnership and co-operation agreement with the **European Union** (EU) came into force in 1998, its provisions including one for EU financial assistance with the closure of the remaining reactors at the **Chernobyl** nuclear plant, site of the world's worst nuclear accident to date in 1986. Ukraine's longer-term aspirations to full membership of the EU and NATO were seen as much more likely following the accession of Yushchenko in 2005, though their remains concern over levels of government corruption. The return of Yanukovych as Prime Minister put a brake on Ukraine's push for Western integration.

Ukraine's lengthy dispute with Russia over ownership of the **Black Sea Fleet** was officially resolved under a framework agreement concluded in 1997 (with final resolution due in 2017). A separate dispute between the two countries over control of the shared Sea of Azov prompted the despatch of Ukrainian border guards to the region in late 2003. An agreement delineating maritime boundaries was eventually reached in December, but relations were severely strained when Russian president Vladimir **Putin** openly backed Yanukovych in the lead up to the Orange Revolution. In March 2006 tensions increased as Ukraine appeared to step in on the side of the Moldovan Government in its dispute with the pro-Russian breakaway forces in **Transdnestria**, by introducing more stringent border controls on Transdnestrian goods.

More pressing was the question of Ukraine's payment for Russian gas. Anger over attempts by the Ukrainian Government to reject price increases from the Russian Government-controlled supplier, **Gazprom**, prompted temporary cut-offs of supplies in early 2006 and 2007. Following pressure to resolve the dispute from the EU, whose own supplies were reduced as a knock-on effect of the disagreement, the Ukrainian Government agreed to accept a near-doubling of costs in June 2006 and a further price rise was agreed for 2007, though Ukraine is also looking to central Asian states as future suppliers.

Ukraine's defence budget for 2006 amounted to some US $1,740m., equivalent to about 0.2% of GDP. The size of the armed forces at August 2006 was some 187,600 personnel, including those serving under compulsory conscription of 18–24 months, while reservists numbered an estimated one million.

Ukraine, economy

An economy shaped by the central planning system of the **Soviet** era, which went into virtual free-fall following independence in 1991, until economic growth returned from 2000.

GNP: US $71,377m. (2005); *GNP per capita*: $1,520 (2005); *GDP at PPP*: $320,561m. (2005); *GDP per capita at PPP*: $6,804 (2005); *exports*: $39,716m. (2004); *imports*: $40,103m. (2005); *currency*: hryvna (plural: hryvnas; US $1=H5.05 at the end of December 2006).

In 2005 industry was estimated to account for 34.2% of GDP, agriculture for 10.8% and services for 55%. Of the 22.3 million workforce, about 30% are engaged in industry, 19% in agriculture and 51% in services. About 56% of the land is arable, 2% under permanent crops, 13% permanent pastures and 17% forests and woodland. Ukraine is self-sufficient in most aspects of agricultural production, with large areas devoted to grain, as well as to sugar beet, potatoes and other vegetables; animal husbandry is also important, though in particular decline in the 1990s. Agricultural output was seriously affected by the 1986 **Chernobyl** nuclear reactor disaster, which made large areas of land unusable.

Ukraine has large resources of hard coal and iron ore as well as brown coal (lignite), titanium, graphite and manganese ore. There are also small reserves of petroleum (395m. barrels in 2004) and of natural gas (39,000,000m. cu ft at the end of 2005), but post-independence oil output has fallen steadily, and most petroleum and natural gas needs are met from imports, notably from the **Russian Federation** and Turkmenistan. The main industries are the extraction of coal, ferrous and non-ferrous metals, machinery and equipment, chemicals and food processing. In 2003 about 45% of Ukraine's electricity requirements were met through nuclear generation, but the future of the nuclear industry remains uncertain in the wake of the 1986 accident at the Chernobyl nuclear power station (where the remaining reactors were finally closed in December 2000).

Ukraine's main exports by value in 2005 were base metals—mainly comprising iron and steel (41% of the total), mineral products (14%), chemicals and related products (9%) and machinery and electrical equipment (8%). Principal imports in 2005 were mineral fuels and products (32%), machinery and electrical equipment (18%), vehicles, aircraft and transport equipment (9%) and chemicals and related products (9%). Some 22% of Ukraine's exports in 2005 went to the Russian Federation, and 6% each to Turkey and Italy. The main sources of imports in 2005 were the Russian Federation (36%), Germany (9%) and Turkmenistan (7%).

Prior to independence Ukraine was the 'bread-basket' of the **Soviet Union**, its rich agricultural land providing 25% of Soviet grain production, 20% of meat and dairy products and over 50% of sugar beet output. Soviet Ukraine also developed a substantial heavy industrial sector and was a principal producer of defence-related equipment. The disappearance of the Soviet framework exposed the chronic inefficiencies of both sectors, with the result that in the period 1991–96 GDP declined in real terms by an average rate of 14% a year, while consumer price inflation rose massively to over 1,000% in 1992 and to some 10,000% in 1993.

The election of Leonid **Kuchma** as President in mid-1994 heralded a serious attempt at economic reform. A comprehensive **IMF**-prescribed programme was introduced under which most price controls were lifted, a new currency (the hryvna) was launched in 1996 with a unified exchange rate, bread and utility subsidies were reduced and export quotas eliminated. The results were initially encouraging, in that the rate of GDP contraction was limited to about 3% in 1997, while inflation fell sharply to an annualized rate of about 10% at the end of 1997. Exports to Western markets also began to increase, more than offsetting a continuing fall in trade with the Russian Federation and other former Soviet republics.

The limited progress was halted by the mid-1998 Russian financial crisis (*see* **Russian Federation, economy**), which highlighted similar deficiencies in the Ukrainian economy. Although GDP contraction was reduced to 2% in 1998, inflation rose to 20% and the hryvna lost more than half its external value in the latter part of the year, being further devalued in early 1999. Although GDP contracted by only 0.4% in 1999, inflation remained high at around 20% and Ukraine experienced serious problems in funding essential oil and gas imports, while the Kosovo crisis restricted Ukraine's trade routes along the Danube river. The IMF noted in March 1999 that reform in the agricultural and energy sectors had been inadequate and delayed, that continued friction between the **Supreme Council** and Government added uncertainty to the economic climate and that stronger fiscal adjustment was necessary to ensure progress towards macroeconomic stability. It also urged that higher priority should be accorded to structural reforms in the energy, coal and agricultural sectors, to a further downsizing in government and rationalization of the public sector, and to greater progress in deregulation and privatization. The appearance of evidence in early 2000 that IMF loans had been embezzled by Ukrainian officials caused the IMF to suspend further disbursements under a three-year facility agreed in 1998.

The re-election of Kuchma in November 1999 and the appointment of the Governor of the **National Bank of Ukraine** Viktor **Yushchenko**, as Prime Minister signalled an apparent determination to step up reform efforts. A new five-year 'Reform for Prosperity' programme was quickly introduced, the hryvna was allowed to float from late February 2000 and the restructuring of foreign debt was agreed in April. These efforts yielded speedy success to the extent that in 2000 Ukraine achieved real GDP growth—of 6%—for the first time since independence, while in December 2000 the IMF agreed to reactivate the 1998 financial support facility. However, inflation advanced to 26% in 2000, real unemployment was believed to be up to eight times higher than the official rate of around 5% and an estimated 60% of economic activity took place in the 'black' economy. Moreover, the major political crisis surrounding Kuchma in early 2001 and the dismissal of Yushchenko in April gave rise to renewed doubts about Ukraine's ability to pursue real economic reform.

By 2001 GDP was less than half of its pre-independence level. Growth of 9% that year, 5% in 2002 and 9% in 2003 marked a significant recovery. Fiscal reforms in 2003 included a restructuring of the tax system; measures to combat money 'laundering' led to the removal of Ukraine from the list of 'non-compliant' countries and the ending of sanctions by the USA and Canada.

High global prices for metals spurred growth of 12% in 2004, though the political instability of the **Orange Revolution** at the end of the year caused widespread concern. The return to power of Yushchenko, this time as President, was outweighed by the economic mismanagement that ensued under the Government of Prime Minister Yuliya Tymoshenko. Cohabitation with former foe Prime Minister Viktor **Yanukovych** from 2006 did nothing to restore stability, though foreign investment levels did remain robust.

Growth slowed to 3% in 2005 as the prices for metals declined and the price of imported gas rose, particularly as souring relations with Russia led to ongoing battles over removing the subsides on Russian gas. This also caused a drop in the current account surplus, falling from a high of 11% of GDP in 2004 to 3% in

2005 and entering the deficit zone thereafter. Growth is expected to continue around 6% for the next few years, though it will be vital for the Government to contain the threat of rising inflation.

Ambitious privatization plans announced in 1992 proved difficult to implement for political reasons, notably the strong opposition to them of the powerful **Communist Party of Ukraine** (KPU) and its parliamentary allies. After further partially-aborted efforts, fresh measures were introduced in March 1996 and had some success, especially with smaller enterprises, although the process was tarnished by pervasive corruption. By mid-2000 over 67,000 concerns had been privatized, including over 7,000 medium-sized and large industrial enterprises, and the decollectivization of agriculture was officially stated to have been completed by the restructuring of some 10,500 collective farms into 11,000 joint-stock companies and co-operatives.

New plans for the privatization of some 600 large and strategic enterprises still under state ownership, including the power supply sector and telecommunications, received parliamentary approval in May 2000. The private sale of farmland was approved in 2001, to take effect from 2004. Also in 2001 the Government announced it would denationalize all coal mines and sell them to strategic investors. By 2003, however, the privatizations had been delayed, and the mines were restructured into state enterprises.

The new Government in 2005 began a wholesale review of the earlier privatization of thousands of businesses under ex-President Kuchma. Prime Minister Yuliya Tymoshenko indicated that 3,000 businesses out of 90,000 sold off since 1992 were on a list of companies being reviewed, though Yushchenko hastened to reassure investors that only a few dozen sales would be closely re-examined. The first sale to be annulled was that of a 90% stake in the country's largest steel plant Kryvorizhstal to a consortium headed by Kuchma's son-in-law for a paltry US $800m.—the stake was resold in October 2005 to multinational Mittal Steel for six times the sum.

Ukrainian Chamber of Commerce and Industry

The principal organization in **Ukraine** for promoting business contacts, both internally and externally, in the post-communist era. Originally founded in 1972.

Chair: Serhiy P. Skrypchencko.
Address: vul. Velyka Zhytomyrska 33, 01601 Kiev.
Telephone: (44) 2722911.
Fax: (44) 2723353.
E-mail: ucci@ucci.org.ua
Internet: www.ucci.org.ua

Ukrainian Stock Exchange (USE)

One of eight stock markets on which securities are traded in **Ukraine** (and one of the two main stock markets based in **Kiev**, the others being regional stock markets).

Founded in 1991, the USE had 121 members and nine listed companies as at December 2006. Total market capitalization was US $331.29m. In terms of volume of trading the USE has now been overtaken by the **First Stock Trading System** (PFTS).

Chair: Valentin Oskolsky.
Address: Rylsky Provulok 10, 01025 Kiev.
Telephone: (44) 2794158.
Fax: (44) 2785140.
E-mail: use@ukrse.kiev.ua
Internet: www.ukrse.kiev.ua

Ukrainians

An east **Slavic people** dominant in **Ukraine**, formerly known as **Ruthenians**. The Ukrainians are linguistically and culturally very close to the other east Slavs—**Belarusians** and **Russians**. Their language, like Belarusian, has a large number of Polish loan words. It is transcribed using the **Cyrillic alphabet**. The Ukrainians adopted Christianity in the 10th century; a significant minority are **Uniates** but the majority now follow Eastern **Orthodoxy**. The autocephalous Ukrainian Church re-emerged in 1990 having spent over 200 years as part of the **Russian Orthodox Church**.

Ukrainian nationalism and identity have traditionally been denied by the neighbouring Russians. The medieval Kievan Rus is seen as the cradle of east Slavic civilization and for many centuries Ukrainian was considered to be merely a dialect of Russian. Under the **Soviet** regime, the Ukrainian people bore the brunt of the famine in the early 1920s and civilian casualties during the Second World War. In all some 15 million people are estimated to have died between 1917 and 1945. Like many nationalities, Ukrainians were allowed a greater degree of cultural identity under Khrushchev in the 1950s. From the time of *glasnost* in the late 1980s, through independence in 1991, Ukrainian nationalism and culture flourished.

The largest community outside Ukraine is in the **Russian Federation** where there are 2.9 million Ukrainians, although, because they have their own established 'homeland' outside Russia, they receive little official aid there for cultural and linguistic programmes. Over 800,000 Ukrainians joined Russians and Belarusians in emigrating to Kazakhstan during the Soviet era, but many of them have returned since 1991. A further 600,000 live in **Moldova**, over a quarter of them in **Transdnestria**. This group, heavily russified, has largely allied itself with Moldova's Russian community.

UkrExImBank *see* **State Export–Import Bank of Ukraine**.

UkrInform
Ukrainske Nationalne Informaziyine Agentstvo
(Ukrainian National Information Agency)

The main independent news agency in **Ukraine**. UkrInform was reorganized as an independent agency in 1990, when it was separated from the Telegraph Agency of the Soviet Union (TASS—*see* **ITAR-TASS**), of which it had been the Ukrainian branch since 1918.

> *Director-General*: Viktor Chamara.
> *Address*: vul. Bogdan Khmelnytsky 8/16в, 01001 Kiev.
> *Telephone*: (44) 2292242.
> *Fax*: (44) 2298152.
> *E-mail*: chiefadm@ukrinform.com
> *Internet:* www.ukrinform.com

Uniate Church

A denomination of Christianity significant mainly in **Ukraine**, which recognizes the primacy of the **Roman Catholic** Pope, but maintains traditional **Orthodox Christian** rites. Also known as Greek-Catholicism. The 'Uniate' Church was formed in 1596 when Orthodox Bishops in Ruthenia (*see* **Transcarpathia**) submitted to the authority of Rome but kept their Orthodox traditions, including allowing the clergy to marry. The Church has retained a strong sense of identification with ethnic '**Ruthenians**' (**Ukrainians**). When Transcarpathia was integrated into the **Soviet Union** in 1946 the Uniate Church was persecuted and forced to reintegrate into the **Russian Orthodox Church**. However, the situation was reversed in 1989.

In **Belarus** the Church was abolished altogether by the occupying tsarist Russian authorities in 1839 and was only restarted in the final days of communism in March 1990. The Uniate Church claims around 4.5 million followers in Ukraine but remains very much a minority religion elsewhere. Relations with the Roman Catholic Church remain close whereas the Orthodox Church is hostile to what it sees as a Catholic attempt to divide the Eastern Church.

Union of Right Forces
Soyuz Pravikh Sil (SPS)

A pro-market conservative political party in the **Russian Federation**. The SPS was created prior to the December 1999 elections to the State Duma (lower house of the **Federal Assembly**) as an alliance of parties and groups broadly descended, through many bewildering changes of name and alignment, from those which had supported the 'shock therapy' economic policies of the early 1990s, notably Yegor Gaidar's Russia's Democratic Choice. These formations had lost influence in the more conservative later years of the presidency of Boris **Yeltsin**, with whom Gaidar broke irrevocably in 1996, and were widely blamed for the deterioration and corruption engendered by the early rush to a market economy.

The SPS won 29 Duma seats in the December 1999 elections, with 8.5% of the proportional vote, and subsequently gave broad support to the new presidency of Vladimir **Putin**, while maintaining its distance from the main pro-Putin Unity Inter-regional Movement (Medved—*see* **United Russia**). In May 2000 the SPS alliance formally constituted itself as a national organization with former Prime Minister Boris Nemtsov being elected Chairman and Gaidar one of four Co-Chairmen. A merger with **Yabloko** was mooted in 2000 but never came about. The process of SPS consolidation was continued in 2001 when, at a party conference in May, all nine constituent parties within the SPS voted to officially merge into a single party.

The SPS made a dismal showing at Duma elections in December 2003, when it won just 4% of the vote and only three seats. All three Chairmen resigned in January 2004 and were not replaced until the party conference in May 2005, when Nikita Belykh was chosen as the new, single Chairman. Significantly, Belykh represents the pro-government faction within the party, openly calling for an end to its opposition stance.

Leadership: Nikita Belykh (Chair).
Address: ul. M. Andronyevskaya 15, 109544 Moscow.
Telephone and Fax: (495) 9562909.
E-mail: edit@sps.ru
Internet: www.sps.ru

Union of Soviet Socialist Republics (USSR) *see* **Soviet Union**.

United Labour Party
Miavorvats Ashkhatankayin Kusaksutyun (MAK)

A minor party in **Armenia** formed in 2002. Under the leadership of wealthy businessman Gurgen Arsenian, the MAK won six seats in **National Assembly**

elections held in May 2003 and joined the governing coalition in May 2006.
Leadership: Gurgen Arsenian (Chair).
Address: Yerevan.
Telephone: (91) 425504.
Internet: www.ulp.am

United Russia
Yedinaya Rossiya (YR)

The largest single party in the **Russian Federation** supporting the presidency of Vladimir **Putin** and consequently known as the 'power party'. YR was formed in April 2001 as a merger of the major nationalist parties, the Unity Inter-regional Movement (Mezhregional'noye Dvizhenie Yedinstvo—Medved) and Fatherland-All Russia (Otechestvo-Vsya Rossiya—OVR).

Fatherland had been founded as a conservative nationalist political grouping in November 1998 by Yurii Luzhkov, the popular Mayor of **Moscow**. It was an outspoken critic of then President Boris **Yeltsin** and attracted considerable support from regional governors and business leaders. In April 1999 it formed the OVR bloc with the regionalist All Russia movement. Coming third in elections to the State Duma (lower house of the **Federal Assembly**) in December 1999, winning 66 seats, the OVR fell in behind acting President Putin following Yeltsin's surprise resignation after the elections. In 2000 the OVR moved purposefully closer to Medved and signed a formal union in April 2001.

Medved had been formed by supporters of Yeltsin in 1999 as a counter to the growth of the OVR. It quickly became the political vehicle for then Prime Minister Putin, though he did not join the party and remains a nominal independent. It took second place in the December 1999 elections to the State Duma, winning 72 seats and matching the more successful **Communist Party of the Russian Federation** (KPRF) by attracting support from independents. Following Putin's election as President, Medved began a process of swallowing other pro-market, rightist groups, absorbing Our Home is Russia in February 2001 and uniting with the OVR in April.

The creation of YR as a single entity instantly created an overwhelming bloc in the Duma, immediately drawing in the support of some smaller groups to command 234 seats.

In Duma elections in December 2003, YR swept the board winning 222 seats for itself based on 37% of the vote. It easily dwarfed the KPRF, its nearest rival, which won just 52 seats. With the allegiance of many of the 60-plus independents and the majority of the **People's Party of the Russian Federation**, YR headed all committees in the Duma and commanded enough votes to change the Constitution effectively at will. In April 2005, under the personal direction of Putin, it banned the formation of electoral blocs in a process seen as a direct effort

to consolidate the Government's hegemony.
Leadership: Boris Gryzlov (Chair).
Address: Bannyi per. 4, 129110 Moscow.
Telephone and Fax: (495) 9800308.
E-mail: info@edinros.ru
Internet: www.edinros.ru

USSR *see* **Soviet Union.**

V

V-Plus *see* **People's Coalition Five Plus**.

Verkhovna Rada *see* **Supreme Council**.

Vlachs
(also known as Aromani)

An Indo-European people of the Romance linguistic family, spread across the southern **Balkans** and ethnically similar to modern **Romanians/Moldovans**. Vlachs proudly claim descent from Romans who established the province of Dacia in what is now Romania.

They are thought to have stayed in the region since the 3rd century, adopting a nomadic and pastoral way of life. A majority of Vlachs are still shepherds in remote regions of their host countries. Spreading around the region they gave their **Slavic** loan name, Vlach (they are generally known to themselves as Aromani), to the Wallachia region north of the lower Danube, and became dominant in **Bessarabia**. Their Romance language, which is divided into regional dialects, is most similar to Romanian. Most Vlachs, like Romanians, profess **Orthodox Christianity**.

In the 12th and 13th centuries an independent Vlach state is thought to have flourished around the Greek region of Pindus. It is in Greece that the greatest number of Vlachs reside, and where during the Second World War they established a fascist-inspired Principality of Pindus. Estimates of their numbers vary widely as the Greek government officially does not recognize any ethnic divisions.

Vneshtorgbank *see* **Bank for Foreign Trade**.

Volga region

The region of **European Russia** defined by the Volga river, which flows southeast from east of **St Petersburg** to the north of the Caspian Sea at **Astrakhan**. The major cities of Yaroslavl, Nizhny Novgorod, Kazan, Ulyanovsk, Volgograd and Astrakhan mark the river's route. The Volga was used by the early **Russians** to colonize the region and to trade with Byzantium and the **Muslim** east. It came under the rule of the Russian Empire after the fall of the Kazan khanate in 1552 and then began the long process of settlement and economic exploitation.

The Volga region is home to a significant number of the Russian Federation's major ethnic groups. The various **Turkic** and **Finno-Ugric** peoples united briefly in 1918 in a loosely-conceived separate **Idel-Ural** state (Idel is the Turkic name for the Volga). As well as these long-established groups, there is a community of Volga **Germans** in the area, although most of the 800,000 Germans were deported to **Siberia** during the Second World War. The principal non-Russian republics of the Volga region are **Mari El** and **Tatarstan**.

Voronin, Vladimir

President of **Moldova**. Vladimir Voronin is a charismatic former baker, who worked his way up through the ranks of the Moldovan Communist hierarchy for 30 years, reaching the presidency (to the considerable alarm of foreign investors) in 2001. Despite campaigning against the presidential system in the late 1990s, he attempted to increase presidential powers after his election. The failure of his proposals of federalization, aimed at breaking the deadlock over the separatist **Transdnestria** region where he himself was born, and at limiting the increasing interference of **Russia** in Moldovan affairs, have led Voronin to a complete U-turn on foreign policy. He has exchanged his staunchly pro-Russian platform for a pro-Western stance, aiming for European integration.

Vladimir Nikolayevich Voronin was born on 25 May 1941 in Corjova, a village in the **Chişinau** district but now within the breakaway Transdnester Republic. In 1958 Voronin enrolled at the Chişinau Consumer Co-operation College and graduated in 1961 to become manager of a bakery in Criuleni, on the River Dnester. He moved on in 1966 to become the director of a municipal bakery in the town of Dubossary across the river.

Voronin retrained in 1971 as an economist at the Moscow Food Industry Institute and then returned to Moldova to begin work within the republican branch of the Communist Party. Between then and 1989 he was an active party official in Dubossary, in the western border town of Ungeny, and in Bendery (back on the Dnester). He also became a deputy in the Moldovan Supreme Soviet in 1980 and retrained as a political scientist at the Academy of Social Sciences, graduating in 1983.

Entering the Moldovan Government as Minister of Internal Affairs in 1989 (and given the rank of major-general), he left the Government before it declared Moldovan independence in 1991 and spent two years out of the limelight, studying law. During this time he was also a reservist in the Russian police force. In 1993 he returned to mainstream Moldovan politics. He helped to co-ordinate the rebirth of the **Communist Party of the Republic of Moldova** (PCRM) and was elected its First Secretary at the December 1994 party congress.

When Voronin stood as the party's candidate in the 1996 presidential elections, he came third out of nine with just over 10% of the vote. Two years later, in the country's second multi-party legislative elections, the PCRM secured 40 seats in **Parliament**, Voronin's among them. Within Parliament, Voronin led the PCRM in campaigns against the weak presidential system and the country's increasingly painful economic reforms. Constitutional amendments in 2000 saw Parliament take over responsibility for electing the President, but after repeated failures by any candidate to gain a victory, the legislature was dissolved. Legislative elections in February 2001 produced a dramatic and overwhelming PCRM victory. With 71 seats in the 101-seat chamber, the party's deputies had no difficulty in electing Voronin to the presidency in a ballot held on 4 April.

At the start of his presidency, Voronin personally led renewed negotiations with the self-proclaimed President of separatist Transdnestria, Igor Smirnov, although these talks achieved few tangible results to match their many headlines. Voronin was also eager to expand his own constitutional powers. It was even suggested that he intended to merge the presidency with the premiership. His appointment of the independent businessman Vasile Tarlev as Prime Minister left him as the most influential member of the PCRM in Government. The choice of Tarlev, coupled with his own pledges of commitment to a market economy, went some way to placate reformists and foreign investors alarmed by his post-election proclamation that 'I have been, am and will remain a Communist'. Nevertheless, during this period his Government distanced Moldova from Western Europe and he even expressed interest in making the country a third member of a proposed **Belarus-Russia Union**. His Government's failure to hold referendums on Moldova's application for membership of the **European Union** and the **North Atlantic Treaty Organization** (NATO) caused opposition parties to boycott Parliament.

In 2003 Voronin staked his office on plans for a new federal Constitution, backed by Russia, proposing that Transdnestria should be a fully autonomous region with its own national symbols and budget, and that Russian would be an equal official language. Popular protests, arguing that the plans aimed to cement Moldova in the Russian sphere of influence, forced him to backtrack in December in favour of a more vague US-sponsored plan. This involved the deployment of international—rather than just Russian—peacekeepers ahead of a political reorganization of the country.

Relations with the Transdnestrian Government and with Russia soured during

2004. Voronin labelled the Transdnestrian authorities a 'transnational criminal group' and a dispute over the Transdnestrian closure of schools using the Latin script spiralled into mutual recriminations, an economic blockade and Voronin's snubbing of Russia by refusing to attend a summit of the **Commonwealth of Independent States**. By the run-up to the 2005 elections Voronin had turned firmly towards the West, repeatedly accusing Russia of interfering in Moldova, and he pledged to continue the impoverished country's push towards European integration. The PCRM won a reduced majority in the poll in March 2005, and Voronin was re-elected by the new Parliament on 4 April with the support of the **Christian Democratic People's Party**, and reinaugurated three days later.

Vladimir Voronin is married to Taissia Voronina with one son and one daughter.

Address: Office of the President, Blvd Ştefan cel Mare 154, Chişinau.

Telephone: (22) 504244.

Fax: (22) 245089.

Internet: www.president.md

Voucher privatization

An innovative way of promoting a transition to free-market economics in post-communist countries, which involved moving companies from state to private ownership by 'selling' shares for vouchers which had been issued free of charge to all citizens. This had the apparent advantage that it theoretically gave everyone the opportunity of share ownership, but the disadvantage that the process brought neither capital nor management expertise into the firms concerned, many of which subsequently failed. The first voucher privatization initiative was implemented in Czechoslovakia in 1992, on a large scale, covering about 30% of the total value of all state-held assets scheduled to be privatized. All Czechoslovak citizens aged 18 and above received a booklet of vouchers, which they could use to bid for shares, either directly or (the more popular route) by investing in one of the Investment Privatization Funds. The two waves of Czechoslovak voucher privatization ultimately achieved the transfer into private ownership of 2,200 companies with an approximate book value of US \$14,000m. In practice, however, the outcome was very rarely that ordinary citizens became long-term shareholders. Instead, they sold off their shares immediately, in many cases to foreign companies intent on asset stripping. A voucher privatization scheme was also implemented in the **Russian Federation** in the latter part of 1992 (with Bosnia and Herzegovina and Montenegro among those following this route later in the decade). Ostensibly the Russian scheme resulted in over 40 million individuals becoming shareholders, and the privatization of nearly 16,000 medium and large enterprises. Again, however, more than half the vouchers were either sold on, or used to buy into the investment funds, and a significant

Voucher privatization

proportion were simply never used.

VTB *see* **Bank for Foreign Trade**.

W

Warsaw Pact

A collective security agreement between the then communist states of **eastern Europe**, signed, and subsequently headquartered, in Warsaw on 1 May 1955 and dissolved in June 1991. Also known as the Warsaw Treaty Organization.

Members: Albania (excluded from 1962 and withdrew in 1968), Bulgaria, Czechoslovakia, East Germany, Hungary, Poland, Romania and the **Soviet Union**.

The Pact members agreed to place the control of their armed forces under a central military command based in **Moscow**.

The Warsaw Pact effectively served as a Soviet-led counterweight to the **North Atlantic Treaty Organization** (NATO). The signatories were bound together to provide mutual assistance against foreign aggressors, and, in practice, to a great extent surrendered control of their foreign policies to the Soviet Union. The Warsaw Pact–NATO rivalry formed the basis of the **Cold War**.

The most dramatic action undertaken by the Warsaw Pact was the suppression of the 1968 Czechoslovak liberal communist experiment, the so-called Prague Spring. Whereas the suppression of the Hungarian uprising 12 years earlier had been carried out by the Soviet army, the forces which entered Czechoslovakia on 20–21 August 1968, nominally at the invitation of hardline communists there, were explicitly identified as Warsaw Pact forces (excluding Romania which had refused to participate). The Prague Spring movement's leaders were arrested and taken to the Soviet Union where they were compelled to resign. A 'normalizing' occupation force remained in Czechoslovakia until 1988.

White House

The name given to the building housing the Russian Federal Government in **Moscow**. Built with a white marble façade in the 1980s, the so-called White (or Government) House served as the home of the Russian Republic's Government until the dissolution of the **Soviet Union** in 1991 when it became the centre of power for the new Russian legislature. It came to international prominence as the scene of two dramatic attempted coups, in 1991 and 1993. In the first, Russian President Boris **Yeltsin** held out against Soviet hardliners from within the building (*see* **August coup**). In the second it was Yeltsin who had the White House surrounded. Elements of the Government opposed to his proposed political reforms—strengthening the presidency at the expense of parliament—refused to accept the Government's dissolution and the calling of fresh elections to a new **Federal Assembly**. Parliamentarians, led by Vice-President Aleksandr Rutskoi, barricaded themselves in the White House in September 1993 while their supporters attempted to seize other strategic buildings in the capital. Yeltsin forced the rebels to surrender in early October after ordering the bombardment of the parliament building by heavy artillery. The White House was badly damaged but was subsequently restored, and continues to house the offices of the Federal Assembly, along with those of the Prime Minister. Other government offices are found in the **Kremlin**.

White Russians

(1): The political term used for the anti-Bolsheviks/monarchists in the Russian Revolution (as opposed to the Bolshevik 'Reds') that was derived from the white banner of the **Romanov dynasty**.

(2): The literal translation of Belarusians, supposedly derived from the association in Russian culture of the colour white with the concept of freedom—relating to the fact that the region was never conquered by the Mongols.

World Bank

The UN's main multilateral lending agency. Established in December 1945, the World Bank was concerned initially with financing post-war reconstruction but it has broadened its objectives to promoting the overall economic development of member nations. Its role is to make loans where private capital is not available on reasonable terms to finance productive investments. Loans are made either directly to governments, or to private enterprises with the guarantee of their governments. The World Bank comprises the International Bank for Reconstruction and Development (IBRD) and the International Development Association (IDA).

Members: 185 countries. Only members of the **International Monetary Fund** are eligible, so in the case of most **eastern European** countries it was not until the 1990s that they were able to join. Those that are now members include **Armenia**, **Azerbaijan**, **Belarus**, **Georgia**, **Moldova**, **Russian Federation** and **Ukraine**.
President and Chair of Exec. Directors: Paul Wolfowitz.
Address: 1818 H St, NW, Washington, DC 20433, USA.
Telephone: (202) 4731000.
Fax: (202) 4776391.
E-mail: pic@worldbank.org
Internet: www.worldbank.org

World Trade Organization (WTO)

The world body established on 1 January 1995 to give an institutional and legal foundation to the multilateral trading system. The successor to the General Agreement on Tariffs and Trade (GATT), it is intended to ensure that trading arrangements conform to an explicit set of rules. It provides procedures for the settlement of disputes, where WTO rulings are binding on member countries.

As of March 2007 the WTO had 150 members. **Georgia** had joined on 14 June 2000, **Moldova** on 26 July 2001 and **Armenia** on 5 February 2003. As of March 2007 there were also 29 countries in the process of applying for WTO membership. These included (with date of first establishment of a WTO working party on their application), **Azerbaijan** (1997), **Belarus** (1993), **Russian Federation** (1993) and **Ukraine** (1993). Russia's membership bid is well advanced and likely to take effect during 2007; it secured US backing for its membership in November 2006, and signed accords with Georgia and Moldova in early 2007, despite recent tensions in bilateral relations.
Director-General: Pascal Lamy.
Address: Centre William Rappard, rue de Lausanne 154, 1211 Geneva 21, Switzerland.
Telephone: (22) 7395111.
Fax: (22) 7314206.
E-mail: enquiries@wto.org
Internet: www.wto.org

Y

Yabloko
(Yavlinskii-Boldyrev-Lukin Bloc)

A centrist political party in the **Russian Federation** supporting gradual transition
to a market economy. The formation was launched in 1993 as the Yavlinskii-
Boldyrev-Lukin Bloc, named after its three founders, who were economist
Grigorii Yavlinskii, scientist Yurii Boldyrev and former Ambassador Vladimir
Lukin. It became generally known by its Yabloko acronym (meaning 'apple' in
Russian) and Yavlinskii emerged as its leader. Opposing the 'shock therapy' of
the administration of Boris **Yeltsin** in pursuit of a market economy, Yabloko won
33 seats and 7.8% of the proportional vote in the December 1993 elections to the
State Duma (lower house of the **Federal Assembly**). Having condemned the
Russian military operation in **Chechnya** launched in December 1994, Yabloko
took fourth place in the December 1995 State Duma elections by advancing to 45
seats, although its proportional vote share fell to 6.9%.

Yabloko's candidate in the mid-1996 presidential election was Yavlinskii, who
came fourth in the first round with 7.3% of the vote and gave qualified support to
Yeltsin in the second. The party nevertheless opposed many aspects of the
Government's subsequent economic policy, drawing particular support from
older professionals. In the December 1999 Duma elections, Yabloko fell back to
21 seats with 5.9% of the proportional vote, while Yavlinskii obtained virtually
the same percentage vote in the March 2000 presidential elections, which were
won by Vladimir **Putin**. Yabloko thereafter adopted a stance of 'constructive
opposition' to the Putin administration.

Plans were announced in June 2000 for an alliance between Yabloko and the
Union of Right Forces (SPS), providing initially for the presentation of joint
candidates in forthcoming elections and possibly leading to a full merger.
However, although the two formations had similar pro-market economic and
social programmes, doubts about the viability of the alliance centred on whether
it would follow Yabloko's line of opposing the Putin administration or the SPS
line of giving it qualified support. Despite setting a two-year timeframe, the
merger never came about.

Yabloko suffered heavily at the polls in December 2003, gaining just 4.3% of the vote and four seats in the Duma. Though there has been further talk of a renewed unification with SPS, Yavlinskii's re-election as Chairman in July 2004 represented the defeat of the pro-SPS faction.

Leadership: Grigorii Yavlinskii (Chair).
Address: M. Levshinskii per. 7/3, Moscow.
Telephone: (495) 2014379.
Fax: (495) 2923450.
E-mail: admin@yabloko.ru
Internet: www.yabloko.ru

Yalta Agreements

The conclusion of the famous summit between the Governments of the UK, the USA and the **Soviet Union** in the final stages of the Second World War. Meeting in Yalta (in modern-day **Ukraine**) in February 1945, the Allies unofficially parcelled up post-war Europe into spheres of influence, implicitly accepting that the Soviet Union would oversee the political future of the east. The conference also established the 1920 Curzon Line as the eastern frontier of Poland, granted international recognition, and support, to the Government of Marshal Tito in Yugoslavia, gave the Soviet Union its permanent seat (now **Russia**'s) on the UN Security Council and agreed to the mass repatriation of ethnic **German** and **Russian** populations across **eastern Europe**. *See also* **Potsdam Agreements**.

Yanukovych, Viktor

Prime Minister of **Ukraine**. Viktor Yanukovych, who trained as a mechanical engineer, served as Governor of the politically turbulent but economically vital eastern region of Donetsk before being appointed Prime Minister on 21 November 2002. A pro-**Russian** hardline politician and close ally of former President Leonid **Kuchma**, he heads the **Party of Regions**.

Viktor Fyedorovich Yanukovych was born on 9 July 1950 in Yenakiyeva, in the eastern Donetsk region. Ukraine was then part of the **Soviet Union**. When he was later appointed Prime Minister he disclosed that in 1968 he had been briefly detained in a juvenile correction camp for an undisclosed crime, and that he was found guilty in 1970 of 'medium' assault, though he did not say if he was imprisoned at all for this. He is now married and has two children.

In 1969 Yanukovych began his career as a metalworker at the Yenakiyeva metallurgical works. After working at the plant for seven years, he moved on to find greater responsibility at larger engineering firms in the region—between 1976 and 1996 he was Director-General of Donbastransremant and

Vuglyepromtrans (both state-run)—and at the Donetsk Regional Association of Motor Transport. In the meantime he studied for a qualification in mechanical engineering at the Donetsk Polytechnical Institute, graduating in 1980.

Yanukovych switched from business management to politics in 1996 when he was appointed Deputy Governor of the Donetsk region with special responsibility for industry. In March 1997 he was made full Governor. Over the course of his five-and-a-half-year period in office he earned a reputation for being capable, but hardline. From June 1998 he was also a member of the Donetsk regional council, of which he was Chair from May 1999.

Over the course of 2002 President Kuchma faced increasing hostility from the public and from the international community. Amidst a smouldering row over the alleged sale of military hardware to Iraq and the murder of journalist Giorgiy Gongadze, Kuchma dismissed his entire Government on 16 November and appointed Yanukovych as Prime Minister five days later.

A staunch ally of Kuchma, Yanukovych became his preferred candidate as successor at the 2004 presidential election. When official results from the 21 November run-off disagreed with exit polls and proclaimed victory for Yanukovych, opposition supporters cried foul and took to the streets in what became known as the **Orange Revolution**. The Supreme Court upheld the claims of fraud and ordered a re-run of the second-round vote in December, which was won by pro-Western opposition leader Viktor **Yushchenko**.

The 2006 legislative elections turned the tables again, with Yanukovych's Party of Regions securing the largest share of the vote and Yushchenko's **Our Ukraine** bloc pushed to third behind his former ally's **Yuliya Tymoshenko bloc**. Yushchenko and Tymoshenko negotiated for months to build a coalition to keep Yanukovych out of office, but when the small but pivotal **Socialist Party of Ukraine** swung its support behind Yanukovych, Yushchenko was forced to appoint his arch-rival as his Prime Minister. Yanukovych took office on 4 August.

Address: Office of the Prime Minister, M. Grushevskogo St 12/2, 01008 Kiev.
Telephone: (44) 2535762.
Fax: (44) 2535762.
E-mail: pr@kmu.gov.ua
Internet: www.kmu.gov.ua

YAP *see* **New Azerbaijan Party**.

Yavlinsky–Boldyrev–Lukin Bloc *see* **Yabloko**.

Yeltsin, Boris

The **Russian Federation**'s first President of the post-communist era and dominant political figure of the 1990s.

Boris Nikolayevich Yeltsin was born on 1 February 1931 in Butka in Sverdlovsk *oblast* (region) in a working class family with a peasant farming background. Despite a youthful accident in which he lost two fingers playing with a grenade, he played professional volleyball for Sverdlovsk, one of the leading Soviet teams, during his student days. He completed his degree in construction engineering in 1955 and married a fellow graduate, Naina Iosifovna Girina (with whom he has had two daughters). Working initially as an industrial manager, he became increasingly involved in politics, joining the **Communist Party of the Soviet Union** (KPSS) in 1961, rising to chair the party's Regional Committee in Sverdlovsk, and in 1980 became a member of the KPSS Central Committee. The election of Mikhail **Gorbachev** as General Secretary in 1985 marked a turning point in Yeltsin's career. Moving to **Moscow**, he was made First Secretary of the KPSS in the city, joined the Central Committee's powerful Secretariat and became a candidate member of the Politburo.

His radical style and informal manner won him popularity in Moscow, where people identified with his willingness to criticize the failures of the Soviet system which condemned them to poor housing and empty shops. Apparently disillusioned with the pace of *perestroika* (restructuring), he became involved in open confrontation with leading conservatives in the party at the end of 1987, and was dropped from the Politburo and shunted from the Moscow leadership to a minor ministerial job.

The election of the **Soviet Union**'s newly-restyled Congress of People's Deputies in March 1989 gave him a chance to build a political support base. Representing a Moscow constituency, he became a founder member of the oppositional Inter-regional Group, openly discussed multi-partyism and called passionately for the transfer of more power from the centre to the republics. He became a member of the Russian Republic's Congress of People's Deputies, elected in March 1990, and in May that body chose him as Chairman of the Russian Federation Supreme Soviet—thus making him *de facto* Russian President. Deciding that this was incompatible with party membership, he threw his party card on the floor in front of Gorbachev at the party congress in July 1990, expressing disgust with the slow pace of reforms

Within the Russian Republic Yeltsin decided to go for more radical change with a 500-day 'dash to the market economy' package and a declaration of sovereignty. He also managed a temporary reconciliation with Gorbachev to ward off a conservative backlash. Yeltsin strengthened his own hand, as Gorbachev did not, by obtaining a popular mandate for his leadership, winning the first ever direct election for the Russian presidency with 57% of the vote in June 1991. Two months later, Yeltsin famously led the resistance to the hardline **August**

coup in Moscow, rallying the crowds outside the Russian parliament building (the **White House**), and retaining the political initiative when the coup collapsed.

The dissolution of the Soviet Union in December 1991 left Yeltsin leading a newly independent Russian Federation, as its executive President. In the course of 1992, he moved to strengthen his own powers, but became locked in a struggle with the conservative forces in the Congress of People's Deputies over economic reforms. Narrowly surviving an impeachment vote in March 1993, he won a vote of confidence in a popular referendum, but in September, when he issued a decree disbanding the Congress, conservative communist and right-wing nationalist forces combined to resist him by force. The ensuing violent power struggle exposed Yeltsin's authoritarian intolerance of opposition. The shelling of the White House on his orders sent out a powerful negative image, from which his liberal democratic credentials never recovered. Elections to a new **Federal Assembly** in December 1993 returned large numbers of communists and ultra-nationalists, although Yeltsin did get his way with the narrow endorsement of a new Constitution giving him stronger presidential powers.

Yeltsin's popularity touched a low point in 1995, as Russian troops fought a long and bloody war in **Chechnya** and the **Russian economy** languished in serious recession. A populist campaign nevertheless saw Yeltsin lead in the first-round poll of presidential elections in June 1996. He effectively disappeared from sight between the first and second rounds of voting and it was confirmed much later that he had had three heart attacks during the campaign. His support held up, however, and he defeated the communist leader Gennadii **Zyuganov** in the run-off on 3 July, with almost 54% of the vote.

Sworn in again on 9 August, Yeltsin suffered another collapse and needed quintuple coronary bypass surgery in November. His health became a major political factor, owing not only to his heart condition, but to pneumonia, stomach ulcers, 'high blood pressure and fatigue' and persistent evidence that he was unable to bring a long-standing drink problem under control. His domestic policy oscillated between commitment to economic reform and periods of retreat in the face of unpopularity. Attempting to assert himself in 1998 and promising vigorous action on the economy, he sacked Prime Minister Viktor Chernomyrdin, then decided in August to reappoint him. The State Duma (lower house of the Federal Assembly) resisted the first change and blocked the second, stepping up its moves to impeach Yeltsin. An eventual compromise allowed the President to continue until elections due in 2000, but not seek a further term, while giving the Prime Minister and Duma greater power over ministerial appointments. New economic proposals were heavily influenced by the communist insistence on greater government intervention. In May 1999 he survived the impeachment votes, and the Duma backed off from confrontations over his choice of successive new Prime Ministers, allowing him to see out the year before stepping down as President on 31 December 1999 and handing over power to his latest Prime Minister and chosen successor-designate, Vladimir **Putin**.

Yerevan

The capital city and main urban centre of **Armenia** situated near the country's southern border. *Population*: 1.1m. (2005 estimate). The city is built on extremely ancient foundations, with archaeological evidence suggesting settlement in the region as early as 8,000 years ago. From the 6th century BC it was a part of the Armenian Kingdom. In its long history it has fallen to a series of conquerors including Romans, Arabs, Mongols, **Turks** and eventually **Russians** in 1827. After the fall of the Russian Empire in 1917, Yerevan became the capital of the Armenian Republic and has retained that role ever since.

Hydroelectric power from a plant on the nearby Hrazdan river fuelled Yerevan's industrialization under **Soviet** rule. Industry in the city is associated particularly with petroleum products, and there is also aluminium smelting.

YeS *see* **New Policy**.

Yezidis *see* **Kurds**.

YMP-Musavat *see* **Equality**.

YR *see* **United Russia**.

Yukos

Major private oil company in the **Russian Federation**, targeted for tax fraud and declared bankrupt in 2006. The travails of the company are widely seen as revenge for the political ambitions of its former CEO Mikhail Khodorkovsky.

Yukos was founded in 1993 from the privatization of *Yu*ganskneftegaz and *K*uybyshevnefte*org*s*i*ntez, and became one of the world's largest non-state oil companies, accounting for almost a fifth of Russia's total oil production and employing around 100,000 people, under the leadership of '**oligarch**' Khodorkovsky, who joined the company as CEO in 1996 from Menatep Bank. In April 2003 Yukos announced a merger with Sibneft, to make it Russia's largest oil firm.

Khodorkovsky, who had become the richest man in Russia and highly influential in politics, was arrested in October 2003 for fraud and tax evasion of US \$1,000m., and the Sibneft merger was scrapped shortly therafter. In July 2004 Yukos was charged with tax evasion amounting ultimately to \$28,000m. It was accused of using tax havens to reduce its tax bill—a trick used by many oil companies, but only Yukos was targeted. The uncertainty over whether the company would be able to continue production helped push global oil prices to record highs. In December the Government forced the auctioning off of

Yuganskneftegaz, the main production unit, bought for US $8,600m. (well below the recent valuation of $15,000m.–17,000m.) by Baikalfinansgrup; **Gazprom** had been banned from bidding for the unit by a court ruling in the USA, as part of Yukos's unsuccessful attempt to file for bankruptcy there. Gazprom denied any links with the financing of Baikalfinansgrup's purchase. Yugansk was then sold on to state-owned Rosneft, who merged with Gazprom in 2005, though Yugansk remained separate.

Yukos has accused the Russian Government of 'an unprecedented campaign of illegal, discriminatory, and disproportionate tax claims escalating into raids and confiscations, culminating in intimidation and arrests'. In July 2006 the creditors filed for bankruptcy in Russia, declared by the courts on 1 August. Rosneft was the second largest creditor behind the state tax service. Meanwhile Khodorkovsky had been sentenced to nine years in prison in 2005.

Yuliya Tymoshenko bloc
Blok Yuliyi Tymoshenko (BYT)

A pro-market electoral alliance and political bloc in **Ukraine** formed in November 2001 to back the political ambitions of Yuliya Tymoshenko. The BYT was initially founded as the National Salvation Front (NSF) in February 2001 as one of two major political groups in opposition to then President Leonid **Kuchma**. It was formed from the union of Tymoshenko's own Fatherland party and other right-of-centre parties.

Fatherland (Batkivshchyna) was launched in 1999 by a faction of the Hromada All-Ukrainian Association after Hromada leader Pavlo Lazarenko had fled to the USA to escape charges of financial corruption when he was Prime Minister in 1996–97. In January 2000 Fatherland leader Tymoshenko was appointed Deputy Prime Minister and put in charge of the energy sector. In August 2000 her husband was among several state energy officials arrested on embezzlement charges and was later also accused of paying large bribes to Lazarenko when he was Prime Minister. Tymoshenko was then herself charged with corruption when she had been a state energy official, and was dismissed from the Government in January 2001 and briefly arrested in mid-February.

Tymoshenko's adept use of the media and her 'youthful' image helped generate wide support for Fatherland as it embarked on the process of attracting a wider power base in 2001. The NSF was cemented in February and renamed itself the BYT in November in recognition of its role in promoting Tymoshenko's position. It went on to secure 7% of the vote in elections in 2002, giving it 21 seats in the **Supreme Council**. Tymoshenko placed herself at the forefront of the opposition, working increasingly closely with her ex-boss, former Prime Minister Viktor **Yushchenko**, in the lead up to the 2004 presidential poll. She showed an impassioned edge when pressing Kuchma on his apparent involvement in the murder of journalist Giorgiy Gongadze, though the campaign ultimately failed to unseat the President.

Declining the opportunity to stand for herself, Tymoshenko swung the BYT behind Yushchenko's presidential bid and participated staunchly in the protests which followed the Government's attempt to prevent him from taking office—the Orange Revolution. Her loyalty was rewarded with the premiership in early 2005.

While Tymoshenko's commitment to pro-market reforms was rarely in doubt, concerns grew over her inability to guide her Cabinet to effective leadership on key issues, especially as her differences with the less radical Yushchenko came to the fore. After a series of high-profile resignations her Government was dismissed in September 2005.

Though not officially in opposition to Yushchenko, the BYT proved its status as a direct competitor to the President's hold on power. It polled an impressive 22.3% of the vote in the March 2006 elections, winning 129 seats and becoming the second biggest party in the Supreme Council behind the opposition **Party of Regions** (PR). To keep the PR out of power, Tymoshenko began negotiations to re-form the old coalition with Yushchenko's **Our Ukraine** bloc and the **Socialist Party of Ukraine** (SPU). After several months, agreement was reached, with Our Ukraine offered the post of Speaker and Tymoshenko to be nominated for the premiership. However, the political manoeuvring required to secure the election of the Speaker was considered unconstitutional by the PR, who blocked the Supreme Council, and mistrust between the former allies saw the SPU switch its pivotal support to the PR. Piqued by the betrayal, Tymoshenko led her bloc into opposition, where it gained the support of several defectors.

Leadership: Yuliya Tymoshenko (Chair).
Address: bulv. Lesi Ukrainki 26/916, 01133 Kiev.
Telephone: (44) 2845221.
E-mail: sector@byti.org.ua
Internet: www.tymoshenko.org.ua

Yushchenko, Viktor

President of the **Ukraine**. Viktor Yushchenko is a banker who was a surprise choice as Prime Minister under President Leonid **Kuchma** in 1999. Removed from office in a confidence vote two years later, he went into opposition to the Kuchma Government, setting up the **Our Ukraine** (NU) movement. In 2004, with Kuchma retiring, Yushchenko stood for the presidency against Kuchma's handpicked successor, Viktor **Yanukovych**. The **Orange Revolution** by his supporters led to the run-off's result being overturned. Yushchenko won the re-run and was sworn in on 23 January 2005.

Viktor Yushchenko, the son of two teachers, was born on 23 February 1954 in the village of Khoruzhivka in Sumska *oblast* in northern Ukraine. He studied economics at university in Ternopil, graduating in 1975, then trained as a village accountant before national service, after which he moved into the banking system of the then **Soviet Union**.

Yushchenko worked for the USSR State Bank from 1976, heading the Ulyanovsk department for nine years and then as Deputy Director of the Ukrainian regional office until 1988 when he was promoted to a managerial position in the Ukrainian Agro-Industrial Bank, based in **Kiev**. He remained at the bank, later named Ukraina, until 1993, when he was invited to join the central **National Bank of Ukraine** and was swiftly promoted to Chairman and Governor. Yushchenko played a central role in creating Ukraine's new national currency (the hryvna) and a new regulatory system for commercial banking.

In 1999 Yushchenko was a surprise nomination for Prime Minister after President Kuchma's previous choice was rejected by the **Supreme Council** by a single vote. Yushchenko's nomination by contrast was ratified by 296 votes to 12. However, his Government, and in particular Deputy Prime Minister Yuliya Tymoshenko, became involved in a series of bruising confrontations with the 'oligarchs' who had control of the country's gas and coal reserves. Tymoshenko was sacked in January 2001 amidst allegations of embezzlement and Yushchenko was removed from office by a vote of no confidence in April, despite last-minute support from Kuchma. The vote was regarded with dismay in many quarters; four million signatures were gathered in support of Yushchenko and 10,000 people rallied in the centre of Kiev to protest over his dismissal.

In July 2001 Yushchenko launched the Our Ukraine coalition, which, by the time of the legislative elections the following year, had built up sufficient support to become the largest single bloc in the Supreme Council. However it proved unable to form a government, and Yushchenko took on the role of heading the anti-Kuchma opposition.

In 2004, as Kuchma's term in office drew to a close, Yushchenko announced his intention to stand for the presidency. With Kuchma not standing again, Yushchenko faced the President's chosen successor, Prime Minister Viktor **Yanukovych**. The election campaign was bitterly contested and split the country both politically and geographically, much of Yanukovych's support coming from the industrialized and largely Russian-speaking east. In September 2004 Yushchenko became seriously ill and was flown to Austria for emergency treatment for what was later diagnosed as dioxin poisoning. The incident left Yushchenko with permanent facial scarring.

The initial presidential poll on 31 October saw Yushchenko garner 39.9% of the vote to Yanukovych's 39.3%, and a second round of voting was scheduled for 21 November. Accusations of vote rigging and intimidation in this second round were rampant, and there were serious discrepancies between exit polls showing Yushchenko with an 11% lead and the final result indicating that he had lost by 3%. Yushchenko and his supporters refused to recognize the results and so began 12 days of popular protest in the central squares of Kiev; this became known as the **Orange Revolution**, after the colour of ribbons and scarves worn by protesters. The election results were eventually overturned by the Supreme Court and a re-run of the second round was scheduled for 26 December, which Yushchenko won by an 8% margin.

Yushchenko was sworn in on 23 January 2005 and appointed Tymoshenko as Prime Minister. The new administration had a distinctly pro-Western bent, as opposed to Kuchma and Yanukovych's pro-Russian orientation. This was prompted at least partly by **Russian** President Vladimir **Putin**'s steadfast defence of Kuchma and Yanukovych throughout the popular protests against them.

Allegations of widespread corruption in the administration forced Yushchenko to dismiss Tymoshenko and her entire Government in September, and it took two attempts for the Supreme Council to approve a successor.

The 2006 legislative elections again highlighted the east–west political divide in the country, though this time the poll was won by Yanukovych's **Party of Regions**, with Our Ukraine pushed into third place behind the **Yuliya Tymoshenko bloc**. Months of negotiations ensued as Yushchenko struggled to rebuild his partnership with Tymoshenko in order to keep Yanukovych out of power. However, the defection of the small but pivotal **Socialist Party of Ukraine** to support Yanukovych forced Yushchenko to accept an uncomfortable cohabitation with Yanukovych as Prime Minister.

Yushchenko is married with five children.

Address: Office of the President, vul. Bankova 11, 01220 Kiev.

Telephone: (44) 2556128.

Fax: (44) 2931001.

E-mail: viktor@yushchenko.com.ua

Internet: www.president.gov.ua

Z

Zviadists

Supporters of former Georgian President Zviad Gamsakhurdia who formed a right-wing paramilitary organization to combat the regime of President Eduard **Shevardnadze** after 1991. Based largely in the western Samegrelo district, they were the subject of a ruthless campaign by the pro-government **Mkhedrioni** militia in 1992, and their insurgency was effectively ended the following year. The regime has attempted to prosecute Zviadists, most of whom are in exile in the **Russian Federation**, but has recently edged towards reconciliation. Konstantine Gamsakhurdia, eldest son of Zviad, returned to Georgia in 2004. He heads the nationalist Tavisupleba (Liberty) party, one of several parties set up by Zviadist supporters.

Zyuganov, Gennadii

Chairman of the **Communist Party of the Russian Federation** (KPRF). Gennadii Andreyevich Zyuganov rose up the ranks of the **Communist Party of the Soviet Union** (KPSS) in the 1970s–80s to become a champion of the party's more nationalist 'right wing', in opposition to reformist Head of State Mikhail **Gorbachev**. He has been Chairman of the KPRF since it was unbanned in 1993. He has twice been defeated in presidential elections, once by Boris **Yeltsin**, and most recently by the current President Vladimir **Putin** in 2000; Putin's victory then was so emphatic that Zyuganov did not even bother to stand against him in the 2004 poll. Zyuganov's philosophies are a somewhat paradoxical mix of communism and overt nationalism—complete with a rejection of Marxist 'class struggle' in favour of racist rhetoric upholding the righteousness of the **Slavic people** in the face of Western capitalist imperialism. He opposes market reforms, but is in favour of a mixed economy and is also a champion of the voluntary restoration of a **Greater Russia**, while spouting invective against the **Commonwealth of Independent States** (CIS).

Born on 26 June 1944 in the village of Mymrino, near Orel in western **Russia**, he enrolled in 1962 as a student in the Department of Physics and Mathematics of the Orel Pedagogical Institute. Between 1963 and 1966 he served in Soviet military intelligence, but returned to his studies as soon as he was demobilized. He also joined the KPSS and entered the Communist Youth League (Komsomol) in 1966. He continued his education at the Institute, from where he graduated in 1969 and where he lectured until 1983, and also at the KPSS Academy of Social Sciences where he eventually received a doctorate in philosophy in 1995.

As a communist, Zyuganov advanced his career rapidly from positions within Komsomol, to a local Party Secretary from 1974 and finally into the 'Propaganda Department' of the central KPSS in 1983. By the time the **Soviet Union** was disintegrating in the late 1980s he had become a Deputy Head of Department and an outspoken critic of Gorbachev's *glasnost* (openness). In 1990 he was a founding member of the breakaway KPRF and a leader of its right-wing 'popular patriotic' faction. In opposition to the reformist authorities, Zyuganov was largely in accord with the various emerging nationalist and ultra-conservative movements. He was fortunate enough to be on holiday during the hardline Soviet **August coup** in 1991, which led to the banning of the Communist Party. Zyuganov was a key figure in the move to align opposition nationalist groups under the banner of the National Salvation Front in 1992 and was elected Chairman of the KPRF when the party was re-registered in 1993. The party maintained a large share of the vote in the 1995 and 1999 elections, making it the largest single party in the **Federal Assembly**. However after the election of President Putin in 2000, the alliance of various pro-Putin blocs gained control in the Duma (lower house), and at the 2003 legislative poll the KPRF was reduced to a mere 52 seats, well behind the 222 held by **United Russia**.

Zyuganov's personal standing has been damaged by his uncharismatic style. His controversial philosophies include suspicion of the **Jews** and an insistence that Slavs are not meant to be capitalists. His opposition to the popular war in **Chechnya** is seen as a political disadvantage, although it helps to distance the KPRF from the nationalist fringe. In his most recent presidential battle, in March 2000, he was easily defeated by Putin in the first round, receiving just 29.2% of the vote. He did not stand in the 2004 poll in which Putin easily secured re-election, but has announced his intention to stand in 2008, when Putin will have to step down.

Country-by-Country Listing

Armenia

All Armenian Labour Party
Armenian Apostolic Church
Armenian Development
 Agency
Armenian question
Armenian Revolutionary
 Federation
Armenian Stock Exchange
Armenians
Armenpress
Caucasus region
Central Bank of the Republic
 of Armenia
Chamber of Commerce and
 Industry of Armenia
Communist Party of
 Armenia
Country of Law Party
Democratic Party of
 Armenia
Deported nationalities
Javakheti
Jehovah's Witnesses
Justice
Khachatrian, Vartan
Kocharian, Robert
Kurds
Markarian, Andranik
Nagorno-Karabakh
National Assembly
National Democratic
 Alliance Party
National Democratic Party
National Democratic Union
National Unity Party
Oskanian, Vardan
Pan-Armenian National
 Movement
People's Party of Armenia
Republic
Republican Party of Armenia
Soviet Union
TRACECA
Transcaucasia
United Labour Party
Yerevan

Azerbaijan

Aliyev, Heydar
Aliyev, Ilham
Armenians
AzarTAc
Azerbaijan Popular Front
 Party
Azerbaijani Export and
 Investment Promotion
 Foundation
Azeris
Baku
Baku Stock Exchange
Baku–Tbilisi–Ceyhan
 pipeline
Caucasus region
Caviar
Chamber of Commerce and
 Industry of Azerbaijan
Equality
Freedom
Kurds
Lezghins
Mammadyarov, Elmar
Muslim peoples
Nagorno-Karabakh
Nakhichevan
National Assembly
National Bank of Azerbaijan
New Azerbaijan Party
New Policy
Pan-Turkism
Rasizade, Artur
Russians
Sharifov, Samir
Soviet Union
TRACECA
Transcaucasia
Turkic peoples

Belarus

Agrarian Party of Belarus
Belarus-Russia Union
Belarusian Chamber of
 Commerce and Industry
Belarusian Currency and
 Stock Exchange
Belarusian Popular Front-
 Renaissance
Belarusians
BelTA
Chernobyl
Communist Party of Belarus
Council of the Republic
Cyrillic alphabet
House of Representatives
Jehovah's Witnesses
Jews
Korbut, Nikolay
Liberal Democratic Party of
 Belarus
Lukashenka, Alyaksandr
Martynov, Sergei
Minsk
National Assembly
National Bank of the
 Republic of Belarus
National Investment Agency
People's Coalition Five Plus
Poles
Pripet Marshes
Rouble zone
Russians
Sidorsky, Sergei
Single Economic Space
Slavic peoples
Soviet Union
START

Georgia

Abkhazia
Adzharia
Aleksishvili, Aleksi
Armenians
Baku–Tbilisi–Ceyhan
  pipeline
Bezhuashvili, Gela
Caucasus region
Chamber of Commerce and
  Industry of Georgia
Citizens' Union of Georgia
Colour revolutions
Department of Privatization
Deported nationalities
Georgian National
  Investment Agency
Georgian Orthodox Church
Georgian Stock Exchange
Georgians
Industry Will Save Georgia
Javakheti
Kodori Gorge
Kurds
Meskhetians
Mkhedrioni
Muslim peoples
National Bank of Georgia
National Movement-
  Democrats
New Rights
Noghaideli, Zurab
Ossetia question
Pankisi Gorge
Parliament of Georgia
Pontic Greeks
Republican Party of Georgia
Rightist Opposition
Rose Revolution
Russians
Saakashvili, Mikhail
Shevardnadze, Eduard
Soviet Union
Tbilisi
TRACECA
Transcaucasia
Turkic peoples
Zviadists

Moldova

AIDS
Balkans
Bessarabia question
Bessarabian Church
Bulgarians
Chamber of Commerce and
  Industry of Moldova
Chişinau
Christian Democratic
  People's Party
Communist Party of the
  Moldovan Republic
Cyrillic alphabet
Democratic Moldova Bloc
Democratic Party of
  Moldova
Gagauzia
Greater Romania
Infotag News Agency
Moldovan Export Promotion
  Organization
Moldovan Stock Exchange
Moldovans
Moldpres-State Information
  Agency
National Bank of Moldova
Our Moldova Alliance
Parliament
Pop, Mihail
Russians
Social Liberal Party
Soviet Union
State Department for
  Privatization of the
  Republic of Moldova
Stratan, Andrei
Taraclia
Tarlev, Vasile
TRACECA
Transdnestria
Ukrainians
Vlachs
Voronin, Vladimir

Russian Federation

Abaza
Abrene question
Adygeya
Agrarian Party of Russia
AIDS
Alfa-Bank
Archangel
Astrakhan
August coup
Aum Shinrikyo
Avars
Bank for Foreign Trade
Bashkortostan
Belarus-Russia Union
Belarusians
Beslan school siege
Black Sea Fleet
Buddhism
Caucasus region
Caviar
Central Bank of the Russian
  Federation
Chamber of Commerce and
  Industry of the Russian
  Federation
Chavash Republic
Chechnya
Cherkess
Common Economic Spaces
Communist Party of the
  Russian Federation
Communist Party of the
  Soviet Union
Cossacks
Cyrillic alphabet
Dagestan
Dargins
Deported nationalities
Don Basin
European Russia
Federal Assembly
Federal Security Service
Finno-Ugric peoples
Fradkov, Mikhail
Gazprom
Germans
Glasnost
Gorbachev, Mikhail
Greater Russia
Idel-Ural
Ingushetia
International Space Station
ITAR-TASS
Jaanilinn question
Jehovah's Witnesses

Ukraine

International Organizations

Arctic Council
Baltic Marine Environment Protection Commission
  (or Helsinki Commission, HELCOM)
Bank for International Settlements (BIS)
Barents Euro-Arctic Council (BEAC)
Central European Initiative (CEI)
Centre for the Prevention of Conflict (CPC)
Centrist Democrat International (CDI)
Charter of Paris for a New Europe
Collective Security Treaty Organization (CSTO)
Commonwealth of Independent States (CIS)
Contact Group (for the former Yugoslavia)
Council for Mutual Economic Assistance
  (CMEA or Comecon)
Council of Europe
Council of the Baltic Sea States (CBSS)
Danube Commission
Economic Commission for Europe (ECE)
Economic Co-operation Organization (ECO)
Eurasian Economic Community (EAEC or EurAsEC)
Euro-Atlantic Partnership Council (EAPC)
European Bank for Reconstruction and
  Development (EBRD)
European Court of Human Rights
European Organization for Nuclear Research (CERN)
European Union (EU)
Group of Eight (G8)
GUAM group
International Atomic Energy Agency (IAEA)
International Bank for Reconstruction and Development
  (IBRD)
International Court of Justice (ICJ)
International Democrat Union (IDU)
International Monetary Fund (IMF)
International Organization for Migration (IOM)
International Whaling Commission (IWC)
Liberal International
Minsk Group
NATO-Russia Council
Non-Aligned Movement (NAM)
North Atlantic Co-operation Council (NACC)
North Atlantic Treaty Organization (NATO)
Organization for Economic Co-operation and
  Development (OECD)
Organization for Security and Co-operation in Europe (OSCE)
Organization of the Black Sea Economic Co-operation (BSEC)
Organization of the Islamic Conference (OIC)
Partnership for Peace (PfP)
Permanent Court of Arbitration (PCA)
Shanghai Co-operation Organization (SCO)
Socialist International
Warsaw Pact
World Bank
World Trade Organization (WTO)

Other Entries

Baltic States
Central Europe
Cold War
Conventional Forces in
  Europe
Eastern Europe
Helsinki Final Act
Helsinki process
Islamic fundamentalism
Nomenklatura
Nuclear Non-Proliferation
  Treaty
Nuclear Suppliers' Group
Orthodox Christianity
Pan-Germanism
Pan-Slavism
Potsdam Agreements
Protestantism
Roma
Roman Catholic Church
White Russians
Yalta Agreements

Index of Personal Names

310

Y

Yanukovych, Viktor, 22, 69, 142, 183, 187, 188, 196, 202, 204, 214, 233, 252, 273, 277, 293, 299, 300
Yarov, Yurii, 69
Yavlinskii, Grigorii, 292, 293
Yekhanurov, Yuriy, 196, 273
Yeltsin, Boris, 21, 43, 62, 73, 76, 78, 98, 114, 116, 142, 149, 166, 194, 211, 228, 236, 249, 264, 281, 282, 290, 292, 295, 302
Yushchenko, Viktor, 76, 142, 187, 188, 195, 196, 197, 203, 252, 254, 272, 277, 294, 298, 299

Z

Zarandia, Badri, 157
Zarya, Irina, 98
Zhang, Deguang, 247
Zhirinovskii, Vladimir, 146, 147, 148
Zhuk, Dimitriy, 47
Zhvania, Zurab, 7, 66, 106, 181, 241, 242
Zinoviev, Oleg, 176
Zoryan, Hrayr, 20
Zulfagarov, Tofik, 26
Zyazikov, Murat, 121
Zyuganov, Gennadii, 6, 73, 74, 212, 229, 296, 302